AVATAR EMERGENCY

New Media Theory
Series Editor, Byron Hawk

The New Media Theory series investigates both media and new media as a complex ecological and rhetorical context. The merger of media and new media creates a global social sphere that is changing the ways we work, play, write, teach, think, and connect. Because this new context operates through evolving arrangements, theories of new media have yet to establish a rhetorical and theoretical paradigm that fully articulates this emerging digital life.

The series includes books that combine social, cultural, political, textual, rhetorical, aesthetic, and material theories in order to understand moments in the lives that operate in these emerging contexts. Such works typically bring rhetorical and critical theories to bear on media and new media in a way that elaborates a burgeoning post-disciplinary "medial turn" as one further development of the rhetorical and visual turns that have already influenced scholarly work.

Other Books in the Series

Mics, Cameras, Symbolic Action: Audio-Visual Rhetoric for Writing Teachers, by Bump Halbritter (2012)
The Available Means of Persuasion: Mapping a Theory and Pedagogy of Multimodal Public Rhetoric, by David M. Sheridan, Jim Ridolfo, and Anthony J. Michel (2012)
New Media/New Methods: The Academic Turn from Literacy to Electracy, edited by Jeff Rice and Marcel O'Gorman (2008)
The Two Virtuals: New Media and Composition, by Alexander Reid (2007). Honorable Mention, W. Ross Winterowd/*JAC* Award for Best Book in Composition Theory, 2007.

AVATAR EMERGENCY

Gregory L. Ulmer

Parlor Press
Anderson, South Carolina
www.parlorpress.com

Parlor Press LLC, Anderson, South Carolina, USA

Printed in the United States of America

S A N: 2 5 4 - 8 8 7 9

Library of Congress Cataloging-in-Publication Data

Ulmer, Gregory L., 1944-
Avatar emergency / Gregory L. Ulmer.
p. cm. -- (New media theory)
Includes bibliographical references and index.
ISBN 978-1-60235-289-6 (pbk. : alk. paper) -- ISBN 978-1-60235-290-2 (hardcover : alk. paper) -- ISBN 978-1-60235-291-9 (ebook)
1. Digital media--Philosophy. 2. Digital media--Technological innovations. 3. Image (Philosophy) 4. Virtual reality in art. 5. Aesthetics. I. Title.
P90.U42 2012
302.23'1--dc23
2012004380

1 2 3 4 5

Cover design by David Blakesley.

Printed on acid-free paper.

Parlor Press, LLC is an independent publisher of scholarly and trade titles in print and multimedia formats. This book is available in paper, cloth and eBook formats from Parlor Press on the World Wide Web at http://www.parlorpress.com or through online and brick-and-mortar bookstores. For submission information or to find out about Parlor Press publications, write to Parlor Press, 3015 Brackenberry Drive, Anderson, South Carolina, 29621, or email editor@parlorpress.com.

for Anjali Claire

Contents

Figure 1. Titian. *Allegory of Time Governed by Prudence.* 1565.

Preface

Something is happening to us and through us that goes by the name "avatar." Some of us are present in Second Life through an "avatar" or have had our identities stolen digitally, added a photograph to our Facebook account or personalized our blog with an icon, even designed and sold t-shirts, skateboards, coffee mugs and the like branded with our personal logos. But branding is not avatar. We have not yet begun to avatar, although there are futuristic scenarios and scholarly histories, looking forward and back in time, archiving the possibilities and precedents. You can meet avatar, that part of you inhabiting cyberspace (for lack of a better term). You and I need to meet the avatar that we already have, that we already are, now that it may be augmented within the digital apparatus (electracy) beyond branding to become prostheses of counsel and decision. Electrate avatar knows more than you or I do, it knows better than you or I do about what will have happened in our various respective situations. This claim must be not only understood, but undergone. It is not only an idea, a theory, but an experience. The goal of this book is to make it a practice of digital education.

The concept, tradition, and practice of "avatar" are central to the invention of "flash reason," a deliberative rhetoric for public policy formation, making democratically informed decisions in a moment, at light speed, against the threat of a General Accident that happens everywhere simultaneously. Any theorizing of "avatar" must at least acknowledge James Cameron's dramatization in the blockbuster film. It is fortunate for my account (given the influence this film will have in shaping the discussion) that there is an important aspect of electrate avatar captured by Cameron's treatment. Avatar as an experience is an event of counsel. It is an uncanny encounter with one's own possibility (potential), as undergone in various wisdom traditions noted here as analogies for the rhetoric (flash reason) made possible through avatar practice. Through avatar, players come to understand the General Economy (Bataille) of the universe, so to speak, represented as "nature" or the Gaia spirit of Pandora in Cameron's film. The "jarhead" Sully, incarnated in his Na'vi simulation, transcends his Marine training as well as his limitations both physical and mental, to oppose the actions of the military-industrial-complex corporation that are threatening the natural order. It is perhaps understandable, if not inevitable, that the screenplay uses the shorthand of the Frontier myth, in high-concept reconfiguration (genre hybrid), to express its values. Cameron's *Avatar* is a Western.

Concepts are an invention of literacy, created by the Classical Greeks in the Academy and Lyceum in Athens, as a device for developing alphabetic writing as a support for thought. Concepts used the formal technique of definition to identify the properties of an entity constituting its essence, its nature, based on its function or purpose. In addition to these general concepts classifying the things of the world, the Greeks produced a number of specialized concepts designed to do the work of philosophy itself, and philosophy ever since has created a host of these devices. The question today concerns whether or in what way philosophical concepts may survive in, or be adapted to, the apparatus of electracy that emerged at the beginning of the industrial revolution and is displacing literacy (and orality) as the dominant metaphysics (reality construction) of electronic digital civilization. The experiment in this study is to construct a "concept avatar" to support thought in electracy. Avatar is to electracy what "self" is to literacy, or "spirit" to orality. Avatar as concept is needed to understand how theory may still be performed in the image metaphysics of electracy.

Concepts begin in response to some problem field (plane of immanence in the vocabulary of Deleuze and Guattari) that resists or challenges or threatens human thriving. The problem field of *Avatar* is represented in the film as the military industrial complex, allegorized in the conglom attempting to mine unobtainium on Pandora, with the help of a ruthless head of security, a former Marine colonel. We are in an allegory, a mythology whose features are familiar, in that the screenplay conforms not only to the hybrid genre terms of a sci-fi-western, but to the fundamental adventure template of a "hero with a thousand faces" that structures nearly every narrative in Western culture. Sully is a "conceptual persona" whose transformation over the course of the narrative constitutes a "vital anecdote" dramatizing the thought needed to address the problem. It is not a matter of what Cameron intended but what we may learn about avatar as thought.

Avatar as concept may be and must be thought today, in that we already are avatar, or becoming avatar. We avatar (verb) online every day; we put our self into the prosthesis of the Internet, as Jake enters the prosthetic body to explore Pandora, and enter the culture of the Na'vi. The entry into writing produced the experience of "selfhood." An important skill of literacy concerns the management of "voice" in writing. What is the experience of becoming image online? The electrate equivalent of "voice" is not just "image" but "avatar," with the difference being that avatar is an expression you receive, not one that you send. My proposal is to add a conceptual register to the problem, persona, and anecdote referenced in the film. What experience does Jake have in the prosthesis that transforms him from jarhead to champion of the Na'vi fight against the conglom? Structurally we recognize his decision as conventional in our culture. At the end of the second act of a standard Hollywood three-act screenplay, the protagonist is confronted by a choice: to change from the disposition given at the beginning of the adventure in order to become adequate to the problem troubling the special world, and hence to take on the role of hero, or to refuse that role. This moment and opportunity to become what one (already) is, is a threshold position latent in experience, and a primary element in our wisdom and assumptions about identity. The mystery of this change is not only that it happens, but how it happens.

Jake's decision to take the side of the Na'vi (Navi means "prophet" in the Hebrew Bible) against the conglom puts him in the service of a Gaia principle maintaining a balance of nature, not only on Pandora but presumably in the universe as a whole. He learned something prosthetically about the principle of Limit, Measure. Measure is the thought experience of avatar. What in the narrative as a whole might function as detail to articulate more clearly the vital anecdote of concept avatar? There is one scene that perhaps intimates more clearly than any other what our concept requires. It is the scene when Sully first meets Neytiri in the forest of Pandora. This Amazonian warrior intervenes to save Sully and help him (Pocahantas-like, as the reviewers point out), because of a sign of his life-affirming potential. This sign is the attraction to the prosthetic Sully of the Woodsprites (Atokirina), the floating seeds of the Pandoran holy tree, resembling small glowing jellyfish, and understood by the Na'vi as spiritual beings. This scene illustrates the controversial technical achievement of the film, shot in 3-D, in that these glowing sprites extend out from the screen, entering the space of the audience, and fill the auditorium with a soft drifting rain of colored beauty. This effect calls attention to the technology of the medium. The relevant point for concept avatar is just that the effect is accomplished by a technical replication of the way binocular vision produces depth perception, which is by the simultaneous rendering of two views of the same scene, slightly displaced one from the other. The thought of avatar must sustain this parallax dimension, supporting the emergence of a third quality out of a logic of two. Hold this effect as an emblem of what is attempted in *Avatar Emergency* (a rhetorical extra dimension).

Michael

Another popular film, a romantic fantasy in this case, provides a version of avatar more reflective of the traditional personification: *Michael* (1996), directed and written by Nora Ephron. The protagonist is Frank Quinlan (William Hurt), a journalist whose once-promising career was ruined when he refused to compromise his integrity. Having become disenchanted and cynical, Frank works for a sleazy tabloid (*The National Mirror*), whose editor (Bob Hoskins) considers him his top reporter, specializing in celebrity gossip and fanciful counterfactual events. The relevance of the film in our context is that the angel Michael (John Travolta) is using his last permitted visit to Earth to intervene in Frank's affairs, to restore his connection with the life principle, Eros, vitality (Gaia). In this project Michael is acting as Frank's "guardian angel," as this figure was known in the Christian era, updated from the *daimon* or personal genius accompanying each soul entering the world in Ancient cosmology. The project unfolds through a lure, a situation arranged by the angel, that brings a crew from the tabloid to rural Iowa to investigate reports that an actual angel (wings and all) has shown up at the home of Patsy Millband (Jean Stapleton), a fan of the tabloid (especially of its mascot, Sparky the Wonder Dog).

Accompanying Frank and his photographer Huey Driscoll (Robert Pastorelli), owner of Sparky, is Dorothy Winters (Andie MacDowell), added to the group by the editor, claiming that she is an expert on angels. She actually is a professional dog trainer, hired by the editor, who wants to take Sparky away from Huey. Michael agrees to ride with the team back to Chicago, his plan being that Frank will fall in love with Dorothy during the journey. During the trip Michael demonstrates his love for embodiment, which gives him the capacity for sensory experience. He consumes bowls of sugar, smokes constantly, and engages in trysts with the ladies who are instantly attracted to him at all the stops that Michael forces the group to make at tourist sites along the way (world's largest frying pan, biggest ball of twine). A key scene in the narrative involves an evening spent at a café and motel. The group has been expanded by a newlywed couple that helped them with a flat tire. At the café the party discusses their favorite pies. When the waitress comes, they order two slices of every kind of pie on the menu. They sample the slices and banter over which kind is best. Affection has grown between Frank and Dorothy, and that night they sleep together.

Angels have no bodies, and their envy of human sensory experience is a *topos* of the tradition. The film expresses a wisdom that is as commonplace as it is true, but also turns out to be hard to accomplish in practice. Or rather, it is the impossibility to accomplish complete satisfaction and the necessity of supplemental fantasy that are a source of creative disequilibrium governing the dynamics of existence. The Romance genre of the film argues (consistently) the wisdom that falling in love achieves an aspect switch from death to life trajectory (two sides of the same energy). Libido is a moebius strip. The functionality relevant to us is this relationship between Frank and Michael. Michael as Frank's *daimon* demonstrates the tradition of "avatar," whose literal meaning is "descent" (incarnation, descent of spirit into flesh). Avatar in Hindu or Indian religion refers to the descent of God into material existence in a time of crisis, and the functionality to be adapted for electracy is this event of consultation, the occasion of decision requiring wisdom, good judgment, prudence (*phronesis*). "Descent" also refers to human embodiment, whether as the incarnation of spirit in pre-modern cosmologies, or arbitrarily thrown, as in existentialist modernity after the death of God. Ironically, the crisis facing civilization in electracy is precisely the one angels know nothing about: finite sexuated corporeality. Michael's self-indulgences certainly set a bad example for sustainable embodiment. We are going to have to deal with the emergency of the senses on our own. *Avatar Emergency* experiments with a rhetoric of flash reason that, instantiated in digital technology, makes possible a practice of judgment that is the electrate equivalent of what Michael personifies in the life of Frank Quinlan (or that Sully undergoes in his Na'vi prosthesis). This "flash" refers to velocity of thought, an illumination of insight referred to by numerous modern philosophers and writers. Representative of this emblem of illumination is Walter Benjamin, who described the dialectical image as a lighting flash: "What was must be held fast as it flashes its lightning image in the now of recognizability" (Benjamin, 1999: N 9, 7). The phrase is associated with networked communications, everything from short fiction through the animation program to "flash mobs" gathered using social media. These and other practices evolving within electracy are probes within which may be discerned an image (primary process) logic. A purpose of *Avatar Emergency* is to explore the capacities of this emergent logic through the invention of concept avatar.

EmerAgency

Avatar Emergency (AE) completes a tetralogy of books featuring the "EmerAgency," an online virtual consultancy, intended as a collaborative framework for inventing the practices of electracy. As with *Internet Invention* (2003), *Electronic Monuments* (2005), and *Miami Virtue* (2011), AE's point of departure is Paul Virilio's challenge to our information society: every technology brings with it its own disaster. The technology in question is that of our communications infrastructure, the digital media that function at the speed of light. The disasters Virilio has in mind are natural, technical, cultural, and social (he even has a category for "deliberate accidents," such as 9/11). The speed of our digital world has created a dimensional pollution, compressing everything into "now" (ironically, separated from "here"). This condition threatens to render impossible any democratic public sphere since there is no time for the deliberative reason, the persuasion and argument, needed to achieve the consent of the governed.

A similar point about the disparity between computing speed and human reason is made in a more optimistic way by cyber boosters. They predict that by 2050 one personal computer will have the computing power of the entire human population of the earth (Kurzweil. Qtd. in Oosterhuis 42). The challenge is to interface the equipment with human thought. The optimistic proposal is to invent "artificial intuition," which, in the grammatological context, could use the Greek term for intuitive intellect: *nous.* The proposal is for a direct connection between the brain and the machine (cyborg). "To allow yourself to act intuitively behind a computer device is a liberating process. You should allow yourself to have direct access to your distributed project databases. How can you as a designer do that? Invent a process, run the process, jump right into the process and make your split second decisions. Sculpt your information in real time" (Novak 39). Marcos Novak describes his work as constructing the alien. The alien stands for something new. The alien represents the unknown. Although Novak's "alien" may be a cousin of "avatar," the first mistake of this appeal is to isolate "brain" from "body." Electracy rather proposes that direct access to databases must be through "mindbodies," engaging mappings among orifices, brain, culture, and *technics.*

AE is an alternative to both the dystopian and utopian versions of this challenge of speed, arguing that "getting up to speed" is a motivation to take seriously the lesson of apparatus theory, which is that language technologies are not just equipment, but include institution formation (to develop and disseminate the relevant skill-set) and identity experience (individual and collective adaptations and adjustments to the new conditions). Even if we become posthuman (whether or not as cyborgs), the proposed invention must still include a practice or skill set that mediates between user and the equipment, just as the practices of literacy mediate between the person and the library. "Electracy" is to digital media what "literacy" is to alphabetic writing. The method of AE is to draw upon a sampling of elements, representing something of what the Western tradition knows about flash reason, sudden thought, or thinking at the speed of light, associated with the archive of image practices, usually associated with a mode of thought alternative to discursive analytical reason. Concept avatar assists our transition from the discursive to the momental. In fact, the ambition of flash reason is to bring into a rhetorical practice the effect Proust experienced as involuntary memory, referring to an event of time that exceeds the three *ekstases* of past-present-future:

> And now, suddenly, the effect of this harsh law [that we can only imagine what is absent] had been neutralized, temporarily annulled, by a marvelous expedient of nature which had caused a sensation—the noise made both by the spoon and by the hammer, for instance—to be mirrored at one and the same time in the past, so that my imagination was permitted

> to savor it, and in the present, where the actual shock to my sense of the noise, the touch of the linen napkin, or whatever it might be, had added to the dreams of the imagination the concept of 'existence' which they usually lack, and through this subterfuge had made it possible for my being to secure, to isolate, to immobilize—for a moment brief as a flash of lightning—what normally it never apprehends: a fragment of time in the pure state. (*The Past Recaptured* 133)

I had this experience when the Woodsprites floated out of the screen of *Avatar* (a moment to be discussed later).

A review of the tradition, having in mind the qualities of immediate insight, reveals that flash reason is associated with a particular virtue—that virtue without which all other virtues are useless, some have said: prudence, or *phronesis*, as Aristotle called it. There is a renewal of interest not just in ethics but in wisdom, noted in, for example, the Arete Initiative at the University of Chicago, which announced a two million dollar research program on the nature and benefits of wisdom. Two million dollars buys a lot of pie. Prudence is a time-wisdom, a capacity to make an appropriate decision in an instant by taking the measure of a particular situation in its temporal context. This virtue has a history that is not well understood, causing it to fall out of favor or be reduced to caricatures ("expediency") and even to be forgotten entirely. The formal goal for this study is to outline an image metaphysics that will do for electracy what Aristotle's categories did for literacy. A premise is that the path to the invention of general electracy (a fully electrate society) passes through an updating of the virtue of prudence. To approach the design of an interface rhetoric through the history of a virtue is to answer one of the four questions of Marshall McLuhan's heuristic tetrad. With respect to the invention of any artifact one is prompted to ask, what does it: 1) enhance? 2) obsolete? 3) retrieve? 4) produce when taken to its extreme? (*Laws of Media* 7). Our heuretic experiment retrieves from obsolescence the virtue of making an instant judgment in a particular situation as a source for the new logic of now-time as the best hope for thinking in Virilio's dromosphere.

AE is organized, then, around an exercise—the design of a personal allegory of prudence, based on a model of "encounter," in which contemporary artists updated famous paintings from a museum collection. The scene of decision foregrounded in this allegory is a point of departure for thinking about judgment itself as a kind of experience, including collective judgments of the kind archived in cultural traditions. What might wisdom be today, upon what authority might it be grounded, according to what measure, on behalf of what world view, what vision of well-being? The argument is expressed as testimony, not as declaration or prescription, framed in a reflexive account of my attempt to design an allegorical emblem out of my own experience. This exercise in allegory is a means to design and test a conceptual persona through a vital anecdote, as relay for concept avatar. Within this frame I present, in the genre of mystory (Ulmer, *Internet Invention*), what I have come to understand about living, my decision to become a professor of the Humanities and the lifestyle embraced as part of that choice, just enough (a measured contribution) to assist your own reflections, to locate your own place in and out of time. Concept avatar must be not only understood, but undergone.

iDatabase

AE is organized as a theoretical pedagogy, proposing exercises that introduce the operating principles and devices testing an aesthetic deliberative reason. The basic insight of apparatus theory is that the language practices of a civilization are an apparatus (a social machine), involving inventions arrived at autonomously in each of the three principal lines of evolution: technology, institutional practices, identity formation. Flash reason is a synthesis made from parts of historical practices, but for it to function as the general skill set of electracy assumes that it is taught in some form institutionally, augmented by the full power of the digital prosthesis. Reviewing the features of image authoring provided by the iLife suite of programs found on most Mac computers (iPhoto, iMovieHD, iDVD, GarageBand, iWeb) might be sufficient motivation for the invention of an electrate rhetoric, in any case. Despite the ease and ubiquity of these and similar authoring programs, however, the question of interface design is not as straightforward as it might seem. Lev Manovich's *The Language of New Media* gives an idea of some of the challenges facing the transition to electracy.

Since the featured experiment in prudence does not directly discuss new media, a brief inventory of Manovich's description of what is included under this rubric gives an idea of the context assumed for avatar as an image practice.

Technology

1. The convergence of all media in digital form, thus making all media programmable. The post-medium condition.
2. A new data object in information space. The new image ontology is "object-oriented." An info-thing is a collection of diverse multimedia items (text, image, sound, voice, music, animation, clips, links, data streams, and the like) formed as an assemblage.
3. Support for real-time interaction with and modification of data. This capability of authoring "on the fly" is what makes it possible for flash reason to address the dangers of the Internet Accident.

Software

1. The avant-garde revolution of modernism, more or less achieving the full potential of its innovations by the 1920s, offers the best description of digital production tools: the cut-and-paste aesthetics of collage-montage, from Cubism to cinema, continuing in the Fine Arts up to our own time, and culminating in postmodernism. Manovich's list of operations includes (besides cut-and-paste) copy, sort, search, filter, transcode, and rip. These aesthetics have become hegemonic in the tools, in the hardware and software of computing, but not yet in the common sense of everyday life or popular culture. This disparity between the parts of the apparatus (technology and institutional practices being out of joint) is a major challenge for education.
2. Information space is a composite, juxtaposing or superimposing heterogeneous locations. The logic of selection (menus) is modular, involving a range of features from video-keying to the program loop. The related point in grammatological terms is that literacy remains relevant as the category system for creating topics (*topoi*), but these topics are modules assembled into heterogeneous wholes that in turn need a regional category. That category (theorized here and in my previous work) is "chora."

3. Simulation exceeds and incorporates representation. The computer replaces, simulates, and exceeds the lens. The scene created in the computer is not limited to, and is independent of, the parameters of conceptual and perceptible environments. Electracy as an apparatus is challenged to invent the institution, a metaphysics, and its related language/thought practices supporting this new relationship between humans and our equipment. Flash reason separates out and adds "affect" to concept and percept, or "judgment" to reason and will, as an autonomous faculty now accessible to ontology through the capacities of digital technology.

Interface (HCI)

1. The computer screen as equipment is literally and figuratively a frame. Or, the various registers of framing constituting any metaphysics are made more explicit in electracy; the computer screen frames an information space; cinematic editing frames the mise-en-scene of this space-time; image ontology frames what counts as reality for those using the apparatus. The interface displaying the information has a double structure, toggling between the transparent (promoting identification with a mimetic scenography) and the opaque (a critical tool for control and navigation).
2. A new object. Any object, thing, or prop in the represented/simulated scene may function as a sign with all the powers of the "as-structure" of language, meaning that it operates to control and navigate information. Any such sign may serve as a portal or gate switching between the levels of identification and control. In historical terms, this interface construes the equipment as externalized and programmable memory palace.
3. General cultural interface. Popular (entertainment) culture in general, and film (cinematography) in particular have become internalized and naturalized to the point that they comprise a rhetoric capable of organizing any body of information. In Aristotle's terms, we could say that the commonplaces of popular forms and media may be used to structure and communicate the specialized places of knowledge. Any data may be constructed and navigated as if it were a movie.

Electracy then faces the same challenge confronting literacy in the era of Plato and Aristotle. In both cases there is in place a vernacular or endoxal skill-set available and capable of exploiting the new media (alphabetic or digital). Aristotle's logic and rhetoric fashioned that endoxal interface of natural language into the powerful devices of argumentative inference that remain the core of literate education to this very day. Our proposal is that flash reason may do for the general cultural interface of media popular culture what Aristotle did for the natural language vernacular of Greek writing.

This set of features of new media extracted rather crudely from Manovich's sophisticated and detailed argument constitutes nonetheless a useful reminder of the equipmental dimension of the electrate apparatus upon which to map the features of flash reason. Flash reason is the rhetoric citizens will need to become native users of the "language" described by Manovich. Flash reason, that is, as avatar rhetoric, is a second-order conduct, articulating the extant information culture for purposes of personal, professional, and public ends, the way literate rhetoric articulated the resources of natural language (including mythology, epics, ritual performance and the like) in the previous apparatus.

Image Ontological Affect

The flash reason necessary for avatar is the skill set native to new media, in the way that argumentation is native to literacy. It does not replace oral or literate practices, but supplements them with a new authoring, constructing a new metaphysics. This new metaphysics opens a dimension of human experience that until now seemed beyond the reach of education, if not of manipulation. This dimension of human capacity was framed by the Classical Greeks as a matter of virtue, meaning "power" or "capacity" native to a person. Virtue as such could not be taught, it was said, but could be trained by means of habit. A synonym for virtue in this usage is "disposition," "inclination," "habitus."

This aspect of human "being" as life principle or force has been described by various terms: entelechy (Aristotle), *conatus* (Spinoza), monad (Leibniz), eternal return (Nietzsche), unconscious (Freud), *Dasein* (Heidegger). Spinoza's definition of *conatus* summarizes the phenomenon in question: a striving to persevere in one's own being. Striving—to what end? The key point is that this dimension of reality happens within first-person experience, not as an idea or concept, but affectively, as a feeling, the sensation of being alive. This "little sensation" is the site of a struggle for the future of humanity today, just as at one time was the "soul." Most recently "disposition" is the target of neuroscience. An index of this continuity in the tradition is Antonio Damasio's *Looking for Spinoza: Joy, Sorrow, and the Feeling Brain.* Damasio is one of the leading commentators on how neuroscience is explaining physiologically some of the insights of artists and philosophers. This affective dimension of the real is now accessible to image ontology in electracy.

A good account of the technological, artistic, and theoretical context motivating flash reason is Mark Hansen's *New Philosophy for New Media.* Hansen's insight is that in new media the very definition of "image" is transformed. An image is not some external support that we perceive as an object, but is a field of information that we experience as a participant. We are in the image, or rather, even more strongly, the image is a construct produced by the interaction of the equipment with our embodied condition. The theoretical basis for this insight comes from a revisionist reading of Bergson, partially rescued from Deleuze's first retrieval of this philosopher for contemporary media theory.

The current usage of "avatar" is confused with "brand," but "brand" is only my self-promoting ego. In electracy brand is augmented by avatar, beyond the pleasure principle. In the electrate image the individual body functions as filter, selecting from a flood of raw data what counts as real. Moreover, the selection is made coherent, given order, by an underlying intuition of unity that is the subject "I." This unity is fundamentally affective (feeling, not emotion). Affect is distinguished, given its own modality, separate from and equal to the other faculties or virtues (in our terms): concept and percept. Hansen puts together this theory with the features of VR equipment and artists who experiment with and display this embodied affective ordination, such as Jeffrey Shaw. "By transforming the body into a screen that literally 'selects' images by absorbing them, Shaw's environments institute a strict proportional correlation between action and perception: without the activity of the body within the space of the image, there would simply be no perception at all" (*New Philosophy* 54). In *Bodies in Code,* Hansen makes a distinction between a person's body image and body schema (mirror perception versus proprioception), and the importance of the latter for "mixed reality," that outlines a possible technical instatiation of concept avatar in digital media. Body image is projected as brand; body schema maps database information on triggers interfacing self and brand with collective knowledge (avatar).

The purpose of flash reason is to develop the rhetorical practice that allows users within the apparatus to take full advantage of the equipment and forms becoming available for everyday use, as described by Manovich and Hansen. This selective filtering of embodiment is made available for ontology in the equipment, just as alphabetic writing made analytical thinking available for ontology in literacy. What the written verb "to be" is to literacy, digitally designed emblems are to electracy. Literacy augmented the experience of idea (thinking); electracy augments the experience of affect (feeling). Concept avatar thinks feeling (the goal of Proust's novel). Hansen notes that assigning affect its own modality brings forward for further application the experience of vitality, the intensity of a satisfaction in its own right (the value termed "life" made reflexive through avatar). Avatar personifies living. A relevant anecdote reinforcing this point is that of a seminal moment in the creative development of Bill Viola's aesthetics, when he viewed a scene of a children's birthday party filmed using high-speed equipment that produced a saturation of information (384 fps). "Viola recounted being dumbstruck by his observation of joy literally growing and moving through the faces of his subjects … even in a still image [from this footage] there was not only an excess of emotion, but a certain temporal expansion of it beyond the confines of what was captured in the image" (Hansen, *New Philosophy* 260).

The most relevant part of Viola's discoveries for avatar is not that new media actually has the capacity to expand the temporality of a present "now," but that emotion has its own temporality, or exists outside of time (264). The answer to the Internet Accident threatened in the conditions of collapsed dimensionality described by Virilio, is to ontologize this detour, this alternative register of emotion, from within which an electrate deliberative reason may be possible. Within the fully formed apparatus this modality constructs a new dimension of reality, supplementing the realities already informing our world, with unforeseen (unforeseeable) consequences for civilization. To access this dimension for judgment both individual and collective requires avatar simulation today, just as it did in bygone wisdom traditions. Avatar is the practice of netizens that remains for the most part implicit in the theoretical conversation to date. AE's purpose, then, is to explore a category system for "new media." Our experiment complements Hansen's and Manovich's accounts in adding the features for a skill set the electrate user will internalize in order to reason with an affective metaphysics, operating database feeds at light-speed in a dromosphere.

The debts incurred during the research process are numerous. Students at the University of Florida have contributed to Imaging Florida, the EmerAgency, and seminars exploring choragraphy, heuretics, and grammatology. Students and colleagues in the European Graduate School (Saas-Fee, Switzerland) have been a valuable resource for experimentation. My colleagues in the Florida Research Ensemble have been a continuing source of inspiration and help: thanks especially to John Craig Freeman and Barbara Jo Revelle. Colleagues and students in the Rhetorics, Communications, and Information Design program at Clemson University are making an original contribution to the heuretics of electracy. The Office of Research, Technology, and Graduate Education at the University of Florida supported the project with a grant from the Opportunity Fund. The Humanities Institute at the University of Florida funded a conference (February 2007), organized by Kate Casey-Sawicki, bringing together colleagues participating in the listserv Invent-L, where many of the ideas expressed here were first aired. Some of the sections of this study are adapted from essays published in *Digital Humanities Quarterly*, *Discourse*, *Pre/Text*, and in two books published by Routledge Press: *Ecology, Writing Theory and New Media,* and *The Routledge Companion to Experimental Literature.* Thanks to Mark Amerika for including me in the online part of *Remixthebook* (University of Minnesota Press). Special thanks to my wife, Kathy, for her support and understanding, and to my sons, Tyson and Leland, for keeping me humble. The ideas outlined here will continue to evolve in my blog, http://heuretics.wordpress.com.

Avatar Emergency

The eye was placed where one ray should fall, that it might testify of that particular ray.

—Ralph Waldo Emerson, "Self-Reliance"

1 Prudence

Decision

In electracy a new identity behavior and experience are emerging within the tradition of avatar. To understand the full potential of avatar as subject formation (supplementing spirit and self) requires that we go beyond the narrow, partial borrowing of the term in contemporary parlance, to review the new demands placed upon the subject in electracy. A detour through Nietzsche provides an orienatation to the question, undertaken from my own perspective. The first section of *Ecce Homo* is entitled "Why I Am So Wise," uttered in a complex tone. Didactic, a lesson on "wisdom," concerning how I inhabited time: writing. What was "writing" and why did I do it? There will be some delay in getting around to my idiocy but you already have an inkling. It has everything to do with "inkling" (*Ahnung*) as a mode of thought in any case. "You," I am talking to you and me—to the "self" I was in 1966, age twenty-one, and anyone else not put off by the second person. A decision was made or took place or was ratified during that year, a turn, and I am testifying in order to generalize to a "decision" theory for an image metaphysics. Dates: May 1966 / May 2011. Temporality is part of the enigma. In the cineplex watching Cameron's *Avatar* through 3D goggles, when the auditorium filled with the drifting descent of glowing Woodsprites, I suddenly recalled a scene that happened in a Spanish olive orchard, May 1966. We all make decisions, choices, (mistakes) each in our own circumstances, conditions presented as situations. It was (retrospectively) a scene of decision. My decision is a way to think about decision itself, decision today and right now in your present circumstances, concerning some graphical interface for an online database. In this book I am playing avatar, belatedly.

Decision concerns event. There is an event to come but not directly so I will start with experience, to test knowing against living (knowing as living). Nietzsche was the philosopher I read in college. He posed the question that turned out to have set the agenda of my research career, speaking with the benefit of hindsight (but everything here is a delay, retrospeculative, aftering). There is a singularity in your life, Nietzsche advised, marking the intersection of the aphorism of thought with the anecdote of life. In my hands is *Ecce Homo,* the Walter Kaufman translation, the Vintage original, subtitled "How One Becomes What One Is." *Werde der du bist.* It was his motto, adopted from Pindar, to acknowledge the antiquity of this imperative. There is an ambiguity that will have been important, whether "what" or "who" comes. I am testifying that I have learned there is no more important phrase than this one in the history of the Western tradition. Let this be the theme of our consultancy, this session between us, with regard to becoming what you are, and my imparting what I learned about it, as a kind of exit interview, a debriefing, now that I am bygone. You may be curious as well about this intersection and the convergence between thought and life, knowledge and experience, and how elders impart to youth useless *counsel.* Event includes the undergoing and the understanding.

Between the preface and the first numbered entry stands a paragraph designating the time of writing as a perfect day, Nietzsche wrote, everything ripening and not only the grape turning brown, when the eye of the sun fell upon his life. He looked back, looked forward, and never saw so many and such good things at once. He buried his forty-fourth year on this day, buried because saved, rendered immortal, by the works published that year, such as *Twilight of the Idols,* in which he attempted to philosophize with a hammer. "How could I fail to be grateful to my whole life?—and so I tell my life to myself" (*Ecce Homo* 221). Don't I know that feeling, doesn't any scholar, when the printed volume is in your hands? That is part of what should be understood, the materialization of that product, a text, and the experience of making such a thing (here we go again). The nature of any object may be approached through this one, to relieve the illusion of its solidity, isolation, fixity, in order to undergo the force passing through it, materialized there, for what we are tracking is this axis of attraction-repulsion organizing reality in electracy. This concerns you.

Nietzsche addresses us from a site in Switzerland, an Alpine valley known as the Upper Engadine where he summered in the years between 1879—1888. I have some experience of the setting because of the seminars I taught in Saas-Fee for the European Graduate School. Walking the trails through and above that valley reminded me of Nietzsche, and perhaps I could have imagined myself in his place, except that my body was free of the pain and suffering that tormented his existence. That and also not being burdened with genius you might add, except that part of what I learned concerns the unavoidability of what genius names, even for you and me. *Ecce Homo* is a consultation, a book of advice, to be shelved with other self-help works. It seems Nietzsche's books were little known in his own day, and in fact one motivation for *Ecce Homo* was to rectify this obscurity, the invisibility that made it appear as if it were a mere prejudice that he lived.

Against his instincts and habits, it became necessary for Nietzsche to declare: "Hear me! For I am such and such a person. Above all, do not mistake me for someone else" (217). We listen to his *counsel*, vouchsafed in the guise of prudence and self-defense, in the name of self-preservation. The addressees are former colleagues, that is, all of us who do little but thumb books, losing in the process our capacity to think for ourselves. When we don't thumb, we don't think. I don't disagree with Nietzsche's condemnation as I compose in free indirect discourse, *erlebte rede*, paperback propped precariously to leave hands free for keyboarding. *Thumbing* about sums it up. Early in the morning, when day breaks, when all is fresh, in the dawn of one's strength, to read a book at such a time, Nietzsche advised, is simply depraved (253). What would he say about you, sound asleep? He speaks from experience, for he knows himself, on how one becomes merely a reagent, how one reads to ruin, to be merely a match that one has to strike to make it emit sparks (thoughts). But isn't that an allusion to Plato?

Now I must quote, since he invokes the virtue that is our theme, prudence, which is another name for a problem, a guide to the art of decision and the relation of experience to knowledge, in the invention stream leading to electracy.

> At this point the real answer to the question, how one becomes what one is, can no longer be avoided. And thus I touch on the masterpiece of the art of self-preservation—of selfishness. For let us assume that the task, the destiny, the fate of the task transcends the average very significantly: in that case, nothing could be more dangerous than catching sight of oneself with this task. To become what one is, one must not have the faintest notion what one is. From this point of view even

> the blunders of life have their own meaning and value—the occasional side roads and wrong roads, the delays, "modesties," seriousness wasted on tasks that are remote from the task. All this can express a great prudence, even the supreme prudence: where *nosce te ipsum* [know thyself] would be the recipe for ruin, forgetting oneself, misunderstanding oneself, making oneself smaller, narrower, mediocre, become reason itself. (254)

This is a saving caveat, since our prudence will be of this latter sort, found rather than planned. Our prudence is fatal.

No need to quibble about this terminology of "selfishness," since "self" is rather what is exceeded, whether or not there is a unity or a measure guiding one's becoming. Tradition supplies a family of terms, such as *conatus*, in Spinoza: the principle that to live is to strive to persevere in one's own being. Nietzsche is an heir of this fundamental project, assigned various names by different thinkers (Entelechy, Monad, *Dasein*) and so are you, in your striving to become what you are. Striving. And this striving, does it not feel as though it has some direction? This direction is prudence, monitored by avatar. Nietzsche has a task, and this is a crucial point: the transvaluation of all values, aka the eternal return of the same, or the will to power. He gave this task to himself. The existence and nature of "task" is part of our consultation, but even more significant is the experience in which Nietzsche had the thought. It is an event much cited in anthologies and surveys. It is dated August 1881, penned on a sheet with the notation underneath, "6000 feet beyond man and time." That day he was walking through the woods along the lake of Silvaplana, he relates; at a powerful pyramidal rock not far from Surlei he stopped. It was then that the idea came to him (295).

A thought happens to Nietzsche. He has an idea. This is the event in question. He experiences a moment of insight, literally an "inspiration." This is the point, this conjunction of experience and knowledge, which is also a possibility for you, and concerns the functionality of avatar. Right there, if we can zoom in and linger. Everything that we will have said concerns just this event, this quality of thought. I want to understand "what happened," because to the extent that it is an event, it is not over yet, and never will be over. Nor can it be left to the few geniuses of history. *You* need to have an idea. Tradition, and you are a *diadoch*, a successor, meaning that it depends on you, for thinking is not just for experts today. The biographical details include the fascinating young Russian woman, Lou Andreas-Salomé, who behaved for a time during this period as a disciple; and also there was the friend who introduced Lou to Nietzsche. Her name constitutes evidence in favor of "signature" as destiny. The thought of "Zarathustra" intersects with the anecdotes of Nietzsche's walks through various landscapes, along the road to Zoagli past pines with a view of the sea, and also around the bay of Rapallo from Santa Margherita all the way to Portofino. Various landscapes contributed to the process, the unfolding of the idea that had more than one date and place, not only Swtizerland but also Nice and the ascent to the Moorish eyrie at Eza. A composite place of invention. Our tactic is always to take the hint, to look around at our own landscapes, rather than to make pilgrimages to Nietzsche's territory. Nietzsche reported a correlation between his creative energies and the suppleness of his muscles. "The body is inspired; let us keep the 'soul' out of it" (302). Precisely, body, for it is the body that is augmented and thinks within an electrate apparatus.

As for this inspiration itself, it falls within the category of epiphany or revelation. "Revelation in the sense that suddenly, with indescribable certainty and subtlety, something becomes visible, audible, something that shakes one to the last depths and throws one down—that merely describes the facts. One hears, one does not see; one accepts, one does not ask who gives; like lightning, a thought flashes up, with necessity, without hesitation regarding its form—I never had any choice" (300). The physical qualities of the rapture are associated with a feeling of freedom, of power, of capacity summarized as a depth of happiness. "One no longer has a notion of what is an image or a metaphor: everything offers itself as the nearest, most obvious, simplest expression. It actually seems as if the things themselves approached and offered themselves as metaphors" (301). Like lightning, *a thought flashes up*. Such is the functionality we want, to manage what happens in cyberspace when the networked databases deliver a water cannon of information. Nietzsche got it, and we need a practice of getting it.

Happiness, considered as a feeling, along with a warning (it is not what you suppose). Yes, and the task of flash reason is to bring this experience into everyday pedagogy. This experience, this lightning flash of insight, the feeling of capacity or capability, potentiality, in which the world offers itself as a forest of signs composed in one's native code, this is the mode of intelligence taken up in a rhetoric of flash reason, constructed for the quotidian practice of electracy. This experience need not be so esoteric, so Alpine, and must not be, if civilization is to thrive in in a digital apparatus. Not that I am so wise (you heard Nietzsche's irony), but I love wisdom. I am testifying, not explaining.

Decorum

How to generalize into a practice the flash of insight? Flash reason, to accomplish the functionality of avatar as counsel, retrieves and updates the tradition of decorum as readymade wisdom. I don't understand my own selection filter, but avatar does. Reality is ontological sampling. The modern meaning of the word "commonplace," to indicate a banality or triviality, signals the weakness in manuscript pedagogy—its tendency to slide into cliché. The manuals always advised that the method required not just "imitation" but *ingenium* (genius), but the latter capacity was assumed and not considered teachable. The tradition was at its best, on its own terms, in the practice of imitations of complete individual works—even word-by-word or phrase-by-phrase transpositions of a model's style and form, adapted to one's own materials and situation (Moss 63). The postmodern taste for pastiche recovers some of the effects of *imitatio.* The mode included an appreciation for an allusive game in which the original source was partly disguised. Recognizing the model was part of the pleasure of reception of the oration or text. Pastiche is an important device for flash reason, nor am I concealing my reliance on a tradition.

The entire practice is an extension of Aristotle's "category" into the highest orders of literate form. This metaphysical register of the alphabetic apparatus accounts for the grain or propensity of the method that led eventually to the rules of decorum, which in turn rigidified into stereotypes. Painters as much as writers were instructed that "each age, each sex, each type of human being must display its representative character, and [they] must be scrupulous in giving the appropriate physique, gesture, bearing, and facial expression to each of the figures" (Lee 35). Even if it is character RTW (off the rack), this iconizing process has important lessons for electracy, including an insight into the narrowing, pejorative meanings associated with prudence in modernity. "Decorum" came to mean "not only the suitable representation of typical aspects of human life, but also specific conformity to what is decent and proper in taste, and even more in morality and religion"

(37). Through taste lifestyle itself becomes scriptable (reduced to style in early modernity, rhetoric prepared to take responsibility for lifestyle). Electracy requires designer character.

Aristotle recognized in the *Rhetoric* and in the *Nicomachean Ethics* that rhetorical decorum and prudence share a faculty of judgment that is not logical or theoretical, but practical; that does not subordinate an object to a general rule or concept, but responds to the particular per se. This is because both rhetoric and prudence are concerned with "problems about which different points of view [can] be maintained, questions open to debate because they [can] be judged only in terms of probable truth and [are] not susceptible to scientific demonstrations of irrefutable validity" (qtd. in Kahn 30). Thus Aristotle writes in the *Rhetoric*: "The duty of rhetoric is to deal with such matters as we deliberate upon without arts or systems to guide us . . . there are few facts of the 'necessary' type that can form the basis of rhetorical syllogisms. Most of the things about which we make decisions, and into which we therefore inquire, present us with alternative possibilities. For it is about our actions that we deliberate and inquire, and all our actions have a contingent character; hardly any of them are determined by necessity" (qtd. in Kahn 30). The standard of judgment for a proper or appropriate decision, in other words, was based in practical considerations "and derives its authority from the conviction that, in some practical sense, 'what all believe to be true is actually true'" (32). Updated decorum has its point of departure not in shared opinion but singular experience.

Montaigne marks a moment of transition, in which the commonplace practice of manuscript culture passed into the print mode of the essay. Our project is to continue this update through literacy into electrate avatar. He exploited the topic of *in utramque parte*—the applicability of the topics to both sides of a case (to attack or defend a question)—which he extended from a rhetorical to an ontological level. He redefined prudence in terms of Pyrrhonist skepticism (53). This skepticism reflects the new sensibility, the changing worldview of early modernity, the new science and its philosophical proponents such as Descartes or Francis Bacon. For these authors "invention" shifts from finding or recognizing a traditional authority (opinion) to inquiry and the discovery of new knowledge. The authority of the "judge" at the metaphorical heart of "category" is exposed in Montaigne's stance.

> Montaigne's proposition is an ironic or skeptical version of the speculative judgment. Unlike Hegel's dialectic, Montaigne's sentence is not the discovery of the identity of two terms, but a narration of the rhetorical structure of equivalence, or of the failure of dialectic. It does not reveal the "profound tautology of all thought," but rather that an equation is authoritative only because it is apropos. In short, it is the copula itself that is the most appropriate, that is to say the most useful, because finally the most pleasurable and inevitable of human fictions. At first glance it seems to be a simple analogy between the mastery of art and life, or between rhetoric and prudence. But closer examination reveals that analogy is a process, that it is constructed and destroyed in the continual essay of the apropos. The essay as scale turns out to be a very dubious form of judgment. (149)

In the context of commonplace practice it is easy to see the extent to which Montaigne used a topical (readymade) grid to compose his essays. "A glance at one of the essays illustrates this. The essay 'That We Should Not Judge of Our Happiness until after Our Death' begins with a quotation from Ovid's Metamorphoses: 'We must expect of man the latest day, Not, ere he die, hi's happy can we say.' This adage is then paraphrased; it is amplified by examples from ancient history and from myth; quotations from the classics are inserted generously; an exhortation is added; and the essay concludes with a brief epilog applying the moral" (Lechner 218). Kafka's rhetoric continues this tradition in modernism in his appropriation of sayings and revisions of parables. The prototype of the technique (explained by Clayton Koelb), is an indirect reporting of a man seeking directions who asked a policeman the way. The policeman's reply ("Give it up!") indicates he took the question to be metaphysical (from one who has lost his way in life) (Koelb 11). These examples express our theme as well as its method: electrate wisdom.

The intellectual obituary of the commonplaces and the confidence in endoxal wisdom is Flaubert's project for a mock encyclopedia of received ideas. The project reflects his own disgust with French bourgeois culture, dramatized in his novel, *Bouvard et Pécuchet.* He compiled a collection of platitudes and clichés that circulated in middle-class opinion, and also a collection of "stupidities" (the Sottisier) culled from supposedly authoritative or admired publications. He worked on these collections for more than twenty years, and bragged that he had read more than 1,500 books in search of his material. His method was authentically topical, in other words, but his motivation was parodic. The entries were listed alphabetically, and read not as factoids about something but as an annotation of current opinion. The entry for "feudalism" gives the flavor: "No need to have one single precise notion about it: thunder against."

Multitude

The topical tradition went fallow, we could say, and represents now in its retrieval an important resource for an Internet choral counsel. At the conclusion of his review of rhetoric, for example, Barthes noted the "stubborn agreement" between Aristotelianism and mass culture in Western societies: "a practice based, through democracy, on an ideology of the 'greatest number,' of the majority-as-norm, of current opinion: everything suggests that a kind of Aristotelian vulgate still defines a type of trans-historical Occident, a civilization (our own) which is that of the endoxa" ("The Old Rhetoric" 92). He goes on to propose an assignment.

> This observation, disturbing as it is in its foreshortened form, that all our literature, formed by Rhetoric and sublimated by humanism, has emerged from a politico-judicial practice: in those areas where the most brutal conflicts—of money, of property, of class—are taken over, constrained, domesticated, and sustained by state power, where state institutions regulate feigned speech and codifies all recourse to the signifier: there is where our literature is born. This is why reducing Rhetoric to the rank of a merely historical object; seeking, in the name of text, of writing, a new practice of language; and never separating ourselves from revolutionary science—these are one and the same task. (93)

Paolo Virno takes up where Barthes left off, seeing in this fit between Aristotle and the culture industry an opportunity for the recovery of a public sphere by using the "spectacle" against itself. The context for Virno's proposal is the post-Fordist stage of capital, the information economy in which knowledge and invention are primary sources of wealth: wealth is not found in products but in the process of production. "In the spectacle we find exhibited, in a separate and fetishized form, the most relevant productive forces of society, those productive forces on which every contemporary work process must draw: linguistic competence, knowledge, imagination, etc. Thus, the spectacle has a double nature: a specific product of a particular industry, but also, at the same time, the quintessence of the mode of production in its entirety" (60).

The possibility of a new public sphere depends upon the emergence of a new collective identity, appropriate to the conditions of the electrate apparatus (currently embodied in the spectacle), theorized with reference to the writings of Spinoza. Should the collective body of society be constituted as a "people," as a unified identity (as One), as Hobbes proposed? Or as a "multitude," of many individuals, whose coherence does not depend on "identity" politics, as Spinoza thought? The history of modernity worked through the politics of various "peoples" (nationalism, in short). The new politics suggest a public life of the multitude. While this whole argument is relevant to the project of flash reason as a logic of deliberation for electracy, the immediate point to stress is Virno's suggestion that the source of coherence for the multitude is the language capacity itself of human beings (the proprium, in fact, of Aristotle's definition of "man"). To explain the kind of practice he imagines capable of supporting this electrate collectivity (image hegemony), Virno invokes the model of Aristotle's topics and the commonplace tradition, which he sees as a particular embodiment of what Marx called the "general intellect."

> In today's world, the "special places" of discourse and or argumentation are perishing and dissolving, while immediate visibility is being gained by the "common places," or by generic logical-linguistic forms which establish the pattern for all forms of discourse. This means that in order to get a sense of orientation in the world and to protect ourselves from its dangers, we can not rely on those forms of thought, of reasoning, or of discourse which have their niche in one particular context or another. . . . The "common places" (these inadequate principles of the "life of the mind") are moving to the forefront: the connection between more and less, the opposition of opposites, the relationship of reciprocity, etc. these "common places," and these alone, are what exist in terms of offering us a standard of orientation, and thus, some sort of

> refuge from the direction in which the world is going. Being no longer inconspicuous, but rather having been flung into the forefront, the "common places" are the apotropaic resource of the contemporary multitude. They appear on the surface, like a toolbox containing things which are immediately useful. (36–37)

The value of Virno's proposal is his recognition of the need for a shared mode of thought. The action item concerns a movement beyond reliance on expert specialization (techno-science) to the establishment of what used to be called "wisdom," and which in practice represented the authority of tradition. The limitation of Virno's insight and proposal is that he ignores the historical specificity of the apparatus. The commonplace tradition developed out of Aristotle's metaphysics is specific to literacy. Or, the inference to be drawn from Virno's argument is that the task is to do for electracy, the post-Fordist society of the spectacle, what Aristotle did for the Classical world: invent a new metaphysics, a category native to the digital apparatus, and a practice of thought adequate to the "toolbox" evolving so rapidly within new media culture. The project is not to follow in the footsteps of Aristotle, but to seek what he sought. The update from topics to pop culture takes care of itself, as in the genre typified by *All I Really Need to Know I Learned From Watching Star Trek.* Alain de Botton is closer to traditional decorum in *How Proust Can Change Your Life.* Concept avatar is ontological self-help.

Allegory

Avatar as conceptual persona retrieves decorum and the topical tradition, updated as a means for individuals to use the Internet as a commonplace chora. Harold Bloom, in his poetics of the modern crisis poem, noted in poets' dialogical struggle with precursors in the tradition an underlying continuation of commonplace compositional procedures. Bloom traces the tradition of topics from Classical rhetoric, the art of places in Cicero, who listed sixteen topics of invention (devices for generating "copy"). Bloom finds six revisionary ratios persisting in Romantic and modernist poetry, surviving their historical transmittal through Associationist Psychology of the Enlightenment, as in Locke's association of ideas, "founded on the notion of habit and memory as modes of repetition that fixed ideas through the accompaniment of pleasure and pain" ("Poetic Crossing" 516). This diachronic rhetoric continues into the present, with Bloom's useful insight into Freud's dreamwork and the defense mechanisms of unconscious thought as a new terminology for the old tropology of rhetoric. Flash reason extracts from Bloom's ratios a poetics for consulting with the global cultural archive. Modernist crisis poems (from Wordsworth through Ashbery, in Bloom's canon) offer a relay for playing avatar (the meaning of this phrase will deepen as we progress). To say "relay" means that the analogy is loose, heuristic, experimental. Keep in mind that you are inventing a practice of decision, a guide to action.

We need an exercise to ground these detours of history and theory in our own experience. Our consultation falls within the same genre as the one motivating *Ecce Homo*, except that I am working the other side of the aisle, that of the idiot. Already names of the experience to which I am testifying are accumulating on the side of knowledge but we mean to reach across from knowledge to this other lived dimension, sometimes confused with ignorance, stupidity, nescience. Since I can't think without thumbing, let me set up an exercise through which you may approach a version of Nietzsche's moment. I need a form in which to cast the memory of an event, and Titian's *Allegory of Prudence* looks promising. The prudence organizing Nietzsche's advice is what the Greeks called *phronesis*. What I have to impart can be approached as an update, adaptation, appropriation of this tradition, virtue, capacity, faculty. I am speaking of the Western tradition, but not only that, since our concern is with wisdom and its deficit, an ecology of thought for a global consultancy. We all need to be on the same screen, with correlated databases, to make the coming decisions, which require some device with decision as a specific experience and practice. Can there be an electrate decorum? Solve WWXD? for the value avatar (what would avatar do).

The ambition of flash reason is to support collective epiphany, despite the skepticism of pundits today, questioning the very possibility of "defining moments" creative of national unity. The event motivating this concern was the shooting of Representative Gabrielle Giffords in Tucson, and the conversation led to regret that even the sense of community following 9/11 had no lasting effect. "It may just be that modern society is impervious to brilliant flashes of clarity. There is very little shared experience in the nation now; there are only competing versions of the experience, consumed in such a way as to confirm whatever preconceptions you already have, rather than to make you reflect on them" (Bai). Flash reason does not concern opinion, does not operate in the dimension of persuasion. Rather, it takes up the operation itself of "version" that puts us in a spin. It thinks the preconceptual.

We are updating an ancient ambition, concerning how humans might communicate with God/gods. The relay from the tradition indicates that individuals may appropriate for themselves if not absolute comprehension (*nous*), then at least the accumulated potentiality of the archive. Take Titian, for example. Titian's painting is composed as an "emblem," consisting of a picture and a motto, whose relationship poses a certain enigma. The practice we are proposing, flash reason, depends upon a (digital) image metaphysics, just as literacy developed a metaphysics of the written word, and we will use the latter as a relay to construct the former. Emblem is a hinge articulating the two apparati. Titian's picture shows the heads of three men, each posed in alignment with the heads of three animals directly below them. The motto reads, "From the [experience of the] past, the present acts prudently, lest it spoil future action."

> The elements of this inscription are so arranged as to facilitate the interpretation of the parts as well as the whole: the words praeterito, praesens and futura serve as labels, so to speak, for the three human faces in the upper zone, viz., the profile of a very old man turned to the left, the full-face portrait of a middle-aged man in the center, and the profile of a beardless youth turned to the right; whereas the clause praesens prudenter agit gives the impression of summarizing the total content after the fashion of a "headline." We are given to understand, then, that the three faces, in addition to typifying three states of human life (youth, maturity, old age), are meant to symbolize the three modes or forms of time in general: past, present, and future. And we are further asked to connect these three modes or forms of time with the idea of prudence or, more specifically, with the three psychological faculties in the combined exercise of which this virtue consists: memory, which remembers, and learns from, the past; intelligence, which judges of, and acts in, the present; and foresight, which anticipates, and provides for or against, the future. (Panofsky 149)

We may borrow from Titian's *Prudence* the concetto form, his personalizing of the iconography. The role of epigram in an emblem is to resolve the enigma (in this case) of the busts (humans and animals) juxtaposed with the motto invoking prudence. That role is played here by the fact that the three men are Titian and his family: the old man is a self-portrait; the mature man is Titian's younger son; the youth is an adopted grandson. The painting celebrates an occasion of satisfaction, a prudent action—the successful completion of a legal case in which Titian changed his will so that his inheritance would pass not to the oldest (scoundrel) son, but to the younger son (who is shown as the lion) (166). Most of all, it is an encounter with time.

The three animal heads are derived from several iconographic traditions (image commonplaces), as Panofsky explains. The tricephalous monster was a companion of Serapis (Pluto), god of the underworld. The arrangement associates the old man with the wolf (the past devours time); the mature man with the lion (action in the present); the youth with the dog (always trying to please, in hopes of a good outcome). The three heads in the convention are joined by a serpent's body—the serpent being an allusion to the snake swallowing its own tail. Titian's design reflects the Renaissance fascination with hieroglyphic signs popularized by the Neoplatonists. Gombrich cites Ficino as providing the charter for the art of emblematics, setting a precedent from which modern advertising benefitted, for our ads are precisely emblems. Modernity through advertising already absorbed what the tradition knows about thinking fast, about instant comprehension, but there is nothing inherently Capitalist or Christian about the emblem.

> When the Egyptian priests wished to signify divine mysteries, they did not use the small characters of script, but the whole images of plants, trees or animals; for God has knowledge of things not by way of multiple thought but like the pure and firm shape of the thing itself. Your thoughts about time are multiple and shifting, when you say that time is swift or that, by a kind of turning movement, it links the beginning again to the end, that it teaches prudence and that it brings things and carries them away again. But the Egyptian can comprehend the whole of this discourse in one firm image when he paints a winged serpent with its tail in its mouth, and so with the other images which Horus described. (Ficino qtd. in Gombrich 158–59)

Emblematic images support flash reason by means of enigmas that provoke thought to move beyond the given sense.

> Not only can we not think of the sign as representing a real creature, even the event it represents transcends the possibility of our experience—what will happen when the devouring jaws reach the neck and the jaws themselves? It is this paradoxical nature of the image that has made it the archetypal symbol of mystery. The serpent does not represent either time or the Universe, but precisely because it is inexhaustible in its signification it shows us so much "in a flash" that we return from its contemplation as from a dream we can no longer quite recount or explain. (159)

The "flash" of inference produced by such "open signs" does involve some articulation: "the experience of meaning after meaning which is suggested to our mind as we contemplate the enigmatic images becomes an analogue of the mode of apprehension in which the higher intelligence may not only see one particular proposition as in a flash, but all the truth their mind can encompass—in the case of the Divine Mind the totality of all propositions" (159). We could just as well think of the schema as an allegory of rhetoric, sorted out according to temporal responsibility: forensic (past), epideictic (present), deliberative (future). The flash of reason has always been desirable but becomes a necessity when the three time zones collapse into Now. And for "the Divine Mind" read "Internet," since what is at stake in our updating of *Prudence* is the functionality of what was imagined and described in previous eras as the "mind of God." Avatar is how individual and collective (total) beings communicate in a digital apparatus.

Template

In order to exercise the quality of experience augmented in electracy, you may compose your own Allegory of Prudence, using Titian's work as a point of departure. The template includes the formal possibilities (allegory, iconography, portraiture), and also the content (a family incident, cultural mythology and legend). The work celebrates a satisfaction. The purpose of the exercise is to get a feeling for flash reason by composing an image commemorating an act of decision, specifically a decision covered by prudence. It is not that the action was itself prudent, but that im/prudence offers a frame, a measure, of your judgment (your decision). The elements of the template include 1. a grounding in personal experience, specifically some decision made in the past, that is memorable for whatever reason; 2. a framing of this event by the tradition of the virtues, specifically prudence, which measures the decision in the context of time (past-present-future); 3. icons: find some equivalent for the allegorical animals, which are "corporate" in McLuhan's sense, each having an assigned meaning in the cultural encyclopedia, recoded to make specific sense in the setting created by Titian; 4. compose a motto or maxim (even a proverb) that expresses the moral of the event.

The rule of thumb for such assignments, when adopting existing works as a relay for a new composition, is to ask "what is that for me, in my circumstances?" Such is the pedagogy of decorum. I observe prudence in Nietzsche or Titian not as information for an exam, but to notice prudence in my own case. With this rule in mind, it is worth noting that Francesco Clemente did a version of our exercise in a different context, as part of a millennium celebration, in which the National Gallery invited twenty-four contemporary artists to make a new piece based on some historical work in the collection. Clemente chose Titian's *Prudence* as his relay, but the "encounters" idea suggests that a further element in our template puts in play Titian's work itself: the point of departure may be Titian's allegory, but then some other work of art might be selected to guide the remake, as a relay for the commemoration design. The modified instruction is: select an existing work of any sort, genre, medium, mode, as a reference for your allegory. Clemente's remake indicates also how loose this adaptation may be, since his version expresses ambivalence. The template identifies fields of attention, to provoke thought.

The salient components of Clemente's remake, entitled *Smile Now, Cry Later*, were inventoried in the commentary by the curator of the exhibition, Richard Morphet:

1. The point of departure for the theme came from one of Clemente's friends in Los Angeles, a Chicano, who had a tattoo including a statement of wisdom popular among his peers. On each arm there was tattooed a girl, one smiling, with the words "smile now," one crying, with the words "cry later." Similar wisdom may be found in a number of classic proverbs.

2. Clemente chose to enter a dialogue with Titian's allegory for several reasons, beginning with his own admiration for the emblem as a form and tradition. Ezra Pound's imagism, or vorticism, was one resource, taking the poetics of the ideogram as an updating of the emblem, with its capacity to create an internal flash of coherence through the juxtaposition of heterogeneous materials.
3. Clemente riffed on Titian's iconography (relating the three ages of man with three totem animals) which Clemente associated with the gryllus, a representation for Medieval people of the baser instincts of life. The gryllus theme is evoked through the growing vine, each of whose leaves depicts a naked black man, each one either smiling or crying and holding a paper with the appropriate half of the title proverb. Superimposed over the entire scene is a winged phallus, an ancient symbol associated with sexual cosmic vitality. The gryllus and the winged phallus may be read as conflicting attitudes towards embodied desire.
4. The painting fills a wall (92 x 184 ins), done in a style evoking graffiti art, including spray painting, referring to the setting in which Clemente's Chicano friend lived (the vulgar gryllus).

How do I go on from here? What is the vector of the relay from Titian through Clemente to me, intimating how I may configure my own relationship with prudence? It is worth remembering that the purpose of this exercise is to learn from the history of prudence (good judgment) how to deliberate at the speed of light. The reason prudence works in a flash is because the response is "character" (given). "It is plain that the word 'character' must be taken here in a stronger sense than the one we ordinarily associate with it: as meaning not just firmness, but rather inalterability of character. Because of such an intransigence, of such a single-mindedness, so to speak, the ancient concept of character, which Goethe properly translates with *daimon* and not with *ethos*, must be assigned to the sphere of nature, and not to that of ethics. The moral of the fable, as Shaftesbury puts it, can only be an ostensive gesture: 'such a one he is! Such he is – *Sic, Crito est hic!* This is the creature!'" (Stimilli, The Face, 51). The Allegory exercise uses decorum to help you map the sources of this response. Our task differs in its motivation from nostalgia for the classical virtues expressed by William J. Bennett, whose *The Book of Virtues* was a best seller for some time. (How uncouth). That book, and its companion volume, *The Moral Compass,* amount to florilegia-- collections of moral exempla, which are useful as far as they go, exhibiting the alliance of prudence and decorum. What we want to retrieve is not the old virtues (the Allegory is not mimetic), but a time-image for decision-making in electracy, in vicious circumstances.

2 Concept

Hypotyposis

The metaphysics of digital imaging dates from the Industrial Revolution, but its genealogy draws upon the traditions of image invention. The Prudence exercise introduces you to electracy as a particular kind of experience, and as a practice that foregrounds individual capacity for experience as such. Titian's Allegory references his family, which is to say his manner of undergoing love and death. This context is a good one for our relay, since the tradition has counted on the shared undergoing of Eros (want) as an introduction to wisdom. Immanuel Kant is considered to be the last philosopher in the tradition of particular intellect that begins in Classical Greece and runs through Leonardo DaVinci. In this tradition thought is fundamentally sign-based, a showing of images to the mind's eye, which is what recommends it as a resource for the invention of an image metaphysics. Kant received the tradition as posing the problem of a fundamental gap or chasm dividing human faculties between pure and practical reason (science and morality, knowledge and belief, the sensible and supersensible, phenomenal and noumenal). In his project of the three Critiques to determine the limits of philosophy, Kant introduced "judgment" as a faculty in its own right, grounded in aesthetic experience, functioning as a bridge crossing the chasm and connecting the other faculties of mind. Flash reason is this bridge.

A feature of special relevance to electracy of Kant's Third Critique is his description of reflective judgment in which a person spontaneously recognizes some form in nature, a body, or art, and judges it to be "beautiful," without benefit of a concept or rule guiding the judgment. This process of thinking without concepts provides a transition from the literate to an electrate apparatus (from conceptual categories to a new image category). The judgment of "beauty" assumes the existence of "common sense," forming a community of persons sharing not any specific "taste," but the capacity to experience beauty. The phrase refers not to our modern meaning of "good sense" or shared opinion, or even the "straight talk" of Thomas Paine, but to the inner or "sixth" sense that unified and synthesized the perceptions gathered from each of the five bodily senses. To convey the immediate and spontaneous certainty of reflective feeling, Kant associated it with the sense of taste. The Latin languages indicate a relationship between taste and knowledge with the near pun, sapore and sapere, relaying the flash of awareness between mouth and intellect measuring the range between sweet and bitter.

Concept avatar takes after reflective judgment, which works in the middle voice (auto-affection). "Beauty" is not a property of an object or thing, but a feeling by which subjects become aware of a harmony among their own faculties (auto-perception). A concept or rule is lacking for the feeling. The judgment operates formally, rather, by means of the proportional analogy "hypotyposis." The bridge between the empirical causal world of sensible things and the moral realm of desire is accomplished analogically, with "beauty" (some sensible example) constituting a "symbol" of the supersensible "good."

> Knowledge by analogy, Kant explains, "means not, as the word is commonly taken, an imperfect similarity of two things, but a perfect similarity of two relations between quite dissimilar things." This definition, supported by examples that Kant gives of analogy in the *Critique of Judgment,* a definition that neither abolishes the heterogeneity of the things to be related nor affirms their complete separation, shows these dissimilar things to be similar merely in the way they themselves relate or depend on certain other things. To take Kant's own example: a hand mill can be shown to represent a despotic state in spite of the absence of any similarity between the two "items," because both function only if manipulated by an individual absolute will. Thus, analogical presentation does two things, as Kant notes. First, it applies the concept (here the despotic state) to the object of a sensible intuition (the hand mill), and then it applies "the mere rule of the reflection made upon the intuition [on the type of causality it implies] to a quite different object of which the first is only the symbol." (Gasché 212)

Hannah Arendt noted that Kant's use of analogy in his logic of judgment was in fact the operation responsible for the formation of most philosophical concepts. The relay with our personification of prudence is explicit.

> All philosophical terms are metaphors, frozen analogies, as it were, whose true meaning discloses itself when we dissolve the term into the original context, which must have been vividly in the mind of the first philosopher to use it. When Plato introduced the everyday words "soul" and "idea" into philosophical language—connecting an invisible organ in man, the soul, with something invisible present in the world of invisibles, the ideas—he still must have heard the words as they were used in ordinary pre-philosophical language. . . . The underlying analogy of Plato's doctrine of the soul runs as follows: As the breath of life relates to the body it leaves, that is, to the corpse, so the soul from now on will be supposed to relate to the living body. The analogy underlying his doctrine of ideas can be reconstructed in a similar manner; as the craftsman's mental image directs his hand in fabrication and is the measurement of the objects' success or failure, so all materially and sensorily given data in the world of appearances relate to and are evaluated according to an invisible pattern, localized in the sky of ideas. (Arendt 1:104)

Paul Ricoeur further elaborates on the philosophical productivity of the mathematical notion of analogy (A is to B as C is to D):

> The closest application is provided by the definition of distributive justice in the *Nicomachean Ethics* 5:3. The definition rests on the idea that this virtue implies four terms, two persons (equal or unequal) and two shares (advantages and disadvantages in the realms of honor or wealth); and that it establishes proportional equality in distribution between these four terms. But the application here of the idea of number, proposed by Aristotle, concerns extension not of the idea of number to irrationals but of proportion to non-homogeneous terms, provided that they can be said to be equal or unequal in some particular relation. In biology, the same formal conception of proportion permits not only classification (by saying, for example, that flying is to wings as swimming is to fins),

> but also demonstration (e.g., if certain animals have lungs and others do not, the latter possess an organ that takes the place of a lung). By lending themselves to proportional relationship such as these, functions and organs provide the outline of a general biology. (Ricoeur 270–71)

Kant clarified that his four-part ratios were not mathematical (not quantitative) but qualitative. Kant's analogical bridge, the commentators point out, retraces the path of ascent from physical love to love of wisdom mapped by Plato (for example, in *The Symposium*). In Plato's story Eros is not beauty but seeks beauty (Fictioc 21). The search begins with a spontaneous experience of sexual attraction. The "disinterestedness" of the feeling is the *sensus communis* of the universality of physical attraction. Kant's insistence on the disinterestedness of the reflective judgment is just to distinguish aesthetic feeling from other kinds of feelings. This foregrounding of aesthetic judgment as a power in its own right is important to flash reason, to establish in the larger context of the conflicts working in deliberative rhetoric the specific dimension of aesthetic pleasure-pain and the values associated with it, separated from the representations and values of knowledge and belief.

The immediate lesson for our allegory is the assumption that my experience of embodiment may be extended through a proportional ratio as a means for moving through information of any kind. One task of flash reason is the need to update the measure of "ratio" and "proportion" to reflect the discoveries of vanguard arts. Bloom finds this option already at work in the tradition of ratio in Hellenism: one branch favored analogy (equivalence in substitution); the other branch favored anomaly (disruption, the breaking of ratio in substitution) ("The Breaking of Form" 13). Hannah Arendt was convinced of the contemporary relevance of reflective judgment, which she called

> the most political of man's mental abilities. It is the faculty that judges particulars without subsuming them under general rules which can be taught and learned until they grow into habits that can be replaced by other habits and rules. The faculty of judging particulars (as brought to light by Kant), the ability to say "this is wrong," "this is beautiful," and so on, is not the same as the faculty of thinking. Thinking deals with invisibles, with representations of things that are absent; judging always concerns particulars and things close at hand.

> But the two are interrelated, as are consciousness and conscience. (1: 193)

Bittersweet

The attraction to beauty in the beloved holds attention and stimulates reflection, revealing a harmony among the lover's faculties (*concinnitas*) that gives pleasure distinct from sexual desire, motivating the lover to begin the journey of becoming human. The process begins in sensory judgment, and leads into belief through custom, the social forms ordering human relationships, revealing the larger guiding patterns at work in society (habitus, *dharma*). Attention shifts away from the self to the other, to beauty of character and of social order. The third stage is knowledge, learning the sciences of form, such as mathematics. The final stage is wisdom: an intution of Form as such (Fictioc 85–86). Philosophers from Pythagoras to Kant (and beyond) based their optimism about the educability of the multitude (and their enlistment in an enlightened politics) on proportional ratios (music of the spheres). It is worth dwelling on this point, since it is possible in one respect to reduce the shift from literacy to electracy to a mutation in the standard of ratio (proportion). This discussion of Alberti and architecture shows what is at stake.

> The unlearned (or unskilled) person cannot do what the learned person can do, but he can judge the results of what the learned person does. Cicero speaks throughout of various arts, and he grounds this argument in a general principle of the relation of art and nature. . . . The "nature" from which art begins, and to which it must appeal to achieve anything, is our nature (which, of course, does not necessarily preclude its consonance with nature in a large sense, that is, it does not preclude the possibility that the same mean is in ourselves and in what we apprehend, and that this similarity is fact makes our apprehension of them possible). Just such an ambivalence runs through Alberti's remarks about pulchritude and concinnitas, the latter of which is a principle of both human sense and nature at large. "Beauty is a certain consensus and unison of the parts of a thing with regard to definite number, fin-

> ish and collocation, as demanded by concinnitas, the absolute and primary reason of nature" (Summers 134).

The project of concept avatar (a transition of conceptual thinking from literacy into electracy) may be seen relative to the use of "nature" in Summers's observation. The literate concept remains responsible for "nature" proper, which it was invented to address as ontology. Concept avatar (electracy), extends the concept analogically into second nature (habitus, popular media), to attempt an image metaphysics. The fundamental analogy of the tradition is that between love and wisdom (philosophy), concerned with the desire to know. The relationship or ratio between love and knowledge has to be adjusted in each epoch, not to mention for each apparatus, with implications for individual experience and behavior. As love goes, so goes wisdom. Anne Carson identifies exactly the hinge of the ratio.

> There would seem to be some resemblance between the way Eros acts in the mind of a lover and the way knowing acts in the mind of a thinker. It has been an endeavour of philosophy from the time of Socrates to understand the nature and uses of that resemblance. But not only philosophers are intrigued to do so. I would like to grasp why it is that these two activities, falling in love and coming to know, make me feel genuinely alive. There is something like an electrification in them. They are not like anything else, but they are like each other. (Carson 70)

The peculiar taste of this "electrification" identified by the ancient poets was, in Sappho's term, *glukupikron* (bittersweet). It is the samba feeling, celebrated in every variation (*saudade*, blues, tango): glad to be feeling . . . sad. Arendt agrees with this extension of Eros into the "life" principle. The delights of thinking are ineffable, she says.

> The only possible metaphor one may conceive of for the life of the mind is the sensation of being alive. Without the breath of life the human body is a corpse; without thinking the human mind is dead. This in fact is the metaphor Aristotle tried out in the famous seventh chapter of "Book Lambda" of the *Metaphysics:* "The activity of thinking [*energeia* that has its end in itself] is life." Its inherent law, which only a god can tolerate forever, man merely now and then, during which time he is

> godlike, is "unceasing motion, which is motion in a circle"—the only movement, that is, that never reaches an end or results in an end product. (Vol I 123)

Lacan (psychoanalysis) updates Aristotle by showing the complexity of this motion, whose territory may be figured only by topology. This feeling of being alive is what the Allegory of Prudence attempts to access and bring into an emblem, to serve as axiom for a new ratio.

Kant's reflective judgment assumes precisely the reality and universal irrefutability of this basic feeling (life).

> One of the main aims of the Third Critique is to show that sensuousness is not alien to reason. It is the architectonic of reason itself, its systematic "organic" structure constructed through the analogous techne with nature—that is "signaled" in the apprehension of the beautiful. The feeling of life [*lebensgefuhl*] brought forth (experienced) in this apprehension marks the self as at once body and ethical being, because this realization of the self as body is concomitant with the realization of the "*mit*" [*gefuhl*] of being with the other, the feeling of the *sensus communis* and with the ethical as such. (Japaridze 41)

Concept avatar is designed to bring into thought this life feeling. What could be easier, you might say, but Nietzsche reminds us: that I live may just be a prejudice. In metaphysical terms, this life feeling creates a space, an opening in the world, giving a sense of something "more" (possibility, potentiality) that unfolds into an experience of freedom beyond or within necessity.

> Reaching for an object that proves to be outside and beyond himself, the lover is provoked to notice that self and its limits. From a new vantage point, which we might call self-consciousness, he looks back and sees a hole. Where does that hole come from? It comes from the lover's classificatory process. Desire for an object that he never knew he lacked is defined, by a shift of distance, as desire for a necessary part of himself. Not a new acquisition but something that was always, properly, his. Two lacks become one. (Carson 33)

Carson alerts us to the difficulty of the allegory: it must personify this hole.

Alberto Perez-Gomez generalizes this erotic character of space as fundamental to the entire Western tradition, and classifies it as a quality of chora.

> Erotic space is not an a priori concept, nor an objectified geometric or topological reality. It is both the physical space of architecture at the inception of the Western tradition and the linguistic space of a metaphor, the electrified void between two terms that are brought together but kept apart. While this significant gap is the underlying subject of art (including love poems), bounded space is the underlying subject of architecture. It is the space for political and religious action and for theatrical performance, where drama produces katharsis and festival time occurs. It is limited space: in architecture, the creation of limits is crucial and cannot be reduced to material walls. Beyond the city wall of the Greek polis was a regional zone known as chora, a thick limit that was believed to be protected by specific divinities. This regional chora is a quasi-homophone of the central choros or dance platform that mediated between the spectators in the amphitheater and the actors on the skene in a dramatic performance. (Perez-Gomez 36–37).

The Greek understanding of beauty as "harmony" grew gradually out of experience with "joints" or arranging parts into satisfying wholes. The primary erotic "joint" refers to human genitals, and the gap between two people and all the related negotiations is included in the general art of "joining" (116). An electrate public sphere creates participation through this apprehension of the erotic character of dimensionality. Such is the tradition tested in our Allegory of Prudence, articulating the lived dimension of well-being. I will compose a scene of decision, as an experiment in electrate thinking: to think the life feeling that our tutors characterize as hole.

Tautegory

Prudence is a kind of "wind tunnel" testing flash reason. In the experience of the beautiful, central to the tradition we must upgrade, the mind's eye is able to take in the whole of a situation in one glance (*Augenblick*). Prudence requires this power of ingenium, to run through the ratio of hypotyposis and grasp the proportion in one instant of wit. The goal of Renaissance pedagogy was to bridge the gap separating *ars* (teachable techniques) from *ingenium* (natural talent). The goal was to merge two kinds of instantaneous analytical insights.

> The first is *perspicacia*, which "penetrates the most distant and minute circumstances of every subject." This analysis is accomplished in terms of a supplementary list of Aristotle's categories. The second is *versabilita*, which "rapidly compares all those circumstances among themselves, or with the subject; it joins and divides them, decides one from the other, indicates one by the other, and with marvelous dexterity puts one in the place of the other." There is, [Tesauro] says, little difference between ingegno and prudence. (Summers 100)

Kant's innovation in this tradition was to add consideration of the "sublime," referring to conditions that exceed the capacities of both the outer and inner eye, the glimpse in a moment that takes the measure of a situation. Within the conditions of decorum, (beauty), the faculties are in harmony.

> To every empirical concept, namely, there belong three actions of the self-active faculty of cognition: 1. the apprehension of the manifold of intuition; 2. the comprehension, i.e. the synthetic unity of consciousness of this manifold in the concept of an object; 3. the presentation (exhibitio) [*darstellung*] of the object corresponding to this concept in intuition. For the first action imagination is required, for the second understanding, for the third the power of judgment, which, if it is an empirical concept that is at issue, would be the determining power of judgment. (Kant qtd. in Fictioc 128)

Confronted with some phenomenon or event in nature that exceeds the capacity of imagination to present an image adequate to the concepts of understanding, the harmony is destroyed, producing displeasure. The interest of the judgment of the sublime in conditions that expose the empirical impotence of a subject, however, is the paradoxical transformation of this displeasure into the bittersweet revelation of moral freedom.

> The experience of the sublime constitutes a sudden aspect change, where the intelligible point of view somehow breaks

> into the empirical through a "negative pleasure." We feel the presence of the other perspective, and are made aware of the primacy of the intelligible over the empirical, which can be expressed through the idea of freedom. This neither leads to concrete actions nor gives any insight in how to deal with moral dilemmas, but has its importance in signifying our moral vocation, which is tied to our rational nature. (Myskja 130)

At stake in this experience is the capacity of the limitations of aesthetic form to evoke ethical intuitions that exceed form and experience alike.

Commentators agree that Kant's sublime becomes the norm in conditions created by the industrial revolution, just beginning in Kant's lifetime. Exemplifying the project to update hypotyposis, Jean-Francois Lyotard's interest in the Analytic of the Sublime (just one part of Kant's Third Critique) is due to the clue it offers for thought and action in an industrial and post-industrial society. In our terms, Lyotard's adaptation of Kant's sublime is an outline for deliberative rhetoric in electracy. The point that recommends Lyotard's reading of Kant as a relay for flash reason (electrate prudence) is the support for thought provided by affect as a sublime feeling, and the rhetorical powers revealed in this experience of negative presentation. A theme of electracy (apparatus invention) is that the Western tradition already knows a great deal about flash reason (image metaphysics), and that in some respects flash reason has been an aspiration of this tradition all along, couched as speculation about the mind of God.

Lyotard calls attention to the ontological and metaphysical innovations of his project, to emphasize that the aesthetic judgments of taste and of the sublime are not approached in terms of objects and properties, essences and accidents, but as feelings that organize the heterogeneous manifold by means of mood or atmosphere (*Stimmung*). This affective order involves not categories, but "tautegories."

> For "logically" reflection is called judgment, but "psychologically," if we may be permitted the improper use of this term for a moment, it is nothing but the feeling of pleasure and displeasure. As a faculty of knowledge, it is devoted to the heuristic, and in procuring "sensations," the meaning of which will become clear, it fully discloses its tautegorical character, a term by which I designate the remarkable fact that pleasure

> and displeasure are at once both a "state" of the soul and the "information" collected by the soul relative to its state. (*Lessons* 4)

A tautegory is constructed according to the "manner" of its maker, a term that evokes the "concetto" of practical reason.

> The apparent sitter in a Renaissance portrait was thus an external appearance showing an inward truth, and so, it might be said, were Renaissance works of art in general. The spirit they expressed, however, was not simply that of their subject, it was also that of the artist, who gave the painting its "life." The *Mona Lisa* is a painting of—taken from the appearance of—a Florentine merchant's wife and at the same time a painting of—from the hand and sensibility of—Leonardo da Vinci. This second, genetic relation between artist and image was fully recognized in the Renaissance commonplace "every painter paints himself," and the idea adds another dimension to the central paradox that the objective world is only evident from a point of view. Individual style, or manner, developed together with portraiture (and naturalism in general), so that the work itself became "physiognomic" at the same time that physiognomy became a part of the science of painting. (Summers 111)

Tautegories are physiognomic, "singularities" rather than universals, opening as they do a space of "rendezvous" hosting events of decision in practical reason. Tautegories are anchored in feeling (this is the key), and are useful for inquiry in conditions that exceed understanding and knowledge, for the sublime formlessness of experience in the (post)industrial city (dromosphere). The further reflective judgment moves from what in our context is "literate" metaphysics, into the unknowns of electracy,

> the more manifest the tautegorical aspect of reflection becomes. There are signs of it in the more frequent occurrence of operators such as regulation (in the "regulative Idea"), guidance (in the guiding thread), and analogy (in the "as if"), which are not categories but can be identified as heuristic tautegories. Because of these curious "subjective operators," critical thought gives itself or discovers processes of synthesis

> that have not received the imprimatur of knowledge. Knowledge can only draw on them reflexively, inventing them as it does according to its feeling, though it may have to legitimate their objective validity afterward. (*Lessons* 33)

A first step for the invention of flash judgment, as Lyotard makes clear, is the introduction of thinkers to what might be called the new "decorum," the relationship among thought, art, and conduct in the sublime city. The place of individual "manner" in electracy, and the role of physiognomy in guiding inquiry, suggest what is at stake. In traditional emblematics, "virtue" is represented by a scene (hypotyposis) of a beautiful woman beating an ugly woman with a stick. To persist with traditional ratios, and to neglect a necessary reeducation of common sense in the sublime judgment (that works with the full range of the bittersweet, repulsion as well as attraction, "ugly" as well as "beautiful")—in short, a literal and uncritical physiognomy—leaves citizens unprepared to make prudent policy decisions not just with respect to cosmetic glamour or even Nazi racism but the coming revolution in DNA manipulation (the knowledge accident most feared by Virilio).

In his reading of Kant, Lyotard identifies what thinkers at light-speed may experience, which also helps target faculties in need of prosthetic augmentation. "The mountain masses, the pyramids of ice, the overhanging, threatening rocks, thunderclouds, oceans rising with rebellious force, volcanoes, everything 'rude' to be found in nature is sublime in presentation because it is at the limit of what can be grasped in a single intuition. . . . This effort is similar to the effort of the will that aims for virtue" (127). The now-time of electracy demands an enlarged capacity of the single glance against all rudeness. Lyotard finds in the rhetorical figure of "retortion" (a dialectical figure that affirms by denial) an anticipation of the extreme discordance to be negotiated by sublime judgment at light-speed (128). We learn from Kant how to notice in the manifest unhappiness of finitude the latent happiness of infinity.

Theory: Persona

The method of concept avatar is to adapt the literate concept structure to function in an electrate apparatus. Critical thinking is a practice specific to literacy, so to speak of an electrate concept for digital reasoning is like referring to an automobile as a horseless carriage. We live in a transitional moment, however, with experimental modernist literature serving as a bridge between epochs. Flash reason adapts philosophy to Internet culture. We still need theoretical thinking in electracy, but the old alphabetic techniques of inference are no longer adequate to or sufficient for the task. A methodology for our project is "heuretics" (the logic of invention). Heuretics appropriated from the history of discourses on method a generative formula for the creation of new forms and practices (Ulmer, *Heuretics*). The acronym CATTt identifies the set of resources needed for our invention: Contrast, Analogy, Theory, Target, tale. This generator guides a proposal for a hybrid concept (combining features of word and image), as well as the larger experiment in creating flash reason.

The ambition is to create a practice capable of conveying the accumulated potential of literate metaphysics, archived in databases, to an electrate player in a sublime glance. A hyperbolic goal, but no less worthy than curing cancer. For purposes of our exercise, I have zipped this archive into Nietzsche's personal motto: *werde der du bist*. The particular quality of thought that we need our concept to support is judgment, individual decision making (prudence). The larger goal is to orient our compositional practice to the specific site from which will have emerged the metaphysics of electracy (the capacity of the body to undergo *jouissance*). Thus the exercise to compose an Allegory of Prudence is at the same time an experimental construction of an electrate concept. The Theory for inventing this transitional concept is derived from Deleuze and Guattari, especially from their final collaboration, *What Is Philosophy?* They argue that the concept as practiced in philosophy still has a role to play in contemporary civilization. Such concepts function through a kind of cinematic mise-en-scene. A philosophical concept includes the following parts:

1. Name: The "concept proper" slot in our template assigns a name to the idea (e.g. Descartes's *cogito*). Deleuze and Guattari call for a stand (stance or attitude towards thought) that replaces subject/object orientation of thinking. Deleuze and Guattari name their replacement for the subject stand "event." They call for a concept for thinking the position of "event," rather than from the position of subject. Event thinks in and through me. It is a collective dimension of thinking that I receive readymade, to try on or adjust as needed to my expression. In the

case of our electrate concept, we foreground the function of "stand," the attitude in terms of turn, direction and posture, that operates through a concept. "Stand" differs from opinion (argument) or will (narrative).

2. Problem: Deleuze and Guattari replace subject thinking on a "plane of transcendence," with event thinking on a "plane of immanence." This plane or field is selected by our intervention in it, by our creative activity in relation to it, when we frame a field of discourse as problem. The problem Deleuze and Guattari select is that the construction of concepts initiated by Philosophy as part of the invention of literacy has been taken over by Commerce. The commodity form has already displaced Philosophy as the source for defining what constitutes the good life, happiness, satisfaction, well-being (one of the original questions of philosophy). Commercial discourse functions in our CATTt as Contrast.
3. Conceptual Persona: Concept construction includes a third feature, a persona that dramatizes in a vital anecdote how the proposed thought mediates the relation of a person to world. Instruction: personify the thought proposed by the concept in an appropriate character type or role, enacting the attitude and orientation of the thought (the stand). The examples of conceptual personae favored by Deleuze and Guattari include Socrates, Diogenes, and Empedocles. The anecdote(s) reported in each case allegorize or figuratively enact a mode of reasoning. Socrates: allegory of the cave. The way of the heavens. Conversion = movement through the inference procedures: abduction, deduction, induction. Diogenes: lived in a barrel on the public square, performed all his intimate functions in full view of the citizens. The way of the surface. Perversion = dramatize the metaphor in the idea. Empedocles: threw himself into Mt. Etna (he needed to disappear to corroborate his claim of transmigration of souls), but his (bronze?) sandal floating to the surface betrayed his action. The way of the depths. Subversion = transgression and destruction of forms (madness).
4. Presentation: The conceptual persona models how the concept thinks the problem plane. It remains to add to this instruction

the manner of this modeling, its aesthetic premises. A text with a relevant instruction is the following:

> The history of philosophy is comparable to the art of the portrait. It is not a matter of 'making lifelike,' that is, of repeating what a philosopher said but rather of producing resemblance by separating out both the plane of immanence he instituted and the new concepts he created. These are mental, noetic, and machinic portraits. Although they are usually created with philosophical tools, they can also be produced aesthetically. Thus Tinguely recently presented some monumental machinic portraits of philosophers, working with powerful, linked or alternating, infinite movements that can be folded over or spread out, with sounds, lightning flashes, substances of being, and images of thought according to complex curved planes. (*What is Philosophy?* 55–56)

Deleuze and Guattari's opposition to "resemblance" or "representation" throughout the argument, with references to Cézanne, Klee, or Francis Bacon as relays, reinforces the instruction: do for the concept what modernist and vanguard arts did for the image. With this theme Deleuze and Guattari identify the Analogy of our CATTt (modernist art practice). In electracy, the conceptual persona will take a more important role, altering the hierarchy of the literate concept, in which problem and persona are subordinate to name (term). "The difference between conceptual personae and aesthetic figures consists first of all in this: the former are powers of concepts, and the latter are the powers of affects and percepts. The former take effect on a plane of immanence that is an image of Thought-Being (noumenon), and the latter take effect on a plane of composition as image of a Universe (phenomenon)" (65).

Socrates, as presented in Plato's dialogues, is the prototype. Socrates embodied the persona of "gadfly," buttonholing citizens in the streets of Athens in search of someone wiser than himself, in order to refute the Delphic oracle's declaration that no man was wiser than Socrates. He dramatized "dialectic" as a mode of thought. We need to generate similar features for our conceptual avatar. Avatar is a conceptual persona, and this performance is a position that you ultimately learn to play (playing avatar). It becomes your Socrates, playing Virgil to your Dante, a spirit guide of your choosing. The function of avatar is to advise me on my decision, to consult on all matters of prudence. What statistics are to calculation (quantity), avatar is to prudence (quality). With the appropriated term "avatar" we are referring (paleologically) to a functionality, to be reverse-designed into a rhetorical (ontological) practice. As a transitional concept, avatar must support both thought and feeling. To get avatar you have to do the exercise, not just read about it. It is not a psychological but an ontological subject.

An electrate concept is not confined to the professional or disciplinary parameters of philosophy, but is a means for theoretical thinking native to a civilization of the Internet, in which digital imaging supersedes alphabetic writing. The historical record shows that each innovation in forms and practices of thought preserves some parts of the previous mode, abandons some parts, and adds some new elements. An electrate concept, in this spirit, does not simply reproduce Deleuze and Guattari's proposal, but revises it with our purpose in mind, looking for those aspects of their poetics that lend themselves to digital imaging, while deemphasizing other aspects relevant only to the literate apparatus. The following discussion makes one pass through the generator, to propose a style of written reasoning adapted for electracy. Here is the CATTt: Theory, Deleuze and Guattari; Contrast, Commercial advertising; Analogy, experimental modernist arts; Target, the public sphere, deliberative rhetoric, the practice of consulting needed for a democratic society; tale (the tail of the CATT), referring to the form used to organize the other resources: Allegory of Prudence. This version is an invitation to test your own pass, revising the recipe to taste. The Allegory of Prudence we are composing is an experiment testing the electrate concept "avatar." This is heuretics: learning as making-doing.

Contrast: Commerce

Deleuze and Guattari complained that Commerce took over concept production in our era, along with everything else in the order of public discourse. Roland Marchand's history of the creation of the commodity sign is a useful resource to document our Contrast. He begins in the 1920s, which is not the beginning of advertising, but the first full separation of exchange value from use value in guiding promotional thought. Contrast is not a rejection of its source, but an inventory of materials to discover what sorts of concepts Commerce makes. Philosophy can learn something from Commerce about how to adapt to the conditions of electracy. We accept the formal discoveries of Commerce (use of icons, schemas, scenarios, tableaux and the like) but reject its propaganda stance on behalf of corporate profit. Our goal is thinking, not selling/buying. The real craft of using the CATTt generator comes at this point: How do we create (invent) a synthesis, a hybrid of our Theory and Contrast, to formulate an emergent set of instructions for constructing an electrate concept?

Our inventory of Marchand covers what Commerce got right, understanding that the emergence of electracy in a capitalist society is a contingency of history. Marchand describes advertising as the discourse primarily responsible for converting the citizens of the industrial city to the worldview of the new apparatus, which dates from the beginnings of the industrial revolution. This worldview is based in aesthetics, referring to the sensory faculty of taste described by Immanuel Kant in the eighteenth century. The aesthetic image is to electracy what the analytical word is to literacy. The commodity form, separating exchange value from use value, desire from product, expression from object, allowed the pedagogy of aesthetic judgment to operate autonomously. Advertisers realized they were selling not the steak but the sizzle. Electrate intelligence, not just commerce but civics and ethics (practical reason), functions in the dimension of sizzle. Advertising discourse disseminated throughout America (and the emerging global economy) the inventions of Paris, including not only "fashion" but the new logic of taste, and the design styles of modernist arts. The appropriation in ad practices of popular culture forms from tabloid magazines to celebrity gossip and movies contributed to the didactic value, assisting the public in internalizing the new native discourse of the image apparatus. They were learning brand, but not avatar.

Within this general frame of Commerce as advice on modernization, the ads specifically demonstrated how to construct concepts in the emerging mass media discourse, and this is what Deleuze and Guattari recognized as a direct challenge to Philosophy. An important point of alignment between Deleuze and Guattari and Marchand is precisely here. The philosophical concept includes a conceptual persona to mediate between the "name" of the concept (the idea) and the problem plane or discursive field addressed by the idea (between the general and the particular). Literate concepts foreground idea; commercial concepts foreground persona. Everything that Marchand describes about the strategies of ad campaigns is relevant to the design of conceptual personae: social tableaux, parables, visual clichés, fantasies and icons. Betty Crocker and her peers are to Commerce what Socrates is to Philosophy. Plato's parable of the cave in the Republic dramatizes the essential gesture of philosophy: conversion. One prisoner turns around, away from the shadows cast on the walls of the cave, to behold the true light of the sun outside the cave. Diversion (the "vert," turn or trope of Commerce) is a conceptual stand of reassurance, crystallizing majority opinion around a few key figures (scenes). A prisoner. Turns. Such is the invention scene of philosophy.

The functionality of avatar concerns the ability of the persona and anecdote to materialize the attitude or stand (position, gesture) of thought as event. "Truth can only be defined on the plane [of immanence] by a 'turning toward' or by 'that toward which thought turns'; but this does not provide us with a concept of truth" (*What is Philosophy?* 39). Kenneth Burke provides some context for the turning (the vert of version) enabled by "concept." "Turn" refers to "trope" in rhetoric, and is the stylistic operation relevant to the "directionality" and movement of thought within writing. In his study of St. Augustine's *Confessions,* generalized as *The Rhetoric of Religion,* Burke forgrounded the vert family in relation to decision-making ("voting or purchasing, giving answers to questionnaires, taking of risks calculated on the basis of probability") (101). "I sometimes wonder whether the good Bishop of Hippo could ever have written that work were it not for the many Latin words that grow from this root, meaning turn" (*Langauge as Symbolic Action* 242). Augustine's moment of conversion to Christianity (the famous scene in Book VIII) is analyzed dramatistically:

> There are the tense moments of decision in formal drama, when the protagonist debates whether to make a certain move, and finally makes the choice that shapes his destiny, though he still has to discover what that destiny is. . . . We are interested in the kind of decision, if it can be called decision at all: the kind of development that usually takes place in the third act of a five-act drama. Despite his great stress upon the will, and despite his extraordinary energy in theological controversy, Augustine seems to have felt rather that, at the critical moment of his conversion, something was decided for him. Act III is the point at which some new quality of motivation enters. And however active one may be henceforth, the

course is more like a rolling downhill than like a straining uphill. (*Rhetoric of Religion* 63)

The feeling that "something was decided for him" is the avatar function. This is the level of decision that concerns us: not some superficial choice, but the indictment of destiny (so to speak). This moment of decision and change is taught as the turning-point of the standard Hollywood screenplay, instructions for which may be found in countless primers on scriptwriting (coming in this genre at the end of the second act of a three-act script). There is a narrative or dramatistic dimension in our thought, but "concept" separates, isolates, and develops as an alternative to any particular turn or direction, the pivot or switch site, the Archimedian lever upon which turning of thought as such depends. Augustine contrasts his con-version with the per-version of his pagan experience. "As regards Augustine's Confessions, the most notable use of the -vert family is in the contrast between Book II, concerned with what he calls his adolescent perversity, in stealing pears (a Gidean *acte gratuit*), and Book VIII, that describes his conversion" (93). Augustine, that is, decided to turn away from embodied pleasure. This turn is one version, one take, among possible attitudes. He tutors us on turning, but his movement cannot be ours. The instruction from Contrast is to foreground a persona to dramatize our idea, to show how to stand and turn in a problem field (understanding "turn" as "trope"). Each resource of the CATTt contributes to the final emergent poetics of our concept in an unpredictable way. The framing imperative is that we take responsibility for our own turning, and test it now with an Allegory of Prudence.

Analogy: Cabaret

Electracy dates from the late eighteenth century, the epoch of revolutions (industrial, bourgeois, representational, technological). We orient ourselves to our own epoch by analogy with the invention of literacy in Classical Greece. The term "apparatus" in this context (derived and expanded from media studies) is used to notice that the invention is a matrix including institution formation and identity behavior (individual and collective). A relevant point of the analogy is that in Athens Plato and his students (including Aristotle) created a new institution (the Academy) that opened a new zone in the city within which they invented the devices of "pure thought." This new kind of thought was different from the oral apparatus (religion, ritual, spirit, tribe). It has been dubbed "natural history" retroactively, and eventually became hegemonic, or at least fully independent, in the seventeenth century, the inception of "science" in the modern sense. "Science" as a stand first became possible within the literate apparatus. The related identity inventions are "selfhood" as experience and behavior, and the democratic political state. Our present moment is the heir of the two previous apparati (orality and literacy), providing two axes guiding (in unstable syncretism) our collective deliberations: right/wrong (oral); true/false (literate). Electracy does not eliminate or replace these two historical orientations, but supplements them with a third stand. The formal practices of electracy are invented primarily in nineteenth-century Paris. Paris is the Athens of electracy. The template from Athens maps the dynamics of apparatus creation. Simultaneous with the emergence of bourgeois hegemony, a counterculture zone opened first in Paris, known as "bohemia." The original bohemia was the neighborhood of Montmartre, on the outskirts of Paris. The taverns and bistros of the area provided cheap wine, prostitution, song and dance (all the vices). The first official cabaret associated with the avant-garde is Le Chat Noir, founded in 1881, followed by the Lapin Agile and the Moulin Rouge. These Cabarets are to electracy what the Academy and Lyceum were to literacy.

A good account of the institution formation related to this scene is Pierre Bourdieu. Aesthetic experience is the relevant human capacity to be augmented in the prosthesis (the electrate apparatus), and pure art is the means. Bourdieu identifies Baudelaire and Flaubert as the inventors of this stand and formal operation, with Manet as their equivalent in painting. "Before Baudelaire," Walter Benjamin wrote in his study of Paris as the capital of the nineteenth century, "the apache, who lived out his life within the precincts of society and of the big city, had had no place in literature. The most striking depiction of this subject in *Les fleurs du mal*, '*Le Vin de l'Assassin*,' inaugurated a Parisian genre. The café known as Le Chat Noir became its 'artistic headquarters.' '*Passant, sois moderne*!' was the inscription it bore during its early, heroic period" (*Writing of Modern Life* 108). The monumental importance of Benjamin's unfinished Arcades project is its ambition to reconstruct through documentation the milieu from which emerged the metaphysics of the new apparatus. The vanguard revolution more generally subsequently develops and institutionalizes this stand or attitude. The future of electracy involves unfolding the potential of pure art, just as the history of literacy records the unfolding of the potential of pure reason. The new form is an adaptation to the shock of life in the industrial city.

The philosophical account of this historical gambit is familiar, beginning with Kant's promotion of aesthetic judgment (the faculty of taste) to equal status with pure and practical reason. The third faculty added to the axes orienting thought is that of pleasure/pain (Spinoza's joy/sadness). Embodied sensory experience, in other words, is the ground of electrate intelligence. The responsibility of this dimension (distinct from oral salvation or literate engineering) is well-being (thriving). The commodity form contributes to the invention of electracy by initiating a reformation in Western identity, the most profound since Rome converted to Christianity, and in the same league as the Protestant Reformation. In this case it is the conversion to "pleasure" (sensory satisfaction) albeit in the guise of consumerism: the old values of "character" (self-denial) are displaced by "personality" (self-promotion), opening a new dimension of identity formation (brand). The implications for politics and ethics are substantial: what happens when pleasure/pain (attraction/repulsion) has equal status relative to right/wrong and true/false in contemporary civic life? The difference between a language and a dialect, some wit observed, is that a language is a dialect with an army. Well-being needs an army (an institution). Concept avatar is intended to think this register of experience, the capacity to be affected. Both branches of the Western tradition (Greco-Roman and Judeo-Christian) deprecated visceral experience and even condemned human embodiment as misfortune or sin. The challenge of electracy is to design practices of thought for an augmented aesthetic prosthesis that make affect intelligent.

What is the state of mind (stance) to be dramatized in the conceptual persona of avatar? The "pure art" created in Cabaret achieved international recognition ultimately in Dadaism, product of Cabaret Voltaire in Zurich (where the cabaret scene moved during the World War). The readymades in general, and *Fountain* in particular (the urinal submitted as a joke to a supposedly non-juried exhibition) make Marcel Duchamp the Aristotle of electracy. *Mona Lisa with a Pipe* (by the artist known as Sapeck, 1887) is emblematic of the attitude that is the "Spirit of Montmartre" expressed in these works. The attitude is *fumisme*, used to name the mocking humor that characterized the cabaret scene of bohemian Paris. The anchoring term is the verb *fumer* (to smoke), but with a usage in agriculture, "to manure." A *fumiste* is a chimney sweep, with slang extension to name a joker, crackpot, fraud. An immediate point of interest is the background that Sapeck's *Mona Lisa* provides for Duchamp's more famous readymade (the mustachioed Mona Lisa), composed much later. The choice of iconic image to profane is motivated in part by the term *fumisme* itself. The hazy smoke referenced in this semantic field resonates with one of the important terms used to identify Leonardo's style: *sfumato. Sfumato* is a term coined by Leonardo to refer to a painting technique which overlays translucent layers of color to create perceptions of depth, volume and form. In Italian *sfumato* means "blended" or "smoky" and is derived from the Italian word *fumo* meaning "smoke." Duchamp was "blowing smoke."

A "wit" is different from a *fumiste*, a distinction used to clarify the intent of Sapeck's illustrations:

> Whereas the former made fun of idiots in terms that they were not always able to understand, the fumiste accepts the ideas of the idiot and expresses their quintessence. . . . The *fumiste* avoids discussions of ideas, he does not set up a specific target, he adopts a posture of withdrawal that makes all distinctions hazy, and he internalizes Universal Stupidity by postulating the illusory nature of values and of the Beautiful, whence his denial of the established order and of official hierarchies. From this point of view, which is that of the sage, the dandy, the observer, and the skeptic, everything has the same value, everything is one and the same thing. (Grojnowski 104)

The Sfumato effect invented by Leonardo was a solution to a compositional problem relevant to flash reason. The problem was that of physiognomy, the capacity of external features to express character, disposition. Leonardo codified an emerging analogy in his era between the air of a face and the atmosphere of a landscape. The historical precedent concerns how one of the primordial elements (air) was adapted to expressing the uniqueness of "face" (prosopon) (Stimilli, 65). Andy Warhol emulating Duchamp gave this stand its purest performance to date, by transforming celebrity portraits into a pop iconography. The image of thought mocked in *fumisme* is Descartes's *cogito*, since, as Deleuze and Guattari observed, the stand of the subject in Descartes's radical doubt (I think, therefore I am) is that of "idiot" in the classical sense of "private person," one who does not participate in the public sphere. This alienated subject finally goes crazy in modernity, they explain, with reference to Dostoevsky.

Avatar personifies attitude. "Attitude" concerns the state of mind within which the thought happens, concerning belief or desire (for example) directed towards our Target (the practice of judgment or decision). Taken as a whole, or as a position of enunciation within the culture, comedy implies a certain attitude towards reality, for example, which is one answer to a fundamental question of philosophy—the transcendental question (where are we when we think?). Alenka Zupancic describes the comedic stand:

> There is something very real in comedy's supposedly unrealistic insistence on the indestructible, on something that persists, keeps reasserting itself and won't go away, like a tic that goes on even though its "owner" is already dead. In this respect, one could say that the flaws, extravagances, excesses, and so-called human weaknesses of comic characters are precisely what account for their not being "only human." More precisely, they show us that what is "human" exists only in this kind of excess over itself. (*The Odd One In* 49)

Although the spirit of Montmartre (our Analogy) is comedic or even parodic, the important lesson is not any one specific attitude, but attitude as such. The design lesson is to notice that parody works explicitly from a source.

The key to concept avatar is to learn from the CATTt how a vital anecdote associated with a conceptual persona produces thought. The relevant documentation in *What Is Philosophy?* is the references to modernist arts practices (literature, painting, music). The mental landscape of thinking relates to the problem plane by means analogous to those invented by Cézanne (for example) to express the physical landscape. The CATTt directs us to adopt the modernist arts plane of composition (invented in Paris) as a relay (Analogy) for treating the conceptual anecdote, in order to create a vector or a different turning within the problem, to challenge the commodity version of contemporary embodiment. The short-hand instruction from our Analogy, then, for how to compose a vital anecdote, is Duchamp's readymade. An example of a readymade is a postcard representation of Leonardo's *Mona*

Lisa, to which Duchamp (alluding to Sapeck as much as to Leonardo) added a mustache and goatee, plus a caption, L. H. O. O. Q. (the letters punning on a phrase in French meaning "she has a hot ass"). So much for the Dark Lady. The formal instruction includes not only the attitude, but the device: take a picture. The phrase alludes to the technology of imaging, and suggests a nickname for our conceptual procedure: take (verb/noun). Avatar takes thought (as birds take flight).

Bachelor Machine

Flash reason includes the readymade as logic (it shows what the readymade is for). The *Documents of Contemporary Art* series includes a collection on *The Artist's Joke.* Marcel Duchamp anchors this collection, as he does the one on "Appropriation." Pressed by an interviewer to accept sophisticated hermeneutic readings of his Readymades (such as the geometry book left out in the rain), Duchamp replied that it was a joke. A pure joke. To denigrate the solemnity of a book of principles. The rhetorical form exemplified in Duchamp's work is that of the "bachelor machine." Lyotard contributed an essay to the catalog of the famous exhibit in which Michel Carrouges established bachelor machines as a modern myth. These bachelors are imaginary machines, related to the absurdist science of "pataphysics" (Bok), whose machinations symbolized and allegorized human sexuality. The fate of Eros in modernity is expressed in these delirious devices, whose proliferation in art and literature Carrouges documented in his exhibition.

The simplest prototype of a bachelor machine is Lautreamont's formula, adopted by Surrealism as one of its emblems: "he is beautiful . . . like the chance meeting of a sewing-machine and an umbrella on a dissecting-table!" (22). Among the more famous examples are the ones described in Raymond Roussel's novels, some of Kafka's stories such as "In the Penal Colony," or Poe's "The Pit and the Pendulum." Works by Picabia and other artists associated with Dada and Surrealism created these mental mechanisms, articulating at once the new beauty and the new Eros, with Duchamp's *Large Glass* one of the foremost examples. They are apotropaic in defending against the anxieties of the industrial sublime. The first bachelor machine, Lyotard proposes, was Pandora's Box, closing the circle (Blumenberg would say) with the fault of Epimetheus (*Duchamp's Trans/formers* 45). Eureka! Lyotard considers the contradictory structure of bachelor machines to fall within the tradition of topical *dissoi logoi*, the technique of arguing both sides of any question (47). We are in the neighborhood of an industrial scale concept for thinking *technics*.

As Lyotard observed in the case of Duchamp's anamorphic machines, the new topological and non-Euclidean geometries created new kinds of spaces, enabling new manners of relating in every respect. The result, central to our project, was a "new cunning" (58). Thierry de Duve's discussion of Duchamp's invention of the readymade establishes its importance as a model of a new decision logic. What becomes clear in de Duve's account is that the readymade is not an "object" but an action, a statement in a discourse, modeling how to author in electracy (it anticipates Lacan's object @). De Duve foregrounds an aspect of readymades of special relevance to our context: judgment as event rather than choice.

> The *Bottle Dryer* of 1914 was Duchamp's first pure Readymade. Alternately entitled a *Bottle Drainer*, *Bottle Rack*, and *Hedge-Hog*, this piece was selected by Duchamp without the addition of other items or alterations. Essentially this object appears to be a work of "open" abstract sculpture, a symmetrical form that could have been made by some artist anywhere from the 1920s to the late 1960s. But in titling it by its literal designation *Bottle Dryer*, Duchamp was simply reinforcing an internal contradiction already established in many viewers' minds. These facts simply define its claim to be called art. But Duchamp's appellation of "hedgehog" for this restaurant appliance runs somewhat deeper. In an essay by Isaiah Berlin there is a comment on a line written by the Greek poet Archilochus, "mark one of the deepest differences which divides writers and thinkers, and, it may be human beings in general. The one type, 'the fox,' consists of men who live by ideas scattered and often unrelated to one another. But the man of the other type, the 'hedgehog,' relates 'everything to a central vision, one system more or less coherent or articulate . . . a single, universal, organizing principle.' " Not only does this appliance resemble a hedgehog, apparently it suggests a unified vision. (Burnham 83)

Burnham read *Bottle Dryer* as emblem expressing aura (evoking "hedgehog" as a type of thinker). The readymade is a relay for the new judgment, for operant-idiots of anticipation. Readymades are a part of a larger context in which painters responded to the industrial revolution (the beginning of electracy) including the impact on their medium of the invention of photography and also of commercial tubes of paint. Duchamp's solution to the crisis of painting was more extreme than that of his colleagues, in that, while they were willing to strip away nearly every attribute of their practice, to reduce it to some essential property (e.g. flatness), Duchamp took the final step and abandoned painting altogether. The point that de Duve stresses, is that the readymade is an act of pure judgment . It is an act of reflective judgment (in Kant's terms) that puts the maker in the position of spectator, whose reception produces art. In contrast with literacy, this act of selection is empty of intention, the opposite of identity as self-presence.

This act of randomized selection and remotivation of the received or given is the point of departure for electrate decision. The device is neither mimetic nor expressive, but conative: the aim is to receive event (in the manner of consulting an oracle). That most of the Readymades are commodities, commercial objects, is an important part of the invention, demonstrating that electrate authoring shifts to a meta-level, taking as the material of its discourse the commodity-information sphere. Again, a crucial point is that this judgment is distinct from both understanding and reason (conceptual knowledge and moral belief) and represents a distinct region of valuation (the life feeling of "little sensations"—the infra-thin—what Lacan called *lichettes*). The equivalent of the natural written language from which the Greeks crafted the working concepts of philosophy is the discourse of popular culture, including Commerce, in all its forms and genres, the manipulation of which generates an ad hoc semantics (second nature).

De Duve's detailed review of the R. Mutt case recognizes that the readymade is an utterance in a discourse and not an object, and hence to appreciate its status as a relay for electrate judgment. In our context we recognize it also as a move in a language game. What it means to position oneself temporally in the hinge of Now (as Lyotard described Duchamp's stance, showing its relevance for flash reason), becomes clear in the cunning manifested in the process that resulted, eventually, in the recognition of a urinal, entitled *Fountain,* signed by one R. Mutt, as a work of art. A further Kantian element of de Duve's history of this delay is his use of the formal ratio of hypotyposis, or the "algebraic comparison" as Duchamp called it, to articulate the steps

Duchamp undertook to create his invention. As the story goes, Duchamp learned from his experience with *Nude Descending a Staircase* about the power of scandal to create publicity and status. He submitted *Fountain* anonymously, to test his colleagues' declaration that any work by any person would be admitted to the exhibition of independent artists, for which Duchamp himself was one of the organizers. The submission was a provocation, an experiment, a joke, a gambit, a wager on the future of art, a wager that Duchamp won. *Ingenium.*

The significant point for our purposes is that Duchamp did not simply submit the assisted readymade and leave it at that. He manipulated the situation as a mediated image, to get not the object, but the picture of the object as provocation, into public circulation. Following the logic of a bachelor machine, Duchamp was able to attach or link his statement to other statements, and then to let the ratios of information circulation do their work as transformers. Duchamp's strategy meets the requirements of an operator in the dromosphere, to manage expectation and anticipation, the belated temporality of prudence.

> Making avant-garde art of true significance means anticipating a verdict that can only be retrospective. It means delivering the unexpected in lieu of the expected in such a way that betrayed and disappointed expectations show themselves, in the end, to have been fulfilled. Because it is in the nature of expectations not to depend on factual verification for their truth as expectations—that is, as projected scenarios—the scenario that I have described as the chain of fulfilled expectations proves to be the right one. Indeed, let's reestablish the facts: instead of the *Chessplayers*, the Paris Independents were presented with the *Nude Descending a Staircase*, and they rejected it; instead of going directly to Stieglitz in order to gain avant-garde legitimacy for *Fountain*, Richard Mutt went to the Independents, and they rejected it. The last formula, the one that happily linked the two chains of algebraic comparisons, translates back into one that is familiar: *Nude*/Paris Indeps = (*Nude*)/(Armory Show) = *Fountain*/N.Y.Indeps. (de Duve 141)

Duchamp put an emblem (an image, an idea, a label) into the temporal loop of time, the after-effect or retrospective emergence of meaning, the future anterior, in order to influence the values and practices of his institution. Duchamp raised "joke" to its highest power, confirming Koestler's claim about the shared features of wit and creativity. The adjustment to be made for our rehearsal is to shift the setting away from art proper, to follow Duchamp's creation of the possibility of making art in general, rather than working in any specific medium. His answer to the question of the ontology of art (what is painting?) becomes the analogy for an art of ontology, that is, using the readymade as a unit of discourse, to articulate an image category for electrate metaphysics. The readymade opens the possibility not just of art in general, but of general electracy. Duchamp occupies temporarily the position of conceptual persona, along with the vital anecdote of the R. Mutt joke. Concept avatar does not rely on any one persona, however, but facilitates a practice of adopting tutor anecdotes.

Target: Judgment

How is judgment as bachelor machine applied in flash reason? How does one take a stand or make a turn away from or towards a position by means of avatar? Paolo Virno provides a source for Target (specifying the need or lack to be supplied by our concept). Conceptual thinking continues to be relevant in electracy to the extent that a democratic public sphere is still possible in an Internet civilization. Our concept must support judgment in decision making. Judgment (practical reason) means drawing upon the lessons of the past to make a decision in the present situation promising the best outcome for the future well-being of the community. Good judgment requires the virtue of *phronesis.* Prudence is a virtue, meaning that it is a matter of disposition, a quality of character. The practice of deliberative rhetoric in the civic sphere follows the paths of inference, beginning with abduction from the particular conditions to the rules (an archive of maxims and proverbs representing the wisdom of experience or tradition and its associated respected authorities). Commonsense rules supplied the premises for deductions formulating hypothetical cases, which in turn inductively were applied to the situation. The problem with practical reason today, Virno observes, is that there is not now, and never has been, a rule for applying the rule to a case. The application requires a decision, arbitrary in itself, and this decision represents the aporia (impasse) of ethics. The dilemma is moot, in any case, since there is no reservoir of tradition to supply authoritative proverbs in the first place. Or rather, tradition has been replaced by Commerce (entertainment).

The aporia is implacable, since in the sublime conditions of the industrial city the archive of maxims and proverbs recording the wisdom of collective experience lost all authority. Moreover, the locus of causality disappeared from everyday life, to become accessible only to scientific expertise supported by technology. Commerce filled the void, promoting through advertising the conversion of citizens to an entirely new stand, oriented along the axis of pleasure-pain (attraction/repulsion). Wisdom is reduced to taste. Marchand cites a pronouncement made by one advertising agency in the 1920s to note the role Commerce attempted to play:

> The product of advertising is public opinion; and in a democracy public opinion is the uncrowned king. It is the advertising agency's business to write the speeches from the throne of that king; to help his subjects decide what they should eat and wear; how they should invest their savings; by what courses they can improve their minds; and even what laws they should make, and by what faith they may be saved. (Marchand 31)

We see what is at stake in our invention: who or what gives counsel in the electrate public sphere?

Virno's proposal assumes that we are now living in conditions of a permanent "state of exception," in which the rules guiding judgment may be open to revision, to innovation, to testing against experience (a ratio of anomaly, not equivalence, is needed). Here is an opportunity for flash reason. His suggestion to replace valid reasoning with the deliberate use of fallacies, in order to expose the enthymemes, the assumptions and values determining the ineffective deductions guiding decision-making, acknowledges the unconscious as a site of ethical decision unsuspected in pre-modern philosophy. Ethics we now understand is beyond the reach of both reason and will. Fallacies and joke-work are transitional forms manifesting the fourth mode of inference invented in Cabaret: conduction. The primary instruction derived from Virno is based on his proposal to adopt logical fallacies (exploiting the structure of joke-work: condensation, displacement, secondary elaboration) as sources of innovative inference practice in conditions of ethical/political crisis. "Jokes and innovative action displace the 'rotational axis' of a form of life by means of an openly 'fallacious' conjecture, one that nonetheless reveals in a flash a different way of applying the rules of the game: contrary to the way it seemed before, it is entirely possible to embark on a side path or to escape from Pharaoh's Egypt" (*Multitude* 163). Joke-work surprises thought from an unexpected direction.

Virno's proposal shows the relevance of *fumisme* as a rhetoric. The pragmatics of laughter and the forms that elicit it are guides to the site of interface, the moebius twist, crossing body and language. The two sides of language (biology and culture) are hinged here, enabling discourse and desire (unconscious satisfaction, that the French call *jouissance*) to coexist in one practice. This is the point of departure for electracy as metaphysics. Literacy ontologized the semantic register of writing; electracy ontologizes the libidinal register (the signifier).

> The logic of crisis is most evident in the articulation between instinctual apparatus and propositional structure, between drives and grammar. Each attempt at delineating a different normative "substratum," though it unravels within wholly contingent sociopolitical circumstances, retraces and compounds, on a reduced scale, the passage from life in general to linguistic life. Anomalous inferences are the precision instrument by virtue of which verbal thought, delineating a different normative 'substratum,' recalls, each time anew, the anthropogenetic passage. Their anomaly lies in the manner in which language preserves within itself, though transfigured to the point of being barely recognizable, the original nonlinguistic drive. (*Multitude* 160)

Virno's insight introduces the topic of "letter" (a hybrid of language and body), theorized in Lacan's psychoanalysis (to which we will return).

Instruction: Style gives access to embodied (sensory, aesthetic) thought. The lesson of our Target resource, then, is to create a concept persona supporting judgment (decision) conducted in an aesthetic style. This style sheet is the one invented by the Parisian avant-garde. The goal is to activate and administer in writing the embodied (unconscious) drives that accompany meaning. Aesthetics is the area of philosophy that remains functional in electracy.

Experience Ontology

It is worth remembering that in the context of apparatus invention the bachelor machine is as practical for the pleasure-pain axis as is dialectic for the true-false axis. Inquiry is conducted in at least two modalities: the high focus of specific questions, guided by methodological presuppositions, and low focus browsing, relying on intuition and associative or lateral thinking. Literate schooling teaches the former and assumes the latter. Intuition is actually the default mode, in research and quotidian thought alike, in conditions of massive complexity with rich redundancy in the information. It is also the mode in which fields of knowledge are invented, and sometimes transformed (creative discovery, sudden insight). If Kant were alive today, his example for the "sublime" might be "information" rather than "ocean storm." The institutional pragmatic goal of concept avatar is to adapt the logic or mechanisms of intuitive inquiry to interface design for semantic web databasing.

The analogy with the sublime is apt, since, as Kant explained, in those conditions the site of world measure shifts from the objective order of things (the order of beauty), to personal embodied experience. Kant's Copernican revolution in metaphysics (shifting the locus of categories from the world to the [transcendental] mind) was the point of departure for what has evolved into a new ontology of experience, made viable by digital imaging technologies. The notion of experience ontology is proposed by analogy with the invention of semantic ontology by the Classical Greeks at the beginnings of literacy. Being (ontology) is not in the world, but is a classification system made possible by alphabetic writing. Semantic ontology, based on the categories invented by Aristotle (substance and accidents), uses rules of definition to extract certain features from observed entities. The salient features that count as "essence" are those manifesting function (purpose, end): "form follows function" was in Greek metaphysics before it became the mantra of modern design. Certainly things had functions before literacy, but literacy put this quality of experience into a tool and institutionalized it. In recent decades these ancient categories have been made more flexible, but are no match for the information sublime.

Similarly, experience ontology is relative to the apparatus (social machine) that makes it possible or functional (digital imaging). The quality of experience made accessible to ontology in electracy is that of affective memory in the individual body. Affective memory is the deepest order of memory, existing only as somatic markers informing kinesthetic intelligence. It is "enactive," resulting from the accumulation of routines, habitus, acquired through daily life, and carrying emotional charges associated in idiosyncratic (singular) ways with individual enculturation. Anyone who has reacted "automatically" in an emergency situation of instant reflex has drawn on this kind of experience (blink). More immediately relevant in our context is the fact that this dimension of emotionally cathected sensori-motor enactions is also the source of coherence for intuition and creative insight. This affective network does not depend on specific image representations, but is encoded across the senses, multimodally. The event of insight, in which irrelevant semantic domains are superimposed, yielding a eureka moment, is due to an affective match that is not in the semantics of the domains but in the idiosyncratic experience of the seeker.

The most extensive analysis of these sorts of matches is by Gerald Holton, historian of science, who introduced the phrase "image of wide scope" (wide image) to account for his observations (Ulmer, *Internet Invention*). Although Holton and others using his methods have studied hundreds of cases of the most productive people across the full range of sciences, arts, and society, the prototype is Albert Einstein. Einstein himself mentioned in his autobiography the importance of the memory of a gift from his father of a compass when Albert was four-years old. Albert was fascinated by the fixity of the arrow regardless of the movements of the compass. The attunement of Albert's disposition or temperament was manifested in this fixity, which Holton abstracts as the "invariant principle." This disposition found a match with "speed of light" in the physics problem set Albert addressed as an adult. Holton's argument is that this affective trace is the reason Einstein and not Poincaré or some other equally well-prepared scientist solved the problem of electromagnetism.

The image of wide scope is present in cases not covered by Holton, such as that of Frank Gehry, designer of the Guggenheim Museum in Bilbao. Gehry reported that one of his most vivid memories was of the carp that his grandmother would bring home live from the market. Frank loved to watch the carp swimming in the bathtub, before it was served for Sabbath supper. The movements of this fish are now observed in the sweeping curved geometries of Gehry's designs. The wide image accounts for Gehry's recognition of this feeling in the geometries, which he began to use even before he had access to the computers that made them practical.

The immediate point of relevance is to note the interface feature, equivalent in experience ontology of essence in semantic metaphysics. This feature is the kinetic gesture, the motion charged with affect, in the scene (e-motion). For Einstein it was the one fixed feature within a turning frame; for Gehry it was the undulations of a swimming fish. Commentators from a diversity of fields have made similar observations of this feature as the appropriate interface between the affective body and the archive of documents. Gelernter, arguing for adding intuition and poetry to the AI model, used a reading of Genesis to show the feature: a series of stories, whose coherence was provided by scenes of Moses making a certain gesture of "a powerful arm outstretched." Deleuze and Guattari, in their study of Kafka, similarly opened a new network of intertext within the oeuvre, a system consisting of an oppositional pair: bent head + portrait photo / straightened head + musical sound. The implication is that the phrases expressing such patterns are present in the surface text, and may be extracted as features, designed as hooks or attractors addressing potential matches in the idiosyncratic backstories of researchers, supporting browsing or low-focus inquiry.

The further implication is that experience ontology is inherently supported in audiovisual media. The fact that film (AV media) simulates the presentation of the world to perception enables it to record the event situations that trigger the somatic markers of enactive memory. Digital simulations of lens photography further enhance the ability of audiovisualization to enhance, augment, and bring into awareness and articulation this dimension of intelligence that until now has remained "unconscious." Commentators in the Humanities are especially excited by the possibility that database simulation allows reflection upon the dispositions that are a primary source of judgments and decisions in ethics and politics (not to mention aesthetics). The positive aspect of this discovery is that filmic presentation, in its capacity to trigger deep memory, in principle allows individuals to examine under the hood of their bachelor machine. The caveat directed to promotors of neuroaesthetics comes from the philosophical aptitude of German language. Presentation (*Darstellung*) is an improvement on representation (*Vorstellung*). However, as Sam Weber pointed out in several books, both of these modalities are framed and repurposed by a third kind discovered by Freud, distortion (*Entstellung*). *Star Trek* already taught us that in VR, the most convincingly authentic experience is in fact a kind of dream. Its *Stelle* results from all the turns of tropology—condensation, displacement, rationalization, representability. Concept avatar does not propose any one place, stand, location (*Stelle*), but the functionality of place (chora).

After the Greeks had spent some time with their epics in written form they began to notice some clustering and patterns emerging within the words, the phenomenon of *paronomasia*, with a variety of words formed out of a shared or similar roots. "*Dike*" or "justice" was the first word that was studied systematically for these patterns, and became the first concept constructed in philosophy (in Plato's Republic). Similarly, commentators today are noticing the presence of affective intensities emerging within image work. The next step is to do for these image patterns what the Greeks did for their word patterns: put them into an ontology, that is, a system for storage and retrieval of information on a massive scale, opening a further dimension to reality. The purpose of concept avatar is to support this passage from one style of concept to another. Avatar does not eliminate essence, but redirects attention to a different aspect of a scene, to different traits, that gather into an alternative pattern expressing and constructing an affective metaphysics. "Experience ontology" is a reminder of this background of flash reason, joining data extraction, visualization, and collaboration tools, to integrate data and interface design. Virtual worlds, or mixed (augmented) realities, may be designed to support experience ontology, both for pedagogy and research, by addressing the somatic markers of affective memory, enhanced by information retrieval. The proposal is that experience ontology is to creative discovery what semantic ontologies have been to scientific method. On the side of *technics*, we need an experience web to supplement the semantic web. The Allegory of Prudence probes this dimension of experience, accessing this feeling that motivates your image of wide scope. Electracy augments the sensory capacity of your body to know that your foot is in the fire, extended into the dimension of thriving, so that you (we) know when there is an emergency of well-being.

3 Joke

Attitude

Concept avatar learns from bachelor machines informed by *fumisme.* The Allegory of Prudence does not require a certain attitude, but counsels on attitude formation as such, advising me on how attitude "turns out." "The biolinguistic conditions of so-called 'evil' are the same biolinguistic conditions that animate 'virtue,'" Paolo Virno says. "They both feed off the uncertainty experienced in the face of 'that which can be different from the way it is' [Aristotle's ethics]" (Virno, Multitude Between 21). The axis of Aesthetic Reason (of pleasure-pain, or joy-sadness) supplements Practical Reason at this contingent moment of choice. It answers the question: what is the measure guiding decision? Agamben states the question within the frame of a philosophical tradition, represented by Spinoza.

> The Irreparable is that things are just as they are, in this or that mode, consigned without remedy to their way of being. States of things are irreparable, whatever they may be: sad or happy, atrocious or blessed. How you are, how the world is—that is the Irreparable . . . According to Spinoza the two forms of the irreparable, confidence or safety (*securitas*) and despair (*desperatio*), are identical from this point of view. What is essential is only that every cause of doubt has been removed, that things are certainly and definitively thus; it does not matter whether this brings joy or sadness. As a state of things, heaven is perfectly equivalent to hell even though it has the opposite sign. (But if we could feel confident in despair, or desperate in confidence, then we would be able to perceive in the state of things a margin, a limbo that cannot be contained within it). The root of all pure joy and sadness is that the world is as it is. Joy or sadness that arises because the world is

> not what it seems or what we want it to be is impure or provisional. But in the highest degree of their purity, in the so be it said to the world when every legitimate cause of doubt and hope has been removed, sadness and joy refer not to negative or positive qualities, but to a pure being-thus without any attributes. (*The Coming Community* 90)

Electracy is the apparatus of joy/sadness, hence our concern with augmented attitude. Agamben is glossing the "consolation" of philosophy, the contingent relationship between how the world is and our attitude within that world. Wisdom proposes that we work on our attitude rather than on the world, with the recommended answer to the transcendental question of stand (at least up to modernity) being *ataraxy* (suppression of desire). In electracy this pair is not an either-or, since attitude now is ontological (world-creating). Avatar emergency concerns precisely the relation between attitude and action. We take up this question of stand, orientation, direction (attitude) anew, appropriating as a relay for the inference procedure of flash reason (conduction) in electracy the stand-up routine as a practice of concept avatar. We are learning how to play with avatar, in the persona of wiseacre. "Attitude is the heartbeat of an act," advises one handbook of the craft.

> Material cannot be emotionally neutral. Your subject matter has to disgust you, pain you, thrill you, because audiences don't respond to words, they respond to feelings. Every piece of material has a specific attitude, such as "I'm worried about . . ." or "I love . . ." or "I'm angry about . . ." This Margaret Smith piece comes out of how she feels about her manager: "I hate my manager. He's always giving me advice like 'Wear red lipstick up there. Look pretty.' What if I'm not funny and it's coming out of these big old red lips? It's like being a crummy outfielder with a paiseley mitt." (Carter 18)

Prudence involves attitude. The attempt to learn something about attitude from the tradition of the wise fool is further indication of what separates concept avatar from philosophy, in that Deleuze and Guattari reject the entire history of the sages, whose figures they say remain within a transcendental metaphysics. Heuretics uses our sources as relays, not to recommend them literally. We have something to learn about attitude adjustment (about orientation) from the sages.

Take for example this report of an incident involving a Yogi, a Priest, and a Sufi. It is an example of persona and anecdote.

Nasrudin put on a Sufi robe and decided to make a pious journey. On his way he met a priest and a yogi, and they decided to team up together. When they got to a village the others asked him to seek donations while they carried out their devotions. Nasrudin collected some money and bought halwa with it. He suggested that they divide the food, but the others, who were not yet hungry enough, said that it should be postponed until night. They continued on their way; and when night fell Nasrudin asked for the first portion "because I was the means of getting the food." The others disagreed: the priest on the grounds that he represented a properly organized hierarchical body, and should therefore have preference; the yogi because he ate only once in three days and should therefore have more.

Finally they decided to sleep. In the morning, the one who related the best dream should have first choice of the halwa. In the morning, the priest said: "in my dream I saw the founder of my religion, who made a sign of benediction, singling me out as especially blessed." The others were impressed, but the Yogi said: "I dreamt that I visited Nirvana, and was utterly absorbed into nothing." They turned to the Mulla. "I dreamt that I saw the Sufi teacher Khidr, who appears only to the most sanctified. He said "Nasrudin, eat the halwa—now!" And of course I had to obey. (Shah 75)

9/11—20/20

There is an arresting statement deep within the *9/11 Commission Report*, that makes explicit an organizing theme, suggesting an opening for attitude adjustment, or reorientation. "It is therefore crucial to find a way of routinizing, even bureaucratizing the exercise of imagination" (344). The immediate context is concern that security experts had not foreseen the scenario of the hijack attacks, despite many contextual signals. The comment is made in a chapter entitled "Foresight—And Hindsight," in which imagination is listed, along with policy, capabilities, and management, as the four categories of failure demonstrated by the surprise attack. We may be witnessing the creation of an addition to the list of oxymoron jokes: military intelligence, jumbo shrimp, bureaucratic imagination. Scenario of a bureaucratized imagination: You: "I need an idea, now!" It: "Take a number!" or "Please hold while I transfer your call."

The wording in the *Report* suggests a misunderstanding about imagination, as if it were a way to eliminate surprise, when the reality is just the opposite: the function of the imagination is to enhance "surprisability" (the capacity for surprise). "In composing this narrative, we have tried to remember that we write with the benefit and the handicap of hindsight. Hindsight can sometimes see the past clearly—with 20/20 vision. But the path of what happened is so brightly lit that it places everything else more deeply into shadow" (339). We are reminded of Kierkegaard's observation, that life can only be understood backwards; but it must be lived forwards. Here is our singularity as sequence: the intersection of the aphorism of thought and the anecdote of life. The point in our context is to propose that the *Report's* observation about the value of imagination applies not only to strategic planners but to citizens in general. To admit this truth is already a proposal for a transvaluation of values. Meanwhile, the Department of Homeland Security created the Analytic Red Cell Unit, in which such authors as Brad Thor (who claims Glenn Beck is his Oprah Winfrey), and Brad Meltzer, both specializing in thrillers, consulted on various disaster scenarios. Why don't they consult with the EmerAgency?

Mythology

Edith Hamilton provides convenient summaries of Greek mythology. The aspect of the story of Prometheus (Foresight), Epimetheus (Hindsight), and Pandora (Disaster), to be noted in our context of image metaphysics is the role of prank, joke, trick, governing relationships among the characters. Prometheus first tricked Zeus over the matter of animal sacrifice.

> Prometheus had not only stolen fire for men; he had also arranged that they should get the best part of any animal sacrificed and the gods the worst. He cut up a great ox and wrapped the good eatable parts in the hide, disguising them further by piling entrails on top. Beside this heap he put another of all the bones, dressed up with cunning and covered with shining fat, and bade Zeus choose between them. Zeus took up the white fat and was angry when he saw the bones craftily tricked out. (Hamilton 70)

A case of originary *fumisme*. Spin and sting: the ways of the gods.

Zeus's revenge for this prank was to create his own bait-and-switch device in the form of the first woman, Pandora ("The-Gift-Of-All"), so-named because each of the gods endowed her with a favor. Pandora (Cameron no doubt courted the bachelor machine echo) is "gift" in that sense developed in Derrida's discussion of *pharmakon*, generalized from the German word, meaning both "gift" in the English sense, and "poison." Derrida activates this terminology to work within his own critique of "present," to exploit its amphibology to provoke thought about the role of temporality in metaphysics. One version of the story attributes Pandora's motivation not to malice but curiosity. "The gods presented her with a box into which each had put something harmful, and forbade her ever to open it. They then sent her to Epimetheus, who took her gladly although Prometheus had warned him never to accept anything from Zeus. He took her, and afterward when that dangerous thing, a woman, was his, he understood how good his brother's advice had been" (Hamilton 70). When Pandora opened her box, "out flew plagues innumerable, sorrow and mischief for mankind. In terror Pandora clapped the lid down, but too late. One good thing, however, was there—Hope." The iconography of this (X) "box" evolved from the original giant round jar used in ancient times for storage through a small, square cosmetics or jewelry box to (in modernism) the female sex organ (Panofsky and Panofsky): the mandorla as guiding emblem (celebrity girls-gone-wild). Flash reason searches the euphemist detours of tropology.

In which I Laugh

I took a break from the perplexities of concept avatar to watch *Mad Men,* Season 4, Episode 3, "The Good News." In a scene of domestic relations between Joan Harris (the redhead office manager) and her doctor husband Greg, Greg tells Joan a joke. Freud commented that we do not know what we are laughing at when we laugh at a joke. It is an involuntary reflex associated with unconscious motivations. Here is a version of the joke.

> Hillbilly 1: Let's play twenty questions.
> Hillbilly 2: What's that?
> Hillbilly 1: I write something down on this piece of paper, and you can ask me up to twenty questions to try to guess what it is.

> (Hillbilly 1 writes down "donkey dong" and tells his friend to start guessing).
> Hillbilly 2: Is it something you can eat?
> Hillbilly 1: I suppose so.
> Hillbilly 2: Is it donkey dong?

Laughter. How many stories have I read about Eureka moments in history? Some hero of heuretics struggling with an impacted interrogative, in a distracted moment during a quotidian activity, due to the mysteries of incubated learning, suddenly gets it. Will history record—along with Archimedes' bath, Newton's apple, Poincare's bus—Ulmer's donkey dong? Perhaps not, since it remains to be seen if the knowledge triggered by this laugh proves fruitful. Handbooks teaching the craft of comedy have no trouble explaining the formula for a joke of this type (Dean). The formula is simple to state: compose a set-up through exposition that creates in the audience a certain expectation, based on shared cultural background (habitus). This habitus constitutes your wisdom. For example, your expectation that I am speaking of prudence. It turns out, in fact, that *dharma*, as Krishna explains it to Arjuna, resembles what we call habitus. Expectation, anticipation, foresight: these are the powers of prudence we are probing.

For purposes of the larger argument, I will make explicit what we already recognize. The expectation in this case is our understanding and experience of the game Twenty Questions. The word or phrase will be difficult to guess, and Hillbilly 2, having never played the game before, might run out of questions without success. When we learn that the phrase in question is "donkey dong" (which is funny in itself), the challenge seems even more impossible, since we would never ask questions that would get us into that neighborhood (parages). This joke is well-designed, in that it milks the set-up for comic effect with each exchange. The joke formula then is to create a Punch by switching to a different scenario, in order to violate our expectations and surprise us. In the scenario of Hillbillies, "donkey dong" apparently is commonly consumed in some form or other left to the imagination. We did not expect Hillbilly 2 to get it with the second guess. That he got it so quickly, and with that specific question, surprised me. Aha! I took the bait, and the punch landed: a sucker punch.

Bisociation

Arthur Koestler in his classic study on creativity proposed a name for the juxtaposition and interaction of stories or planes of information at work in the Hillbilly joke: bisociation. Koestler's insight was prescient in part because he based his claims linking thought in comedy, science, and arts on physiological processes, now the commonplaces of neuroaesthetics. The relevant point is the experiential similarity between getting a joke and solving a problem.

> The creative act of the humorist consisted in bringing about a momentary fusion between two habitually incompatible matrices. Scientific discovery can be described in very similar terms—as the permanent fusion of matrices of thought previously believed to be incompatible. Until the seventeenth century the Copernican hypothesis of the earth's motion was considered as obviously incompatible with commonsense experience; it was accordingly treated as a huge joke by the majority of Galileo's contemporaries. (94)

Koestler's review of the history of invention, of the great discoveries from Archimedes to Einstein, foregrounds the place of surprise, of violated expectations, accidents, mishaps, and contingency, that seem to be inherent in innovation. One of his many examples is the familiar story of Pasteur and the discovery of vaccine, when laboratory experiments were spoiled by an obnoxious mould. A related story is that of Fleming, whose breakthrough after fifteen years work came when a gust of wind blew through the lab window a spore of the mould *penicillim notatum* (194). The surprise happens to someone in the process of seeking, or inquiry, who grasps the unforeseen relationship. "The essence of discovery is that unlikely marriage of cabbages and kings—of previously unrelated frames of reference or universes of discourse—whose union will solve the previously insoluble problem. The search for the improbable partner involves long and arduous striving—but the ultimate matchmaker is the unconscious" (201). In short, bachelor machine.

Koestler understands the "unconscious" as a kind of reasoning based on rules derived from the arts rather than from logic. His choice of "matchmaker" as the personification of this procedure alludes to Freud's study of jokes as a version of unconscious method. The genre of joke most cited by Freud is that of the *Schadchen*, or marriage broker. These jokes show the *Schadchen* to be a sophist who in selling the bride to the prospective groom either lets slip some fundamental flaw in the woman, or, if the flaw is already known, selling it as a virtue (Oring 27). We can imagine how a *Schadchen* might arrange the meeting between Epimetheus and Pandora. Discourse, language in other words, mediates in some form the coupling of incompatibles. Insight is a gestalt shift in communication, a figure-ground reversal, a switch in which noise (parasite) becomes information (to borrow Michel Serres's terms) (*The Parasite).* Electracy admits that Eros may be personified by a *Schadchen.* Prudence is not prim and proper. A measure of the difference in attitude between literacy and electracy is seen by comparing Boticelli's didactic "Birth of Venus" with Freud's *Schadchen* jokes.

Rehearsal

Dean's instructions for creating a stand-up routine, in the context of Koestler's analogy between jokes and discovery, supply a form for a vital anecdote, within which my conceptual persona may perform the thought of a problem field. This proposal is preliminay, a "rehearsal," the backstage planning and preparations, constructing a place or site, a position, within which a possible thought may appear. For mnemonic purposes, Dean's advice is to locate our wit (discovery) within a fully imagined situation. The principle is that a bit is a particular situation and our response to it, dramatized as our own experience. The heuretic rule is to substitute our problem field (the dialogical struggle over the function of avatar) for the joke situation. The joke mechanism, and the mining procedures for filling the slots of the mechanism, constitute inferential steps for thinking the unthought (conduction, bachelor machine). The joke mechanism consists of two stories, two interpretations of one situation. To use a Margaret Smith version of one of Dean's examples, take the situation of Smith visiting her parents. The parents wonder why she doesn't visit more often. The cultural expectation guiding the first story concerns what is appropriate according to norms, etiquette, values: families respect and care for and about one another. The connector (pivot, switch, hinge) prompting this norm (expectation) is "visit." Dean's advice is to locate a connector open to a second interpretation, a different assumption. This second assumption is

Smith's attitude, the assumption of her persona, which is hostile to her family. She tells a second story from the point of view of this minority assumption: *I would visit more often, but I can't get Delta to have its plane wait in the yard while I run in.* The mechanism as a whole is this conjunction of two stories around a shared term. The instruction is to translate the family visit situation into my situation of constructing a concept (or whatever your task may be), in which we imagine ourselves as a participant with an attitude.

Smith's joke takes a Machiavellian approach to the cultural rules/expectations, one that is more cynical. The second assumption in Smith's bit is that most families do not get along. This assumption is just as familiar as the normative behavior, but violates decorum. This point is important: the official and unofficial attitudes are equally familiar. Freud might say the violation releases the energy used to repress this unofficial attitude, and so we laugh. This energy is ontologized in electracy. Alenka Zupancic noted that the unofficial attitude is familiar, and yet surprising when it appears (because repressed). The comedic stand, she says, is that when a husband returns home unexpectedly, one may assume that there is a lover hiding in the wife's closet. In tragedy the husband (Othello for example) assumes this as well, but is wrong. The relevant point for our consultation concerns its purpose of an inference leading to the unthought. The unthought is not absolute, but is relative to a habitus, meaning that it includes the unofficial as well as the official expectations. The conceptual persona must be surprisable. To be noted for now in documenting the rehearsal is this instruction to apply the generative mechanism not only to the expectations or assumptions of a research theme, but also to the assumptions motivating our attitude to the debate. The gambit is that if we construct a place for an insight to appear, it will come. The difficulty in shifting from joking to creativity is the requirement, following Baudelaire's lead, that I invent a new commonplace (*poncif*) to supply the assumptions for the joke. Insight as fashion.

The Idiot

Bernard Stiegler addresses Paul Virilio's warning about our contemporary condition of dromosphere (dimension collapse) produced by Real Time of *technics*, using the Prometheus story as an emblem for the human condition. The subtitle of Volume 1 of *Technics and Time* is "The

Fault of Epimetheus." How did we create for ourselves a dromosphere? Is the dromosphere itself the Internet Accident? The empirical point challenges traditional philosophical categories distinguishing nature, technology, and language, to argue that there is an irreducible symbiosis (rhizome) between humans and tools, such that human evolution occurred through tool creation. Tools have their own being, constituting a third dimension along with nature and humans, to be accounted for in ontology. In the era of electracy, beginning with the industrial revolution, technology finally (or once again) exceeded human capacities of intention, will, control. Invoking Virilio's account as shorthand for the present conditions of *technics* (the human-machine rhizome), Stiegler uses Epimetheus as an interface, to bring the empirical evolutionary account into relation with the resources of philosophy.

What is the fault of Epimetheus and why is it so important to *technics*? Epimetheus is an idiot, albeit a Titan idiot. Prometheus the potter made humans out of clay. We are "thrown" like pots (adding a further nuance to Heidegger's reference to *Dasein*'s thrownness). Prometheus assigned to his brother the job of providing the new creatures with qualities, with attributes like those that determine the nature of every other entity in the world. Epimetheus forgot his responsibility, and so humans have no assigned place in the Chain of Being. We have to make a place and even a nature for ourselves (second nature)—the Timaeic gambit. One of the first implications of this story is the recognition that we are all "Cylons," Cyborgs, Galateas, Pinocchios, Pandoras, meaning that this ambivalent relationship among maker, machine, and snare goes all the way back to the origins of humanity itself and before. This context is crucial to the task of becoming what you are, since one "is" precisely nothing determined. Concept avatar proposes to think this potentiality.

In the historical debate about whether Epimetheus and Pandora are a happy or fatal accident, Stiegler takes the side of Epimetheus (the *Schadchen* dimension) as a role model for humans to regain parity with tools (nor is he the first to do so).

> The figure of Prometheus makes no sense by itself. It is only consistent through its doubling by Epimetheus, who in turn doubles up on himself—first, in committing the fault of forgetting, which amounts to witlessness, distractedness, imbecility, and idiocy, and . . . second, in reflecting upon it, in a re-turn that is always too late. This is the very quality of

> reflectivity, knowledge, wisdom, and of the quite different figure of remembering, that of experience. Everyday Greek language roots reflective knowledge in *epimetheia*, namely, in the essential technicity that makes up (the condition of) finitude. (*Technics and Time, Vol. 1*186)

The belatedness ("aftering") of human being is the metaphysical condition underlying the capacity of prudence (how to anticipate through experience, how to step out of time). But this anticipation is not the ratio of planning, calculation, rationality (it is not literacy).

Cogito

We recall Deleuze and Guattari's formula that the working concepts invented for philosophy have three elements: a problem field (plane of immanence) provoking thought, the "idea" or concept proper responding to the provocation, and a conceptual persona that performs a "vital anecdote" demonstrating the character of the thought. A prototype is Plato's Socrates, and they inventory a number of the most representative examples throughout the Western tradition. A primary example is Descartes's *cogito*, since this concept is the one against which much of contemporary philosophy (including Deleuze and Guattari) defines itself, in order to produce a new orientation of thought in the world. The persona of modernity that becomes hegemonic in Descartes, the position of transcendental "I," is that of "idiot." "The idiot is the private thinker, in contrast to the public teacher (the schoolman): the teacher refers constantly to taught concepts, whereas the private thinker forms a concept with innate forces that everyone possesses on their own account by right ('I think')" (*What is Philosophy?* 62). Precursors for this persona include Nicholas of Cusa who opposed the scholastic organization of Christianity.

> The idiot will reappear in another age, in a different context that is still Christian, but Russian now. In becoming a Slav, the idiot is still the singular individual or private thinker, but with a different singularity. It is Chestov who finds in Dostoyevski the power of a new opposition between private thinker and public teacher. The old idiot wanted indubitable truths at which he could arrive by himself: in the meantime he would doubt everything, even that 3 + 2 = 5; he would

> doubt every truth of Nature. The new idiot has no wish for indubitable truths; he will never be "resigned" to the fact that 3 + 2 = 5 and wills the absurd—this is not the same image of thought. The old idiot wanted truth, but the new idiot wants to turn the absurd into the highest power of thought—in other words, to create. (62)

An example of the complementary relationship between literacy and electracy (electracy as supplement of literacy), is the different positions within discourse established for subjects in each case. Literacy formed a subject of reason, providing procedures of method and logic to avoid error, contradiction, and that ambition continues in Descartes and on through the Enlightenment (literacy is Promethean). However, in conditions of the dromosphere, of industrialized memory, this subject as individual self, is overwhelmed. The new concept emerging in contemporary philosophy shifts the site of thought from individual subject to collective event, a shift made practical within the digital prosthesis. The individual subject in electracy continues to function, necessarily, and its relation to event is that of "idiot" in this "modernist" (Russian) sense, activating the connotations of fool (perhaps wise fool). Here is what is to be constructed for electracy, this subject position of stupidity, the stance of Hindsight, complementing his brother Foresight, and fooled by Pandora. The cosmological implication is an understanding that the world is a prank, and that in the story we are what came out of the jar (box).

Today the overwhelming power in relation to which individuals must continue to think and act is not the gods, or God, but *technics.* Nicholas of Cusa, one of the few thinkers acknowledged as direct ancestor by Deleuze and Guattari, extracted from the tradition a particular distinction with fundamental importance for technicity—potentiality—introduced originally by Aristotle as the difference between *dunamis* and *energeia,* echoed in Deleuze's Virtual and Actual (don't be distracted by disavowals of this precedent for the Virtual). Cusa's "instructed ignorance," developed in such works as *Idiotae,* took up the thought of *posse.*

> Nicholas says in *De apice theoriae* that he once thought that the truth about God is found better in darkness or obscurity than in clarity and he adds that the idea of *posse,* of power or being able, is easy to understand. What boy or youth is ig-

> norant of the nature of *posse*, when he knows very well that he can eat, run and speak? And if he were asked whether he could do anything, carry a stone, for example, without the power to do so, he would judge such a question to be entirely superfluous. Now, God is the absolute *posse ipsum*. (Copleston 44–45)

Velle est posse (to be willing is to be able; where there's a will there's a way). But the idiot is not Caesar. Concept avatar enables player to receive thought. We are in the neighborhood of Walter Benjamin's "program for a coming philosophy," whose purpose is to orient philosophy within this horizon of "potentiality" rather than of contemplation or of action. Sam Weber's *Benjamin's–abilities* unpacks the implications, as does Giorgio Agamben's *Potentialities,* in which we finally understand the attraction of Bartleby the Scrivener to so many modern thinkers ("I prefer not to"). He is a conceptual persona dramatizing Virtuality, whose verso is im/potence. The third axis emerging in electracy adds to knowledge and will an attitude (I can/not) concerning relative power. From this context we infer an approach to electrate learning: it is "for dummies," but not in the sense intended by that business model. It is not about being educable, but surprisable. It is the position cultivated by the analyst in psychotherapy, who listens to the analysand's discourse with a third ear (to receive the bachelor machine).

Event-ization

The rehearsal includes Stiegler's use of mythology to frame a grammatology of *technics*. Hans Blumenberg explains that mythos is already doing the work of logos by distancing humans from the Overwhelming, the problem field of the existential world (dread). The motivation for creating myth is as defense against the "absolutism of reality" experienced as impotence and anxiety. Myth is evasion, the lie that preserves life. Stiegler is working on myth, in Blumenberg's terms, meaning that he is participating in a living tradition. Epimetheus the idiot is a conceptual persona showing thought in the dromosphere. *Technics* names our contemporary circumstances in which technology has its own evolutionary tendency, separate from both nature and culture. Concept avatar assumes a machine-human rhizome.

Human subject position is not that of creator whose intentions are fulfilled in and whose capacities are extended by the machine. That experience of full meaning or intentionality is the stand of "self" that Derrida devoted so much effort to deconstructing. The experience of electracy is rather that of being interrupted from out of the blue, to be presented with a pattern or gestalt (a *poncif*) that may or may not mean something. In the world of *daimons*, such as the one described by Heraclitus, the oracle at Delphi (for example) neither reveals nor conceals, but intimates. Here is the imperative: you must get it, this intimation. Or better yet, learn to *take* it. What is the logic of intimation? The electrate subject (the self as idiot receptive to event) is operator, whose function is "anticipation" (the idiot is wise in the ways of surprisability). "If there is a dynamic proper to the technical object tending toward its concretization, it nevertheless supposes a possibility of anticipation on the part of the operator, of the driving force, the human qua efficient cause of the technical object. We shall seek to show here that this capacity of anticipation itself supposes the technical object, and no more precedes it than does form matter" (*Technics and Time, Vol. 1* 81). Myth is apotropaic in that it ministers to the anxiety that accompanies the human capacity to anticipate the future, and hence there is no getting rid of myth, as the Enlightenment proposed to do. From anxiety emerges avatar.

What humans bring to the mix of *technics* is indeterminacy, unpredictability, an idiom of singularity best embodied in aesthetic sensibility at work in the practices of art. Prometheus was a potter, among other things. Epimetheus today is an artist.

> [Style] is indeterminable and undetermined and, as such, it is the mark, the cipher, the gramme, and the weight of the undetermined, the default—while it is created out of the defaults of the stylist, conceived as the withdrawn and marginal figure of the artist who appears along with industrial society, as pariah, handicapped social specialist of the undetermined of the idios. What penetrates through the artist, the focal point of style, is always the originary default of origin. It is the most immediate expression of *epimetheia* and of its idiocy, evident everywhere, making use of everything, finding support in any and every material. (*Technics and Time, Vol. 2* 85)

We recognize in Stiegler's "operator" what is at stake in the project articulated most clearly by Nietzsche, to become what you are. At the interface of transformation, two tendencies converge (culture and technology), and we may recognize bisociation as the art relevant to the operator. The bachelor machine is a Rosetta Stone articulating the rhizome. Gregory Bateson proposed an analogy between evolution and creative thinking, in which the formal factors are reduced to two functions: random generation of possibilities; a principle of selection (Bateson 205). Stiegler refers to a similar articulation in *technics* as "event-ization." The function of the operator is selection, and the design principle of selection derives in part from the structure of mythology. Selection is an element of event. These are the dynamics of decision rehearsed through concept avatar. Stiegler clarifies the stakes: y/our becoming is the measure orienting the turn of *technics*. Your becoming is ontological (constructive of reality). What then is the measure of your becoming (because the operator is distributed)?

Myth

Myth (Plato's "bastard reasoning") performs the cultural function of selection by using formal devices to focus attention, to transform indifferent perception into observation. The rhetorical device was given the name "significance" in Gestalt theory, the shaping of events into meaning. Any attempt to put an end to myth, Blumenberg notes, forgets the human need for meaning that myth addresses. The principle of significance is that

> . . . in man's historical world of culture things have "valences" for attention and for vital distance different from those they have in the objective world of thing that is studied by the exact sciences, in which the distribution of subjective value to phenomena that are studied tends, in the norm, toward zero. The theoretical subject is only able to strive for indifference because it is not identical with the individual subject and its finitude, but has developed forms of integration that have an open temporal horizon. "Significance" is related to finitude. It arises under the imposed requirement that one renounce the "*vogliamo tutto*" ["I want everything"], which remains the secret drive for the impossible. (*Legitimacy of the Modern Age* 67)

Love and death (family) are integral to the rhizome managed by concept avatar.

"Meaning," in the context of electracy, is interface. Significance (or gestalt *pregnance*) in myth is constructed with any materials (fiction, history, philosophical concepts) by establishing "the simultaneity of things that do not seem to belong together and whose meaningful structures collide in time, as material objects do in space" (102). Koestler refines the encounter according to context: collision produces laughter in comedy; fusion produces intellectual synthesis in science; confrontation produces aesthetic experience in art (45). The prototype for significance is simply aesthetic taste, Blumenberg says. Significance is an aesthetic effect, and the simultaneity and "closing circles" of repetition that produce the effect throughout the tradition have been identified as the primary operative feature of modernist arts. Perhaps the best-known example of closing circles is Homer's *Odyssey*. The Allegory of Prudence probes "significance" as circular (or rather, topological) motion.

In his history of the origin of the avant-garde in France, Roger Shattuck in his conclusion replaces "juxtaposition" with "simultanism" to name the primary technique and attitude shared by the experimental arts in modernism. "Ultimately it becomes apparent that the mutually conflicting elements of montage—be it movie or poem or painting—are to be conceived not successively but simultaneously, to converge in our minds as contemporaneous events. The conflict between them prevents us from fitting them smoothly end to end; what appeared an arbitrary juxtaposition of parts can now take its true shape of enforced superposition" (345). One of the names Apollinaire (who supplied many of the terms for Montmartre invention) applied to this formal operation was "Orphism." The relevance of this logic in the Now conditions of dromosphere are obvious (we will return to this point).

Blumenberg's insight is that work on myth continues in the present epoch, and we can point to Stiegler's text as evidence. Like Stiegler, Blumenberg gives special attention to the Prometheus tale as a prototype. The tale survives in modernism, translated and adapted to what Apollinaire called the "new spirit," to name the ridiculous and grotesque qualities of parody and joke that informed the attitude of Parisian Bohemia (Montmartre cabarets) from which the avant-garde emerged. Andre Gide's treatment of the story, set in Paris, concludes Blumenberg's study. In this updated farce Prometheus feeds the eagle that had tormented him to his guests at a totem banquet (appropriate for the "banquet years").

> "When on the summit of the Caucasus, Prometheus had become fully aware that his chains, fetters, strait-waistcoats, prison walls and other scruples, taking them all in all, were giving him pins and needles, in order to change his posture he rose on his left side, stretched out his right arm, and, between four and five o'clock on an autumn afternoon, walked down the boulevard which leads from the Madaleine to the Opera." This is a pure representation of Gide's aesthetic central idea, of the *acte gratuit*, a descendant of the theological concept of God's unearnable and rationally inexplicable act of grace, and here the structural principle of the grotesque (*sotie*), of its constant demonstrative resistance to any inquiry as to its motive and what it is "doing." (Blumenberg 628)

Blumenberg helps clarify that our Real Time idiot is a dadaist. We attend closely, since at the core of prudence is a feeling of constraint.

4 Descent

Internet Accident

Avatar descends (the phrase is redundant) in times of crisis. "Crisis" is from Krinein, naming a perspective that distinguishes, discerns, makes the "cut" of decision, situated between past and future (the betweenness of prudence). The present time of emergency is represented by an exhibit, curated for the Museum of Accidents proposed by Paul Virilio. The Museum is an idea that hardly needs a space, since it is available "without walls" 24/7 on television. Nonetheless, it began its existence as an exhibition and catalogue, both entitled *Unknown Quantity,* presented at the Fondation Cartier pour l'art Contemporain in Paris, from November 29, 2002, to March 30, 2003 (Virilio, *Unknown Quantity* 226). Having directed a television program on this project in Japan, Virilio collaborated with the Japanese on creating an actual museum (*Politics of the Very Worst* 93). This Museum constitutes a paradigm, or exemplary problematic, which has the potential to gather all specialized academic disciplines around a single project, in order (despite Virilio's warning against this effect) to synchronize contemporary knowledge.

The catalogue of the exhibit included Virilio's text, summarizing and expanding upon the thesis argued in a number of his published works, such as *The Politics of the Very Worst, Open Sky,* and *The Original Accident;* an excerpt from the Chernobyl diary of Svetlana Aleksievich (Chernobyl is foregrounded as the emblem of the modern accident with global consequences); extensive illustrations—photographs representing a gallery of modern disasters both natural and man-made; reproductions of art works belonging to an eschatological genre, classical and contemporary, such as Jan Van Scorel, *The Universal Deluge* and Walter de Maria, *Lightning Field.*

Virilio's argument looks at the epoch of electracy from the perspective of the rise and fall of the ideology of progress. The extraordinary technological innovations of the industrial and post-industrial eras, including the invention of the recording technologies of the electrate apparatus, occurred within a shifting horizon of negative expectations. The eighteenth century introduced revolution; the nineteenth century added the expectation of war; the twentieth century culminated in the expectation of an integral accident, referring to an accident of knowledge itself. The basic insight derives from a glance at the history of progress—that every invention brought with it its own disaster: with the ship, train, car, plane, came their respective wrecks. There are no exceptions to this rule, hence, as we contemplate the possibilities of inventing life itself now (cloning, genetic engineering) we may anticipate corresponding disasters (the knowledge accident).

The claim most directly relevant to electracy concerns the Internet accident, with the "Internet" serving as a metonym for the digital technologies of new media rapidly replacing the literate apparatus as the support for the language function in society. The Internet accident is a General Accident that occurs everywhere simultaneously, an event made possible by the light-speed connectivity and global reach of digital media, especially as these capacities are extended into such features as telepresence. Virilio posed the question: what is the integral accident that may be expected to follow upon the invention and general adoption of the Internet? In our context, he is asking: what are the consequences of electracy? Avatar, as personification of flash reason (simultanism), mediates two catastrophes (one outside, one inside).

Virilio introduces the neologism "dromosphere" (from "dromos," race) to name the conditions likely to produce the General Accident. The dromosphere refers to the pollution of dimensions that follows from electronic augmentation of human thought and language. Instant communication is constricting time, eliminating the past and the future, reducing human temporality to Now-time. If the oral apparatus ran on cyclical time, and literacy on linear time, electracy operates within the moment of Now. All trajectory disappears, eliminating the journey with its departure and passages, leaving us only with pure arrival. The mood of this condition is claustrophobic, a sense of being trapped. The human condition in the dromosphere is that of being caught and held within Now-time. The paradox of this confinement is that, augmented by the technologies of telepresence, the experience of Now is separated from place, even from being-there (*Dasein*).

> It is now the immobility of all possible journeys or paths. The time-light barrier then blocks off—along with the horizon of appearances—the horizon of action, the very reality of a space where all succession dissolves, where it is as though hours and days had ceased to flow; surfaces ceased to extend; what cropped up yesterday, here or there, now happens everywhere at once. The accident to end all accidents spreads in a flash and the center of time—the endless present—leaves behind the center of fixed space for good. There is no longer any "here," everything is "now." (Virilio, *Open Sky* 142)

Virilio's argument is that teletechnologies through their instantaneous interactivity have produced a "single time"—Real Time—whose milieu is speed. This unprecedented immediacy and ubiquity makes democracy impossible, he argues. Public space in Real Time becomes an image in some medium—photography, cinema, television. These images replace the "trajectories" of the city, the face-to-face interaction of the public sphere and the encounter of subject with object in the agora, the forum. The question he raises is whether a virtual city is possible—whether it is possible to urbanize real time. "If the answer is no, then a general accident is inevitable, the accident of history, the accident of accidents that Epicurus spoke of regarding history. If we are not capable of urbanizing the real time of exchange, in other words the live city-world, the city-world in real time, through the globalization of telecommunications, then both history and politics will be called into question. This is an extraordinary drama" (40).

The conditions described by Virilio pose a challenge, calling for invention within a new apparatus (social machine), that does for digital media what literacy in Classical Greece did for alphabetic writing. The EmerAgency is our response (a framework for avatar consulting). The creators of philosophy in the Academy and Lyceum invented the very institution of school, and within it the practices of logic, rhetoric, poetics to support ultimately scientific and democratic civilization. Plato warned in the first discourse on method in the Western tradition, *Phaedrus*, that writing separated the speaker's voice from embodied presence, allowing it to wander abroad without protection. The experience of one's own voice returning in writing contributed to the formation of a new identity—the self—as Eric Havelock demonstrated in several books. In electracy the evolution of identity continues, this time through the phenomenon of brand, of one's image and reputation circulating through the Internet, subject to sampling and mixing, to return in the form of scandal, libel, fame, fortune. The invention of a logic adequate to the dromosphere (flash reason, a practice of epiphany for authoring on the fly in database environments functioning at light speed) begins with an investigation of the opportunity for further subject formation opened by avatar. Self appears in cyberspace as brand, to play with another dimension of subject formerly known as *daimon*. In electracy, however, the return (the loop) of agency is experienced as uncanny, since we fail to recognize our own. Hence the need for Heidegger's *Ereignis* (Enownment), to facilitate reappropriation of one's agency.

Dromosphere

The guiding scene and proposed attunement for thought and action in electracy is player with avatar. "Play" is justified in this context not only because of the game analogy invoking a familiar online skill, but more properly in the ludic terms developed by Johan Huizinga, who argues that culture and even civilization emerge out of play. The historical or cultural source of this scene is the Sanskrit poem, "*Bhagavad Gita*" ("Song of God," Book VI of the *Mahabharata*), a major work of Hindu religion. The setting is the battlefield of Kuruksetra (a place of religious pilgrimage), with two armies in conditions of civil war in position to engage. Prince Arjuna is assisted in his battle chariot by Krishna, his friend, who turns out to be an incarnation of the god Vishnu. Arjuna, seeing many friends and family among both armies, expresses to Krishna his ambivalence about the situation, and the decision he has to make. The poem dramatizes the subsequent conversation between the friends about *dharma* (duty, virtue), and the meaning of life in general, the metaphysics of the Hindu worldview. Krishna is one of nine avatars of Vishnu that have incarnated, appearing at times of emergency, whenever *dharma* is in decline. Vishnu's avatars include fish, tortoise, boar, man-lion, dwarf, Rama the ax-wielder, Rama, Krishna, Buddha. A tenth avatar, Kalki, will appear in human form, riding a white horse, at the time of the crisis of our present age. The term "avatar" in Sanskrit literally means "descent."

The secular meaning of avatar refers to the personification in human form of abstract principles or intangible qualities. Aaron Britt surveyed the usage.

> The proliferation of avatar's second meaning can be traced to Second Life, a multiplayer online virtual world, where players fashion their own online personae called avatars. The popularity of the game has shot the term into the mainstream. Philip Rosedale, the creator of Second Life, defines avatar in the gaming sense as "the representation of your chosen embodied appearance to other people in a virtual world." Considering that Second Life avatars may assume literally any guise—wings, a dragon's head, gills and flippers—the key to avatarness, in Rosedale's view, is user control. And insofar as a Second Life avatar does and is precisely what the player wants, not just a little Mario who can be made to run and jump or a shapely diva gyrating of her own programmed will, it comes far closer to being a full-fledged virtual persona. (MM12)

Yes, it is a persona, but not in the way Rosedale suggests. The value of "avatar" for us is that the name tags the site of electrate identity experience, and in its religious, secular, and literal senses indexes cultural resources that have yet to be explored for the insight they may offer into our question of deliberation in the dromosphere. Rosedal's definition, however, confuses brand with avatar. It is indeed a relationship with self, but it is not merely a kind of branding of the ego, finding a logo for one's fantasy. In Second Life, you play a brand. The functionality of avatar according to tradition is as counselor, consultant communicating to humans the measure of the universe intended by God. Concept avatar seeks an interface practice (flash reason) that, treating total Internet information as "god," creates an interface practice of contemporary wisdom in which individuals experience the measure of collective well-being. The initial step, addressd in the Allegory of Prudence, is just your capacity to be affected, to be augmented as measure for the electrate apparatus. Avatar is a chiasmus circulating energy between macrocosmic information and microcosmic embodiment. To avatar is an experience of reception.

Our point of entry into electracy is this question of avatar: what it is, what it is for, how to do it (how to avatar, avatar as verb). A first lesson of our guiding scene for contemporary decision making—Arjuna with Krishna on the verge of battle—signals a shift in our approach to this usage, extending it to identify the site of subject formation itself in electracy. The scene shows us a relationship between self (player) and avatar. Self is Arjuna; avatar is Krishna. This relationship is a relay for understanding the condition of one's image (reputation, status, brand) in cyberspace. An online incarnation is not "self" or ego, but a dimension of identity emerging in the new apparatus that is unfamiliar to modern people, and for which the analogy, helping us to imagine what is happening and to guide the invention of this new formation, is avatar or (in the Western tradition), *daimon*. The function of avatar is counsel in a situation of emergency requiring decision, and it is this functionality addressed in concept avatar. Through avatar you go beyond the limits of "self" to understand action from the position of communal well-being (event).

Uncanny

The tradition already shows how avatar separates from brand, in order to turn and return upon self. The purpose of avatar is as consultant for decision, with the relation player-avatar constituting a passage between idiot and collective subject. The experience of concept avatar as first-person undergoing of collective wisdom is uncanny. You participate in an electrate public sphere (dromosphere) through avatar, beyond commodity. The experience of identity specific to the epoch of electracy is the uncanny. Both Freud and Heidegger were influenced in their choice of the term "*unheimlich*" to name the feeling of contemporary identity by their readings of Schelling (who defined the uncanny "as something which ought to have been kept concealed but which has nevertheless come to light") and the other German Romantics who thought of life in terms of a circuitous odyssean roundtrip home. The anxiety that marked the fundamental mood of Being in Heidegger served rather for Freud as a symptom of repression. The feeling of dread he identified as the uncanny arises in our experience of encountering "something familiar and old-established in the mind that has been estranged only by the process of repression." The multitude of different experiences that produce in us the uncanny effect all turn out to be transformations of a more basic experience (he inscribes the odyssean circuit into biology).

> This *unheimlich* place is the entrance to the former *heim* ["home"] of all human beings, to the place where everyone dwelt once upon a time and in the beginning. There is a humorous saying: "Love is home-sickness"; and whenever a man dreams of a place or a country and says to himself, still in the

> dream, "this place is familiar to me, I have been there before," we may interpret the place as being his mother's genitals or her body. In this case, too, the *unheimlich* is what was once *heimisch*, homelike, familiar; the prefix "un" is the token of repression. (Freud, " 'The Uncanny' " 152–53)

The importance of Freud and of psychoanalysis in general for electracy is this return of metaphysics to the physical sexed and gendered body, since it is this particular Real in the modalities of attraction-repulsion, pleasure-pain, that is ontologized by means of the aesthetic practices of electracy. In our context of icons and emblems we may refer to this place as the *mandorla* or the "almond" schematized by Duchamp and impersonated by the girls-gone-wild celebrity type, such as Britney Spears. Celebrities are in the electrate vanguard, testing the new dynamics of image brand.

"Home" as the measure of what is canny is undergoing mutation, which has stirred up the *daimonic* dimension of experience, since *daimons* are domestic threshold guardians, and hang around doorways. The relevance for electracy is the desublimation in Freud's comparison, the deflation of an idealized experience into an abject corporeal memory. The vulvan gains parity with the phallic in the coming community. It is important to remember that Schelling used *unheimlich* to translate Greek "Nemesis" (Stimilli 109). Nemesis (Retribution) is the name of one of the five demi-gods that enter the world to be "guardians" of the incarnated soul. "Avatar" means "descent," and in the old cosmology souls descended into flesh and managed their temporary sojourn with the help of these donors or spirit guides. The other companion demi-gods include Daimon (Genius), Tyche (Chance), Ananke (Necessity), and Eros (Desire). These figures personify the forces shaping destiny or fate. This context of Ancient identity experience reveals the selectivity of the pedagogical tradition that draws exclusively on Eros as the analogy for the ratio with wisdom. Eros is inseparable in practice from the full council governing the soul's embodiment. The task of concept avatar is to extract from this tradition a functionality of consultation, a fatal pedagogy, to restore to experience the full ratio of limit and measure guiding decision (fatal because originating in character, disposition, that part of identity that may not be persuaded). Electracy adds a further dimension to the institutionalization of human faculties. Orality gives us right-wrong; literacy gives us true-false. We still need judgment (prudence), to discern these distinctions in lived situations. Through avatar, we discover the readymade decision.

For concept avatar the uncanny is a logic of emergence. Historically the uncanny is an effect of the Industrial Revolution and the invention of the commodity form. As Marx explained, in these new conditions (the impoverishment of experience), individuals lost their sense of agency. They no longer were able to recognize their productions as their own, resulting in behavior and attitudes that Marx compared to magic, the fetishism of "savages"—alienation, reification, objectification. Concept avatar restores the experience of collective agency. The formal site of emergence begins within narrative, functioning as myth. Avatar as practice takes up this enunciative position in order to make it self-conscious, the goal being to enframe and transform narrative in turn by means of the figural. The collective event of mythology (continued today in popular culture) is taken over by avatar as a personal oracle. The strategy is to write from the position of receiver, in actantial terms, the conative position (in Jakobson's set of functions).

To function as consultant, you accept an event of catastrophe as disclosure, as oracle or parable addressed to me, showing me the limits of being, as my own threshold or bifurcation point. The catastrophe (the emergency) is event (its persona could be Epimetheus, or Oedipus). The figure does not record essence or telos, but a habitus accessible to revision (in principle). The Allegory of Prudence is an identity experiment. The rhetorical premise is that the only one capable of changing your mind at the level of embodiment (habitus) is you yourself. The figure discloses deep disposition, constituting your feeling of "limit," constraint, with neurophysiology replacing the *daimonic* explanation of the effect today. Neuroaesthetics explains how body states are mapped in the brain. Art provides a means for mapping habitus configurations into media. Habitus is *dharma* (is ethos), and embodiment is pathos.

The task of flash reason is to design the interface practice capable of supporting individual interface with Internet global information. The larger ambition is the creation of a distributed collective Allegory of Prudence, designed to organize this information flow into wisdom (choragraphy). The persona of concept avatar provides the vehicle of this counsel. Jurij Lotman made the point that an art text is a second-order modeling system. The primary system is natural language itself, which is used to model everyday life. Lotman demystifies the aesthetic effect by noting that a work of art creates its particular world (diegesis) by recoding the primary set of semantic equivalences into a secondary set that holds for that world exclusively. In the world of Lermontov's poetry, to give a simple example, a semantic equivalence is established among a wheel of cheese, a particular kind of shield, and the moon. There is no dictionary or thesaurus for this collection. Theorists such as Greimas have developed descriptions that map the logical systems that produce these aesthetic equivalences. Literacy produced an ontology out of natural language. Electracy takes up where literacy left off, to produce an ontology out of popular culture multi-modality discourse.

The methodological implication for flash reason is that we include both the primary and secondary ontologies in our consultation. In the dimension of technology, the databases are just beginning to manage literate (dictionary) semantics (text mining). Second-order (aesthetic) semantics, the figurative level of cultural conduct, is not yet attempted (perhaps IBM's Watson, champion of Jeopardy, is a first step). The challenge for electrate data mining is an experience web ontology capable of processing dream work (*Entstellung*, anomaly). Avatar event happens in the dimension of more. Meanwhile, the first ontology is literate, structuring most of the documentation of a chosen policy disaster, targeted for consultation. You need to recognize your agency in this scene (enowning). The figure in which I experience limit (encounter avatar) is composed the way an artist creates second-order ad hoc semantic equivalencies using the primary modeling system. The first emergent effect might well be a tertiary modeling system that recodes individual art works in order to produce new meaning (in the way that literature recodes natural language). In short: pastiche (as a shorthand name for cabaret creativity) is a general schema for avatar consulting. James Joyce's *Ulysses* is an example of this phenomenon, recoding not only natural language, but Homer's *Odyssey* as well. Francis Bacon's *Screaming Pope*, revising Velazquez's portrait of Pope Innocent X, is a visual example. The point is that these practices, invented within modernism (and before) now must be extended to general electracy and taught as such in the public schools. The entire Internet archive is the "natural language" for electrate metaphysics, using bachelor machine (cabaret) logic. The name of flash semantics is aura (Benjamin), ordering "air" or "manner."

Avatar as vehicle of electrate identity begins as a formal possibility, then, within the conventional structure of narrative, in the relationship between the subject and the object of value (desire). Value. This narrative situation models the position of practical reason, responsible for making a decision ad hoc, on the spot. This is the primal formal analogy on which all other analogies are grounded. Avatar emerges out of our capacity for narrative identification (symptom of self) the way Athena was born from the head of Zeus. The analogy alludes to Algirdas Greimas's study of the thymic (passional) dimension of discourse, in which he noted the great instability of actantial roles in passional configurations. In the passion of love, for example, we see the loved object transformed into a subject.

> This effect of animation is all the more impressive when the object in question is not an animated being, in the narrative of the fantastic, among others, but also more tritely in fetishistic behavior. Curiosity also tends to transform its object into a subject, even into an antisubject that resists, flees, dissimulates, and so on. There is also no want of misers who treat their "coffers" as subjects, as actual alter egos. In short, in passion the object has a tendency to become the subject-partner of the impassioned subject. Hence the hypothesis that the only generalizable structure to describe passion is an intersubjective structure, or, more precisely, a structure wherein each objectal relation encompasses potential intersubjectivity, a sort of fuzzily contoured interactantiality. (Greimas and Fontanille 68)

The argument is that avatar is the culmination of a process through which "things," a category of the real ontologized in Classical Greece, ultimately are coming into their own, so to speak, separating, becoming autonomous, as described in various theories such as existentialist alienation, Marxist commodity reification, or psychoanalytic fetishism. The assumption is that we are dealing with a specific kind of energy (embodied *jouissance*) to be developed as a new resource in the digital apparatus. An electrate "object" is emerging from the literate "thing," then. The ultimate separation of things from culture is *technics* (Stiegler), in which technological evolution becomes autonomous. Modernist aesthetics in its variations on "objective correlative" produced the logic for working with this dimension of extimate experience in which "subject" finds itself distributed through the "outside."

Smart toasters are the continuation of an ancient dream. Avatar is a kind of sentient doll or surrealist mannequin: "Feeling" (from *sentire*), capable of sensory experience, senses, sensation, capacity for emotion, passion, conscious, aware, living; "doll," small model of a human figure. Pinocchio fits this scenario, especially in Stephen Spielberg's *A. I.*, as do the Cylons in *Battlestar Galactica,* (referred to contemptuously by the humans as "toasters"), signaling the relevance of our question to the identity conditions known as the posthuman. Sentient dolls, animate objects, are found in proximity to impassioned subjects. In this phenomenon we begin to see the complexity of Eros as ratio. My self-image (brand) broadcast through the public sphere, is a kind of Pinocchio, a Gingerbread Man, whose animation has unforeseen consequences. Pygmalion and Galatea. This event is codified in the rhetorical figure of prosopopoeia, central to deconstruction and faciality in Deleuze and Guattari. Avatar arises out of the ashes of a narcissism that opens the path to the recovery of a particular kind of experience: consultation of player with avatar. We recognize in this history the thematics of Freud's theory of the uncanny, which references E. T. A. Hoffmann's story "The Sandman." Krishna shows Arjuna the civilizational decision incarnated in him (warrior).

Procession

There is a tradition of avatar in the West, whose terms help to locate a set-up for concept avatar. What are the elements, for which we will develop an upgrade path?

1. Theory: Neoplatonism describes human being as a fall (a breaking off) from pure spirit into matter. The original descent is "natural" (birth). Embodied, one chooses between a vicious or virtuous descent (to embrace or reject sensory pleasure). Wisdom prescribes a practice of "attention," devoting one's life to a "return" to pure spirit.
2. Allegory: Plotinus treated Homer's *Odyssey* as an allegory, to dramatize the circular journey of descent and return. Ulysses demonstrates the middle stage of striving, between Procession (the going down) and Epistrophe (return) (M. H. Abrams). The fourth mode of descent is "artificial," undertaken for purposes of wisdom, experiment, education. Ulysses leaves Circe,

and follows her instructions to enter Hades (via ritual sacrifice), to learn from the shade (*manes*) of Tiresias how to return home.

3. Trajectory (movement, path, *Weg*): The shape shared by the theory and the allegory, extracted as measure. A lesson of this vocabulary is that "descent" entails three other stages of "avatar." Up to modernity Western culture was devoted almost entirely to "return" or "ascent," to escape the "prison of embodiment."

Such is the chief lesson of the Passion of the Christ. The stage that survives into modernity, however, with its commitment to immanence against all transcendence (after the death of God), is that of striving or dwelling. There are Sanskrit words for these other stages as well, although not applied to this context. Usage dictates that we retain "avatar" as metonym for the whole cycle, as raw material for our conceptual persona. The caveat for prudence is to note the ambivalence inherent within striving (to what end?). Concept avatar consults on the vicissitudes of striving.

Ezra Pound begins his *Cantos* with a version of Ulysses's descent into Hades to consult Tiresias (one of the classic accounts of avatar). His method of access involved much sacrifice:

> Dark blood flowed in the fosse,
> Souls out of Erebus, cadaverous dead, of brides
> Of youths and of the old who had borne much;
> Souls stained with recent tears, girls tender,
> Men many, mauled with bronze lance heads,
> Battle spoil, bearing yet dreory arms,
> These many crowded about me; with shouting,
> Pallor upon me, cried to my men for more beasts;
> Slaughtered the herds, sheep slain of bronze;
> Poured ointment, cried to the gods
> To Pluto the strong, and praised Proserpine;
> Unsheathed the narrow sword,
> I sat to keep off the impetuous impotent dead,
> Till I should hear Tiresias. (I 3)

The whole of the *Cantos* constitutes a relay for concept avatar, portraying as it does the search through the past (the dead) for guides, counseling on how to live today. Harold Bloom updates this tradition through the modernist (post-Miltonic) crisis poem (poetry responding to emergency). He exposes beneath the "anxiety of influence" the dialogue with the dead that Odysseus seeks in Hades. Our poets demonstrate how to receive counsel from the tradition, which turns out to be the skill of talking to yourself.

The heuretic analogies continue: avatar descends into media spectacle as Ulysses into Hades, a fourth mode of descent, to question and to learn. The structural pattern repeats across civilizations and media. In Plato's version, the Real is a realm of Ideas (Christianity placed Plato's Ideas in the mind of God). Spirit enters a body when it is born, and this material *kosmos* is an image of the Real. In Plato's revision of oral ritual, this world itself is Hades. The parable of the cave in the Republic, recounting the turn away from the shadow play in the cave, and the journey outside to the true light of the sun, is an appropriation for Philosophy of the wisdom descent central to ritual celebrations of the mysteries. Journeys to Hades are examples of the fourth descent, the probe (Dante's tour of Inferno). Science Fiction has run ahead to predict the coming relationship of player and avatar, but the point of view tends to be reactionary (witness *The Matrix*). Our Allegory of Prudence requires us to compose our own parable, exploring our own turning. The task now is not escape from embodiment, but an embracing (enowning) of immanence.

Synderesis

Giorgio Agamben suggests a point of departure guiding the analogies for a conceptual persona.

> *Synderesis* is a technical term used in the Neoplatonic mysticism of the Middle Ages and the Renaissance to designate the highest and most delicate area of the soul; it is in direct communication with the supersensory, and has never been corrupted by original sin. Perhaps these pages give us a glimpse of the future experience of the *ego cogito*, and furnish one more proof of the close proximity between two poles of our culture. We see that the *cogito*, like mystical synderesis, is what remains of the soul when, at the end of a "dark night," it is

> stripped of all its attributes and content. The heart of this transcendental experience of the I has been signally described by an Arab mystic, Al-Hallaj: "I am I and the attributes are no more; I am I and the qualifications are no more . . . I am the pure subject of the verb." (*Infancy and History* 34)

This "obsolete" notion of *synderesis* may be retrieved for thinking about the connection of telepresence between player and avatar. The new attitude introduced within electracy (beginning with aesthetics) is the embracing of "pleasure-pain," characterized in the tradition as the "vicious" descent. In apparatus theory, dreams (visions, fantasies) motivate invention as much as does practical necessity. The functionality we seek to emulate is this interface with the Real.

We may elaborate our Allegory of Prudence (good judgment based on wise counsel) following Agamben: to articulate a new experience of time, for a practice of judgment native to image spectacle. Even as our idea of history has changed, our model of time has remained within literate metaphysics. Time in this metaphysics has been thought through two shapes (two ideas, *eidos* = shape). The Greek shape is a circle. The Christian shape is a line: circularity and linearity. Modern time is a secularized line. But in the dromosphere there is no time for round trips or progress, when before and after, here and there, have collapsed into Now. But what is this Now? Agamben has one answer, alluding to Walter Benjamin's *Jetztzeit* (now-time). The shape of this temporality derives from a tradition of emergency (as Benjamin put it): an experience of the normal condition as a state of emergency. Agamben locates a third model in the Gnostic time of interruption, figured as a broken line. In this experience everything has already happened (the worst, the best, revolution, the resurrection). Time stands still, and nothing may be expected from the future. All that history has deprecated must be revisited. This stillness is the condition addressed through concept avatar. The Allegory of Prudence attempts to locate and undergo this stillness, recognized as the measure of becoming what you are.

Agamben recommends retrieval as the method for expressing the new experience of time (a grammatology of the archive). He proposes two topics for further inquiry. First is the tradition of kairos (even a "kairology"), with its roots in *metis*. In practice metic time breaks with the vulgar time of streaming instants, to recognize a moment of opportunity (an opening in time). The conventional emblem of a weaver throwing the shuttle does disservice to kairos, since the moment may not be awaited with such certainty or rhythm, but it has the advantage of its association with the fates as weavers. The other topic Agamben proposes as the basis for a new time shape is pleasure. "Yet for everyone there is an immediate and available experience on which a new concept of time could be founded. This is an experience so essential to human beings that an ancient Western myth makes it humankind's original home: it is pleasure" (114). Never mind that Aristotle himself said that only the gods may sustain such an experience. The time of pleasure is neither that of precise continuous time nor of eternity. It is rather the time of history, Agamben says, but a kairological history. The name for this time out of time (out of joint) is "moment" (*Augenblick*). Here is the primary issue for electrate experience: avatar as prosthesis of temporal "pleasure," but with this caveat: we must account for the full axis, pleasure-pain (Freud's original term was the unpleasure principle). Michel Foucault alludes to this challenge, in his last project, *The Care of the Self*, the third volume of his *History of Sexuality*, in which he retrieved Classical models for socializing embodiment as guides for a contemporary invention of behavior. Proust already alerted us that this temporality is a mere fragment (a quality).

The invention of flash reason may approach a new operation of time through shape (a time of consultation with avatar). We keep in mind that we are not replacing the received temporalities of our institutions, but opening a third orientation to be augmented in electracy. There is no shape given in the intuition of time as inner experience (Kant). Since no shape is given (thus opening a history of time), we resort to a graphic analogy (the *gramme*). Here is the problematic of trace, according to Derrida. It is not a question of any one shape, a fourth graphic, for example, but the differance of time space and the embodied experience of belatedness, delay and dispersal. It is important for our allegory to realize that this entire question never leaves the problematic of prudence (judgment expressing a wisdom of time). Thus we become aware of this other dimension, the undecidable trace working within any particular configuration of time space (chronotope). This is the trace included in the term "electracy" (electricity + trace).

Once this problematic is thematized, the practices associated with a new kairotic temporality become accessible to invention. Momentary time-out interfacing light-speed information. The preliminary problem addressed in our practice, however, is how or in what way this temporality may be experienced. More precisely, we learn from the tradition of encounters with the dead, as well as with the analogy from the invention of literate metaphysics, that this event happens only through a compositional practice relative to an apparatus. How may we undergo through design a differantial prudence (decision, judgment)? Most of the disappointments reported regarding social networking experience are made from the position of selfhood (of ego, of literate identity projected into brand), concerned about attracting and holding attention upon a fixed identity. But "self" is not one in cyberspace, and maintains a tenuous alliance with brand. Avatar is no more self or brand than Krishna is Arjuna, or Tiresias is Odysseus. The instructions are analogies. What is avatar, as practice and experience? It is like consulting with incarnate Vishnu in a moment of emergency.

Metis

The Allegory of Prudence probes my own relationship with this third temporality. The ambition is to generalize concept avatar as judgment relevant to public policy politics in the dromosphere. Dromosphere serves as figure for all the forces at work in your moment of decision. Paul Virilio's choice of the Greek term for "race" (*dromos*) to name the condition of dimension collapse in electracy is a clue guiding the heuretics of flash reason. The method poses a question: what is the reasoning that wins races; specifically (continuing with the tactic of retrieval), what was the logic of the race course in Classical Greece (grammatology, inventing electracy by analogy)? The oral Greeks called this reason *metis*, (after Zeus's first wife) and it survived in literacy as prudence, *phronesis*, practical reason. Plato configured it as his contrast while inventing the pure or contemplative reason and its logic of identity organizing the philosophy of Being. *Metis*, rather, is the logic of Becoming, useful in conditions of contingency such as those concerning ethics and politics, when the outcome depends on human judgment. A *phronimos* or prudent person is one capable of immediately assessing the givens of a particular situation, and drawing upon maxims formulated from past experience, making a decision to act in a way that foresees the best outcome in the future. In short, prudence is time-logic. Prudence is grounded in our original question, expressing the imperative to become what you are.

The details of prudence (*metis*) in their oral version are exemplified by Odysseus, who relies on cunning and deceit to overcome more powerful adversaries and forces. The same vocabulary was used in early literacy in manuals teaching hunting and fishing. The emblematic figure of *metis*, in fact, is the fishing net, especially the cast net with its encircling meshes. The "net" of "network" in electracy resonates with this skill of creating or escaping snares, traps, lures, or any sort of aporia—mastery of circles and binds. Marcel Detienne and Jean-Pierre Vernant use the race course (*dromos*) to map the operating features of *metis* that may be projected onto any situation (Arjuna and Krishna in the battle chariot). But we need to keep track of who or what is entangled. Prudence means not caution but foresight that prepares one for success in open circumstances requiring improvisation and instant thought. The challenge of electrate *metis* is our idiocy.

The race course holds three sites and moments of danger and opportunity: the starting line, the turn (bend), and the finish line. Here is the entire map (choragraphy) of concept avatar. The charioteer stands in for any pilot (Arjuna in his chariot with Krishna), with the vocabulary of navigation, cybernauts, cybernetics, helping translate practical reason into flash reason. The ultimate test of wayfinding is that of a stormy sea at night, when all guidemarks disappear (the scene of aporia), whether this night sea is literal or figurative (projected into the arts of medicine, politics, rhetoric). Avatar as guide through Tartarus (the trackless realm beneath the underworld, the outer dark). The crisis opportunity happens in the turn. Such is the event addressed in the Allegory of Prudence: to map the turn in the *dromos* of becoming. You only go around once, the saying goes, and it refers precisely to *dromos*. Narrative and argument both provide training maps, institutionalized within the historical apparati of orality and literacy. These designs are too slow, and must be gathered into a trope (turn) in electracy.

What makes the dromosphere so challenging is that it requires the invention of a new mode of governance. The rhetorical skills of deliberative reason within a public sphere that made democracy possible were inventions of literacy, and are not necessarily sustainable within electracy. The time of decision, the civic process of critical analysis and persuasion through argumentation, is a luxury we do not have in the conditions of Right Now. We need a rhetoric that is forensic, epideictic, and deliberative at once. What happened, who is responsible, what do we do now? This is the point of departure for flash reason, the image logic of concept avatar, responsible for introducing measure into Tartarus. Avatar logic is as compressed as the compression ratios of the equipment supporting it. An apparatus is not only equipment, but also practices of thinking developed within emerging institutions, and behaviors of identity (individual and collective). Our exercise is training: your turn will have come.

5 Moment

Intensity

Against Now there is Moment. Heidegger's second volume on Nietzsche helps identify Zarathustra's Gateway as the emblem of concept avatar. The turn in Heidegger's understanding of modern *phronesis* came in part through a long meditation on this scene. The second volume is devoted to the theme of the eternal return of the same, and its correlates—the transvaluation of all values, and the will to power. The lectures foreground *Zarathustra* and its context in Nietzsche's other writings. Nietzsche's "idea," the illumination when he received his thought of eternal return, was the point of departure of our experiment with an Allegory of Prudence. Now we look more closely at the details of that thought. The relevant point in reviewing Nietzsche's thought of the eternal return is that Heidegger proposes it as a marker of an epochal shift in Western thought, as significant as St. Paul's letters to the Romans. If St. Paul's letters are the beginning (if not the inception) of willing in the West, Nietzsche's Zarathustra is the beginning (if not the inception) of a new modality; but what to call it? Judgment, decision, life? "That which first and last obtains, that which accordingly constitutes the condition of 'life' as such, Nietzsche calls value" (Heidegger, *Nietzsche* 171). Value, specifically: well-being, as the primary site of invention in electracy.

Heidegger reads Nietzsche in his own terms, concerned with prudence as the capacity of appropriate decisions in a particular situation. His purpose is to open up the "black box" of "virtue," to understand and describe "decision." "The present which is held in authentic temporality and which thus is authentic itself, we call the 'moment,'" Heidegger writes.

> The moment is a phenomenon which in principle can not be clarified in terms of the "now." The "now" is a temporal phenomenon which belongs to time as within-time-ness; the "now" "in which" something arises, passes away, or is present-at-hand. "In the moment" nothing can occur; but as the authentic present, the moment makes it possible to encounter for the first time what can be "in a time" as something at hand or objectively present. (Heidegger qtd. in Beistegui 124)

Moment opens up the dromospheric Now. The Moment, in other words, makes room for a "step" (Derrida's *pas*), allowing the "decider" to take an attitude or stand, and create a second-order relationship to the given now-circumstance. The Moment (the Open) is Heidegger's version of the empty space required to keep life in play (the opening of chora).

> Unlike the "now," as the empty form within which events and facts take place, Moment marks the very advent or gathering of time, the fold at which and within which past and future are folded into one another, thus transforming the present into a site of intensity, so that *Dasein* reenters the world or repeats its own existential facticity with a renewed and heightened sense of itself as the power, and thus also the freedom to be (Being), as the power and freedom of Being itself. (qtd. in Beistegui 125)

This feeling of intensity is precisely the value (life). Concept avatar is moderator of intensity.

Zarathustra

Heidegger's lecture course, delivered during the war years, was intended (according to sympathetic accounts) to separate Nietzsche from the version of him created by Nazi propaganda. The scene of the Gateway Moment is in Part Three, the section entitled "Of the Vision and the Riddle." An inventory of the relevant parts in our context begins with the scene itself, the allegorical dramatization of the flash of insight (*Augenblick*), and the fact that Nietzsche resorted to the "parable" form in order to intimate his thought. Commentators have noted, in fact, that *Zarathustra* thematizes the problem of form, of how to communicate a new thought (how to change the hegemonic system of values), since Zarathustra is shown trying out most of the available devices for expressing wisdom.

Nietzsche's intentions with this work have been established by reading his more essayistic writings as commentaries on *Zarathustra.* Nietzsche's insight, his changed attitude, is against the ascetic values of the entire Western tradition, the rejection of "life" as it is, including its pain and suffering, the "spirit of revenge" against the passage of time, and the like. The crisis of Will is that it may not be exerted backwards, upon the past. Against all "nihilism" of Will, Nietzsche says "yes" to his own life, in its embodied finitude, whose materiality affords in recompense the capacity to be affected, to possess a moment of happiness, an event of joy. It is this *gaya scienza* that interests Heidegger in the Moment as an event of appropriation of one's own life. The instruction concerns how to become what you are, beginning with assessing your attitude.

> This is where ethics begins to take place, namely, in the movement of appropriation, whereby one becomes what one already is, in the peculiar doubling of truth that ek-sistence is. And in this doubling, in this turn back onto itself as the self that is turned outward, *Dasein* moves deeper into being, persists in it, in such a way that it now exists its own being to the full, thus increasing its own ontological potentia as the power to be being, thus elevating to another power. And it will not come as a surprise, then, that Heidegger, in a remarkable proximity with Spinoza, will celebrate the feeling of "joy" that overwhelms him or her, as this redoubling elevates his or her being to another power (Beistegui 118).

Such is the will to power: the commitment to human potential, measured on a scale of increasing/decreasing "power" from joy to sadness (the bittersweet of Eros; the saltysour of Nemesis). Spinoza's *Ethics* is devoted to an account of human being, or essence, in this materialist way, as *conatus*: the striving of every creature to persevere in its own being. Nietzsche takes up this same conative principle, the value of the preservation of life as that which is "beyond good and evil." Spinoza anticipates Nietzsche's "death of God" with his metaphysics of immanence, expressed in his motto, "God or Nature." Our Allegory exercise is a means to test and undergo this peculiar Moment.

There are several dimensions of Moment that need to be articulated, since it identifies precisely the dimension of reality ontologized in electracy. Nietzsche may be to electracy something like what Socrates is to literacy: Socrates could manage dialectics "in his head" so to speak, without writing. Nietzsche could have Moment "in his body," without imaging. Ordinary people, however, need the help of a prosthesis and practice to bring these capacities into everyday usage. It is important to follow Heidegger's unpacking of the thought of eternal return, but it is also necessary to make explicit the formal procedures that enable flash reason to support Moment. Nietzsche is existential in making his own life a test of his philosophy. One of his maxims is to look for that secret point at which the aphorism of thought intersects with the anecdote of life. This crossroads is the locus that provides the raw material for putting the stamp of being on becoming, as Nietzsche described his personal Moment, when he decided on the "yes" that transformed contingency into necessity and brought into appearance his singular *eidos*, the shape of his life as a whole. The everyday means for writing a similar effect is art. This crossroads is where player consults avatar. The purpose of the Allegory of Prudence is to locate such a crossroads. Before considering the formal structure of the Gateway, we may review a further context of the thought.

Daimon

A feature of Heidegger's turn is a shift away from *Dasein* or individual being to the collective dimension of being-together. The guide-word for this new orientation is "*Ereignis*," meaning "event," but which Heidegger's creative etymology and paranomasic extensions define as "appropriation," alluding to the Moment of glimpsing the whole. The site that supports Being, the receptacle that allows Being to appear, is now thought topologically, as a region of dwelling. The individual subject is no longer the center of meaning, but is one dimension of a four-dimensional "square" (the four-fold network of mortals and gods, world and earth). The region or chora gathers and holds this relationship together (a field dynamics). The site of Nietzsche's life, the setting of his creative process, is part of his thought, then, always with the existential pointer back to our own situations. Heidegger cites Nietzsche as writing, at the time of first thinking the eternal return: "Let us imprint the emblem of eternity on our life!" (*Nietzsche* 201). In *Ecce*

Homo (our point of departure) Nietzsche recorded the time and place of his inspiration.

> The fundamental conception of this work, the idea of the eternal recurrence, this highest formula of affirmation that is at all attainable, belongs in August 1881: it was penned on a sheet with the notation underneath, "6000 feet beyond man and time." That day I was walking through the woods along the lake of Silvaplana; at a powerful pyramidal rock not far from Surlei I stopped. It was then that this idea came to me. (*Ecce Homo* 295)

Nietzsche records the ingredients that accumulated during that period, a perfect day in short, giving a stretch of intensity that is his time regained (Proust). In *The Good European* David Krell and Donald Bates document the work sites of Nietzsche's career, his movements motivated by health problems, between summers in the Swiss Alps (the Engadine region), and winters along the Italian and French Riviera. Part of their purpose is to consider possible relationships between the character of the thoughts and the spirit (genius) of the places, the philosophy and the setting (as an essay in Heideggerian chora). In a letter to Koselitz (August 14, 1881) in which Nietzsche told of his thought of eternal recurrence, he also declares the importance of the landscape of Sils Maria.

> I take it as a kind of reward that this year has shown me two things that belong to me and are intensely intimate to me-- namely, your music and this landscape. This isn't Switzerland, isn't Recoaro; it is something altogether different, at all events something far more southern—I would have to travel to the highlands of Mexico, near the Pacific, in order to find something similar (for example, Oaxaca), and even then it would have to be with tropical vegetation. Now, I shall ty to retain this Sils-Maria in my life. (Krell and Bates 149)

The high mountains next to deep lakes was the scene of *Zarathustra.* Friends who visited Nietzsche during these summers were given a walking tour, retracing the literal path of discovery, including always a stop at the "memorial rock." One visitor reported that, "the hike around Lake Silvaplana [some twelve kilometers] was at first so strenuous for him that he used to recline in a fold in the 'Zarathustra Stone' until he felt recovered enough to head back through the woods to Sils" (156). Krell and Bates pick up a resonance with one of Heidegger's terms used to articulate *Ereignis* (enowning) when he describes the specific place of inspiration as "the cleavage of the gigantic boulder not far from the village of Surlej" (133). "The cleavage," Heidegger wrote in his first attempt to state explicitly the nature of Event, "is the inner, incalculable settledness of en-ownment; of the essential swaying of be-ing as the midpoint that is used and that grants belonging—the midpoint that continues to be related to the passing of god and the history of man at the same time" (*Contributions* 197).

This division, marked by the hyphens introduced into the terminology (be-ing), points to the formal structure of Moment, and also to its Ancient pedigree in the mythology of fate or destiny. This background working of a cleavage, split, gap, abyss, fissure, hole (the regioning of chora) throughout the history of Being is fundamental to flash reason. It is personified in some eras as the effect of a *daimon*, a version of consultation with avatar. Heidegger introduces this theme in relation to everything that is uncanny about human being. The root is *daio*, in which are nested two verbs: to kindle a fire (the fire of life); to divide (active voice); to be torn asunder (passive voice); to distribute or allot (middle voice); to feast on (celebrate) what has been distributed (aorist voice) (Krell 20). This inner split is recognized by contemporary neuroscience as what makes human decision-making possible. "Action proceeds from an exchange between the body and its double; deliberation and decision express this fundamental dialogue. We have two bodies, the physical body and the virtual body. The virtual body consists of all the internal models that comprise the elements of the body schema and allow the brain to simulate and to emulate reality. This body is the one we perceive when we are dreaming. It, too, has a phenomenal reality" (Berthoz 128). Consciousness, Berthoz proposes, is the product of a dialogue between these two bodies, between "I" and "me." In short, imagination. Concept avatar supports an autocommunication of decision, a dialogue of my two bodies.

Heidegger calls attention to the place assigned to a "*daimon*" in the genesis of Moment, especially in the first mention of the thought of eternal recurrence near the end of *The Gay Science* (number 341).

> What, if some day or night a demon were to steal after you into your loneliest loneliness and say to you: "This life as you now live it and have lived it, you will have to live once more and

> innumerable times more; and there will be nothing new in it, but every pain and every joy and every thought and sigh and everything unutterably small or great in your life will have to return to you, all in the same succession and sequence—even this spider and this moonlight between the trees, and even this moment and I myself. The eternal hourglass of existence is turned upside down again and again, and you with it, speck of dust!" Would you not throw yourself down and gnash your teeth and curse the demon who spoke thus? Or have you once experienced a tremendous moment when you would have answered him: "you are a god and never have I heard anything more divine." (273)

This particular way of framing the inspiration is an important clue to the nature of "judgment" as a distinct modality of wisdom. The specific meaning of the *daimon*ic for Nietzsche is clarified by Krell and Bates who note in their biography the range of settings in which Nietzsche used this allusion. Nietzsche was a philologist and a classicist, and as such was intimately familiar with the importance of the *daimonic* in the Ancient world. He associated it with the Dionysian aspect of that civilization. He credits a *daimon* for the happy chance that led him to discover the work of Schopenhauer in a used book stall. "I don't know what daimon it was that whispered to me, 'Take this book home with you'" (Krell and Bates 40). No circumstance was too trivial for the possible intervention of the god. In a letter suggesting that his friend, Erwin Rohde, should visit him while he was in military service (the cavalry), Nietzsche wrote: "Yes, my dear friend, if someday a daimon should direct you early in the morning, say, between five and six, to Naumburg and, as luck would have it, guide your steps in my direction . . ." (qtd. in Krell and Bates 42). In Basel Nietzsche celebrated with his colleagues the "greeting of the Daimons" by making a libation (81).

In the context of apparatus theory the changing status of *daimon* tracks the gradual emergence of a new identity formation, specifically (as Eric Havelock has shown) the experience of being a "self," based on the recognition of thought as being one's "own" (and not an external spirit voice). For the Ancients any sudden thought or insight was attributed to the intervention of a *daimon*. The genealogy of "self" may be told as the movement of the *daimon* from outside into the inside of the individual. People had tutelary spirits (guardian angel) that were born with them and died with them and provided counsel throughout life. The Latin translation of "*daimon*" as "genius" makes it easier to recognize the completion of this internalization or privatization of experience, whose culmination was the Romantic celebration of the special talent with which some fortunate individuals were naturally endowed. This genealogy of "genius" continues in the electrate apparatus, most self-consciously in New Age self-help instructions for contacting one's "spirit guide," or even one's "angel." New Age popularizations are useful as revivals of an obsolete mythology, but fail by taking the tradition literally. Concept avatar is not literally an annunciation scene, but a rhetorical practice (flash reason), designed to create a counselor effect.

Constructing Thresholds

Flash reason becomes practical as a "general electracy" only within the digital apparatus, meaning that it requires a technological prosthesis. Concept avatar inventories the functionality of Moment, to help notice those features that might lend themselves to technological augmentation, and those features that need to be put into the rhetorical skill-set of electrate citizens. What is required, then, is the design of an institution, including all three dimensions of the apparatus, that enables us to receive the voice (*Stimme*) or gesture of our *daimon* (genius). To appreciate exactly what this reception entails requires us to take into account the entire tradition of "genius," and not just the most recent versions of it found within Romanticism. Perhaps the best-known *daimon* is the one associated with Socrates. As E. R. Dodds explained, *daimons* originally were associated with *Até*, an action of poor judgment or any "unaccountable" or destructive action (5). *Até* was a consequence of imprudence, and in modern terms would be explained as "temporary insanity." Events manifesting *Até* provided the story line for tragedy, in whose poetics the term was understood to mean "blindness" for the individual, and "calamity" for the community. *Daimons* could also be the source of extra energy affecting will, which today would be described as an "adrenaline rush," or in traditional terms as having "heart" or showing "courage" (8).

The passage of "genius" from "tutelary spirit" through "disposition" to "native talent" traces, as noted, the consolidation of literate identity as an inner integrity confined to the individual mind-body

(Murray 2). An associated term is *ingenium*: Italian *ingegno*, French *esprit*, English wit (3). Histories of commonplace pedagogy record educators' agreement that topical learning required wit for its application, but that wit was not teachable. A claim (and challenge) of flash reason is that electracy is to "wit" (understood in this broader historical context) what literacy is to commonplaces, with the reminder that the two are interdependent. The case of Socrates helps clarify exactly what is involved with this claim (Hans). As the paradigmatic figure of emergent literacy, Socrates was a syncretic figure, combining qualities of oral and literate culture. Plato represented both sides of the hybrid in the dialogues, recording a number of situations in which Socrates encountered his *daimon*. Socrates characterized his *daimon* as being much reduced, nothing like the full presence of a god, but merely a voice (*daimonion*). Perhaps the best-known example was the day of the trial (dramatized in the *Apology*). Before leaving home that day, Socrates paused at the threshold to "consult" his *daimon*. His *daimon* was so attenuated (that is, Socrates was so far along in becoming literate), that it only made itself felt negatively, as a "no," intimating that an action or behavior was not appropriate (imprudent). In fact one reason that Socrates gave for avoiding a more public or political role was that his *daimon* was suited only for personal work, lacking a more collective capacity. Since the voice did not reply to the consultation, Socrates considered his decision to be appropriate, and so he showed up in court.

The Socratic persona has several relevant features of genius. The first is that the *daimon* in this transitional period was associated not just with the person, but with the household, the family (Murray 2). Second, the *daimonion* anticipates not just the voice of conscience, but the sense of judgment specific to decisions leading to action–- to "agency," in short. The commentators point out that Socrates's *daimonion* was an aberration, an innovation in its personal adoption of one individual, in the context of his cultural norms (Nicholls 63). Socrates's uniqueness was his ability to operate in both modes (oral and literate) simultaneously, so that the logical rational skills and the mantic divinatory abilities could collaborate. The unmediated encounter with a *daimon*, that is, was an event of possession.

The point for us is the co-existence of dialectic and mantic practices. The literate celebration of Socrates established the hegemony of his dialectic and the erasure of divining. At the beginning of Romanticism, however, the mantic (oral, religious, irrational) Socrates was revived and championed by several German thinkers culminating in the work of Goethe, the figure most credited with reviving and converting the *daimon* into modern genius (defined as exceptional creative talent naturally possessed by a few elite individuals). A study of Goethe's transmittal of genius, however, shows another aspect of the tradition that brings out a different understanding of this "creativity" which must be taken into account in the invention of concept avatar. The *daimon* is a personification of the fundamental life force of an individual. To be able to hear this *Stimme* is to be in communication with one's authentic being, one's true nature or essence, one's disposition or temperament, source of the independent capacity for judgment. In Classical terms, it is an experience of fate or fatality, a constraint with veto power over one's actions. In the case of Socrates, all his friends, and even his accusers at the trial, wanted him to leave town, go into exile, but *daimonion* intimated otherwise. The functionality of our electrate Moment (as concept avatar) is to give users access to this voice, drowned out, according to this Romantic revival, by the they, the crowd, the mass, and its augmentation in the institutions of the spectacle. Goethe continued updating the experience of *daimon* by retranslating "genius" as *Grenze* or limit. This is the upgrade path continued in concept avatar. Such is the feeling to be accessed, noticed, enhanced, studied in the Allegory of Prudence. The life feeling is your measure, limit, a paradoxically liberating constraint of freedom.

The Gate

To ask about the functionality of Zarathustra's Gateway as a relay for concept avatar is to notice the relationship between Nietzsche and his work. To put the stamp of being on becoming literally involves not only a decision but composition. As a practice for an electrate apparatus, concept avatar teaches image metaphysics. The gap between being and becoming (the choral zone) is crossed by art, which is to say that the newly ontologized body is experienced in the mode of design (such is the purpose of the Allegory of Prudence).

> *Ecce Homo* is nothing other than the attempt to constitute a body for oneself by writing oneself in granite words, by fixing the divine instants of a life, sparkling, like precious stones; it is nothing other than the effort to erect oneself as a monument

> by fixing oneself with the steely point of a pen. For Nietzsche himself, Nietzsche as body, is nothing other than an event, an instant in which an untimeliness outside time erupted into the time of decadence, and in which, in order to last, it had to turn to stone. (Gasché, *Of Minimal Things* 24)

Concept avatar guides the passage from literacy to electracy. The first Being was possible only through writing. The second-order metaphysics of electracy similarly emerges and is sustainable within digital media. Moment happens in the middle voice, in the practice of flash reason. Moment offers a taste of my own mood, including a feeling for the historical forces at work sedimented in and haunting the Now but that are not present, neither sensible nor intelligible. Instantiating concept avatar, the Gate shows how *duende* happens, as a mantic measure (Grenze), giving what belongs to me, is properly mine (enowning). The fundamental point motivating all this conversation is that humans are not given Being in advance (the fault of Epimetheus); we become what we are, and this becoming requires guidance (what culture adds to nature). Moreover, we tend to resist and deny this enowning, since (as the philosophers relentlessly remind us), what is most our own is death (finitude, mortality). Nonetheless, Nietzsche says, there is joy to be found in destiny, now, in this pattern, comportment, disposition, fashion, that is my potential. The first function of the Gate is to let me undergo my condition as a relationship of finitude. The advanced function is to provide a distributed ratio, a hypotyposis for an Internet wisdom supporting global policy formation on behalf of well-being.

The updated *daimon*, understood as a formal feature of language, is explained by Agamben (expanding on Heidegger) as the reflexive "*se*," as in the archaic Spanish verb *pasearse* ("to walk oneself") that Agamben associates with Spinoza's heritage as a Sephardic Jew. Agamben shows that Heidegger's *Ereignis* (in which Heidegger hears the verb *eignen*, "to appropriate," and the adjective *eigen*, "proper" or "own") is close to the meaning of **se*. He reminds us also that this etymology extends to *ouga*, "eye": *ereignen*, *ir-ougen*, "to place before one's eyes," which is one of the meanings of "hypotyposis" and of *Darstellung* also (*Potentialities* 117). The connection between the reflexive *se and the *daimon* occurs through Heraclitus, fragment 119.

> The usual translation of this fragment is "for man, character is the demon." But ethos (character) originally indicates what

> is proper in the sense of "dwelling place, habit." As for the term *daimon*, it neither simply indicates a divine figure nor merely refers to the one who determines destiny. Considered according to its etymological root (which refers it to the verb *daiomai*, "to divide, lacerate"), *daimon* means "the lacerator, he who divides and fractures." . . . The same semantic development can be found in a word that is derived from the same root: *demos*, "people," which originally means "division of a territory," "assigned part." Once restored to its etymological origin, Heraclitus's fragment then reads: "For man, ethos, the dwelling in the 'self' that is what is most proper and habitual for him, is what lacerates and divides, the principle and place of a fracture." Man is such that, to be himself, he must necessarily divide himself. (*Potentialities* 118)

Flash reason supports this recursive loop, a movement of division that permits "eternal return," the repetition of drive (Freud might say) that is my character. The *daio* of the *daimon*, in other words, may be simulated and augmented in both the equipment and rhetoric of flash reason. Alenka Zupancic, referring specifically to Nietzsche, calls this structure the "logic of the two."

> It means that the very core of truth involves a temporal paradox in which the truth only "becomes what it is." The temporal mode of truth is that of existing as its own antecedent. Or, to use Lacan's formula (which is quite Nietzschean in this respect), "the truth, in this sense, is that which runs after truth." This temporal mode of antecedence is correlative to the temporal mode of the (notion of) subject, caught in a "loop" wherein the subject will have to appear at the point of the Real which inaugurated her in some "other time." Or, to put it slightly differently the subject will have to appear at the point of the Real where she is inaugurated as if "from elsewhere." The Nietzschean theory of the event (or of the philosophical act) actually implies that, in the event, the subject encounters herself. (*The Shortest Shadow* 13–14)

This self-encounter is the event of prudence activated through concept avatar.

This principle of aftering (Bloom's belatedness), a formal version of the fault of Epimetheus, indicates the challenge facing human ontology as operator of *technics*, given a fundamental disjunction between the dromosphere's Now and human temporality. The critique of presence central to deconstruction indicates that it is nearly impossible for humans to be-here-now, as wisdom advises and as the dromosphere necessitates. The recursive loop of *daio* describes the structural dynamics of avatar as prudence. The structural, formal, and functional issue is that the Gate and its rhetoric operate with (are enabled by) a metaphysical gap, that human themselves (potentially) are. This gap is characterized differently in different epochs, as in Plato's dual worlds of visible and invisible, matter and spirit. The divide always must be bridged or traversed, always involving relations of ratio among areas of a topology. The bridge requires a revision of the traditional modalities of Being, Nothingness, Appearance. In Nietzsche's case, the traditional gap between appearance and reality is abandoned, in favor of a different orientation. The point to stress in our context is the value foregrounded in this new arrangement: Nietzsche's self-encounter was achieved by shifting away from the epoch of will (the Christian era), no longer judging (against) life, and instead accepting "life" as he had lived it as the measure of appropriation. Yet this encounter with (my) life is not straightforward (it is as if we lack the spiritual equivalent of the opposable thumb assumed in the root of Begriff as grasp). Nietzsche admitted that his orientation substituted a lie for truth (an evasion of death). This shift must be appreciated as a move into a new apparatus, not against empirical truth, appropriate to the literate axis true-false (let alone the oral axis of right-wrong relevant to religion), but for the electrate axis of pleasure-pain, learning to be embodied. The lie is not against truth but for well-being.

The task, then, is to articulate what the "life" associated with the Gate entails. Nietzsche's strategy to step out of the ascetic ideal (later understood as of the same character as Freud's superego, with its imperative of Enjoyment) was to say "yes": "a 'yes' not to the imperative of enjoyment, but to the little bit of enjoyment that keeps persisting on the subject's part" (*The Shortest Shadow* 82). This little bit of actual enjoyment is sensory (*aisthesis*), and involves an inheritance from Kant's reflective judgment. Zupancic unpacks Nietzsche's "yes" in relation to a simple aesthetic experience, using Kant's own example of a "green meadow." The objective judgment is that "meadows are green." The subjective second "yes" is to the agreeableness of the color sensation, that is, to the object of satisfaction. "The third stage is a 'yes,' not to the object (the green color of meadows), but to the agreeable feeling itself. This is a 'yes' not to the object that gratifies us, but to the gratification itself (to the 'satisfaction as object'), namely, a 'yes' to the previous 'yes.' In this case, the feeling itself, the sensation, becomes an object (of judgment)" (143). The more says yes. This is the site (*dromos*) of image ontology, this little sensation giving a bit of satisfaction through this articulation of three movements (*metis*). Electracy promises to do for this sensory capacity to be affected what literacy did for the capacity to calculate. The ambition of the Allegory of Prudence is confined for now just to test this claim, to notice in our own experience this little sensation, this *Augenblick*, that somehow, in memory, turns out to be worth eternity.

The vital anecdote of concept avatar captures this fold or turn in its figure. This third move creates the hinge structure, the slippery or pivot position supporting a second-order judgment, the reflexive *se that introduces separation and connection at once, making possible freedom, the taking up of a (different) attitude on how things stand with me (*Befindlichkeit*). The second phase of self-encounter, in other words, is a possible change of mind, a new behavior, a different orientation. It facilitates a step away, from actuality into potentiality, meaning it is augmented by the negative power of language. Nietzsche's perspectivism; Heidegger's "step back." The logic of the two (the *daimonic* split) has a simple enough mechanism, which Zupancic stresses is not the simplistic "everyone has a point of view." We are reviewing the design of the *dromos* (the track of trope).

> The presupposition of the truth as perspective is that the gaze can appear on the level of what is seen (producing an effect of decentering). Yet this occurs not through reflecting on our perspective, but through its change or its shift. This is Nietzsche's crucial insight and emphasis. The effect of this shift of perspective is not simply a relativization (and/or an accumulation of numerous perspectives), but the emergence of a stain (or a blind spot) that blurs the transparency of what we see (or know)—this being the objective element in what we see. In order for this effect to take place, we do not need to embrace a thousand different perspectives—a change between two can be enough. One could also express this as follows: there is a perspective (on things) that emerges only when one shifts

> perspectives: . . . the point of disjunction introduced into the reality of a given situation by the shift of perspective. (112–13)

Zupancic recommends the *mise-en-abyme* device as a common way this shift (parallax) may be represented (the play within the play in *Hamlet;* the parable "Before the Law" in Kafka's *The Trial,* the parable of the cave in Plato's *Republic*). The paintings of Malevich give directly a sensation that alerts us to the possibility of this shift. Chris Marker's *La Jetée,* (in which a man was marked by an image from a childhood event that turned out to be the scene of his own death), is the emblem of the two (19). Cézanne's realization of the motif produced a new spatialization of shifting perspective that was made hyperbolic in cubism. A rhetorical figure, *metalepsis* (a second instance makes the first possible), is in this collection, as is Derrida's trace and Deleuze's fold. What are the political implications of a citizenry educated in *daio* logic?

Duende

The genealogy of the *daimon* merged with the history of Being in the West. Aristotle described being as *phusis,* "nature," the upsurge of the life force. To name exactly how this force worked Aristotle coined the term "entelechy."

> *Daimon/daemon* can refer specifically to the fate of an individual, or more generally to a kind of hidden or numinous force that shapes a person's life. This particular meaning of the term is most readily found in Orphic beliefs. It is also in this sense that one speaks of an individual being possessed by his or her *daemon* as by an alter ego or "other self." A person's *daemon* is thus seen as his or her life principle or entelechy—the entelechy being Aristotle's term for the indwellilng biological law or determinant characteristic of all living organisms. Heraclitus also spoke of this notion of the *daemonic* when he stated that a man's *daemon* is his fate. (Nicholls 11–12)

In modernity the life force was secularized and psychologized in the philosophy of Spinoza: "the *conatus* with which every thing endeavors to persist in its own being is nothing but the actual essence of the thing itself" (Spinoza 108). *Conatus,* manifested as "striving," goes back to Cicero, and was associated with the instinct for self-preservation (108). Leibniz's monad also was an updating of Aristotle's entelechy, used to explain the fundamental integrity and shape of an individual identity. "For Leibniz, the monad operates as the organism's biological prototype or telos of its full development or perfectibility. In the case of conscious organisms like animals and humans, Leibniz holds that the monad is in fact the soul—the internal source of appetite, striving or Kraft that animates the organism and regulates its development" (Nicholls 93). Goethe's association of entelechy and the *daimonic* was derived from his reading of Leibniz and the influence of the *Monadology* on Herder's notion of Kraft (94).

The relevant point in our context, thinking about the functionality of Moment, is this family relationship of the notions of daimon, entelechy, genius, and *conatus* with avatar—all updating the enigma of fate, destiny. An important aspect of Aristotle's metaphysics was the temporal movement of Being implied by entelechy, indicating that essence existed as a potential (*dunamis*), that may or may not become actual (*energeia*). This attribute of entelechy motivated the Germans to emphasize the importance of *Bildung*, the education necessary to actualize human potential (98). The artist genius provided a site (a choral receptacle) where nature could reflect upon itself in the medium of language and form of art. This locus condensed the traditional association with the genius of the household, the city, an entire people (the *Volk*) (103). The spirit of these collective entities could be channeled through the artist's voice, constituting an ontological function, bringing into appearance the truth of nature, justifying the role of literature in decorum.

Federico Garcia Lorca's lecture on *duende* is a statement of the virtue of "life" as the autonomous value to be institutionalized in electracy that shifts our analogy from narrative to cabaret performance. "*Duende*" is a survival of "*daimon*" that, as Lorca (and every other modern who used the term, including Heidegger) explained, had nothing to do with Christian "demons." "The *duende* I am talking about is the dark, shuddering descendant of the happy marble-and-salt demon of Socrates, whom he angrily scratched on the day Socrates swallowed the hemlock, and of that melancholy demon of Descartes, a demon who was small as a green almond and who sickened of circles and lines and escaped down the canals to listen to the songs of blurry sailors" (43). Lorca lists Nietzsche as one of those scorched by this spirit of the earth, "who looked for its external forms on the Rialto Bridge and in the music of Bizet" (Nietzsche noted the change in his musical tastes, away from Wagner toward Bizet, that occurred as part of his insight into eternal recurrence).

Lorca's identification of *duende* with the genius of a specific region (Andalucia) and the soul of its people manifests the modifications in this Ancient spirit passed along through Romanticism. His description of the evening the Andalusian singer Pastora Pavon was performing in a little tavern in Cadiz is one of the best evocations of the peculiar nature of "genius" as *conatus*, in clarifying that this Kraft has nothing to do with craftsmanship or technical ability, but only with soul capacity. Pastora is a master of craft. "For a while she played with her voice of shadow, of beaten tin, her moss-covered voice, braiding it into her hair or soaking it in wine or letting it wander away to the farthest, darkest bramble patches. No use. Nothing" (45). Lorca identifies by name and description several members of the legendary tough crowd. A tiny man sarcastically murmured from somewhere "Viva Paris!" implying "here we care nothing about ability, technique, skill. Here we are after something else." He was alluding to the cabaret singers of Montmartre.

> As though crazy, torn like a medieval weeper, La Niña de los Peines got to her feet, tossed off a big glass of firewater and began to sing with a scorched throat, without voice, without breath or color, but with *duende*. She was able to kill all the scaffolding of the song and leave way for a furious, enslaving *duende*, friend of sand winds, who made the listeners rip their clothes with the same rhythm as do the blacks of the Antillis when, in the "*lucumi*" rite, they huddle in heaps before the statue of Santa Barbara. (45–46)

Lorca places "*duende*" in the family of terms for the bittersweet feeling of Eros, in all the versions that spread through the Black Atlantic, the creole cultures that invented the musics of tango, samba, jazz—each with its own mood (*mufarse*, *saudade*, blues). Concept avatar attempts the thought of this popular feeling. The blues express *duende*, but *duende* is not confined to music. A key element in the description is that *duende* may be invited, but it comes and goes on its own terms, but is most likely to appear when "death" is a possibility and its preference is for the rim of the wound. No philosopher has ever been able to account for it, but Lorca as poet gathers a series of images to convey the sensory quality of the feeling: "The hut and the cart wheel and the razor and the prickly beards of the shepherds and the peeled moon and the fly and moist pantry shelves and torn-down buildings and lace-covered saints and lime and the wounding line of eaves and miradors possess, in Spain, fine weeds of death, the allusions and murmurings (perceptible to any alert spirit) that fill our memory with the stale air of our own passage" (48).

Lorca distinguishes *duende* from the muse and from angels, who have a different relationship with inspiration and external visitation. Edward Hirsch in his study of artistic inspiration treats these three modes together, to account for the widest range of art examples. Michel Serres's *Angels* explicitly develops the idea of the angels and *daimons* as messengers between mortals and gods, whose function has been taken over in modernity by information technologies. The connection with the Gateway, in the context of Trickster stories, is pointed out by Lewis Hyde.

> All tricksters like to hang around the doorway, that being one of the places where deep-change accidents occur. Eshu is no exception. He likes especially the doorway between heaven and earth, which is why his face appears on the divination board. The art of divination makes heaven and earth briefly coincident. Eshu is a sort of slippery joint at the point of their contingency, revealing fate or reversing it depending on the disposition of things. It may well be that fate is set in heaven, but it must be played out here on earth, and between heaven and earth there is a gap inhabited by this shifty mediator. (124)

Marcos Novak brings all these threads together in his discussion of liquid architecture when he suggests that cyberspace may be constructed in accord with the old dreams of magic. *Duende* is the mood of dwelling in information, and poetry is its logic (Novak 228). This thread emphatically shows that concept avatar is a thought of feeling as a dimension of civilization.

6 Memory

Vocation

In 1965, after your junior year in college, you went to Spain, the official (practical) reason being to study language, literature, history. You enrolled in classes, but the fantasy of departure from home was narrated by Hemingway. What was the motive? A desire for "experience," assumed to require adventure, risking disappointment as we know from the tale of Parzifal who did not recognize the Grail as such when it was presented to him. During the first few weeks in Madrid, still working on the language and not yet acquainted with anyone, you went to a bookstore. What were you seeking, when you entered that store? An inventory of the attractors governing your life trajectory must begin with the book, books as such. You already were in the orbit of writing. From bedtime stories to choice of major in college the book as object and experience was the attractor, the desire to read leading to the desire to write. You wanted to Be a Writer. The book acquired that day was the diaries of Franz Kafka, 1910–1923, edited by Max Brod. Did a *daimon* intervene, as Nietzsche wondered about his discovery of Schopenhauer at a book stall?

On the back cover there was a description.

> Kafka's diaries reveal to us the extraordinary inner world in which he lived. Here he describes, perhaps to relieve the pain that they caused him, his fear, isolation, and frustration, his feelings of guilt and his sense of being an outcast. In between come quick glimpses of the real world, of the father he worshipped, and of the woman he could not bring himself to marry. And throughout this personal journal Kafka the writer is experimenting, searching for his true mode of expression.

You opened the fat volume at random, and happened upon this passage: "To be pulled in through the ground-floor window of a house by a rope tied around one's neck and to be yanked up, bloody and ragged, through all the ceilings, furniture, walls, and attics, without consideration, as if by a person who is paying no attention, until the empty noose, dropping the last fragments of me when it breaks through the roof tiles, is seen on the roof" (Kafka, *Diaries* 224). Sold. That rope, it recognized you. Here was a way to study your presumed vocation, by immersing yourself in the diaries of a writer. You could apprentice yourself to the diaries, and discover the backstory of one of the stars of the syllabus. Did you appreciate that Kafka was not so much crafting images as reporting an actual feeling? What feeling? An event. Truth (it compels your attention when it appears). Your next stop was a *papeleria* to get a notebook. This choice determined a certain mood, attunement, filtering the encounter with the Spain of 1965–66, still governed by General Franco. Prague in Madrid. A fateful choice? You went in search of your rope (did you believe it was only a trope?).

The very copy of the diaries is in my hands, with the pencil marks and underlinings now seeming almost random. Kafka lived within a suspended decision (aporia). His ambivalence about his plans to marry Felice Bauer crystallized a general dilemma, a tension at the center of life that Sartre formulated as live or tell. Entries dated 1913 inventory reasons for and against the marriage. The choice was: either Felice, or Writing. Listen to her name. Does it not say *happiness*? Several times he wonders if the only solution is to throw himself out a window, not without his gallows humor. "I have come to believe that there are possibilities in my ever-increasing inner decisiveness and conviction which may enable me to pass the test of marriage in spite of everything . . . Of course, to a certain extent this is a belief that I grasp at when I am already on the window sill" (229). Aporia. The impasse is constitutive of experience as such, with Eros being one name for it. You framed your own options in similar terms, casually accepting Kafka as a default advisor (decorum).

In Spain there was a turn. You learned later, reading Harold Bloom, that you are an example of an "American religion," a stock character if you like, in the typology of "self-reliance" (*Agon*). Poets working the Romantic Sublime are a recent incarnation of Epimetheus (belated). The tradition of player with avatar drawing upon Ancient *gnosis*, encountering the god within, the uncanny *daimon*, through Romantic genius, to modern anxiety and the event of text—this history informs Bloom's theory of literature. "Avatar" has an exotic, esoteric provenance, but it also is as familiar to American culture as Thoreau's *Walden* and the spirit guides of self-help gurus. In reading we learn how to talk to ourselves (such is the scene of decision) (Bloom, "Poetic Crossings"). In short, reading is uncanny. In Bloom's terms, what happened in Spain was an encounter with a strong precursor (Kafka). You passed through the three crossings that inform the *agon* of such encounters, passage across thresholds, following the *dromos* (the oblong race course). An abstract version of the experience begins with the anxiety of doubt about your vocation, your potential to write, a feeling of loss, of emptying out, that Bloom associates with kenosis, one of three Greek concepts of space (along with *topos* and chora). Kenotic space is nothingness, emptiness, and was used in Christian theology to name the opening of Christ's incarnation in Mary's womb. The second crossing (threshold) is doubt about your capacity for love, solipsism, putting self-preservation above desire. The saving third crossing occurs if the sensory undergoing finds its trope in language, or design, by means of which you enter (descend) into writing. The lost time of living is regained in telling (as Proust would say). The ethos as experience of limit (failure, loss) is countered by pathos, a representation that paradoxically inverts your relation with the precursor (better a living dog than a dead lion, Achilles advised from the afterlife).

The turn pivots on some sensory experience, some trait emergent from the external setting to trigger self-appearance, the stamp of Being. Because your body is pathos (character, that which may not be persuaded). My search for an Allegory of Prudence takes an olive orchard in bloom as a metonym for a year in Spain. By early winter you were far from equilibrium. You tried on several personae: ex-patriot writer, student of flamenco, bohemian artist, goliard minstrel. The only criterion for role was "other than bourgeois," an evasion of habitus. You balked at "salesman" as Arjuna did at "warrior." An olive tree is a dialectical image in this scene, meaning that it conjoins past and present. It records an event (May 1966), a memory, a site that through its persistence and attraction has become a measure, a reference point tracking how I became what I am. My undergoing of prudence is indexed here, recording Limit (*Grenze*). The flowers of the olive tree are small and creamy white, hidden within the thick leaves, is how the guidebooks put it. *The blossoms usually begin appearing in April and can continue for many months. A wild, seedling olive tree normally begins to flower and produce fruit at the age of eight years. The size of the olive fruit is variable, even on the same tree, and the shape ranges from round to oval with pointed ends. The fruit is gathered in mid October and should be processed as soon as possible to prevent fermentation and a decline in quality. The leaves of olive trees are gray-green and are replaced at two to three year intervals during the spring after new growth appears. An olive tree can grow to fifty feet with a limb spread of thirty feet. New sprouts and trees will emerge from the olive tree stump roots, even if the trees are cut down. Some olive trees are believed to be over a thousand-years old, and most will live to the ripe old age of five-hundred years.*

You hitchhiked with your American friend from Madrid, as you had done many times that year. You were a good team, with her vocabulary and your pronunciation. The Spaniards always stopped for the attractive blonde woman, and then you appeared as the guitar-toting companion. At the border with Portugal (Valencia de Alcántara) she discovered that her passport was still in a drawer back in the Madrid apartment. She wanted you to go on with the family from Lisbon but that was not an option. There were no hotels, only rooms in private homes. Three Guardia Civil questioned you casually when you left the bodega. They were friendly, bantering with the American woman. It was unusual to see foreigners in this village in those days, so you were an item of conversation, suspicion, and undisguised attention from the inhabitants. We walked out of town along the narrow highway. The orchards in the evening light stretched into the hills, colors fading out to silhouettes, offering a place for picnic supper: wine, cured ham, bread, cheese. Olives. Fermented, cured in brine, green olives taste salty sour. What was your conversation about? Did you describe Kafka again to her, or recite one of your own parables? She hadn't shaved her legs in months, she explained, and this custom became a leitmotif, comparing manners and behaviors noted that year. It was a night in an olive orchard, on the border between Spain and Portugal, May 1966. Isn't this why you left home? You will have arrived at the outermost limit, the end of your rope.

At dawn you awoke in early light covered in flowers. A complete carpet of blooms. The transfer from above to below was total. The ground as far as you could see and throughout the entire orchard was a carpet of petals. The trees in unison all dropped their flowers during the night and had moved on to the next stage of their cycle. An intersection occurred, between the annual revolution and your linear trajectory. The locals see this scene once each year, in this season, nothing remarkable, however beautiful, but you were the event for them. A Gestalt, figure-ground switch, depending on stand. You remained together in the sleeping bag for some while as the scene happened. Beauty. You departed from the orchard, leaving the site as you found it, and walked to the station. A train for Madrid came through later that morning and you were on it. You agreed that the orchard addressed you, intimated something, but what? There is the turn (the idiot). The momentum of the round trip, *ida y vuelta*, however many delays or detours, was now irreversible. Review the scene: the Spanish border of Portugal, the hinterlands of Extremadura, the missing passport, the Guardia Civil with their patent leather souls, an olive orchard with picnic, the May night outside, one sleeping bag for two friends, and most of all the seasonal morning blanket of flowers. What are you overlooking?

The experience returned unexpectedly as a Proustian moment, viewing Cameron's *Avatar.* The floating glowing Woodsprites, seeds of the Pandoran holy tree, projected into the dark auditorum in 3-D, triggered the memory of the orchard (uncanny). Proust's experience was of an exact match of one sensation (a spoon clanging on a plate, the banging of a hammer) in two different time-space locations. In my case, the orchard shed its petals during the night while we slept. The visualization of a million white flowers falling through a moonlit midnight existed only in fantasy. Cameron's 3-D cinematography matched the fantasy scene. What is the contribution to my Allegory of Prudence? Extremadura was where you will have turned for home, and from this decision all the others followed. You are still in transit through the third crossing, attempting to accomplish the metalepsis of writing that salvages the doubts of vocation and love in a trope. Bloom (a fatal signature) explains the call and response: ethos is character (limit); pathos is response (representation). The latter salvages the former (belatedness is finessed with a trope of transumption, by means of which time is regained). The relevant instruction in our context is Spain as Moment. In Spain I glimpsed life as possibility, potentiality, as having options (the logic of two). Spain exposed a pattern, but was not yet the figure, which is formed through the fermentation of delay and displacement (*Erfahrung*). The gesture of reaching (of desire) opened the hole and you felt the t/rope. The orchard provided the vehicle of Moment, but it took some time for the tenor to reveal itself as prudence. The doubt was that if Kafka was the measure (and after a year of modeling a journal on his diaries I recognized him as The Writer), then I was not one and could not be one (the crossing of Election). The crossing of Solipsism went by unattended in the night (the option of love). The choice was self-preservation, in any case, which is to say, the feeling was not bittersweet, but saltysour.

At an existential level I committed implicitly to knowledge. It will have been as if, having undergone one epiphany, I needed to pause, to take stock of what happened, to understand it and have it, not only to undergo it (Nietzsche's going under), not only as event but also as text and concept. Is my capacity to be affected so modest? I am testifying. It was as if Aladdin said *Open Sesame*, and called it a day when the magic worked. You didn't realize that as a rule epiphanies must be constructed. They don't happen (there are not Moments galore). In May 2011 I got it and laughed, and these one hundred thousand words unspooled as *Nachträglichkeit*. I understand it now in actantial terms: taking the relay of the *Bhagavad Gita* as narrative, in which both Arjuna and Krishna are characters, I identify with Krishna, not Arjuna (in the persona of "friend"). I wanted to be sage, not hero, but there is no place for this role in our ethos. The bizarre quality of that announcement to myself, since I am explaining myself to myself (*Ecce Homo*), is that in some way I believed that, once I understood, I could rejoin you in the orchard or just after. I forgot time. But then, isn't this forgetting against anxiety the bonus of kairotic (a)temporality? The larger point is that your capacity for Moment (Time Regained) is what is augmented in electracy as apparatus. What is the institutional form of time regained (kairotic interruption), and what is its accident? But all of this is just relay, testimony.

Orpheus

What, then, is a Writer? The updating of avatar function as flash reason takes McLuhan's advice about the laws of media: that with any artifact one must ask, what does it render obsolete, and what does it retrieve from the past? As our guiding scene suggests, avatar's history includes various incarnations and theorizations, as god, soul, self, text. It is not that literate selfhood is rendered obsolete in our context, seeking a practice of flash reason adequate to the demands of the dromosphere, but that this experience of being an autonomous individual is brought into relationship with a new dimension of reality produced within the epoch of electracy. Bloom reminds us that the Classical Greeks, who invented "self" in the first place, considered *daimon* to be as intrinsic to personhood as talent or beauty. Concept avatar retrieves this dimension of identity experience suppressed during high literacy. The Allegory of Prudence is an experiment designed to bring us into contact with this feeling of *daimon* and its functionality of providing measure of decision. *Daimon* says No, and it is in fact the personification of negation, negativity, "negentity," as such. Negentity is Merleau-Ponty's term, and his usage is worth citing at this point, to mark a philosophical parallel to the Orchard event. Let me cite Merleau-Ponty, to confirm my choice.

> A philosophy of negativity, which lays down nothing qua nothing (and consequently being qua being) as the principle of its research, thinks these invisibles in their unity, and at the same time admits that the knowing of nothingness is a nothingness of knowing, that nothingness is accessible only in bastard forms, is incorporated into being. The philosophy of negativity is indissolubly logic and experience: in it the dialectic of being and nothingness is only a preparation for experience, and in return experience, such as it has described it, is sustained and elaborated by the pure entity of being, the pure negentity of nothingness. . . . If I identify myself with my view of the world, if I consider it in act and without any reflective withdrawal, it is indeed the concentration in a point of nothingness, where being itself, being such as it is in itself, becomes being-seen. What there is common to both the concrete descriptions and the logical analysis—even more: what in a philosophy of the negative identifies the absolute distinction between being and nothingness and the description of nothingness sunken into being—is that they are two forms of immediate thought. (86)

What is wrong with you, that you love this mode of expression? You didn't know any of that in 1966 in any case, but the *vuelta* from the Orchard brought you to chora (this enabling nothing that may be addressed only with bastard reasoning). Isn't this what Plato wanted for you, to undergo a passage from your companion's desirable unshaven legs to the contemplation of negentity? Orchard avatar. This account wants to bridge the passage, show both ends of the rainbow, from *duende* to negentity, as a map for you. Avatar in our Internet public sphere is a relationship, and depends upon a certain kind of experience. Another relay (rather than model) for this approach to avatar is provided by Maurice Blanchot's appropriation of the Orpheus myth as an emblem of his theory of writing (*The Space of Literature* 171). The Greek myth recounts the life and death of Orpheus, credited as the inventor of writing. Blanchot focuses on Orpheus's descent (avatar) into Hades, which he was able to enter through the power of his art. His purpose was to retrieve his beloved Eurydice, who died in an accident. Blanchot focused his retelling, more or less faithful to the original, on the moment when Orpheus broke the agreement with the demi-gods and turned to look at Eurydice before they exited Hades. "Thracian Orpheus took her and with her the command that he not turn back his gaze until he had left the groves of Avernus, or the gift would be revoked," as Ovid wrote. "Through the mute silence, they wrest their steep way, arduous, dark, and thick with black vapors. They were not far form the border of the world above; here frightened that she might not be well and yearning to see her with his own eyes, through love he turned and looked, and with his gaze she slipped away and down" (Ovid qtd. in Morford and Lenardon 273).

The Greek terms for descent (*catabasis*) and ascent (*anabasis*) remind us that the West has its own tradition of avatar and *aarohat* (Sanskrit "ascent"). "*Catabasis*" (Greek *kata*, "down," and "base" or "foot") is the essential epic convention of the hero's trip into the underworld. A hero necessarily braves a *catabasis*, such as the descent of Orpheus into the lower world in order to charm Hades and Persephone to bring his wife, Eurydice, back to the living world. Most *catabases* take place in the Underworld, such as the descent of Heraklês, or in Hell, such as that of Dante. However a *catabasis* can also be other dystopic areas such as what Odysseus encounters on his twenty-year journey from Troy to Ithaca. Christ's Harrowing of Hell appropriates this pagan narrative. *Catabasis* connects avatar with the very structure of narrative, codified in the templates of screenplay authoring: the protagonist becomes hero by leaving home, entering the special world of the narrative (that is, descends into the realm of death). This model is only the point of departure for our project (becoming image), since brand as the identity experience of electracy no longer possesses the coherence of narrative form.

Jacques Offenbach's *Orpheus in the Underworld* formalized the *cancan* music hall dance that became emblematic of Parisian cabaret decadence. Blanchot's appropriation of the myth typifies a device of existentialist authors of his period (Camus and Sisyphus, for example), of updating legends, fables, myths, as allegories for contemporary experience. The lesson passed along for us is the analogy between the writer's relation with the work and the relation of player with avatar. Blanchot developed his poetics in explicit opposition to Sartre's endorsement of prose and an activist engagement with political polemics. Blanchot takes "the other slope of language," that of poetry, with important implications for EmerAgency consulting. Poetry is "useless" in instrumental terms (and proud of it). Our purpose, rather, is to bring into ontology the disposition, attitude, virtue (desire) of the subject, in order to open a new front in the struggle for survival. Blanchot's lesson is that the "entry into language" by a speaking being (mourning) is a kind of avatar descent. No Eurydice. No Felice. Writing necessarily loses them, but not necessarily in a bad way, to the extent that it accesses the parallax, the double slope of operant subject. There is a General Economy of living that Commerce disavows, countered by concept avatar. And yet, if there were money in it, there would be cruises to hell.

Blanchot was one of the first, and remains one of the most perceptive, French readers of Heidegger. He took up Heidegger's project to introduce a new ontology, doing for the poetic slope of language what the Classical Greeks did for the propositional slope. Heidegger's etymological reading of the Greek word for "truth" (*aletheia*), made explicit the limits of the Greek achievement. "Truth" is an uncovering, in a figure-ground relationship. The Greeks focused on the figure, which they ontologized, and forgot about the ground, the act of disclosure itself. A related point, important for distinguishing this ontology from the direction taken by modern science, is that the Greeks were concerned with what showed itself of its own accord, what attracted attention through the beauty of its form. Heidegger shifted attention to the ground that withdraws in order to disclose, and demonstrated that art with its circumspective devices of indirect intimation offered the means for ontologizing this more reticent Real.

Blanchot takes up this angle, which was continued by Derrida. The moral that Blanchot extracts from the story of Orpheus concerns the author's experience of writing this withdrawal. To write is to descend into the void that language opens in Real, the site of potential that Aristotle called *dunamis* and Deleuze the virtual. Eurydice is the object of desire, indicating that Eros and Thanatos are involved, life, sexuality, the Unconscious. Foucault's reading of what Blanchot attempted has become definitive, when he named this void the "outside." Many other modern writers explored the Orpheus theme, in order to evoke the experience of creativity in which one's personal identity is subordinated or extinguished, replaced by what is more than and beyond the limits of conscious thought, identity, understanding. Blanchot referred to this stance in language as "the neutral," beyond individual identity, in which the subject receives from world, from the outside (such is the experience of avatar). The outside is the new dimension of subject activated in the electrate apparatus. Roland Barthes was teaching a seminar on the Neutral at the time of the accident that killed him, the notes from which are now published. These "accidents" index the General Accident against which flash reason operates. It is worth noting in the context that Kafka (one of Blanchot's favorite exemplars of writing) was a lawyer for the Worker's Accident Insurance Company. Keep in mind what this training is for: dromosphere (Hades).

An instruction of this analogy is that avatar as the enunciation of flash reason performs an entry into image, models the identity experience of chora as opening (as the fault of Epimetheus), and must be designed according to this conative or receptive stance. Avatar is not mimetic of one's ego, but a probe beyond one's ownness, as a relationship with community, with the Other. Freud's topology of the psyche (Ego, Id, Superego) is his version of one's attendant demi-gods. Deleuze and Guattari's "rhizome" is much invoked in association with the Internet. Our use of the figure follows their example of rhizome as a symbiotic relationship between two separate domains brought into mutually beneficial alliance. It is significant that one of their primary examples of rhizome (the wasp and orchid, or bee and flower) was also the chief guiding image for students in manuscript culture, who were advised to compose texts the way bees made honey: by frequenting the best flowers of rhetoric, to retrieve and store their essence, with which to create honey in the hive. Here is another analogy for the avatar relationship: player to avatar is as artist to work (writer to text). The Copernican shift of this analogy calls attention to the experience of Writing, which is that of reception from outside. It is decidedly not the experience of transparent communication of clear and distinct ideas.

Analogy depends upon the familiarity of its ratio. To understand your relationship with avatar, you are offered a comparison with authoring, or with art making in general. Blanchot's allegory specifies the relevant part of the analogy: player with avatar in an Internet dromosphere is like Orpheus with Eurydice in Hades. "Fun" does not apply to the experience referenced in this figure. Such is the counsel provided by our traditions and our artists, said to be the antennae of the race. The project of a general electracy is to adapt the lessons of the experimental arts and theory to the quotidian practices of the new apparatus.

What relay could be more familiar than this one, that player with avatar is writer with text? Bruce Clarke, in *Allegories of Writing,* develops the analogy of writing as *daimon,* with reference to Angus Fletcher on personification. The emphasis on conceptual persona and vital anecdote in our concept avatar gains practical support from this context. The most thorough discussion of how *daimon* functions through writing, however, is that of Bloom (in *Agon*). In the process of writing, or even of reading, the precursor work (in John Ashbery's "Self-Portrait in a Convex Mirror," one of Bloom's examples, the precursor explicitly addressed is a painting by Parmigianino), is in the position of *daimon* (or avatar). Such is the tradition of our Allegory of Prudence, in conversation with Titian. The *gnosis* produced by this encounter of writer with work is precisely knowledge of one's own being, not "self-knowledge" of the Socratic sort, but in the spirit of Nietzsche's stamp of being. In the composition or design of the reading the writer takes over the *daimon's* role, accessing thus the other dimension of subject, across the split or gap, through personification (conceptual persona). Poems are to other poems what people are to themselves (Bloom, *Agon* 237). A free democratic society in electracy requires an interface constructed in the manner of decorum.

The difference between Bloom's revisionary ratios and concept avatar is that the former remains within a Romantic worldview of literacy, in which authors require originality, and so must bury their sources through denial and the whole system of Freudian defense mechanisms. The more electrate attitude is documented in Marjorie Perloff's *Unoriginal Genius: Poetry by Other Means in the New Century.* Our context shows that she is right to retain the term "genius" to name contemporary practices of appropriation (collage-montage). The value of Bloom's insight is that he traces his poetics from the commonplace tradition of generating new texts from *topo*i, such as the comparison more/less, through its mutation in associationist psychology of the eighteenth century, into Freudian metapsychology, in which the rhetorical tropes are refunctioned as evasions of ego defense. The fundamental lesson is in a procedure for receiving counsel from a tradition, to exploit the "aura" (Emerson's lustre) of an existing work, to appropriate its resonance and turn it to one's own purposes. Concept avatar is postmodern, rather than Romantic, in this framing, meaning that appropriation, from Duchamp's readymades to contemporary sampling, is not denied but promoted as legitimate and desirable, since the stand is event, not subject/object. Richard Kearney, in his history of the Imagination, characterized the postmodern imagination as "parodic" (Kearney 250), but the *fumisme* of Montmartre cabaret suggests that this classification applies to the whole of modernism. In this context, I return to Kafka as *daimon*, as occupying the Krishna position in my exercise, to advise me on how to become what I am. The precursor artist, Bloom says, gives you a measure by which to judge and negotiate your ethos, character, fate. "Allusion is concealed measurement, just as echo is repressed quotation" (*Agon* 236). Through Kafka, I learn to talk to myself (that is, to access the faculty of judgment made possible in humans through the *daio* cut in Being).

Destiny

An experiment then, to formalize more fully this measure, this figure of concept avatar, decision consultant. Fate, Luck or Fortune put into your hands a particular guide, that year in Spain, one "Kafka," who manifested a certain relationship with decision, between living or telling, between Felice or Writing, which he experienced as an absolute either/or. Try on this faciality for now, to let avatar descend as conceptual persona. Kafka lived with the anxiety of decision, whose terms you recognized in those days. The disquiet, struggling with an invisible order, apparently free yet bound to some implicit decorum of unknown provenance. The insight has to do with "limit." Limit, border, boundary, edge, dividing inside/outside: constraint. Here exactly is the nature of the experience in question and the question of experience. What is "limit" as event? Kafka mimes my disposition, an irreducible intution, and the fundamental question in an apologue or aphorism. *He is a free and secure citizen of the world because he is on a chain that is long enough to allow him access to all parts of the earth, and yet not so long that he could be swept over the edge of it. At the same time he is a free and secure citizen of heaven because he is also attached to a similar heavenly chain. If he wants to go to earth, the heavenly manacles will throttle him, if he wants to go to heaven, the earthly manacles will. But for all that, all possibilities are open to him, as he is well aware, yes, he even refuses to believe the whole thing is predicated on a mistake going back to the time of his first enchainment* (*The Zurau Aphorisms*).

We are in a primal or archaic experience (first person) ontologized through avatar as practice. The Overwhelming. I am testifying: avatar emergency, the *daimonic* No, personify the anxiety of the human condition in which you come up against your limit (pathos), your finitude, against what is expected and demanded by dharma (ethos). That rope is irreparable. Yes, and from it emerges a struggle for recognition, a striving to persevere in one's own being, a drive for self-preservation, because the rope is uncanny (reified). You may observe this struggle (anxiety) today as Brand—the drive of differentiation, for this bit of absolute uniqueness is what is most uncanny in experience. Avatar counters brand with wisdom. In electracy brand takes care of itself. Our concern rather is with concept avatar. What is undergone in this event of the primal scene, when one stands before the law of two chains? This experience is described in the philosophical tradition as fate. Fate doesn't require belief or proof: it happens. Fate is imaged through weaving, the spinner holding a spindle between the knees. It requires three (the Moirai) to make the web: Lachesis (selects the wool). Clotho (spins the thread), Atropos (weaves the web). Avatar counsels on networked destiny, reminding us of the continuity between the history of the computer (*technics* evolving from the Jacquard Loom through Babbage) and the mythology of weaver Fates. Here is the experience of being: we are bound at birth, our life is constrained by the limit of mortality. These limits constitute raw measure, and their range is figured in the demi-gods or guardian angels: Daimon, Ananke, Tyche, Eros, Nemesis. Finitude in every dimension.

> A man's fate (according to this tradition) is inescapable; it is bound upon him by *peirata*. This term, *peras*, which becomes so important in Plato, was also used in connection with spinning. It meant thread or woof thread, a spun rope, or even a knot. It came also to refer to the cord or thread by which a man's fate was fastened upon him and whose presence is betrayed by its effects. No doubt a cord or thong with which a

> man could bind things together (a bundle of sticks, a group of prisoners) so that he could treat the many as one was a valuable instrument and an impressive source of power. To the primitive mind it could well seem to be a godlike instrument suggestive of the way in which the universe is held together or formed. Later *peras* came to mean boundary, limit, or form, approaching the sense in which Plato used the term. The figure of fate as a woven bond or ligature which limits or circumscribes a man is expressed in many ways. An image running through Homer suggests that in the web which binds a man the warp threads are time or length of life. This time is to be understood as qualitative time, time as lived, its hours differentiated by the varying contents of experience. The woof threads are fate, the ordained events themselves. The tapestry thus woven and bound upon a man, by design of Zeus, is unchangeable. (Ballard 15-16)

This cord is the umbilicus. We know *peras* by Paris (the Athens of electracy). The positive side of this feeling is central to the updating of fate through avatar. This undergoing of an interior sense of limit may function as measure, but not without apparatus invention (coordinating flash reason with cyber technologies). To avatar is to go before the law, but it is not law as justice (Nomos), but Nemesis, meaning "uncanny" because forgotten, denied, secret, ever a surprise when it appears (Stimilli 110). You want something (desire, will), but *daimon* says No. It is to wrestle with angels. I arrived at the border and customs turned me away. Not me exactly, but my companion, avatar. We are not talking about some sort of return of the archaic gods, but an updating of an historical process, to use fate as a grammatological analogy for understanding how a civilization may deliberate intelligently about fatality. Authority begins in this raw intuition of limit, and each apparatus in turn learns how to institutionalize it as the force of obedience. The alternative to fate as the universal measure in literacy was Reason. That place in thought is now open, empty, functioning at best as a floating signifer (mana or *hau* in symbolic exchange, that which compels reciprocity, Laclau's hegemony). Entering this threshold conjures avatar. This feeling of emergency is what we want to notice and bring into representation in the Allegory of Prudence.

I was in the orchard and yet not present. The flowers dropped on my body and distracted spirit (asleep! like K. in *The Castle*). Only later did I remember the bridge in the background. At Alcántara there is an enormous bridge, built by the Romans around 106 CE on the orders of the Emperor Trajan. The ceremonial arch (forming a gate at the center of the span) bears the inscription in Latin: *I have built a bridge that will last forever.* A bridge. Forever. You walked to the river Tagus, rolling up your jeans to wade in the heat of the afternoon. Standing 233 feet high, the spans towered over us. Looking up, we saw several people watching from the bridge. How could I have forgotten this monument? Any reading of the Spanish memory as allegory today (Moment, Time) must take into account this bridge, whose very scale shouts next to the orchard (look at me!). Trajan's gate against the olive orchard. Avatar shows player this arrangement. The keywords of our project are here: bridge, gate. Timing? Temporality? The tree may live a thousand years. The bridge endures. I consult this expanded scene: *Orchard with bridge @ Alcántara.* "Alcántara" is an Arabic word meaning precisely "bridge." Hence we could just say, orchard @ bridge. Does it have to be either/or? Isn't parallax the tactic against aporia?

Interpretation notes a fundamental antagonism (inherent in any social world), emblematized, in Thomas Friedman's account, in the tension between "the Lexus and the Olive Tree" (the Roman bridge in the Lexus position). The human needs and desires expressed in these emblems are equally necessary for everyone, but they reflect the opposing sides, or opposing values, that inform the global conflict of our era. As Friedman explains, globalization has replaced the Cold War as international system.

> Olive trees are important. They represent everything that roots us, anchors us, identifies us and locates us in this world—whether it be belonging to a family, a community, a tribe, a nation, a religion or, most of all, a place called home. Olive trees are what give us the warmth of family, the joy of individuality, the intimacy of personal rituals, the depth of private relationships, as well as the confidence and security to reach out and encounter others. (Friedman 31)

The Lexus emblematizes the opposite pole of human experience. "It represents an equally fundamental, age-old human drive—the drive for sustenance, improvement, prosperity and modernization—as it is played out in today's globalization system. The Lexus represents all the burgeoning global markets, financial institutions and computer technologies with which we pursue higher living standards today" (33). Can flash reason through concept avatar mediate with a new logic of hegemony the contending forces that identify with one or the other of these drives? The olive tree is an icon of politics today in the Middle East.

After the Law

That "Kafka" means "jackdaw" (blackbird, crow) in Czech makes the following apologue even more relevant (Kafka's father used a blackbird as his business logo). *The crows like to insist a single crow is enough to destroy heaven. This is incontestably true, but it says nothing about heaven, because heaven is just another way of saying: the impossibility of crows.* The impossibility of *Kafkas.* We may learn from Kafka how to write, after all, if not how to live, if not that writing is living just as much as not writing also is. Learning from the parodic paradigm, your assignment is to replace his content and experience with your own, and add his methods to your practice of flash reason. Kafka advised that there was hope, but not for him, and envisioned a cage going in search of a bird. He alerts us deliberately to his position within a certain tradition of iconography. The instruction is to exploit the recognizability of traditions, to borrow their aura for your own emblem design. Tradition constitutes authority, adding depth (3-D) to experience, Arendt observed.

Kafka's crow had a well-known association with the personifications of Hope in general, and Hope in turn with the myth of Pandora. The crow's (or raven's) cry (*cras, cras*, as the onomatopoeia was transcribed in Latin) was interpreted as saying "Tomorrow, Tomorrow" (Panofsky and Panofsky 145). Among the attributes of Elpis, or hope, was this companion bird, treated as faithful augur, for when he cannot say, 'All is well,' he says, 'All will be well.'" "Even without the excellent commentary by Claude Mignot, appended to most Alciati editions after 1571, no one could fail to see that the quotation from the 'Ascraean sage' refers to Hesiod's tale of Pandora and her pithos; and the additional references to the crow—who always holds out a promise by saying 'Cras, cras,' 'Tomorrow, tomorrow'—strangely yet lastingly connecting this harsh-voiced bird with Hope, on the one hand, and Pandora, on the other" (29).

Panofsky and Panofsky note the existence of negative connotations in the tradition as well. "Dürer represented the fool given to procrastination accompanied by no less than three crows saying 'crasz'" (29). It may be worth noting in this context that Goethe, in his extensive study of the *daimonic* tradition, replaced Nemesis with Elpis (Hope) in the group of donor demi-gods, in order to bring out the redemptive power of retribution.

The commentators say that in Kafka there is no bridge, no way between the two dimensions of life established in the tradition of Western experience, between the individual and the world, the inside and the outside, matter and spirit, and this aporia is what makes his work and life emblematic of modernity. He advises: find the bridge. What is more important in my scene: Trajan's gate testifying to monumentality, or the very presence of a hyperbolic bridge? In fact, isn't this gate the message of the bridge (the gate bridges Being and Becoming)? Kafka's writing, isn't that Trajan's gate? There are these two worlds, then, and in one of them you are underway, your existential project informing the intentions with which you configure "circumstance" into "situation," experienced as "full meaning," with thought, will, and judgment all in accord. Prudence is the virtue that is your capacity to judge the nature of the situation in an instant of time, make a decision based on experience of the past with the best chance of producing through action a beneficent outcome in the future. Yes, that makes sense if time is a circle, if what goes around comes around, so that what happened before models future probability. But that is not the shape of Now. There is an interior setting modeling the circumstances. Suddenly there is an edge, like a "ha-ha" you didn't see coming in the landscape, a threshold, and something else intervenes, a force from elsewhere but not external either, and you are arrested. You feel the rope. What is that, what has happened? Kafka's protagonists awoke to find themselves under arrest, or turned into vermin. I awoke covered in flowers. Perhaps this threshold is incarnated in the ditch into which Thales tumbled while observing the stars on an evening walk, that made him a laughing stock for milk maids at the very beginnings of philosophy. Heidegger begins one of his books with this story, a parable of the origins of philosophy. We will call that interruption an intuition of *daimon*, when suddenly you feel the choke chain (rope) around your throat. Call it limit, but a better name is "measure." Prudence, but Goethe used "limit" to translate "genius." I am testifying, to invite the upgrading of an old wisdom. Is it possible to learn from the experience of others? Have you felt the t/rope? *Become what you are.*

The parable "Before the Law," introduced as a *mise en abyme* in *The Trial,* gives us a key figure for the event in question: gateway, door, portal, *poros.* The man from the country comes to the city and encounters the *law* as a gateway guarded by a doorkeeper (a threshold guardian, a *daimon*). To avatar means composing a parable. This one is a favorite of theorists: denied entry at that particular time by the guardian, the man from the country, the rube shall we say, like the idiot that you were, is prepared to wait, like a citizen in a bureaucratic waiting room.

> Before his death he gathers in his head all his experiences of the entire time up into one question which he has not yet put to the gatekeeper. He waves to him, since he can no longer lift up his stiffening body. The gatekeeper has to bend way down to him, for the great difference has changed things to the disadvantage of the man. "What do you still want to know, then?" asks the gatekeeper. "You are insatiable." "Everyone strives after the law," says the man, "so how is that in these many years no one except me has requested entry?" The gatekeeper sees that the man is already dying and, in order to reach his diminishing sense of hearing, he shouts at him, "Here no one else can gain entry, since this entrance was assigned only to you. I'm going now to close it." (Franz Kafka, *The Trial* 155)

We are lingering with Kafka, because you encountered him then and set our agenda. Part of the lesson is kairotic (the third shape of time). *The Trial* and *The Castle* both treat this theme of Moment, and the fear of missing it, the missed encounter. In both stories the protagonist comes very close to the bridge, to the condition that would open the link between the two realms (whatever they might be—— the hearth and the uncanny). The paradox of revelation in Kafka's vision is that the closer one is to illumination, the weaker one becomes, to the point of exhaustion or sleep, so that the *Augenblick*, the epiphany, never occurs. The reader, however, infers what is possible.

> Awakening, the bodhi that is continually spoken of in Indian thought from the Vedas to the Buddha, is something that happens during wakefulness, an invisible shift, a sudden

> change in distances and in the mental place, thanks to which consciousness is able to observe itself—and is therefore able to observe itself in its typical role as observer. The most effective metaphor for this event is the awakening from sleep, the passage from dream to wakefulness. (Calasso 226)

A formula (a topic) may be extrapolated from Kafka for the textual aspect of our emblem. He describes in the follow passage the problem of expression:

> 1. Is it possible to think something unconsoling? Or, rather, something unconsoling without the breath of consolation? A way out [*Ausweg*] would seem to lie in the fact that recognition as such is consolation.
> 2. And so one might well think: You must put yourself aside, and yet one might maintain oneself, without falsifying this recognition, by the consciousness of having recognized it.
> 3. That, then, really means having pulled oneself out of the swamp by one's own pigtail.
> 4. What is ridiculous in the physical world is possible in the spiritual world. *There* there is no law of gravity (the angels do not fly, they have not overcome any force of gravity, it is only we observers in the terrestrial world who cannot imagine it in any better way than that), which is, of course, beyond our power of conception, or at any rate conceivable only on a very high level.
> 5. How pathetically scanty my self-knowledge is compared with, say, my knowledge of my room. (Evening). Why? There is no such thing as observation of the inner world, as there is of the outer world. At least descriptive psychology is probably, taken as a whole, a form of anthropomorphism, a nibbling at our own limits. The inner world can only be experienced, not described.
> 6. Psychology is the description of the reflection of the terrestrial world in the heavenly plane, or, more correctly, the description of a reflection such as we, soaked as we are in our terrestrial nature, imagine it, for no reflection actually occurs, only we see earth wherever we turn. (Kafka, *The Blue Octavo Notebooks* 14, numerals added)

Kafka's aphoristic composition may be generalized into a genre for our use. I am adapting this particular one for my "motto" or aphorism, to be part of the Allegory. But you may appropriate any relevant text in the same way. Richard T. Gray's analysis, in *Constructive Destruction: Kafka's Aphorisms,* is the basis for articulating our passage into the following sequence (generalizing from the numbered sections of the original aphorism):

1. Begin with a keyword, contextualized by a thought problem. *Ausweg*—a way out, a dodge or expedient—also evokes the "no way" (*Ausweglos*) of aporia, the impasse whose primary manifestation structuring our lifeworld is mortality. Kafka exploits the multivalence of the term.
2. Take the question literally, or apply it to a concrete circumstance, such as a person contemplating suicide (?). The rhetorical trick: to recognize that there is no consolation is itself a consolation.
3. Find an analogy (or metaphor) in art, in this case in one of the tales attributed to Baron von Munchausen.
4. Recast the analogy as a proposition (the dichotomy dividing the physical and spiritual world). Explain the principles organizing this imaginative stance (free of the laws of physics).
5. Apply to one's own worldview (draw a personal conclusion).
6. Recast the personal insight as a tag line, or generalize it in aphoristic form.

Use this sequence to explore or discover one's own attitude toward the same keyword, or with respect to another such term of one's own repertoire. I put myself by means of pastiche into Kafka as persona, to address myself from the position of avatar, to restate the terms and goals of an Allegory of Prudence. The simulation of style produces a feeling of manner. We are not strong poets, we fumistes, but acknowledge daimon.

Taking Kafka's *Ausweg.*

Is it possible to receive your own post as if for the first time, as if it were news about yourself originating from abroad? This prospect articulates the aporia, the no/way out or im/passe in the circuit of auto-affection. To subscribe to this channel one must use the good offices of an avatar, a go-between (a prosopon). That, then, really means recognizing your autobi-

ography in the schtick of a Punch and Judy show. What is commonplace, even stereotyped, in the material world is obscure, indeterminate in the spiritual one. There there are no stock characters, no plot formulas, or rather, it is only we self-observers who continue to miss the point of our love for puppet shows. How pathetically scanty is my self-knowledge compared with, say, my knowledge of my home town. (Past). And so? Any observation of the inner world is accomplished through sketches of the outer world. At least expression is doubtless a form of improvisational theater, an abstract graphing of one's own shape. The inner life may be figured, not narrated, described, or analyzed. Expression is the opening of a passage between the two sides of life (the im/material). Or, more correctly, the invention of an aesthetic effigy that neither resembles nor indexes either dimension of my nature, since, immersed as we are in spectacle, we only see programming wherever we turn.

Part of the effect of this pastiche is due to Kafka's aura (the kafkaesque). This aura is to flash reason what definitions are to literacy. The importance of Kafka for image metaphysics is that he shows us a world in which the literate category has become total and absolute. Kafka's aesthetic strategy, as Clayton Koelb has shown, is to literalize or extend a commonplace phrase, idiom, figure or trope, to appropriate the aura of a truism as a point of departure for an original thought. *The Trial* may be read in this light as imagining a world in which the accusatory mood present in the etymology of the word "category" (originally associated with the vocabulary of the courts and the practice of indictment) spreads from metaphysics into all experience. As Milan Kundera (among many others) observed, Kafka's vision of a society run by "tribunal" became reality for millions of people, and this is one reason why authority is discredited in the era of Camps. To live "categorically" is a nightmare. "The trial brought by the tribunal is always absolute; meaning that it does not concern an isolated act, a specific crime (theft, fraud, rape), but rather concerns the character of the accused in its entirety: K. searches for his offense in 'the most minute events' of his whole life" (Kundera 227). Heidegger proposes that the metaphor guiding the design of the new (image) category be drawn not from the courts, but from some other practice, such as poetry. Electrate judgment shifts from forensics to aesthetics. His invention strategy is generalizable to the practice of an Internet wisdom. To undergo the avatar effect, you impersonate the precursor, in order to address your self (your brand).

Figure 2. "Olive Orchard @ Alcántara"

7 Measure

Standing Now

In her two-volume study, *The Life of the Mind,* Hannah Arendt filled in the background against which may be figured a practice of concept avatar, of composing an electrate measure of well-being (chora). Measure, that is, *dharma* (to invoke a traditional vocabulary). Arendt works her way from the Ancient Greeks up to Heidegger— specifically to Heidegger's lectures on Nietzsche (you see our focus). Between the first and second volume of the published versions, Heidegger experienced his "turn" (*Kehre*) a change of perspective or attitude, with important implications for electracy. (This turn is in your biography also). Arendt structured her history as a rewriting of Kant's three critiques, because she believed that Kant's third critique (on aesthetic judgment) was the basis for a pedagogy of ethical and political judgment, adapted to our media age. Unfortunately, Arendt died unexpectedly with only two of the three volumes completed (on histories of contemplative reason, and practical will).

Arendt's argument passes through, and stops short, as fate would have it, at an account of Heidegger's reading of Nietzsche, thus calling attention to this text. *The Life of the Mind* is a narrative account of the epoch of literacy. Flash reason continues Arendt's project in its own way, with Kant's aesthetic judgment being one of the earliest outlines of the possibility of thinking without concepts (reflective judgment), giving the body a turn. Arendt's history is organized by two important questions for chora (*Ort*): where are we when we think? What provokes us to think? Some observations that she gleans from the tradition, along with their relevance to us, are: 1) Thinking is swift, because immaterial (thus thinking has an affinity with figure, especially epiphany). 2) Intuition, for example, is distinguished from discursive (step by step) reasoning, as "when a flash of insight (*phronesis*) about everything blazes up, and the mind is flooded with light" (Arendt 1: 117). The "flash" passes through an associative network, such as the one Lowes documented in the imagination of Coleridge. 3) When we think, we are nowhere (or, as Heidegger said, we are "nowhere, without the no"). 4) Discursive thinking is alphabetic, structured by concepts, while intuitive thinking, available naturally to anyone, is instituted formally in ideogram systems. The Chinese ideogram is "emblematic." "For these schemata—sheer abstractions—Kant used the word 'monogram,' and Chinese script can perhaps be best understood as monogrammatical, so to speak. In other words, what for us is 'abstract' and invisible, is for the Chinese emblematically concrete and visibly given in their script, as when, for instance, the image of two united hands serves for the concept of friendship. They think in images, not in words" (Arendt 1: 101). An important clue: the emblem is to imaging what the concept is to alphabetic writing. Eisenstein and Pound both based their modernist innovations on the ideogram. 5) "When" is reason? It is always out of order, out of joint, never confined to the present moment. It "jumps the tracks." What is the rhetorical practice of "jumping out of line?"

Arendt's history removes the radicality, in some ways, from electracy as an image metaphysics, to the extent that she shows the historical character of "being," the degree to which it has evolved and transformed from one epoch to the next, one culture to the other. Each epoch (Greek, Roman, Medieval, Renaissance, Enlightenment, Modern) understood differently the relationship between thought and reality. Foucault's genealogy identified the episteme of each epoch, setting the parameters of any "statement" for that setting (not only what was said, but what it was possible to think in a given epoch). Arendt, however, frames the changes differently, foregrounding another capacity of mind, which is "stance"—to take and maintain a certain "attitude" toward the givens or the parameters of one's own time, such as the stance of "wisdom," or *ataraxy*, for the Romans (1: 154), or the Hindu witness-consciousness. What is the parameter today? *Fumisme.* Accident judged by well-being (player with avatar). As Bloom reminded us, "stance" is one of the original meanings of trope, with rhetorical "figures" based on the fighting positions and strategies of boxers and wrestlers.

Arendt's second volume shifts from "thinking" to "willing." The history of the will, she says, would coincide with a history of the inner life, and could begin with the Christian era and St. Paul's letters. If thinking contemplated the essences of perceptible things, concerned with that which is necessary, permanent, already given, enduring and always present (Classical Greeks), then willing opens the experience of an inner being, located within an individual, producing an awareness of radical freedom, in relation to contingent affairs of the social world, of political ethical action and belief (Medieval Christianity). The will, that is, raises the ontological status of "accidents," *kata symbebekos*, including errant memory of the past and projections or speculations about the future. Aristotle's distinction in his *Metaphysics* between the potential and the actual (*dunamis* and *energeia*)—his solution to the problem of how Being and Becoming are related—became in the individual a feeling that one could choose to act, or not. Arendt asserts that this feeling is a discovery, an invention of behavior (5). Identity formation, in any case, is as much a part of an apparatus as is technology. But all of that was preparation for the missing volume.

The relevant point is that, historically, intelligence has always created its own time and space, relative to an apparatus, and this opening of a place for thought, with its own dimensionality, may be called "chora" (after Plato's term for space, region, or receptacle in *Timaeus*). Concept avatar is designed to develop chora as a practice of flash reason (choragraphy). The history of decision is bound up with that of the will, but draws on all the faculties. Willing specifically opens up the future for human projects, including not just a multiple-choice option among existing possibilities (Ancient *proairesis*), but the introduction of something fundamentally new into the world. The implication, confronted only by Duns Scotus (prior to Nietzsche and Heidegger), is that God acts contingently (Arendt 2: 31). *Sumbebekos*? Willing is lived as expectation, hope and fear, addressed directly through feeling. If the recommended state of mind or attunement (*Stimmung*) available through "thinking" (pure reason) is serenity, accepting necessity, the mood of willing (practical reason) is impatience, tension, associated with an assumption that to will is also to assert "I can" (*velle/posso*) (38). Serenity and impatience: we accept their legacy, but move into a third mood (aesthetic manner).

The Judeo-Christian foregrounding of will inverts the priorities of the Greco-Roman value of contemplation. The new value is not knowledge, but belief (faith). The chief virtue in this frame is "obedience" (2: 68). Greco-Roman ataraxy accommodates world, while Judeo-Christian "no" rejects world. Faith does not involve persuasion, but is pure choice, which is, again, taking a stance, maintaining an attitude. Part of the usefulness of Arendt's history is the clarity with which it outlines the uneasy relationship of the syncretism informing the Western tradition. Every major impasse at work in our policy debates is structured by the tension between the two different civilizational values: pure and practical reason, science and faith, knowledge and belief, the prototype of which is the confrontation between Galileo and the Church, dramatized in Bertolt Brecht's play. Such are the orienting poles of the Western tradition, our handedness, each not knowing and not wanting to know what the other is doing.

Nietzsche warned that we should not take for granted the favorable attitude towards curiosity that has been hegemonic in modern sensibility, since this attitude is recent and nearly unique in the history of the world. The administration of George W. Bush showed the possibility that policy makers at the highest levels of the most "advanced" societies may place faith over knowledge. The authority of science is challenged at every turn in contemporary policy debates (conservative politicians proudly declaring their creationism). This polarity of Western deliberation is a primary target of EmerAgency consulting (the bridge). Arendt's history breaks off at the crucial juncture, with the first page of her volume on judgment rolled into the typewriter, found in her study after her death. She was preparing a third register of the life of the mind (we should say body-mind), introduced by Kant, more or less at the inception of electracy (the beginning of the industrial revolution). The point to emphasize is that "judgment" is an autonomous faculty, equal to and distinct from "thinking" and "willing." We know by analogy that "judgment" has its own stance, attitude, fundamental value, attunement, whose practice is emerging within electracy. Part of the task of concept avatar is as transition (bridge) to this third axis—judgment.

In terms of the EmerAgency as an electrate consultancy, applying to policy formation the operations of choragraphy (flash reason, concept avatar), the promise is that judgment will do for policy disputes just what Kant promised it could do for an individual thinker: create a bridge facilitating communication between the faculties of knowledge and desire, necessity and freedom. The most immediate connection between Arendt's history and chora is the traditional privilege of *nunc stans* (the standing now) over *nunc fluens* (the contingent passing of time). Arendt juxtaposes the parable of the Gateway in *Zarathustra,* with one of Kafka's parables, to make the point that human thought is the only counterforce to the chronological flow of time. Her interpretation of these parables itself concludes with a reference to the kind of sign specific to the formal operations of judgment.

> The gap, though we hear about it first as a nunc stans, the "standing now" in medieval philosophy, where it served, in the form of nunc aeternitatis, as model and metaphor for divine eternity, is not a historical datum; it seems to be coeval with the existence of man on earth. Using a different metaphor, we call it the region of the spirit, but it is perhaps rather the path paved by thinking, the small inconspicuous track of non-time beaten by the activity of thought within the time-space given to natal and mortal men. Following that course, the thought-trains, remembrance and anticipation, save whatever they touch from the ruin of historical and biographical time. This small non-time space in the very heart of time, unlike the world and the culture into which we are born, cannot be inherited and handed down by tradition, although every great book of thought points to it somewhat cryptically—as we found Heraclitus saying of the notoriously cryptic and unreliable Delphic oracle: *oute legei, oute kryptei alla semainei* ("it does not say and it does not hide, it intimates"). (Arendt 1: 210)

Avatar intimates. The Allegory of Prudence constructs an experience of this extra dimension. It is the dimension of potentiality, the (un) realized virtual, concerned with that which in action exceeds the reach of thinking and willing

As Is

What is the formal operation of flash reason that creates this experience of intimation? This alignment relating a specific human capacity (to be affected) with a formal practice (image poetics) requires a fuller discussion of what Lyotard called the tautegory. Although his insight into the epochal nature of metaphysics (its historical character) is fundamental for electracy, Heidegger had no sympathy for the technology and culture of the Entertainment spectacle within which electracy is emerging. While he acknowledged that calculative thinking was as necessary as meditative thinking (the latter being the poetic mode of the Ancient "other beginning"), Heidegger feared that the hegemony of the former had become so dominant that the latter had all but disappeared from Western civilization. An obvious symptom supporting his fear is the confusion today regarding the purpose of the Humanities disciplines. The arts (plastic and poetic) were the resource for a renewal of this other mode of thought, to facilitate the transition into a new, post-literate epoch. Meditative ontology replaces the object with the event (*Ereignis*) of appropriation (the moment of insight into one's own mortal throwness in the world). One of the clearest statements of this insight is "The Origin of the Work of Art," which explains the relationship between the two kinds of thinking. The example is a painting by Van Gogh of a pair of shoes, belonging to a peasant woman, according to Heidegger's reading. As Heidegger established in his review of literate metaphysics, Western ontology practiced a particular way of looking, of noticing what was already there (*essents*) as something, for some use or purpose, and this functionality constituted the essence of the thing as what it is. The shoes for the peasant woman are equipment.

A second order look, another application of the as-structure (a "tautegory"), comes from art, as in the way Van Gogh shows that the shoes have this purpose, showing the worn shoes as a kind of measure of the peasant's world, which Heidegger construes as "reliability." Heidegger characterizes as "unconcealment" (*aletheia*) this revelation of a world. *Aletheia* is "truth" understood as the clearing, the opening that makes it possible for a thing to appear as such.

> The equipmental quality of equipment was discovered. But how? Not by a description and explanation of a pair of shoes actually present; not by a report about the process of making shoes; and also not by the observation of the actual use of shoes occurring here and there; but only by bringing ourselves before Van Gogh's painting. This painting spoke. In the vicinity of the work we were suddenly somewhere else than we usually tend to be. The art work let us know what shoes are in truth. (*Poetry, Language, Thought* 35)

This measure of our local world is what we seek in the Allegory of Prudence.

Art works (verb, rather than noun), to show the Being of being. A non-objective form—a Greek temple— makes the point more clearly, since there is no obvious referent. "Tree and grass, eagle and bull, snake and cricket first enter into their distinctive shapes and thus come to appear as what they are. The Greeks early called this emerging and rising in itself and in all things *phusis.* It clears and illuminates, also, that on which and in which man bases his dwelling. We call this ground the earth" (42). Commentators on modernist arts help fill in the background of Heidegger's point, regarding the kind of experience in question. The basic argument is familiar enough by now, but perhaps not its ontological import. Modernist aesthetics, that is, foregrounds some principles that have always been at work in art. The first one is that arts use style to (in metaphysical terms) make accidents speak of essences. Wallace Stevens, for example, used the paintings of Marcel Gromaire to make the point that art brings into appearance the energies of the maker's being. "By substance he means the spiritual fund of the picture, the fund originating in the thought and feeling of the artist and perceptible in the painting. He speaks of the human spirit seeking its own architecture, its own 'measure' that will enable it to be in harmony with the world. It is from the intensity, the passion, of this search that the quality of works is derived" (Stevens qtd. in Altieri, *Painterly Abstraction* 32). The experience of "measure" (ratio) is the functionality of avatar.

A related principle is the capacity of art to use the as-structure of metaphysical logic in its own way, to make the non-sensory appear. A key feature is that the appearance is given in the most humble or mundane things. "With Kafka a phenomenon bursts onto the scene," writes Roberto Calasso: "the commixture. There is no sordid corner that can't be treated as a vast abstraction, and no vast abstraction that can't be treated as a sordid corner. This phenomenon isn't a reflection of the writer's personal inclinations. It's a matter of fact. Svidrigailov, in *Crime and Punishment,* observes that for him eternity looks like a village bathhouse full of spider-webs. It's a peculiarity of the period, a sign of the times" (22). The formal key giving art the functionality of a metaphysical theater is to assign semantic import to formal properties of the work. The work operates in a middle voice, facilitating an encounter with one's "self," acting on the principle that the "inside" is discovered through the "outside." Composing a pastiche replaces definition as a device for concept avatar. "In art, at least, all appearances clearly depend on the way in which the work constitutes an immediate process of calculated selections, which can be said to reveal the person to his or her self, at the same time as they give a particular tonality to the world" (Altieri, *Painterly Abstraction* 128). This capacity to be affected in an aesthetic mode is the formal core of concept avatar. The pastiche touches its author.

Charles Altieri sorts out the different branches of constructivist aesthetics, articulating three varieties of graphic ontology: Cézanne; Picasso and Braque; Malevich. All three are relevant. But Cézanne connects most directly with late Heidegger's shift from individual *Dasein* to collective "region," the place in which Being takes place (*Ereignis*). Heidegger sought a holistic category, to gather and organize a singular historical situation, to provide a measure for the totality of relationships operating in a moment. Heidegger referred to such a measure as dwelling in a region. Cézanne may be seen as testing "regioning," in the way he makes a site reveal the agent. "To understand how Cézanne opened new directions for painting and poetry, let us concentrate on his ability to establish a dialogue between the two genres of still life and landscape. It was his late landscapes that most dramatically extended realization into an ontology based on the painterly process of subsuming structural modeling into the life of the painterly eye" (*Painterly Abstraction* 181). Cézanne's landscape passages, Picasso's cubist semiotics, or Malevich's geometries, produce for the artists themselves, first of all, and for the viewers as well, an experience of Being, understood as *phusis*, entelechy, the upsurge of energy in the life force (*duende*). Sensitivity to intensity, the capacity to receive this force of feeling, is the dimension of embodiment ontologized in electracy. These devices (and all the other experiments of vanguard arts) are the source of a graphic logic, a "grammar" that supports imaging beyond the reach of written or spoken conceptual thinking.

Poetry pursued a similar aesthetic, often under the influence of innovations in the other arts (and in technology). The goal was not representation, but testimony relating a feeling of being-in-the-world. Matisse, commenting on what he learned from Cézanne, observed that "a Cézanne is a moment of the artist while a Sisley is a moment of nature" (Pleynet 18). "Feeling" in this sense has been taken up in neuroscience, to give an empirical account of this affective capacity. "My hypothesis, presented in the form of a provisional definition," states Antonio Damasio, "is that a feeling is the perception of a certain state of the body along with the perception of a certain mode of thinking and of thoughts with certain themes. Feelings emerge when the sheer accumulation of mapped details reaches a certain stage" (86).

The "mapping" refers to "sensory maps in which neural patterns are instantiated and out of which mental images can be derived. The essential content of feeling is the mapping of a particular body state; the substrate of feelings is the set of neural patterns that map the body state and from which a mental image of the body state can emerge. A feeling in essence is an idea—an idea of the body and, even more particularly, an idea of a certain aspect of the body, its interior, in certain circumstances" (88).

The Allegory of Prudence meets this mapping (choragraphy) coming from the side of poetics, locating correspondences mapping states of feeling through recognition of figures in one's milieu. The goal of flash reason is to ontologize this dimension of embodied capacity by means of aesthetics in general, and arts practices specifically (augmented in the apparatus). Relative to this goal, Altieri's primary example for the text as the mind's exploration of its own energies is Wallace Stevens. "The 'as' offers a fundamental feature of the medium of language, which one can isolate in the same way that painters isolate color and form-- in this case, to define the powers that theorizing makes visible for life" (*Particulars of Rapture* 343). To prove the philosophical power of the "as" in Steven's poetry, Altieri compares it to Wittgenstein's method of the "aspect." The lesson for flash reason, following Heidegger's insight, is to extract instructions from both philosophy and the arts on the generative power of as (to frame one thing as something else). It is the operation of trope, or turn.

> This most basic feature of language makes possible the "saying" that opens a region for Being. To undertake relational ontology in an aesthetic dimension requires practice with the peculiar "iconic" nature of this "as" connector (distinct from the "is" of literate metaphysics). "Revealed in the 'early hours' of Western destiny as Being in order immediately to go back into forgetfulness, this trait is presencing as relation and difference, and is therefore the relation as such, the difference as such. At its deepest level, this trait is only the 'as' as such. Are there any means left by which to excavate the fold of the trait and its unequal overlapping in the retrait? *Fuge,* the fault that joins, the jointure that differs, is another name for the trait. In 'Aletheia' Heidegger notes 'that the jointure [*Fuge*] thanks to which revealing and concealing are mutually joined must remain the invisible of all invisibles, since it bestows shining

> on whatever appears. Joined by being turned toward itself, the fold of the *Fuge,* without any appearance at all, produces all appearing.' " (Gasché, *Of Minimial Things* 218)

Stevens's "Ordinary Evening in New Haven" makes Altieri's case for how poetizing (in Heidegger's terms) helps readers and authors experience their own powers and possibilities. Stevens is also one of Bloom's chief exhibits, teaching the revisionary ratios by which a work of art becomes the site of measure for my Being (letting me experience the shape I am in).

> The simplest acts, like arriving in New Haven or "registering" the weather, take place on a metaphysical stage. The theory of poetry—or better, poetry as theorizing—becomes the theory of life, because it puts within contemplative brackets the essential force that makes value possible: the interdependence of the unreal and the real. The "as" becomes a metaphysical emblem, projecting the endlessly proliferating incarnations of the spirit in the flesh. And what began as Cubist metamorphoses of the world perceived expands to project this 'as' as the body for the giant within whom we think, and from whom we feel at once a clearing and a completing of the forms of desire. (Altieri, *Painterly Abstraction* 347)

This "giant" alludes to Emerson's version of the *daimon,* the god within of self-reliance. An important point, to be developed further, is this discovery and creation of value (Nietzsche). The "as" is the tool of avatar's conceptual persona. The principle is profoundly simple, yet capable of infinite refinement. The formula of correspondences between macrocosm and microcosm was "as above, so below." As the Orchard goes, so I go. "Self-portrait as Orchard with Bridge." Daimon countenancing body.

Conatus

Altieri's *The Particulars of Rapture* is useful for foregrounding the role of modernist and constructivist aesthetics in "sheltering," augmenting, or exercising the individual's conative force (*Particulars of Rapture* 29). The practice of concept avatar, in which a persona performs the vital anecdote dramatizing the thought within the problem field, makes use of the tropical "as." What guides the design is the experience of feeling (allegory is felt, not text). The philosophical relay of *conatus* (the striving to persevere in one's own being) is Spinoza. Synonyms for *conatus* include "essence," "virtue," "power." Concept avatar thinks this feeling of "potency" (potentiality), counseling what can/not be done. Altieri in a series of close readings shows how paintings and poems in their form and theme promote the experience and understanding of a collection of expressionist values: intensity, involvedness, plasticity (34). These are the measure of well-being. The important point for us is that these aesthetic experiences include the dimension of value, not superior to, but distinct from the values associated with the institutions promoting science (knowledge) or religion (belief). A purpose of concept avatar is to understand the possibility of electracy to support a third register within policy formation, to include in its own right the value of self-preservation (*conatus*), experienced as "satisfaction" in an awareness of one's own life force. Such is the wisdom received through avatar. The Allegory of Prudence notices an encounter with such percepts and affects.

Conatus involves one's capacity to be affected. Modernist arts correlate with Heidegger's theory of mood and atmosphere as the holistic organizing powers of image metaphysics. Art in our context is a resource from which to learn a "logic of mood" (*Particulars of Rapture* 56). The paintings of Malevich often serve as a prototype showing this logic in its purest form.

> On one level, psychological life is involvement in these strange and intricate balances among delicately poised shapes, reinforced by quick leaps among related color tones. But the balances cannot be treated simply as momentary states. They suggest, at the least, that there is a power in the psyche to attune itself to elemental forces. The awareness of abstract relatedness depends on and extends the constant perceptual adjustments we make as we feel what color, line, and rhythm can create. (51)

The system of graphic design does for image ontology what Greek grammar did for word ontology. Subject-object was in grammar before it structured metaphysics.

In addition to providing a "receptacle" guiding an experience of one's life force, the arts support a second-order thinking, specifically the formation of an attitude toward the first-order perceptions or sensations. Van Gogh's painting expresses an attitude toward peasant labor, including a feeing of a value, a commitment, an investment, an identification. These are the elements at play in the hegemonic struggle in the political sphere. Altieri's insight is to articulate expression as distinct from cognition, from the established stances of both idea and will (pure and practical reason). Altieri instead associates conative value with manner functioning to construct attitudes (110). Manner (style) allows a second-order reframing that exposes our established investments to review (or even to awareness). An example is Van Gogh's brush work as a manner of treating a subject-matter to lend it ontological import (116). Manner, we might say, is how *duende* is manifested, meaning the life energy of the maker is invested in values of vividness not mimesis, intensity not cognition. The degree of satisfaction felt through identification with a given state depends, according to Spinoza, upon whether it is empowering or the opposite. Registering potentiality, this measure is grasped intuitively, in the degree of joy or sadness experienced in the state (hope and fear). *Conatus*, Altieri explains, anticipates what Nietzsche meant by "will to power" (144). Power and impotence (the sphere of potentiality) register in the body as anxiety. "Will" is one possible stance relative to power, for which Nietzsche sought an alternative. The traditional function of wisdom was to evade the anxiety of impotence.

Ortschaft

The lesson for flash reason in this discussion is the formal one, to learn from painting and poetry a rhetoric of manner and expression, to be applied to the review and creation of attitudes in the public sphere. There is nothing mysterious about "expression," in that it has always been at work in any art, treated in any commentary as the distinction between "story" and "discourse," for example—between the subject matter and the maker's judgment of or attitude towards that matter, to be inferred primarily from the manner of treatment, the style. The usefulness of Altieri's account in the context of Heidegger's metaphysics is the articulation of manner as a distinct source and vehicle of value (the ground of political and ethical conduct). How does the expressive, conative manner work? Any primer on poetry describes it. It is "the secret" of all poetry, or at least all lyric poetry, according to Jane Hirshfield's commentary on "the mind of poetry"— "the use of description of the natural world to explore human feeling" (90). Heidegger's "annotations" on Holderlin's river hymns are based on this principle. Poetizing for Heidegger exploits features of language not relevant to calculative thinking, and so give access to the other modality of Being. He values the circumspective indirection of poetry, which makes appear (in thought, in imagination) the withdrawal or concealment of Being (that which is not and may not be present).

The river Ister (Danube) in Holderlin's hymn, according to Heidegger, is not a symbol, an allegory, or even a metaphor in the usual sense. Forget about interpreting all the personal references in the poem to the poet's biography, Heidegger proposes. Certainly all these conventional attributes of poetry are at work, but they are not what affords the ontological reach of poetizing. From Hölderlin's poems Heidegger learns how language "regions." Poetry opens space, makes room in the sense of "chora," whose effect is to add a sense of "measure" to the world (this is what poets are "for"). The term used is "*Ort*," which may mean place or location, but which also names the point of a spear, the tip that delivers all the force of a blow, and this "point" should be understood in relation to the *punctum* or sting of Barthes's third meanings.

Heidegger in his later period takes a different stance in relation to being-there (*Dasein*), to unfold more fully the "there" or the world in which beings dwell in time. The experience of this complex site called *Ort* emerges within art, where it acquires categorial power. Image ontology emerges within the graphic design of digital simulations, the way word ontology emerged with the grammar of written philosophy. The categories of region or "*Ortschaft*," however, are the inverse of literate categories that articulate subjects and predicates, applying the ratios of calculation to the life-world. Choral (holistic) categories, rather, grasp collections of entities in their interrelationships in a region, to whose forces humans attune themselves through mood. Poetizing makes this process accessible to practical reason in the same way that mathematics makes calculation applicable to scientific experiment. The poetic "as" connects an outside scene with an inner feeling, in order to mediate a conative negotiation with the world. At stake is well-being, individual and collective thriving, whose immediate site of application in the public sphere is "sustainability."

The Western tradition is organized around the gap or fissure, the split into which the "as" is fitted. This divide takes different forms in different epochs, but poetry in its basic effect of circumspection, of commixture, using the visible or sensory percept to evoke something "more" in thought and feeling (affect), testifies to the structure. John Lysaker also uses Stevens to illustrate how *Ort* (the place of encounter) is not given directly but emerges within poetic language (just as Being emerged within propositional logic). His example is "Reality Is an Activity of the Most August Imagination," concerning a drive home from Cornwall to Hartford, "in the big light of last Friday night" (22). A possible gloss is that "the poem is about how the surging presence of a given night cannot be located among things or with the basic concepts that allow us to thematize what moves behind and in things" (23).

> It is not that Stevens's poem is about the *Ort*—as if the *Ort* were some thing, event, or force that the poem, through some poetic medium, represented. How could it be when the *Ort* concerns the "aboutness" relation itself, the very possibility of poetic address, thereby eluding any representation as the condition of its possibility? And yet, I would insist that the *Ort* is found in the language of the poem, marked even as an "argentine abstraction," an abstraction that draws the rest of the poem to itself such that one must read the entire poem in a nocturnal, silvery light. (25)

What manner of composition allows *Ort* to appear? A shorthand version is to observe how the river Ister in Holderlin's language becomes a figure of poetry itself, such that the poem manifests the process of autofiguration that recommends it to Heidegger as ontological. Here is the modernist update, corollary to the *daimon*-writing allegory. The secret, similar to the one Hirshfield found in Japanese poetry, is that the river is named and described for itself, inflected in a way that makes it intimate something other than itself (trope as). The effect could be called "sublime," in Kant's sense, in the way it turns thought back upon itself, to give an experience of one's own powers and energies as present in the world. Lysaker outlines the structure, with reference to a poem by Rilke.

> Initially, one has a traditional saying that is repeated or re-said as a figure of speech or poetry, as an instance of language. The language of the ur-poem does not rest with that repetition, however. Instead, it returns in a third saying (or second repetition) to its own ground and figures it. And in Rilke's case, it

> is a figuration wrought through ur-figures such as nature, the open, the draft, the sphere of life and death, the angel, and so on. (41)

What guides the design is the auto-affection, discovering and mapping one's capacity to be affected. The folded parts correlate with the *ida y vuelta* of a race course (*dromos*) and Bloom's three tropical crossings. The Allegory practices *metis* with respect to our three faculties: thinking, willing, feeling. It is these zones of felt recognition that serve as interface with an Internet public sphere.

The Allegory of Prudence constructs *Ort*. The *Ort* happens in the awareness of an ur-poem, a receptacle (chora) that gives Becoming (first-order experience) the stamp of Being (second-order). The structure (it is worth repeating) is that of a palimpsest, produced through the folding or recursion signaling the arrival of "more" into meaning: "For lurking within certain principal figures, one can find three sayings. Initially, one has a saying that bears a tradition within itself. It is then repeated such that it is translated into the language of the poem, coming to stand as a poetic figure. That figure, that saying, is then said a third time, except that now it coils back on its own ground as poetry, thus participating in an event of autofiguration, addressing us as a figure of poetizing" (41). It is by means of such folds that avatar (as function) appears and becomes available for consultation. This fold is *die Kehre*.

Hölderlin's saying of certain features of the river, evoking its geography and history, and the qualities of its flowing, enfold these three levels. Heidegger anticipates Virilio in his warning that the speed of technologies has collapsed the dimensions of time and space (no departure or arrival, no journey, no distance), but his answer is the opening constructed through poetizing (*Ort*). "The river is the locality of journeying. The river is the journeying of locality. These formulae evoke the impression that we are referring to entirely empty, universal relations. Contrary to this appearance, and in accordance with the word of the hymns, we must think definite and singular relations whose singularity is expressed clearly by way of the proper names that are named in the poem 'The Ister' " (*Hölderlin's Hymn* 43). Hölderlin's decision to use an historical (ancient) name for the Danube (Ister) activates the three levels in one word. Heidegger plays with etymology: Danube (Ister) = the root *ist, est, ister, ester* from which is generated the semantic field of "exist," "subsist," "persist" and the like. Heidegger's concern is that we not mistake ontology for psychology.

Heidegger finds compelling the power of this poem to evoke the historical destiny of the German people, who were gathered together by the force and power of the river to support life. The poet is able to use this historical gathering force of the river as a figure for the gathering power of the poetic word, to compose an image category, extending in turn to the writer and reader, who similarly are made coherent. The third dimension is the one that makes readers aware of their own power, their freedom, their potential, their capacity to act, to change, to intervene, to decide otherwise. Although nearly extinguished in the West, meditative thinking survived to some extent in Asian culture. *Ereignis*, Heidegger said, had most in common with the Tao. And despite Heidegger's insistence on the exceptional status of Hölderlin or Rilke, their poetizing, as noted, is a secret of all poetry. "In its connection of vision and thought we find the first secret of poetry's ability to quarry knowledge by mining the outer for inner ore" (Hirshfield 128). These devices are the tools of flash reason.

The opening (*Ort*, chora) is what concept avatar knows. To receive counsel, compose *Ort*. Walter Benjamin, taking advantage of German language, clarified our proposal. The kind of experience intimated through *Ort* is not *Erlebnis* (immediate perception), but *Erfahrung* (happening reflected through writing). My Allegory is not mimetic memory, but construction now, belated, metaleptic, retroactively finding the coherence of life lived. Proust identifies most directly the shape of time ontologized in electrate image metaphysics, and a host of modern philosophers have endorsed his experience as "unsurpassed." Moment is Proust's Time Regained.

> The truth surely was that the being within me which had enjoyed these impressions had enjoyed them because they had in them something that was common to a day long past and to now, because in some way they were extra-temporal, and this being made its appearance only when, through one of these identifications of the present with the past, it was likely to find itself in the one and only medium in which it could exist and enjoy the essence of things, that is to say: outside time. This explained why it was that my anxiety on the subject of my death had ceased at the moment when I had unconsciously recognized the taste of the little Madeleine, since the being

> which at that moment I had been was an extra-temporal being and therefore unalarmed by the vicissitudes of the future. This being had only come to me, only manifested itself outside of activity and immediate enjoyment, on those rare occasions when the miracle of an analogy had made me escape from the present. And only this being had the power to perform that task which had always defeated the efforts of my memory and my intellect, the power to make me rediscover days that were long past, the Time that was Lost. (*The Past Recaptured* 133)

Cayo Hueso

Flash reason (tested in our Allegory) puts involuntary memory into a device to locate this figure, the pattern of repetition, in temporality (my prudence). To put *Ort* (opening, chora, element, aura) to work, or at least the principle of aesthetic *qualia*, to undergo measure for myself, I consult Key West (accepting Wallace Stevens as guide). It is a portrait of prudence after Titian, meaning that it proposes a vital family anecdote for concept persona (but you are not bound by this choice). Occasional: two families, hinged by my son and daughter-in-law, spending the week before hurricane season, B&B. On Duval, looking in a shop window with large photographs of famous people (Young Elvis, JFK with Frank). Who is that man, the full-length portrait, wearing the Hawaiian shirt? We speculate in conversation. A native bystander says Jimmy Buffett. On the map mark his tone of voice. Pity? Contempt? Then we noticed Margaritaville next door.

The *daimon*'s way (Parmenides). The *daimonion* at least. A force addressing me. This is the dimension for receiving concept avatar, which is not the same in every epoch. Reason? That was before Utility. The ground before that was Heaven. You know the history. The Commodity today, but that is not it. A figure-ground reversal, for this "choragraphy" (the Gestalt graphics of flash reason beyond logic). We will appoint Lacan's *sinthome* eventually. The touristing families are important, as ground for the figure—the circum-stance (love, for short). *Il solito tran-tran di tutti i giorni* except to whom it may concern: everything.

I draw the map, not unlike the one in the Mel Fisher Museum, tracking *Nuestra Senora de Atocha* where it sank. What is an insight worth? It could be a pedagogical metaphor, like the rhizome of bees and flowers, nectar into honey in the hive, used by the medieval apprentices to guide the making of commonplace books. But those were topical, not choral. There is a dimension that electracy brings into appearance, although it will always have been t/here. Passing the cemetery on Windsor Lane, in the middle of the street, a small pink teddy-bear. Leave it be (fetish).

In Seven Fish for dinner, best food on the island? Worst setting? Small, dark, the ambiance is people packed in all talking at once. Notice not the conversation with your partner, inaudible in any case, but the enveloping roar, the noise parasite. Only for a momentito, a glimpse. The plane of immanence. Life a philosopher said simply, but that is too abstract: living. *Conatus* (striving prior to any subject or identity). Outside, the Neutral, stepping there to take thought as in times past a cigarette. What is this feeling, a thought without concept, a force without form (not thinkable, or only duly noted, within literacy). Key West as a whole, gathered t/here. Florida felt.

Where is the measure of this apprehension? It is singular, specific, momentary. A weak ontology, then (*undsoweiter*). In Cayo Hueso the measure (this reading) nonetheless is another rhizome that came (not alone) to the courtyard trees of the B&B, between six and seven in the evening, to feed on the seedpods abundantly offered by the China Palm. When he visited Key West in the 1830s, John James Audubon found eighteen birds he had not seen elsewhere, including the white-crowned pigeon. Endangered now, our host explained (I have a print rolled in a tube from the Audubon house). Endangered.

More is the experience given by this dimension. Every epoch takes it up in turn. Polis. God. Reason. Utility. Money. The universal today is empty, and to keep it from closing I put in a white-crowned pigeon. Reflective judgments start from here, from petals dropped by olive orchards. What we are given is the vehicle, and the tenor is more, something other, the invisible, a form for this matter, even if we call it a plane of immanence. Such is Flesh, in/visible at once, because we are immersed, a moebius outside-in. Today it must be generated out of pure aesthetics. Pure more, which is us. Life. Body and its by-product, the accidental spirit. Who speaks for the late J. J. Audubon? White-crowned pigeon in a China Palm. That's about the size of it. The plane of immanence marked in an emblem (pigeon + palm tree). A choral measure, gathering events into coherence. Today is the day (Mel Fisher t-shirt) for motto. That is the practice to be invented, to bring to the table the *daimonion* (your genius, to speak Latin). And this glass of wine. Ingenium escaping all abstraction.

Wallace Stevens, tell me, if you know, why, when the (pigeon-feeding) ended and we turned toward the town, tell why the glassy lights, the lights in the fishing boats at anchor there, as the night descended, tilting in the air, mastered the night and portioned out the sea, fixing emblazoned zones and fiery poles, arranging, deepening, enchanting night (the idea of order at Key West). That's right. Poetry is the new math. "Pathematics," someone suggested. The more schools reduce arts education, the less relevant they become (to electracy), guaranteeing an opportunity for the usurper, Entertainment. Commerce. To be tube. *The idea of order at Key West*, or anywhere, remains singular, to bring into the matrix the axis attraction-repulsion. It has to be put to work as an institution, this dimension of Time Regained, if well-being is to have a chance. *White-crowned pigeon in a China Palm* above; *today is the day* below. Prudence as endangered species.

Figure 3. "White-Crowned Pigeon @ Key West"

8 Enjoyment

Ethics

The White-crowned pigeon is an electrate *thing*. A primary task for concept avatar is as consultant on embodiment. This consultancy extends reflective judgment from the particular of my individual situation to the public sphere of global policy formation. It promotes a politics of well-being, understood as collective thriving by means of the values of manner. The attitude toward "body" manifested in the traditions of "descent" of spirit into flesh must be transformed in electracy, in which the axis of pleasure-pain is opened to ontology. Within the era of literacy, up to modernity, human subject formation developed as "self" at the individual level and "state" at the collective level (city-state through the manuscript era, and nation-state within print). Concept avatar, manager of a new prudence, assumes that individual and collective subjectivation are mutating. For literate subjects, good judgment included an intrinsic measure, discernible through a *sensus communis* (a shared access to sense, good sense, common sense). As Aristotle explained, any decision to act took place within a three-part matrix: the contingencies of how things happened to be in the circumstances of a situation; the precepts of a rational ethics; how things could be if humans fulfilled the potential of their nature, the telos of their final cause (MacIntyre 53). As MacIntyre complained, with reference to the emotivism of modern identity after Nietzsche, the third dimension of this matrix of judgment has disappeared: there is no telos, or at least no agreement on what human nature may be, by which to measure the appropriateness of a decision. Lacan, from within the discipline of psychoanalysis, proposes an answer that relates "emotivism" to an ontology. This issue is crucial to concept avatar, whose function is precisely to consult on the construction of electrate measure (beyond ends, without telos). Such is the responsibility of operant subject, symbiotically (one hopes) rhizomed with the destiny of *technics*.

To become what we are involves decision. As Hannah Arendt explained, Aristotle and the Greeks invented their new higher reason from an analogy with the know-how of craftsmen. Craftsmen started with a prototype, an idea, and created an artifact by means of the choices or options that Aristotle called *proairesis*, and which he articulated in terms of four causes: material (what is it made from); formal (what is its essence); efficient (what produced it); final (for what purpose). It is worth noting, in the context of MacIntyre's argument that selfhood up until modernity was experienced as inherently narrative, having naturally the coherence of a story within which character (virtue) was manifested in choices (226). This understanding no doubt motivated Roland Barthes to use Aristotle's term to name the code of action in his theory of narrative (*S/Z*). The Greeks had no words for "free will." Aristotle's reasoning led him to the still point of a prime mover, and Christian theologians were happy to name this place "God." Kant continued this structure as a guiding idea of "purpose" in the world, understood as anthropomorphism (not creationism).

Arendt's history of thought, retracing and updating the field outlined by Kant in his three Critiques (of pure, practical, and aesthetic reason), calls attention to the invention of concepts and behaviors to which flash reason also intends to contribute. Christian civilization, beginning with the writings of St. Paul, introduced a new mood of thought, free will, which included a state of mind different from the serenity (and melancholy) of contemplation valued by the Greeks. Will is tense, oriented toward the future, and assumes a capacity to act (Arendt 2: 38). Judeo-Christian theology required a principle of free will, in order to give believers an opportunity to choose good over evil and get credit for it through salvation. Acquinas formulated the decision as a practical syllogism: the ethical rule (thou shalt not steal); an opportunity or temptation to steal; the decision. The unforeseen consequence of this frame of conduct was the possibility of creation, of something new entering the world, a beginning, not merely a choice among existing options (108). This invention path is relevant to concept avatar, since an apparatus includes inventions of behavior as well as of equipment and logic. *You are this possibility.*

The next innovation in ethics (and ontology) was Kant's categorical imperative, duty as the moral, introducing a principle of indifference with respect to how the law is applied to a case: the moral law is something foreign in me; it must be possible to choose against my own interests. The paradox of this choice was the experience of freedom: that one is not determined by nature (biology, disposition). The final revision before our own moment was made by Bentham, who replaced the idealism of duty with an apparently more material understanding of human motivation: utility. Psychoanalysis problematizes this entire evolution by displacing the act of choice (decision) to the Unconscious. Although Christianity changed the worth of humility from negative for the Greeks to positive, the new virtue was not put to the test collectively until modernity. Freud itemized the blows to humankind's pride of place: Copernicus removed us from the center of the cosmos; Darwin showed we were made in the image not of God but of apes; and Freud himself showed that we are not even masters of our own thoughts and actions. He could have included Marx, who showed that our ideals are dictated by our position within the economic mode of production.

Now we confront the complexity of prudence. Lacan takes the measure of this progression. He shows that Kant's categorical imperative is better understood by Freud's notion of the superego. Freud's topological and dynamic models of the psyche diagrammed a possible opening for avatar functionality. The result is an equivalence between Kant's notion of the "good" and that of the infamous Marquis de Sade's "philosopher in the bedroom." The insight is that the moral law is founded on something more basic—desire (Eros and Thanatos)—that puts human choice and decision out of the reach of traditional virtue.

> Psychoanalysis thus introduces a new kind of problem for ethical reflection: not the ancient problem that we may live and act in ignorance of what is truly good for us, but the modern problem that there is something in our desire that goes beyond what would direct us to what we think we want for ourselves. In particular, it raises the question of fortune in our lives in a new way, for it links fortune not to the good we can know, but to the inherent morbidity in our desire which takes us on paths we can never regulate nor foresee. Psychoanalysis holds that the "truth" of our mortal destinies is not one for which there exists a general wisdom, a general means for adequating one's living to what is truly good for it. (Rajchman 36)

Is this inherent morbidity in our desire a matter for tragedy or comedy? That is where you come in. This observation poses a fundamental aporia for prudence (judgment). Psychoanalysis, in other words, is part of the general philosophical turn against the will found in modernity, and the search for another modality, not *proairesis*, free will, or determinism.

> Libidinal necessity, this great *ananke*, does not determine or predetermine what we become. Rather, it puts the unconscious to work; it supplies the unconscious with a chance to work. Libidinal necessity, Lacan says, means that our bodies never stop "writing themselves" in our destinies. Thus, though our fortune as erotic beings can never be foretold, the way it works itself out in the "censored chapters" of our histories can be interpreted. The "law" of "psychical causality" is then neither social nor psychological, but "structural." (39)

The new modality for a community, Rajchman adds, is no longer prudence, duty, or utility, but sublimation (creative energy displaced from eros) (70). Deliberation in electracy must understand conduct in the public sphere as lined with libidinal energy (the new moral imperative is: enjoy!) (67). The keyword is "energy." Rajchman's terminology (allusions to Fortune and Necessity) testifies to an increasing awareness of the forces at work in subject formation (the council of five demigods, with Elpis coming off the bench). Concept avatar personifies the whole council. We have met the Overwhelming, and it is us (our embodiment).

Category

Lacan introduces his ethics as part of an innovation in ontology—the invention of a new "thing," which is what especially recommends his work for electracy. His most important contribution in any case ultimately may be to ontology rather than psychology. But why shouldn't ontology be medicalized? His method in Seminar VII, devoted to the ethics of psychoanalysis, is to review certain aspects of the history of Western civilization, to get a feel for how his predecessors have managed to invent something by means of Eros. He learned from Heidegger not just a vocabulary but a method of ontology. Lacan's project, that is, includes opening a new dimension of being, or of beginning to provide a writing practice that renders accessible to thought and application a dimension of the Real that has resisted the best efforts of the previous apparatus to grasp and hold it. This dimension grounds the experience of attraction-repulsion, and is the axis (and energy) ontologized in electracy.

Heidegger's *Introduction to Metaphysics*—based on a series of lectures delivered at the University of Freiburg in 1935—provides a useful context for concept avatar relative to enjoyment. The paradox at the heart of Heidegger's project should be noted at the outset. His innovation was to shift the study of being from the register of pure reason (science) from where it had been practiced throughout the era of literacy, to the register of practical reason. He is, in other words, a philosopher of prudence in the tradition of Aristotle and Machiavelli. The paradox is that his own judgment in the conditions of his lived situation in Germany of the 1930s was flawed, and not just in retrospect. As others have pointed out, Heidegger's decision to become a Nazi put him in the company of a tradition of would-be philosopher-kings who thought they could influence a tyrant (the "flight from Syracuse," alluding to Plato's failed consultancy with a tyrant, before he retired to his Academy). He realized rather quickly (within a year or two) that National Socialism was not what he had imagined, and that his ability to influence its direction was a fantasy. Those critics who want to link the themes of Heidegger's philosophy to his biography are right, to the extent that he in fact produced an account of practical reason. To not have engaged with the events of his day would have been inauthentic, as if his theories were merely hypothetical or academic, rather than an ethics, a guide for actual living. The risk of *phronesis*, as Aristotle and others in the tradition frequently warned us, is that it is a virtue, based in disposition, and may be learned only with difficulty if at all. Prudence is not a logic, but a *savoir-y-faire*, and Heidegger lacked *sprezzatura*.

Nonetheless, Heidegger's framing of the history of metaphysics is implicitly a grammatology. In our context, we may see that Heidegger's arguments for the end of metaphysics, is better understood as a case for the closure of literacy. As much as he despises the techno-scientific conditions—the age of the world picture—brought about by the complete triumph of the Greek order, he is aware that it is this new order of equipment that created the possibility for a paradigm shift. *Introduction to Metaphysics* outlines the terms of the new direction. The main argument is that the kind of category created in the Academy and Lyceum by Plato and Aristotle represents a decision, an historical choice with profound consequences that determined the course of Western civilization. Concept avatar concerns this dimension of collective historical decision, as well as individual decision (the ambition of Internet wisdom is to correlate these registers). Aristotle's decision to model his invention of the "thing" on the practice of judicial indictment (forensics) left open another possible beginning for literacy. Heidegger's goal, his project of "destruction" (deconstruction) of the history of metaphysics, is to recover and make available again the "other beginning," the "road" (method) tried by the Pre-Socratics but not taken. "Logos and physis move apart, but logos does not yet break away from physis. This is to say, it does not yet confront the being of the essent in such a way, it does not yet take such an attitude 'toward' it, as to appoint itself (as reason) a court of justice over being; it does not yet undertake the task of determining and regulating the being of the essent" (*Introduction* 178).

The important insight for us is Heidegger's point that the Greeks in their invention of philosophy as a practice of the new technology of alphabetic writing encountered or noticed a new dimension of the real that had not been accessible in the oral apparatus: being. Being is an emergent feature (the more) of written language. This fact is crucial as a relay for inventing electracy. The first experience of being in the context of writing was that of disclosure, the upsurge of the world as a force of energy. Heidegger used the term *aletheia* to name this effect of an emergence out of concealment, presencing from nothing into something, while *phusis* names the force of nature. Being involves two moments at least: the apprehension of this appearing; taking the measure of what has appeared after it is already there. The first is a revelation, an epiphany that something is. The second asks after what the thing is, and itemizes the properties, determines which attributes constitute the essence and which the accidents. Noteworthy in Heidegger's reading of the spaces of these two stages is his use of the term *chora*.

> That wherein something becomes refers to what we call "space." The Greeks had no word for "space." This is no accident; for they experienced the spatial on the basis not of extension but of place (topos); they experienced it as chora, which signifies neither place nor space but that which is occupied by what stands there. The place belongs to the thing

> itself. Each of all the various things has its place. That which becomes is placed in this local "space" and emerges from it. But in order that this should be possible, "space" must be free from all the modes of appearance that it might derive from anywhere. For if it were similar to any of the modes of appearance that enter into it, it would in receiving forms of antithetical or totally different essence, manifest its own appearance and so produce a poor realization of the model. That wherein the things in process of becoming are placed must precisely not present an aspect and appearance of its own. (The reference to the passage in *Timaeus* is intended not only to clarify the link between the *paremphainon* and the *on*, between also-appearing and being as permanence, but at the same time to suggest that the transformation of the barely apprehended essence of place [topos] and of chora into a "space" defined by extension was initiated by the Platonic philosophy, i.e. in the interpretation of being as idea. Might chora not mean: that which abstracts itself from every particular, that which withdraws, and in such a way precisely admits and "makes place" for something else?). (66)

This disclosive withdrawal, a creative negation, is the movement that Bloom discovers in the revisionary ratios of the modernist crisis poem (the writing opens a kenotic space in history). This opening movement is not benign, however, as noted in some of its synonyms (abyss, void, catastrophe). The Aristotelian categories focused on taking the measure of the properties to determine the nature of what appeared, after it appeared and was already there. This metaphysics of being forgot about Being, the event of coming into appearance, the creation of the space in which things showed a face. Heidegger's proposal for the new epoch (electracy in our terms) is to recover this experience of the event of emergence as the point of departure for a new orientation to the Real. Avatar "emergency" includes this "emergence." The model for this new orientation to things will not be the court of law, as it was for Aristotle (turning "indictment" into logic), but art in general, and the poetic in particular (in whatever medium), in order to capture the disclosive withdrawal through the manner of appearing. A shorthand version of the difference would match literate "indictment" (correctness) with electrate "epiphany" (insight). Being happens in language, in the relationship between spoken and written discourse.

If literate metaphysics appropriated a forensic rhetoric (propositional logic) for its operational inferences, electrate metaphysics takes as its point of departure epideictic rhetoric, the poetic operations of praise and blame of persons, places, things. And if literate practice favored the visual sense and forgot about the aural dimension of its "category," this sound sense is the site of the other beginning (for Heidegger). The instruction is: synesthesia, the full sensorium as resource.

Appearance

The pre-Socratic Greeks identified three ontological paths: being, non-being (becoming, nothing), appearance. The historically determining decision of philosophy was to take the path of being, reject the path of non-being, and work to reduce the sway of appearance (the realm of *doxa*, illusion, error, opinion: in short, of practical reason). Appearance is not nothing, and not error as such, but it shows only one face that masks essence or truth of its nature. Philosophy worked to take off the mask. In the age of the world picture, however, the society of the spectacle constituting the electrate public sphere, takes the way of appearance, that Heidegger associates with modern "celebrity."

> Truth is inherent in the essence of being. To be an essent—this comprises to come to light, to appear on the scene, to take one's [its] place, to produce something. Nonbeing, on the other hand, means: to withdraw from appearing, from presence. The essence of appearing includes coming-on-the-scene and withdrawing, hither and thither in the truly demonstrative, indicative sense. Being is thus dispersed among the manifold essents. These display themselves as the momentary and close-at-hand. In appearing it gives itself an aspect, *dokei*. Doxa means aspect, regard [*Ansehen*], namely the regard in which one stands. If the regard, in keeping with what emerges in it, is a distinguished one, *doxa* means fame and glory. In Hellenistic theology and in the *New Testament doxa theou*, Gloria Dei, is God's grandeur. To glorify, to attribute regard to, and disclose regard means in Greek: to place in the light and thus endow with permanence, being. For the Greeks glory was not something additional which one might or might not obtain; it was the mode of the highest being. For moderns glory has long been nothing more than celebrity and as such a

> highly dubious affair, an acquisition tossed about and distributed by the newspapers and the radio—almost the opposite of being. (102–03)

Electracy as the apparatus of our image spectacle necessarily commits to a metaphysics of appearances. Édouard Glissant captured this Heideggerian insight in a phrase that clarifies our usage of "flash" reason to name electrate deliberative rhetoric. The phrase is *agents d'éclat,* happily translated by Betsy Wing as "flash agents." Discussing Glissant's use of neologisms, she gives "flash agents" as the example, noting that she rejected a list of alternatives such as "dazzlers" or "glamour mongers."

> This phrase includes, but is not lmited to, our category The Media, with all that this implies for us. But, as always in *Poetics of Relation,* activity in a concrete world is important; physical notions of the dazzling, explosive power of this agency cannot be left out. Think: flash in the pan for shallowness, the strobing flash of momentary glamour, the news flash in a sound byte from our sources. Glissant creates these metaphorical noun phrases to name the reality he sees emerging in the world. (xiii)

Flash reason constructs The Media Spectacle into an ontology of second nature.

Lacan's most influential notion—the gaze—places his ontology on this third path of appearance and regard. He is concerned specifically with the being of the human subject, engaged in a struggle for recognition with the Other. Aristotle placed the being of his categories in the world. Kant's Copernican revolution relocated the categories to the human mind. Now Lacan problematizes that history with a closer look at that mind as "unconscious." The revised site is the sexuated body. He remains within ontology, however, by proposing that the unconscious is structured like a language. His inquiry concerns specifically human essence as speaking beings, and the contribution that embodiment makes to language. He agrees that being happens in and through language, and his addition to the history of being is to investigate the full participation in ontology of the human body, with language as the crossroads or interface between the outer external environment and the inner material physicality of the individual person, especially the sexed nature of human existence. The subject in this framing is nothing substantive or permanent, but "punctiform," momentary, and relational. In fact, what especially recommends his account to electracy is his argument that the human subject is an emergent effect of the poetic operations of language: the condensation and displacement manifested in the conductive work of symptoms of all sorts are directly translatable into the figures and tropes of rhetoric, summarized as metaphor and metonymy (Bloom refered to Lacan in his own review of this appropriation of rhetoric by psychoanalysis to describe the unconscious). We will see that he attempts to evoke an understanding of chora, and hence like everyone else who has ever addressed this region, is forced to use the "bastard" language of figuration, as Plato said. Like Plato, who introduced chora to metaphysics, Lacan also uses mathematics to account for its operations, with the difference that Lacan understands his appropriations of topology and set theory as figural (not "topology" but "topologerie").

The first lesson Lacan provides for thinking with the gaze is his own exploitation of eloquence (style), in order to make his thought memorable. In his television appearance he claimed to be mystified by what attracted the crowds to his seminars, but his theories already answered his own question, since he formulated the ontological question not as "why is there something rather than nothing," but, "what am I, for the Other," or, "what does the Other expect of me." "Recognition" in every sense of the term is in play in human being, with "love" in all its vicissitudes as the primary conduct that is the prototype for all individual and collective association. This theme of attraction-repulsion (economimesis) is of central importance to an image ontology. Socrates is an emblematic figure for everything to do with this question, with the bit from the *Symposium* being one of the touchstone references. Alcibiades, lamenting his inability to seduce the sage, compares him to a statue of Silenus: ugly on the outside, but holding within a treasure (*agalma*). The structure of the question is all here: a space containing a value. Subject with Other (another relay for player with avatar).

Thing

Lacan takes up Heidegger's project as much as he does Freud's, or he takes it up by means of Freud's discovery of the unconscious (the uncanny as boundary object). His contribution, keeping in mind that Aristotle is credited with inventing the "thing," is the creation of a new understanding of "thing" and another "object" that fundamentally transforms ontology. To use the term "ontology" here is to emphasize that this "thing" and "object" open a new dimension of the Real, make this dimension exist as reality, to be developed on behalf of human well-being (or not), just as literate metaphysics opened up the material dimension that historically became science. Thus the usages of language that Lacan proposes and that are being reviewed here are "ontological," in the same way that the Greeks exploited certain aspects of Greek grammar and syntax to produce topical thinking. Inventing flash reason works by analogy to propose choral thinking, that extends writing to include the imaging technologies of electracy.

Lacan positions his project within the same questions informing the old prudence, in order to show the implications and relevance of his different conclusions. The tradition of prudence as practical reason and particular intellect from Plato through Kant relied upon common sense (in the richer sense covered by *sensus communis*) as the basis for judgment in the public sphere. Common sense grounded the innate capacity for judgment on the human ability to recognize beauty in the human and natural world, including sexual desire as a point of departure for "*Bildung*" or education. The tradition proposed a direct continuum between beauty (aesthetics) and ethical and political judgment (decorum). The prototype of this pedagogy in practice is Boticelli's *The Birth of Venus* (a mnemonic trot on Neoplatonic philosophy created for a Medici Prince). Modernity registered the breakdown of this ratio with the notion of the sublime. Lacan draws upon the resources of psychoanalysis (and all the liberal arts and sciences) to introduce "sublimation" into this fracture, and in doing so opens the path to a new common sense (a new Gestalt).

The seminar of 1959–60 reviewed a certain history of Western civilization, to understand how society in the past managed the forces of desire. His understanding of desire resonates with Heidegger's account of the Greek's original insight into being as *phusis*, an upsurging power, with nature experienced as overpowering, overwhelming (sublime).

> But this necessity of disaster can only subsist insofar as what must shatter is driven into such a being-there. Man is forced into such a being-there, hurled into the affliction of such being, because the overpowering as such, in order to appear in its power, requires a place, a scene of disclosure. The es-

> sence of being-human opens up to us only when understood through this need compelled by being itself. The being-there [*Dasein*] of historical man means: to be posited as the breach into which the preponderant power of being bursts in its appearing, in order that this breach itself should shatter against being. (Introduction to Metaphysics 162–63)

In short, *you* disclose (instantiate) disaster. Problems B Us (motto of the EmerAgency).

We should keep in mind that Heidegger is attempting an ontology of practical reason (a contradiction in terms for Aristotle), and his coining of the term "*Dasein*" (being-there) for individual human existence is intended to indicate his concern with what it is to be situated in a particular time and place (chora is existential). To articulate the strange (uncanny) quality of *Dasein* Heidegger and Lacan both refer to the tragedy of *Antigone,* and especially the commentary of the Chorus on Antigone's fate or destiny, as revealing the full measure of the uncanniness of being. The relevance of *Antigone* for Lacan is in part to register the ontological import of his theory, and to situate his ethics against old prudence. Tragedy, that is, is a cultural form that confronts a dimension of experience named *Até* (blindness in the individual leads to disaster for the community). Greek rules of prudence, inscribed on the walls of the temple at Delphi, recommended know thyself and avoid excess, and tragedy shows how difficult it is to hold to this wisdom. Avatar in any case is not "thyself."

Heidegger cites the judgment by the Chorus, the lesson drawn from Antigone's imprudent behavior. Man in his strangeness, the Chorus observes, is able to venture over the land and the seas and extend mastery over all places and creatures: "'Everywhere journeying, inexperienced and without issue, he comes to nothingness.' The essential words are pantoporos aporos. The word poros means: passage through . . . , transition to . . . , path. . . . Beyond all this he becomes the strangest of all being because, without issue on all paths, he is cast out of every relation to the familiar and befallen by *Até*, ruin, catastrophe" (151–52). This ruin is death, mortality, the given nature that culture strives to forget or evade. Freud used Oedipus as the paradigm for intersubjective identity formation. The key ingredient of tragedy that recommends it as a representation of human reality is *Até*, (the aspect of human destiny that has to do with everything that resists the good sense of reason). Lacan translates the term aporia, impasse, as "screwed." "He advances toward nothing that is likely to happen, he advances and he is 'artful,' but he is aporos, always 'screwed.' He knows what he's doing. He always manages to cause things to come crashing down on his head" (*Seminar* 275). What can "prudence" be in such a cosmology?

Antigone and Creon both cross the line of prudence and are destroyed in what in our context suggests the politics and ethics defined by a dilemma over policy formation (the occasion triggering the confrontation, the rebellion and death of Antigone's brother, Polynices). This action of transgression and inhibition maps limit, forces measure to appear, the upsurge of threshold. Another example, central to the point Lacan wants to make about ethics, is the invention of courtly love that hybridized the Greek warrior ethos with the Christian virtues. Lacan uses it to demonstrate the operation of sublimation, manifesting the functioning of the Thing (*das Ding*). The Lacanian Thing is a field of relationships, a force not an essence, not a substance with attributes, and like Heidegger's *Dasein* in the midst of the overwhelming, the subject is situated within this field. To represent the structuration of the field Lacan uses topology (the moebius strip, klein bottle, torus) to show what he calls the "extimate" arrangement of the Thing. The Thing is not an object standing over against a subject, but is at once outside and inside the person. Here is the key to the avatar effect. Concept avatar thinks extimacy.

Modern poets have engaged with this field experience of *Dasein* since Baudelaire, the feeling of mood in which something outside intimates the inside, in which the visible reveals the invisible, and have named it in their various poetics negative capability, correspondences, illumination, objective correlative, *Weltinnenraum*, vortex. Lacan's thing is polluted with subject. Lacan wants to foreground the ontological import of these poetics, to argue that the experience of the uncanny, in which something strange outside of me is at the same time recognized as belonging to me, is the very event of *phusis*, the upsurge of being, called to our attention by Heidegger. The troubadours who invented courtly love worked with this extimate experience. Their invention of a new conduct of love was emblematic for Lacan's Thing, with the troubadours modeling the need to invent behaviors, attitudes, as part of the apparatus. The Thing, like chora, is neither perceptible nor intelligible, in itself, but it is the place of encounter of becoming with being. It is the force of desire entangled with the repetition of drive. It is the energy that operant subject must tap to manage *technics*. The troubadours made this force manifest by elevating women, who in medieval society were of lowly status, to the position of the Lady, the Belle Dame Sans Merci, who was cruel in withholding her favors from the suitor. This figure is a defensive trope. In Lacan's terms, the Lady exemplifies the special object, the object other, *objet petit a* (*autre*), which is often written object (a) or *a*. Let us use what the keyboard offers to register this notion: @—as if the "a" were encased in the "o" of other. The @ may be anything whatever, nothing of any account, something like a fetish object invested with emotional energy (cathexis). Its elevated status, established by the narrative of a fantasy, shows indirectly that the Thing is functioning,

A principal attribute of the Thing is this choral opening of a space, a hole in the Real, within which the @ appears (its function being to maintain this opening, as relay of desire). Lacan alludes again to Heidegger (his essay on the Thing) to articulate this structure. Heidegger's example of the Thing was a clay jug or vase used by the Greeks in a ceremony to pour out a libation to the gods. In Aristotle's terms, the proprium of the jug, determining its essence, is its capacity to contain liquid. Heidegger switches to the other metaphysics, concerned with the upsurge of the overwhelming, which is conveyed in the ceremony by the libation, the sacrifice of the wine that reveals the existence of the gods in the narrative of the mortals. *Dasein* is a four-fold relationship in this scene, interlacing extimately gods and mortals, heaven and earth. What interests Lacan in Heidegger's scene is the role of the jug as signifier—the use of its containing power to signify something else of a different order. "It creates the void and thereby introduces the possibility of filling it. Emptiness and fullness are introduced into a world that by itself knows not of them. It is on the basis of this fabricated signifier, this vase, that emptiness and fullness as such enter the world, neither more nor less, and with the same sense" (*Seminar* 120).

Part of Lacan's point, in his attempt to include in ontology the dimension of the body and its desires and drives, is to observe how sublimation (fantasy individual and collective) mediates the Thing. He shows us how language (speaking writing, the signifier) opens this dimension of desire to access a new kind of sense that he punningly names "jouis-sense," packing in this portmanteau French *jouissance* (enjoyment, orgasm), with plays on "I hear" (*j'ouis*), evoking also the context of sense, good sense, common sense. In electracy we must learn to think and write *bliss sense*. The cavity of the jug allegorizes the relationship between the hole opened in the Real by language, the signifier specifically, and the orifices of the body, articulated through social disciplines into the erogenous zones. Yes, holes or interface openings of the body are central to electrate metaphysics, since every previous metaphysics did everything possible to deny and suppress flesh (for good reason, recalling the fault of Epimetheus). The relationship of these openings is further explored using the topological configurations of knot theory, with the loops formed by the knots figuring the part-objects of the body and their functions. What the troubadours (the "trou" sounding their connection with the "hole") are demonstrating is how to manage the lack or absence, the negativity, from which springs human energy—the lack named desire that may never by satisfied. The courtier uses the fantasy of the Lady protectively, to maintain a safe distance from the Thing, that in one version is the truth of human mortality, the death drive, the reality named in the pun connecting screwing with being fucked (over). Lacan's interest in the hole, the lack, and its management in sublimation, is that paradoxically it opens the possibility of freedom from the determinism of nature. These theories unpack the conditions of the electrate axis of pleasure-pain, the complexity, to be taken into account in flash reason. There is a psychic equivalent to the atomic energy at work in Things (*jouissance*). The Allegory of Prudence records an appearance of this energy, a persona of concept avatar.

9 Letter

Fantasy

What is the wisdom guiding human "absensibility" (negentity)? The absolute center of flash reason, concept avatar, that which is to electracy what contradiction is to literate logic, is the hole as logic (someday this will drive a global economy). The structure operated through flash reason includes three registers: Moment (Time Regained) as the more made reality; the hole as logical device managing information in this shape; *jouissance* as the embodied energy augmented in this ontology (plus the *technics* of the apparatus). Lacan explains how hole manifests itself as inference procedure:

> In Freud, a dream is not a nature that dreams, an archetype that stirs, a matrix for the world, a divine dream, or the heart of the world. Freud describes a dream as a certain knot, an associative network of analyzed verbal forms that intersect as such, not because of what they signify, but thanks to a sort of homonymy. It is when you come across a single word at the intersection of three of the ideas that come to the subject that you notice that the important thing is that word and not something else. It is when you have found the word that concentrates around it the greatest number of threads in the mycelium that you know it is the hidden centre of gravity of the desire in question. That, in a word, is the point I was talking about just now, the nodal point where discourse forms a hole. (*My Teaching* 28)

Player and avatar gather around this hole that, like the black holes of astrophysics, is a manifestation of energy. In a word, that is It. *Flash reason*: this is how and why it works (I laughed when I got it): the functionality of hole.

Chora is *positive immanent material nothing.* We celebrate this fundamental ontology every day. We live it without (necessity of) knowing. It is given, there is (*es gibt, il y a*) a hole, primordial gap, and you are It. Through avatar you play the hole, descend into hole; avatar personifies hole. Synonyms for hole besides chora include entelechy, monad, *conatus, Dasein.* Functionally hole is potentiality, the virtual dimension of event. It is the fault of Epimetheus, condemning humanity to becoming what it is, since there is no essence (or only retrospectively). Is the gap a chaos brought into order, or a clearing opened in plenitude? Both and neither, or rather a dynamic breathing, rhythm (*ruthmos*). Chora names this dynamic *disclosive withdrawal*, the movement by means of which you experience your own activity in the world (the nothing doing). The paradox and mystery of this zero is its power as an active force, whose organizing virtue is experienced in one of its purest forms in any sport involving the configuration of hole, ball, pole, strike (stroke, throw, gesture). The strike zone in baseball is prototypical, manifesting the templum marked in air, in imagination, around it appearing the region of the game (ritual) entire, field drawn out as choros (the dance floor at Knossos designed by Daedalus), the rules and the umpire adjudicating the event, the players, fans, the institution, the way of life ramifying out into culture and society. Sport as secular ritual, as liturgy.

The historical prototype is polo, invented in Ancient Persia. The sacred dimension of this game as ritual provided an allegory of life: you are the ball, the club is chance, the goal is destiny, god is the player (not you, you are not the player but the object in play). In dream logic (hole), we understand that we are the addressee of every aspect of the scene. The word "polo" means "ball," derived from Tibetan "*pulu.*" This allegory was made most explicit in *The Ball and the Polo Stick,* by Arifi of Herat, a fifteenth-century Sufi account of ecstatic, self-sacrificing love (Huson, 21). Huson notes that the allegory is invoked also in the *Rubaiyat* of Omar Khayyam (eleventh-century Sufi poet and astronomer) to figure human helplessness before god. The added value in our context is that the emblems representing the four elements making possible polo play (ball, stick, hole or goal, and stroke) are the historical basis for the four suits of playing cards, most importantly the four suits of the minor arcana of the Tarot (pentacles, wands, cups, swords). Tarot (along with the *I Ching*) are complete image metaphysics, primary sources available for retrieval as relays for an Internet wisdom system. Divination is how the relationship between player and avatar was managed in the pre-modern habitus. A task for concept avatar is the secularization and updating of these traditional image metaphysics, to do for electrate civilization what the oracles did for pre-modern cultures.

A purpose of concept avatar is apprenticeship in hole management. Electrate prudence (concept avatar) finds one model for managing the three ecstasies of time in the clinical practice of psychoanalysis, which deploys the experience of "transference." Transference is the ersatz love (identification) that arises between the analysand (patient) and analyst (doctor) during the course of treatment (the talking cure). In fact, transference could be described as an apprenticeship in prudence, because of the way the patient is brought to undergo the relationship among memories of the past, present circumstances, and future actions. Psychoanalysis contributes to electracy by focusing on encultured embodiment. This capacity of the body for *jouissance* is ontologized in electracy (as a dimension of reality open to augmentation as civilization). The unconscious is a theory of memory, after all.

The argument is that an initial experience of satisfaction in infancy or early childhood (such as suckling at the breast) produces an event that marks the body and creates a "facilitation" or path that directs later behavior. Certainly body orifices are holes, but not "hole" as such. "Dis/Satisfaction" is ontological in electracy, and we need to understand exactly how it functions. Commerce within Entertainment constitutes the vanguard in this enterprise. Concept avatar is a direct response to this institutionalization of electracy (this is *avatar emergency*). The uncanniness of desire results from this creation of a unary trait in the unconscious, for when some detail of present circumstances matches this trait the punctiform subject emerges, shows itself in the manner of *phusis*. For the treatment to succeed, the analyst must be in the position of the Lady in courtly love, that is, as the object-cause-of-desire, the analysand's object @, in order for the Thing to be inferred. Here is the insight that is counter-intuitive, and that resists literate intelligibility: the earliest bit of satisfaction formats hole, and may be ontologized through the little sensations of modernist arts.

The potentiality of electracy emerges in this encounter of satisfaction, sensation, language and design. Part of the value of psychoanalysis as cure is the relay it provides for avatar functionality: by occupying the hole (by playing the dummy) the analyst learns to manage transference (prudence). Here is another analogy for player with avatar: consciousness with the unconscious (analysand with analyst).

Lacan evokes the idea of traces, inscribed in a contingent way on the body, that come from elsewhere. Psychoanalysis demonstrates that the grounding of this knowledge boils down to the fact that the *jouissance* of its acquisition is the very same as the *jouissance* of its experiencing. The body (or rather parts of that body) "knows" something, because it enjoys this something, and this enjoyment brings about an inscription of both this knowledge and this *jouissance* on (part of) the body itself. This inscription does not belong to the signifying order (and, hence, not to the Other) but is brought about through what Lacan tries to understand with the "letter" (Verhaeghe 120). Electracy brings this inscription beyond signification into ontology and metaphysics, to be enhanced through the institutions of the apparatus as augmented (mixed) reality.

Literate metaphysics, thematized most fully by Aristotle, determined Being as substance (what is), articulated between essence and accident. The object @ is not a substance or essence (not a literate thing). The actual object, attribute, or trait is the trigger of a time image, which recommends it as a guide for prudence within flash reason. Proust's involuntary memory is the prototype of the dialectical image, simultaneously past and present (sensations of the madeleine dipped in tea; the uneven paving stones; the clanking of a spoon against a plate). Freud's case studies are valuable in showing how a particular scene triggers a fantasy: a maid on her hands and knees scrubbing a floor, seen from the rear, as in the case of the Wolfman. These examples are generalized as operators of hole. The function of concept avatar is to map these triggers, whose firing makes accessible (and hence open to revision) the forces structuring habitus. It is an energy not directly accessible, any more than is atomic energy. Flash reason is a rhetoric of trigger devices supporting creative innovation (browsing, categorial clustering organized by shared emotion) in networked experience ontology. The object @ manifests itself in everyday experience within the scenario of a fantasy, which is a kind of *sensus communis* (Gestalt). Part of the relevance of the object @ for prudence is that Lacan theorized it using Aristotle's model of causality. The experience of "encounter" associated with love (desire) falls within the sense of "destiny" also addressed in tragedy. The point for prudence is to understand the place of decision and judgment still functional in human events. Aristotle argued that the difference between fortune and chance was that some human choice had to be included within the accidents of a situation.

The symptom is a memorial to a choice, a decision, but one that has been shifted to the unconscious. Fantasies form around an object @, in a scenario that condenses all three dimensions of time: 1. an impression in a present situation arouses desire; 2. the desire is connected with a memory of an originary satisfaction; 3. the imagination creates a future situation in which the desire is accomplished in an action. "Desire can exploit an occasion offered in the present in order to sketch an image of the future based on a model from the past" (Eleb 71). This definition clarifies the similarity among prudence, fantasy and policy formation, in which planners spin out various scenarios of future action, relative to lessons drawn from past events and their outcomes. The old prudence, we could say, has been shifted from an action of character to a defense mechanism. The fantasy is diagrammed as a vortex, a circulation around the Thing, the lost cause, the lack or chora opened in the Real by (infinite) desire. The Allegory of Prudence maps the hole. Is this too much baggage to carry back to Orchard @ Bridge?

Sinthome

Patients seek treatment when there is a disturbance in the usual coping mechanisms (fantasy). A symptom is a "lived epiphany" (Harari 69). Its intensity is a source of enjoyment, but at some point its influence on behavior may become troubling enough to cause one to seek treatment. Freud's case history of an obsessional neurotic known as the Rat Man is exemplary. A typical aspect of this condition is an inability to make a decision, or the deferral of a choice (hence the frequent allusion to *Hamlet* in the literature). The Rat Man's present dilemma was which of two women to marry, and his inability to make a choice. The anxiety associated with a marriage decision is central to Kafka's situation, including his own apprenticeship to Kierkegaard's rejection of his fiancé, Regine. A fantasy that the Rat Man had lived with for some time was motivated by a story he had been told while serving in the military of a torture in which rats chewed into a prisoner's anus. The importance of psychoanalysis for electracy is not only because of the logic of hole that it constructed out of dream work, poetry, misprisions, jokes and the like, but because it discovered how the sexed body expresses itself (*jouissance*) in this way. No previous paradigm granted ontological respect to something like fantasies of an anal rat torture, but this dimension of possibility is fundamental to the aesthetic axis of attraction-repulsion as force operators of *technics*. Fantasy is ontological. Freud, as a post-Champollion practitioner of emblematics, understood the fantasy scene as not mimetic but as an image-rebus, carrying a signifier. The signifying element of the scene was the "Rat" syllable/sound. The animal (*Ratten* = rats) was an active image in a mnemonics joining a set of words including this syllable: *Raten* (installments), *Spielratte* (gambling), *heiraten* (to marry). Freud referred to this punning echo as a "verbal bridge" (Freud, *Three Case Histories* 70). The "Rat Bridge" has become emblematic of this conductive signification in general. Nietzsche's *Rätsel* (riddle, puzzle, mystery, enigma) appears in this series as well. Rat is hole. *Der Rat* = counsel. Player with Rat.

At the end of his career Lacan explicitly associated his therapy with the history of prudence by declaring that the goal of the treatment was to learn how to do something with one's symptom. His phrase is, *savoir-y-faire*. "*Savoir-y-faire* means something like 'dealing with it,' with connotations of 'getting rid of it,' 'untying oneself from it'; it does not involve learning a skill, but sorting something out, getting rid of a burden or irritation. It thus implies an unknotting or denounement" (Harari 121). The "y" in the formula echoes the "y" in the famous essay on the agency of the unconscious, in which Lacan makes use of the conductive signifier, including the shape of the letter, to move from the *arbre* (tree) of Saussure's example of a sign, to the *barre* or line separating the sign into signifier/signified, to the bifurcated pathway in Christian iconography representing the choice between virtue and vice (Chaitin, 43). The treatment aims at changing the analysand's relationship with and attitude toward *jouissance* (attitude adjustment). To recognize the symptom as a trope of destiny, as "belonging-to-me" (echoing Heidegger's *Ereignis*, one of whose senses is "enowning"), is to take responsibility for one's history. Own your symptom, to use current parlance. Symptom in this changed perspective becomes *sinthome*, the word for "symptom" in Medieval French (time of the troubadours). In short, Lacan endorses Nietzsche's program (to become what you are), and goes into detail about the difficulties of implementation.

Lacan acknowledges that he does not know exactly the nature of this know-how or *sprezzatura* (in our context), but the model for it he learned from James Joyce, especially *Finnegans Wake*. This relay makes sense in the context of the ontological hole as verbal bridge. "I let fairevieews in on slobodens," to quote at random from the text, "but ranked rothgardes round wrathmindsers; I bathandbaddend on mendacity and I corocured off the unoculated" Lacan recognized in Joyce's style the Rat Bridge of symptomology; that Joyce exploited all the musical and poetic devices of the poetic function, pushed to the extreme of nonsense, that is, for their own sake, without concern for the signifieds of meaning. Julia Kristiva, in her *Revolution in Poetic Language,* influenced by Lacan, calls this "semiotic" dimension of language "chora." The theory is that language supports a dual process—part meaning (signified) and part *jouissance* (signifier), with the latter associated with "being." Any linguistic practice carries a libidinal lining in this musical register of sound, tone, rhythm, voice (*Stimme*). The famous slips and parapraxes exploited by Freud in his *Psychopathology of Everyday Life* connect at this level, retracing the mnemonic tricks of premodern orators. Aristotle exploited the grammatical feature of paronymy ("wisdom is a paronym of wise") to support his experiment to "say being in many ways." Psychoanalysis continues this experiment, using the resources of language revealed by vanguard writers as well as neurotics and psychotics to open the body to ontology.

Lacan realized in his study of Joyce that the writer had learned how to *savoir-y-faire*, how to enjoy his symptom. Joyce's biography, that is, reflected all the attributes of the foreclosure of the Name-of-the-Father, the loss of the phallus, found commonly among neurotics, if not psychotics (a mutation in habitus and *dharma*). At one level the strategy was just that of sublimation—supplement the phallus (the symbolic measure) by making a name for oneself by becoming a famous author. Joyce went further, by pushing his style to the limits of language and into the nonsense of pure signifiers. His method was the macaronic pun, punning across languages, combined with portmanteau neologisms. Joyce uprooted the quilting point of his symptom, it seems, so he avoided the impasse of neurosis. The quilting point of meaning is gone, in the Wake. What then provides its undeniable coherence? The object @, joining letter and signifier, preserving a piece of the Real in the Symbolic (discourse). The implication for individual and collective identity formation, in the context of the apparatus, is profound. The electrate category emerges at the opposite pole of the literate one. It is not universal, but is a *sinthome*, a non-sense letter sported by a particular body. In Lacan's topologerie, the object @ as *sinthome* is graphed as a trefoil knot, with the loops or rings of the three categories of *Dasein* (Real, Symbolic, Imaginary) knotted by a forth ring or clasp, without which the other three loops would separate, fall apart. The fourth ring is *sinthome*.

It is important to keep in mind that *writing* is ontological, meaning that the potential of language to generate hole meaning constructs and brings into reach a certain reality; not the reality of techno-science (as was the case with the ontology emergent through propositional logic), but a reality of attraction-repulsion (*jouissance*), whose institutional instantiation, at this stage, is primarily Entertainment. It is important to note that sinthome is just the most recent formulation of the fatal tradition covered by concept avatar.

> The compulsion of the soul Leonardo describes in these terms [the tendencey of artists to repeat themselves] is of the same kind as the *conatus* of an element toward its natural *locus* in the ancient cosmos, it is a natural inclination the soul cannot but comply with, like the souls of Dante's penitents, which refashion their bodies out of air as soon as they are assigned to their temporary destination. Leonardo's "judgment" is therefore to be regarded as a power rather akin to Goethe's *daimon* than to Freud's unconscious—if one needs look for a metempsychosis of the concept. For the word *giudizio* must not be taken here in a strictly psychological, but rather in a "wholly naturalistic" sense, as referring to a natural inclination that connot be persuaded. . . . A suitable *trait d'union* between Leonardo's and Goethe's insights is provided by Shaftesbury's enthusiastic aphorism: The characteristic is all in all." Daimon is, according to Goethe's own gloss to the *Urworte*, precisely "the characteristic, through which each one distinguishes oneself from everybody else in spite of an however great similarity;" while, at the same time, this identifying trait vouches for "the immutability of the individual." (Stimilli, 51)

What exactly is the "letter" in Lacan's ontology? The mathematical analogy comes from set theory. The subject is a function, that is, an operation applied to a collection of otherwise unrelated signifiers. Here is the new category: not shared traits or properties showing essence, but a gathering around a hole in the Real activated by the irreducible desire of this speaking being, who, in speaking, "enjoys."

The unity of this scene is provided by the "want-to-be" of the subject (Chaitin 127). This being is created, invented, through the subject's *savoir-y-faire.* Lacan drew also upon grammatology, studying the history of writing to understand the formation of the unconscious, of a writing in, with, and through the body. He observed that writing systems were formed by analogy; letters were distilled from other uses: trademarks on pottery, lines traced from oracular readings of cracked tortoise shells (Chinese). To become a letter the appropriated mark was emptied of its established signification and reattached to a new meaning: first the isolation of a trait; next naming the trait with a signifier; finally, using this signifier to name a different item from the original source of the trait with a shared sound (homonymy). Thus in Egyptian hieroglyphics an image of a scarab meant the verb "to become," because of *phonemes* in common (Chaitin 129–130). The "Rat" in the Rat Man's fantasy worked like the scarab, keeping in mind that the associations with the icon (the vermin) continue to function also, as active agents, as aura, just as they did in the memory theater. The device, however, remains consistent, from Plato through Kant to Lacan: hypotyposis. Bloom's revisionary ratios retrace this same facilitation at the level of poetics. *Dromos* and *metis.*

Lacan proposed that this originary discourse of the body (the unconscious) functioned in this same way, such that the signifiers sounded in the music of writing are capable of directly affecting the letter of a body. What matters is not the "meaning" of the symptom; it is in fact nonsense, and the Other is a fiction. The letter of the *sinthome,* therefore, is explicitly identified as being "acephallic" (Voruz 114). Joyce, in other words is the prototype of a modernist vanguard literature that invented a non-objective writing, that is ontological in opening and augmenting for further thought a new kind of sense, *jouissance,* "blissense." The lesson for flash reason is to add to database design this mode of information management (hole logic). One of the last vestiges of Aristotle's propositional logic is in relational databases: the RDF triples use subject-predicate-object structure to model resources. Concept avatar as a practice should be matched with databases using hole logic to model resources. Hole needs its own Google (inventors welcome).

Firenze

Looking for the attractor of my prudence in another family occasion. Family is the decision, or even the accident. Allegory explores the manner of it. Family is lived in many ways. The unconscious disrupts virtue, meaning that hypotyposis as the device for designing choral measure receives a new ratio. In practice it is not clear that knowledge enters into it, or will. Like every practice of the apparatus, avatar is constructed. Concept avatar is reverse-engineered, its order discovered in your (forced) choice(s), in your situation, to be generalized as emblem, bringing the thought of event (the virtual, the potentiality of which your conduct is one instantiation). It intimates: this is how you become what you are. Who knows with what authority the *daimon* spoke, but Socrates heard it, and so I attempt the update in good faith (to notice *daimon*). A report on a condition of well-being, chora in Italy, then (the idea of order in Florence). Fading in memory, a decay more rapid than anticipated, Italy in October 2007. Scavengers pick it apart by night, dream weather leaves the harder materials in place, those towers of aggregate in the badlands of the Dakotas showing time as erosion. A fractal landscape. This quality of memory is simulated in the prosthesis: the electrate augmentation of human capacities in the machine.

In search of this measure called chora, hole, *Ort*, beyond definition or formula, adapted to your own case, to access an experience beyond signification. The stance happens through miniaturization, a region at once outside and in, extimate as Lacan said, first recognized, perhaps, in those maps often included in certain children's books, such as Milne's *Hundred Acre Woods*, setting for Winnie-the-Pooh, based on Ashdown Forest, Sussex, England. Historically the prototype of this space is the dancing floor at Knossos (*choros*), built by the legendary Daedalus. We recognize the fundamental structuring principle, separating sacred from profane, continued in every receptacle of play and game. Imagination as faculty passes from potential to actual, is formatted in each person, as interface capacity articulating Being and Becoming. Such are the stakes and opportunities of choragraphy, mapping the formatting of the imagination (the outside in me). This mapping formerly projected into macrocosm-microcosm cosmologies, redirected to EmerAgency consulting.

The Ponte Vecchio is behind us ("one of the emblems of Florence"). The street vendors (*vous compra*) arrived carrying loads of knockoffs on their backs in large blankets or drop-cloths, like a cadre of elves on Christmas Eve. Just as quickly as they came, they suddenly rolled up their bags and fled, ahead of two *caribinieri* on motorcycles slowly making their way through the crowd of tourists along the bridge. Our party left a *gelateria* encountered on the way from the Ponte towards Santa Maria Novella. The portions scooped into our *cono* or *coppa* were generous, excessive, double the amount received in the famous Vivoli Gelateria, promoted as the best in Firenze, if not all of Italy. Because it is the best, it can provide exact measure: the quantity you order is the quantity you get, in a cup filled precisely to the rim with the excess scraped off and returned to the vat. Off the beaten track, late at night, the measure is different. What of the quality? Kathy and I shared wedding cake which was the best we had tasted. Lee always gets *stracciatella*, and this flavor became the referent throughout the visit, as we joined in what the guidebook declared to be an Italian passion, no day ending properly without *gelato.* A history of video games explained the origin of PacMan in similar terms: inventors searching for a game that would appeal to females started with the ritual visit of Japanese girls to sweetshops. "They love to eat," so a game about eating. The design was inspired by a pizza with one slice removed (between three and four o'clock of the circle) and a strategically placed pepperoni for the eye. A mugshot of the generic contemporary imagination: front Happy Face; profile PacMan (a contemporary *vanitas*?). This choral measure has something to do with sharing a meal.

It is some time after 10:30 PM in this scene, rain drizzle, the chill in the air qualified by the scarves purchased that morning at the central market. The Uffizi after that was an introduction to Italian bureaucracy, standing in lines in order to stand in lines to get the tickets to stand in line. As we shuffled along, getting acquainted with those assigned to this same limbo, a couple pushing a stroller stopped and the man inquired: "Professor Ulmer?" It was Shannon Banes, a student from 1993, now living in Zurich. Exclamations all around (the first time in Florence for both of us). "This sort of thing happens all the time," I lied afterwards.

Even as I waited my turn for a spoon of wedding cake (a streak of carmel always the surprise) there was one of the Botticelli's that persisted in my ruminations. Lee pointed it out, noting especially the angel's gesture, the formal alignment with the doorframe, the sequence of inner-outer pairings, from the evocation of the Virgin's womb in the right foreground, to the room and the doorway middle ground, and the landscape outside background. Gabriel's hand aligned with the doorframe marks the division between this world and beyond (*The Holy Ghost shall come upon thee,* St. Luke). Concept avatar retrieves this functionality (drawing upon every tradition in which it appears). The image gave me a scene with which to anchor my readings about St. Paul's theology of the Church as institutionalizing the Virgin's womb, this womb understood explicitly as chora, making a place for God's embodiment in a physical world, the event for which icons are the relay, vehicles of a relationship, a ratio, a proportion, not a representation. Avatar. That is the structure, the site of what we seek, quiet annunciations of the vortex around these openings between realms or regions. A doorway, a portal, a threshold, an opportunity to meet the guardian, my *daimon*, now a commonplace of new age gurus. Chora is pre-sold in the marketplace, then, high concept, except electracy must go beyond the tradition and its dilapidated survivals and literalisms to reproduce the functionality, not the metaphor (that is, the illumination conventionally described as "wisdom"). That spirit guide always was just an "itself," that is, a doubling, a fold experienced, when it happens, as satori, the thing (*gelato*) itself. Being (in) itself. Avatar personifies itself.

The brightening of the street ahead was a promise, in retrospect, as we moved into some piazza with better prospects for catching a taxi. The angels are everywhere in the museums of Italy, not just the archangels but swarms of *putti* on the ceilings and walls. The classical heritage underfoot exposes the more ancient *daimons*, surviving as the household imp of Lorca's *duende*, direct descendent of Socrates's *daimonion* that he consulted at the threshold of his home before leaving for his trial. That was the oral Socrates, as distinct from the literate one, who applied dialectic to his fellow citizens and was executed for his trouble (during the rule of the democratic government, not the oligarchy, as it happens). Nietzsche's thought of the eternal return of the same was whispered into his ear by one of these messengers, voice of intuition so hard to hear nowadays. What if you had to repeat your life minute for minute forever? Every pain and every joy and every thought and sigh and everything unutterably small or great in your life will have to return to you, all in the same succession and sequence even this spider and this moonlight between the trees, and even this moment and I myself (*The Gay Science,* #341). Chora simulates this whisper, hummed in database patterns. When you log on, voila. Be prepared.

I already knew it, after three steps into the piazza, that the moment (*Augenblick*) was now here (one I might choose should the *daimon* ask). Feeling as category emerges through a landscape. The rain was more visible backlit by the street lamps, whose reflections from the wet cobblestones turned the atmosphere a fluorescent blue. What is the more of this blue? On the far corner two caribinieri in conversation with a woman were laughing, now, and always will have been. Lee is in front, waving to a taxi up the street just dropping off a passenger. A young man on the sidewalk, seated on the low steps of an oversized doorway, guitar case open before him, plays *allegro con brio* the theme from the animated film *The Triplets of Belleville* (it took a minute to recognize it, and a bit longer to recall the title). The guitar is amplified, channeled through a small black box that seems to be adding effects (knockoff music?). Is he really just a kind of organ grinder? *Ben Charest (creator of the score for the film) fuses the score's snappy, predominantly le hot jazz mindset with everything from hip-hop and Bach to the Italian opera farrago" Cieco Cieco Barber" and 1960s proto-surf-rock of "Pa Pa Pa Palavas." But that conceptual stew isn't the least of Charest's delightful surprises, as he giddily infuses it with his own Django-esque guitar stylings and a hodge-podge of found rhythmic instruments that include bicycle wheels, refrigerator shelves and a vacuum cleaner.* A clue: *farrago.* This musical flea-market blew out of that box, opening one of those existential refrains of which Proust's "Vinteuil's little phrase" is the best known.

In the time it took to recognize the number a scene composed itself, a double perspective by division, the *daio* of the *daimon* that allows me to live and to tell at the same time, in a loop, a circumspection of time, the same capacity through which decision models possible worlds. Today the annunciation is more modest. The universal offers an empty doorway, without God, Polis, Reason, Utility, Commodity or any other content with which to prop it open (the phallus that props open the jaws of the primordial Matrix). A threshold with street musician retains sacred functionality, nonetheless. Our theorists (Serres) chart the legacy of angels in our airports (Perez-Gomez updated *Polyphilo* by setting the erotic dream journey on an airplane). From "angelology" to take-out. The structure comes around again in every epoch, but each time more subtle than the last: not god descending, but a bit of music moving my body. The claims may be reduced as the equipment improves. Everyone knows that art is the new religion, and the new science as well (leaving those institutions to their own apparatus) and now we know what to do about it (in electracy).

What is the message delivered in this way? It is simple enough, self-evident (I repeat myself), as if by Cassandra, even if beyond good and evil, so that to hear it involves a transvaluation of all values, seconded in infinite variation by entertainment narratives, including angels to personify the authority of the insight. *Wings of Desire* (Wenders) got it: the willingness of the angels to exchange their eternity as spirits for the finitude of embodied experience, the heft of a stone, the track of a footprint in the snow. Why do we always go right by it? The American remake misses the point in *City of Angels,* critics agree, unable to believe it is just this little fragment of gruntlement, to foreground the love story instead, which is there only as a bonus. Life (or not). That is the feeling for which chora forms the category and digital technology the prosthesis. Do not underestimate the political implications.

Then chora is the mobile fragment, the categorial metonym that memory finds in the scene, serving as interface for a digital civic sphere. Not quite Stevens's "Anecdote of the Jar." The wilderness rose up to it,/ And sprawled around, no longer wild. Stevens placed the jar in Tennessee upon a hill. In Anecdote of the *Gelato* the trait is there already, not added. Certainly I am selecting it to intimate the moment, readymade, the gateway with its guardian or keeper just for me, for the family, to show me my law, how I become what I am, my striving to persevere in my own being. That is, to live. The Christian Church declared many pagan sites to be basilicas and marked them with crosses. The symmetry of history predicts that someday the Duomo in Florence will be a *gelateria.* The thing is mundane, but in close-up. It is trigger, not dynamite itself.

Behind us in the dark is the glowing cone recognized throughout Italy if not the world. The smooth chill in our mouths orders the chill in the air, dampening mist of October rain, arm in arm, Lee at the taxi, Ty with the umbrella, Kathy spooning wedding cake, Anita finding a euro for the guitar case, Django-style rhythm driving the score. Against the ascetic ideal, the *piazza* shifts into a pose for the snapshot to put in the *daimon*'s album, holding open the doorway for now, as we pass through. A measure for the emerging apparatus, to add to those already institutionalized in Religion and Science. Concept avatar speaks for well-being, and this is the manner of reception. We read about preparations for the coming calamity: India is building a fence to repel refugees when Bangladesh submerges. Is that the best we can do? Religion denies climate science, for example (to oversimplify a complex debate), taken with a grain of salt since embodiment is not real for true believers. Science promises to fix the material order, ironically, since it was the arrogance of techno-science that created the machinery of our possible apocalypse to begin with. There must be a place at the table of policy formation for well-being, based on undergoing (not merely understanding or faith), on the polarity of attraction-repulsion that permits my body to know the difference between *gelato* and *creosote*. It sometimes seems simple enough, until the by-product *daimon* materializes unexpectedly. We need to feel the t/rope. What is the *ponte* again? Just happiness.

Figure 4. "Gelato @ Firenze"

10 Frog

To map the hole for myself I start with *Walden,* by Henry David Thoreau, an exemplar of American Religion of self-reliance (Bloom on Emerson), given over to the god-in-me (the giant, higher being, *daimon*). Let Thoreau labor as a persona of concept avatar for now. It could be any work, for if flash reason is any good it must cover any work in any medium. Thoreau descends, in this instance. I start here because it is this classic that gives me access to my fetish, the attractor configuring hole for me. The starting point may be motivated or random. The motivation need be nothing more than the fact that I cannot forget Thoreau; that *Walden* persists with a vividness in memory. It is a mnemonic strange attractor. I want to inquire into the organizing operations of this attractor, of its ability to live on, to stimulate the imagination into our own time. What might be learned from the force of this one work about writing as living? The future that interests me is not just that of *Walden*, but of literature and even of literacy as such, since this archive is what concept avatar relates.

I confess to mourning literacy. Mourning: the psychodynamics of separating from a nurturing surround, relinquishing this provider at the material level but internalizing, introjecting it, while gaining in exchange for the material loss the symbolic power of a new language. Concept avatar mediates the transition. My method is the remake: to remake *Walden* in an electronic version. The version I am talking about now is not in one medium or the other, but is an encounter, a mode of reasoning into which this mourning introduces me. The form is the take, and the method is the fetish, the fantasy. To justify and rationalize this combination is beyond me. The *Walden* ratio. I leave it to the diadochi. An inadequate substitute for the institution that it would be necessary to establish is the inference that might be drawn from my desire to locate materially, to localize, the emotion, or more deeply, the mood, that the pond in Walden Woods reveals to me as fantasy: not Thoreau's mood, but my own, and the persona of *sage*. I want to learn how to use this feeling as a mode of research. Or, as Proust put it in *Time Regained,* the motivation to write his novel was the need to be able to think what he had felt in living.

When 1 wrote the following pages, or rather the bulk of them, l lived alone, in the woods, a mile from any neighbor, in a house which I had built myself, on the shore of Walden Pond, in Concord, Massachusetts, and earned my living by the labor of my hands only.

Jonas Mekas supplies a relay for my remake in his diary films, *Diaries Notes and Sketches also Known as Walden.*

> Street and subway noise
> Close up of the Author.
> IN NEW YORK WAS STILL WINTER
> Central Park, scattered snow.
> BUT THE WIND WAS FULL OF SPRING
> naked branches in wind
> the author playing accordion
> BARBARA'S FLOWER GARDEN
> Chopin
> Barbara planting flower seeds on the window sill
> Film Makers' Cinematheque, 4th St.
> Street and subway noise
> SITNEY IS FINGERPRINTED BY THE POLICE, AS DIRECTOR OF THE CINEMATHEQUE
> Sitney, CU of his hand
> I CUT MY HAIR, TO RAISE MONEY, HAVING TEAS WITH RICH LADIES
> the Author, showing his haircut, turning around
> daily expense notes
> SUNDAY AT STONES
> the Author, eating: also, David & Barbara Stone
> I WALKED ACROSS THE PARK. THERE WAS A PHANTASTIC FEELING OF SPRING IN THE AIR
> apple blossoms.

A shot list as ratio. Some of my earliest memories are of my father reading books to me. I know that these memories are overdetermined, that they include the dimension of "screen memory," a possibility that makes them all the more useful for my experiment. My favorite books as a preschooler were in the *Mother West Wind* series, by Thornton W. Burgess. I still have several of the books (bindings battered). The inside of the cover displays an illustration of the meadow in which Mother West Wind released the Merry Little Breezes every morning. In the foreground is a pond, surrounded by many of the creatures that populate the stories. In the center of the pond sitting on a lily pad is a large bullfrog. The second chapter of the volume I am holding tells why Grandfather Frog has no tail. Choros.

> *Grandfather Frog was old, very old, indeed, and very, very wise. He wore a green coat and his voice was very deep. When Grandfather Frog spoke, everybody listened very respectfully. In the old days when frogs ruled the world, they kept their tails all through life. The King of the frogs had an especially grand tail, and all he did all day was to sit and admire it. All the other frogs followed the example of their king, and did nothing but eat, sleep, and admire their tails. This behavior so angered Mother Nature that she punished the frogs by causing them to lose their handsome tails as they grew up. "Now you all know that people who do nothing worth while in this world are of no use and there is little room for them." Old Grandfather Frog stopped and looked sadly at a foolish green fly coming his way. "Chugarum."*

I especially liked it when my father read these lines in his bullfrog voice. I realize now that my father believed the lesson imparted by the tale/tail and was speaking for himself through the voice of the frog. What I remember experiencing then, however, was the "magic" of writing. I asked how it worked; how he just looked at the object and told the story. He explained the principles of writing, and promised that one day I would be able to read the stories for myself. I recognized the feeling that this act of reading gave me in accounts of first encounters between literate and oral peoples, how the natives described as "magic" the power to retrieve meanings stored in writing.

One of Heidegger's translators commented on the distinction between the beast fable and the Upanishads as reflecting a difference between two kinds of thought, or even two worldviews. The beast fables describe a science of survival, a calculative view of life and its possibilities. The clear formulations of problems or lessons of the fables contrast with the opaque, obscure, mystical messages of the sort found in the Upanishads that attempt to reveal the ultimate nature of things. It is the difference between Aesop and Hesiod.

> Heidegger finds the outlook of the beast fables represented in modern society by the calculative thinking of contemporary science and its applied disciplines. Here is the clear realism of animal life, the sharp and realistic view, the unsentimental outlook quick to take advantage of circumstances to attain an end. With this Heidegger contrasts another kind of thinking which he calls meditative, and which he says is implicit in man's nature. To think in this way requires two attributes not at all common, two stands which man can take, and which he calls releasement toward things and openness to the mystery. (Anderson in Heidegger 12)

Can you hold both positions simultaneously? Yes, since that is what fetish logic is for: *I know, but still*... How might Thoreau be classified in terms of this opposition? The winter that the pond froze over, for example, a hundred men came to remove the ice and ship it abroad to sell in hot climates. "As I looked out I was reminded of the fable of the lark and the reapers, or the parable of the sower," Thoreau observes (196). Later, drawing water from his well, he thinks about the ice from Walden Pond melting in a drink drawn from the Ganges. "In the morning I bathe my intellect in the stupendous and cosmogonal philosophy of the Bhagvat Geeta. . . . I lay down the book and go to my well for water, and lo there I meet the servant of the Bramin, who still sits in his temple on the Ganges reading the Vedas" (197). Thoreau indicates the possibility that the fable and the cosmology may exchange features or effects. He invokes consultation, the scene of Arjuna with Krishna, and I recall that Jack Kerouac sought out the Bhagavad Gita after reading this passage in Thoreau. *Dharma* bums.

The old pond—/ a frog jumps in,/water's sound (Basho, *Two Western Journeys*).

"Basho was seated in his hut, facing Kikaku. Suddenly, breaking the stillness, a frog jumped into the pond. A sudden shift from stillness (no sound) to movement (sound), and then a return to stillness—this combined with the old pond and a frog, created an atmosphere of infinite yugen and tranquility. And that perfectly matched the sentiment that was ripening within Basho at the time. It symbolized his innermost feelings—Shida" (Ueda 141). *Stillness.* I am immediately attracted to this term naming an experience whose nature I cannot quite understand: *yugen.* The commentators note that the originality of Basho's *hokku* was in the combination of the frog and the pond. The many *waka* and *renga* devoted to frogs always feature their croak. In a standard anthology organized by topics, none of the poems in the section devoted to "ponds" refers to a frog. Moran suggests that to understand a poem this delicate and mysterious requires many years of experience. Gozan on the other hand does not hesitate to name the unexpressed sentiment of this hokku: "I am all alone." With this selection of the leap of the frog Basho created his own style, adds another commentator. The effect is achieved by a perfect balance of the humor, typical of haikai—the emphasis on plainness and familiarity (the "plop" of the frog in the water), juxtaposed with the sense of loneliness and desolation. The poetic mood is evoked in this delicate equilibrium. Kafka's crow spoke Latin to say "hope." Does my frog speak Japanese?

In the mean while all the shore rang with the trump of bullfrogs, the sturdy spirits of ancient winebibbers and wassailers, still unrepentant, trying to sing a catch in their Stygian lake,—if the Walden nymphs will pardon the comparison, for though there are almost no weeds, there are frogs there,—who would fain keep up the hilarious rules of their old festal tables. . . . The most aldermanic, with his chin upon a heartleaf, which serves for a napkin to his drooling chaps, under this northern shore quaffs a deep draught of the once scorned water, and passes round the cup with the ejaculation trrroonk, trrroonk! (85)

Someone might think of the proverb: "I fished and caught a frog," glossed as meaning "to bring little to pass with much ado." Perhaps Thoreau had that piece of wisdom in mind when he mentioned that *at long intervals, some came from the village to fish for pouts,—they plainly fished much more in the Walden Pond of their own nature, and baited their hooks with darkness,—but they soon retreated, usually with light baskets* (88). It is a different story when a philosophical friend comes calling. *We waded so gently and reverently, or we pulled together so smoothly, that the fishes of thought were not scared from the stream, nor feared any angler on the bank, but came and went grandly* (179). The fishes of thought.

Gene Youngblood described *The Reflecting Pool,* a video by Bill Viola, whose work he characterizes as "metaphysical structuralism."

> The sound of a passing airplane announces the solitary image of this work. The setting is mythical—a swimming pool in the forest. The pool, which fills the bottom half of the frame, mirrors the trees above it. We hear the sound of a stream that feeds the pond. Viola emerges from the woods by a winding path that leads to the far end of the pool. After fortyfive seconds he suddenly leaps into the air with a shout—but his image freezes at the zenith of its arc. He is suspended over the pool in a fetal position. Nothing else changes; ambient sounds are heard, the water undulates, but in it there is no reflection of the figure suspended above. On the water, sixteen different images appear over the duration of the piece. (Zeitlin 23)

Viola wrote that Pool concerned "themes of emergence"; the images of transition, motion to stillness, suggested "the spiritual birth of the individual." This passage is my gesture, a fashion statement: motion to stillness.

In the backyard of my Florida home is a swimming pool. It is a relatively old pool, dating from 1962, when the house I now own was built, of a type no longer in fashion. It is an Esther Williams design—walk-in steps at the shallow end, with a shallow walkway all around the pool (excellent for younger children). The shallow half of the pool has a flat bottom at a depth of only a few feet. At the deep end the walls of the pool slant from the ledge in toward the drain, eight feet deep. The design was discontinued because there is no safe place to dive into the pool. Swimmers diving in from the side risk hitting their heads on the slanted wall. Esther Williams did not start out in the swimming pool business. Billed as Hollywood's Mermaid because of the roles that translated her abilities as a champion swimmer into underwater spectaculars, Williams got her start in an "Andy Hardy" film in 1942 (Katz). After my friend, Robert Ray, wrote his book on Andy Hardy meeting the avant-garde (Harvard University Press, 1995), I started to think about my Esther Williams pool. I wished I had a copy of the Edward Ruscha "artist's book" called *Nine Swimming Pools.* The ambivalence I feel, my initial resistance to possessing such a thing, was left over from Spain. Fantasy reconciled us, when it posed as Walden Pond. Then I began documenting its ecosystem, leaf litter, lizards, bats drinking from it at dusk, children playing.

"Whoever inhabits that bull's hide stretched between the Jucar, the Guadalete, the Sil, or the Pisuerga has heard it said with a certain frequency: 'Now that has real *duende*!' " (43). Federico García Lorca "took his Spanish term for *daimonic* inspiration from the Andalucían idiom. While to the rest of Spain the *duende* is nothing but a hobgoblin, to Andalucía it is an obscure power which can speak through every form of human art, including the art of personality" (Arturo Barea qtd. in Rothenberg and Rothenberg 43). The ancient *topos* of the spirit of place; how relevant is it to choragraphy? In Basho the fit between his inner feeling and the sound of the frog leaping into the pool formed a mood that had a name: *yugen*. Lorca had a name from the traditions of his place for the mood upon which he drew for his creativity: *duende*. "Black sounds: behind which there abide, in tenderest intimacy, the volcanoes, the ants, the zephyrs, and the enormous night straining its waist against the Milky Way" (Lorca qtd. in Rothenberg and Rothenberg 43, 51). These names are welcome, since they notice a dimension of experience I might otherwise overlook. What is the name of the feeling documented in my Allegory of Prudence?

We worship not the Graces, nor the Parcae, but Fashion. She spins and weaves and cuts with full authority. The head monkey at Paris puts on a traveller's cap, and all the monkeys in America do the same (16).

If one may judge who rarely looks into the newspapers, nothing new does ever happen in foreign parts, a French Revolution not excepted. Despite, or perhaps because of, the Frenchness of his name, Thoreau shows no sympathy for the French. He never explicitly refers to them as "frogs," but he shares none of my own francophilia. Is my frog a euphemism for "monkey"? *Shall the world be confined to one Paris or one Oxford forever? Cannot students be boarded here and get a liberal education under the skies of Concord?* Here we are in agreement: Paris, Florida. Emulation, not imitation (as Basho advised: do not follow in the footsteps of the masters, but seek what they sought). Van Gogh went to the south of France to find light that, according to the japonaiserie of his day, most simulated that found in Japan, as expressed in the *ukiyo-e* prints he admired.

Chora is a composite zone, a commixture. I am collecting as many of the frogs in Walden as I can find, using a fetish to organize my reading. Fetish: a heterogenous assemblage of materials held together by a trivial contingent detail. *When I ask for a garment of a particular form, my tailoress tells me gravely, "They do not make them so now"* (16). It is unlikely that Thoreau ever requested a coat that buttoned with the ornamental fastening known as a "frog." These frog fastenings are typically to be found on military dress uniforms. I am sure that I have seen a photograph of George Armstrong Custer wearing a dress coat with frog fastenings. Thoreau (like Emerson) reminds us that everything happens locally. The counsel, however, is not to reject fashion as such, but, as Baudelaire advised, to compose a fashion. "*To create a new commonplace* [*poncif*]," Baudelaire declared in *Fusées*, "*that's genius. I must create a commonplace.*" *Poncif* is translated also as cliché, stereotype, in the French sense: a fashion. The imperative of concept avatar: fashion cannot be left to Commerce.

> M is also the first letter of Mureau, one of the more unconventional texts in this book. Mureau departs from conventional syntax. It is a mix of letters, syllables, words, phrases, and sentences. I wrote it by subjecting all the remarks of Henry David Thoreau about music, silence, and sounds he heard that are indexed in the Dover publication of the Journal to a series of I Ching chance operations. Mureau is the first syllable of the word music followed by the second of the name Thoreau. Reading the Journal I had been struck by the twentieth-century way Thoreau listened. He listened, it seemed to me, just as composers using technology nowadays listen. He paid attention to each sound, whether it was 'musical' or not, just as they do; and he explored the neighborhood of Concord with the same appetite with which they explore the possibilities provided by electronics. (Cage i)

Explore your neighborhood.

> Precipitous declines in the populations of some species of frogs, toads, and salamanders around the world have begun to alarm experts on amphibians, many of whom are undertaking new field experiments in an effort to pin down the reasons for

> the mysterious trend. Because amphibians breathe through their skin, lay their eggs in water, and have two stages in their life cycle—one in water and another on land—they come into contact with a wide variety of substances. As a result, many biologists believe amphibians are more sensitive than other kinds of animals to environmental changes and pollutants. Like the canaries once used by coal miners to detect deadly fumes, they say, the amphibians may be providing early warning signs of trouble for other fauna, including humans. (*Chronicle of Higher Education*, 26 March 1999)

Is it worrisome that endangered species are a leitmotif in my signature (anagram *lemur*)? Walden Woods itself is in danger of disappearing, threatened by real estate developers. Don Henley, star of the Rock group the Eagles, has taken on the preservation of Walden Woods as his personal cause. By organizing charity concerts and contributing percentages of the sale of certain albums, Henley has raised millions of dollars to purchase the acreage around Walden Pond. Don Felder, lead guitarist of the Eagles, grew up in Gainesville, Florida. He started his first band at age fourteen. Second guitar in that band was Stephen Stills. Come to think of it, Marilyn Monroe's sister lives in Gainesville.

I would fain say something, not so much concerning the Chinese and Sandwich Islanders as you who read these pages, who are said to live in New England; something about your condition, what it is, whether it is necessary that it be as bad as it is, whether it cannot be improved as well as not. . . . I see young men, my townsmen, whose misfortune it is to have inherited farms, houses, barns, cattle, and farming tools; for these are more easily acquired than got rid of. How many a poor immortal soul have I met well nigh crushed and smothered under its load, creeping down the road of life, pushing before it a barn seventyfive feet by forty (2).

How to maintain my swimming pool? Do I have that look as if I were pushing before me everywhere I go a twenty by forty foot concrete-lined hole sloshing water? No barns for me, was my attitude in Spain. After the rains the bottom breaks out in black spot, requiring immediate applications of poisons and considerable scrubbing with a steel brush on the end of a long pole. The skimmer, still with the original iron pipes, has started to leak, causing the water level to drop. I can only open it now when I have to change the filter, so that all the circulation of water through the filter and back into the pool must come through the drain at the bottom. Storms fill the surface with leaves and pine needles that must be cleared quickly before they become waterlogged and drift to the bottom where they could block the drain, stopping the flow of water to the pump, which would in turn soon burn out. The w/hole catastrophe.

Most important of all, acidity, alkalinity, and the amount of mineral salts in the water must be kept in balance to prevent corrosion of metal parts, scale deposits, and etching of plaster surfaces. All water has an acid-alkaline balance that is measured on a pH scale. The scale runs from zero to fourteen with the center, seven, indicating a neutral state. Controlling the chemical balance of pool water is vital. The ideal range is slightly on the alkaline side. Testing pH is not difficult. The water sample in the test kit will change color according to the pH. For example, a phenol red indicator will turn the sample yellow for acid, orange for little or no alkali, and red for high alkalinity. Every time I do the test for pH, I think of developing a color test for PhD.

My Esther Williams swimming pool is trying to become a frog pond, to return to nature, and I am doing everything in my power to prevent that from happening. Measuring the chemicals and adding the right mixtures to bring the opposites into balance—acidity and alkalinity—is a kind of alchemy, related to the ancient tradition of the music of the spheres. What Heidegger called "mood" or attunement—*Stimmung*—is an allusion to this tradition, to the theory of temperament as a result of the balance or imbalance of the four humours in alchemical psychology. Yet as I carry out this chore of mundane chemistry I experience a sense of chagrin. Concept avatar may offer a kit to test the balance of your state of mind, the concinnitas, bitter and sweet, salty and sour. What is this fifth flavor, *umami* (the term loaned from Japanese)? Savory. You inhabit a microcosm, if you will, by noticing the fold: *Ister.*

> Each time he encounters one of these double words, R.B. insists on keeping both meanings, as if one were winking at the other and as if the word's meaning were in that wink, so that one and the same word, in one and the same sentence, means at one and the same time two different things. This is why such words are often said to be "preciously ambiguous": not in their lexical essence (for any word in the lexicon has several meanings), but because, by a kind of luck, a kind of favor not of language but of discourse, I can actualize their amphibology. In French these amphibologies are extremely (abnormal-

> ly) numerous: absence (lack of person and distraction of the mind), alibi (a different place and a police justification). The fantasy is not to hear everything (anything), it is to hear something else. (Barthes, *Roland Barthes* 72)

These amphibians, these frogs say more.

Let us spend one day as deliberately as Nature and not be thrown off the track by every nutshell and mosquito's wing that falls on the rails (65).

The grooved piece of iron placed at a junction of the rails where one track crosses another is known as a "frog," as in this example from the dictionary illustrating proper usage: "the accident was caused by the train suddenly leaving the rails at a frog." There are many such frogs in Walden, a work exemplifying, after all, the condition of the machine in the garden. Thoreau mentions the train and its tracks frequently. In one sentence he alludes to the semantic sets of two different frogs: *A mink steals out of the marsh before my door and seizes a frog by the shore; the sedge is bending under the weight of the reedbirds flitting hither and thither; and for the last half hour I have heard the rattle of railroad cars, now dying away and then reviving* (77). The Fitchburg Railroad passed the pond near Thoreau's cabin. *I usually go to the village along its causeway, and am related to society by this link.* The workmen along the rails saw Thoreau so often they mistook him for a laborer like themselves. *And so I am. I too would fain be a trackrepairer somewhere in the orbit of the earth.* Decorum: the matching sensation triggered between a presentation and a memory: the switch-engines working all night in the yards of the Northern Pacific (Miles City, Montana).

In their discussions of dream work, the psychoanalysts Sigmund Freud and Jacques Lacan noted that every dream has a railroad switch, a switch word, or what I have called a choral word (a hole). Every dream, that is, to use railroad slang, has a frog. Here is the lesson of Walden I want to generalize as a rule of flash reason—to use the frog as the organizing logic of electrate rhetoric, to let frog emblematize the ratio figuring measure today. It is a common enough device, but Thoreau's example makes the case for it especially convincing. *What I have observed of the pond is no less true in ethics. It is the law of average. Such a rule of the two diameters not only guides us toward the sun in the system and the heart in man, but draw lines through the length and breadth of the aggregate of a man's particular daily behaviors and waves of life into his coves and inlets, and where they intersect will be the height or depth of his character. Perhaps we need only to know how his shores trend and his adjacent country or circumstances, to infer his depth and concealed bottom* (192). What is the cut of your jib, the lay of your land?

Thoreau shows a way to perform choragraphy across the levels of schooling. It is a lesson simple in form and profound in effect. Tim O'Brien applies the device to perfection in his autobiographical account of his service in Vietnam.

> The things they carried were largely determined by necessity. Among the necessities or near-necessities were P38 can openers, pocket knives, heat tabs, wristwatches, dog tags, mosquito repellent, chewing gum, candy, cigarettes, salt tablets, packets of KoolAid, lighters, matches, sewing kits, Military Payment Certificates, C rations, and two or three canteens of water. Together, these items weighed between 15 and 20 pounds, depending upon a man's habits or rate of metabolism. . . . To carry something was to hump it, as when Lieutenant Jimmy Cross humped his love for Martha up the hills and through the swamps. In its intransitive form to hump meant to walk, or to march, but it implied burdens far beyond the intransitive. (45)

The movement from physical burdens to metaphysical ones is treated with telling effect in *The Thinqs They Carried*. Similarly, anything and everything in and around Walden Pond may be turned into a device (trope) for exploring a value, a belief, a question. The principle is as ancient as the theory of correspondences, of an intuited relationship between the macrocosm and the microcosm. The assignment is to position yourself at the crossing, at this switch or frog between the material environment of Gainesville, Alachua County, Florida, and the mood, the emotional frame that tells you how you are situated, where things are "at" for me, my attunement to the world. To hump things (slang). This mood is *gnosis*. I understand in principle or by definition that as a modern person I am alienated, for example. I know what the term means, but I do not get it. By definition, it is an unclaimed experience. I know further or the theory suggests that as the modern condition gives way to the postmodern, so too does the ground mood of dread, of anxiety, give way to another tuning. And if anxiety is *daimonion*? We shifted ethos before, from shame to guilt culture (Dodds), in becoming literate. And today, becoming electrate, a shift from guilt to idiot?

The Allegory explores this tuning collectively in a distributed way, each in our neighborhood (chora), to extrapolate from our models and relays to find the equivalent of *yugen* or *duende* for our own location; or if you can find no equivalent in your local culture, then to invent a word for the mood whose traces you discover running through the collective entries, or to borrow a term from another culture to help find a dimension of your experience previously unattended. The instructions are to form an image—a dialectical image—by juxtaposing a detail in my own setting with a detail or feature of a cultural text—any work of my choosing in arts and letters. Any work in the standard curriculum of the public schools should serve this purpose well enough. The next step is to explore the resonances thus created as an allegory from which I may infer the nature of a personal emotion that may in turn allow me to recognize an underlying collective atmosphere. This inference is a discovery, an expression, not a representation of something that I already knew. It is an invention whose proof is in your recognition of the match, the correspondence, the fit between the outside and the inside, the visible and invisible dimensions of experience. Player consults avatar.

The effect might be a lack of fit, in which for example the juxtaposition of Walden Pond and my Esther Williams swimming pool forms an abyss, a gap of meaning into which I have poured just enough bits and bytes to stabilize the terrain, the ground. The commixture may be mistaken for a parody, as was Georgese Bataille's mysticism, except that in the latter case it was not an instance of the Parisian *poncif.* Aristophanes's *Frogs* is a farce, a parody of the descent scenario, in which Dionysus goes to Hades to retrieve Euripedes, since Athens has no more decent tragedians. The role of the Chorus traditionally was to mediate between the gods and the audience (an avatar function). Here it is a Chorus of Frogs, whose croaking is transcribed to say: Brekekekex ko-ax ko-ax. Google supplies a list of animal-noise Babel. *Afrikaans: kwaak-kwaak; Albanian: kuak; Arabic (Algeria): gar gar; Bengali: gangor-gangor; Catalan: crua-crua; Chinese (Mandarin): guo guo; Croatian: kre-kre; Czech: brekete; Danish: kvaek; Dutch: kwak kwak; Estonian: krooks-krooks; Finnish: kvak kvak; French: coa-coa; German: quaak, quaak; Hebrew: kwa kwa (/qva qva); Hindi: meko-mek meko-mek; Hungarian: bre-ke-ke; Italian: cra cra; Japanese: kerokero;*

Korean: gae-gool-gae-gool; Polish: kum kum; Russian: kva-kva; Spanish (Spain): crua-crua; Spanish (Argentina): berp; Spanish (Peru): croac, croac; Thai: ob ob; and Turkish: vrak vrak.

The frogs display a series, a trajectory, that I may use as a point of reference, a measure, as a reminder that there is more tuning to be done. The juxtaposition of my pool and Thoreau's pond, mediated by the choral frog, produces an effect of triangulation, marking out a site in the unknown to which I may now direct my attention. The slang meaning of my totem? To croak, to die.

The exercise requires that I undertake myself the construction of an allegorical metaphor (my Allegory of Prudence). Walden repeats the device endlessly, as when Thoreau comments on *the forms which thawing sand and clay assume in flowing down the sides of a deep cut on the railroad* (201). His interpretation manifests an explicit use of the traditional schema of correspondences. *What is man but a mass of thawing clay. The fingers and toes flow to their extent from the thawing mass of the body,* he states, and then shifts the vehicle of the figure to that of a leaf. He goes on to declare: *"The Maker of this earth but patented a leaf. What Champollion will decipher this hieroglyphic for us, that we may turn over a new leaf at last?* Such is his poetics—to begin with an observation of something in the material world, and then (appropriating a commonplace) to turn it in the direction of a maxim relating to human conduct.

This turn of figuration is familiar enough to instructors at all levels: *Time is but the stream I go afishing in.* Or, *We have constructed a fate, an Atropos, that never turns aside. (Let that be the name of your engine). . . . Every path but your own is the path of fate. Keep on your own track, then.* What is one's own? *Daimon* knows. We know this figure well, but there is little evidence to suggest that the literalmindedness of our onedimensional culture has changed very much, despite the continuous training in figuration provided by advertising. Narrative is now universally embraced as the humanistic or qualitative supplement to calculation. Everyone has or needs a story, we are told. Yes, and a "figure," a trope (a turn) as well. The challenge of choragraphy is to add heuretics to hermeneutics, fabrication to interpretation. The goal of reading the figures composed in the arts and letters relays is to learn how to make a figure myself, to use the works in the humanities tradition as a chora or place of mediation in which, in the prosthesis of the

Internet, we may think together our personal and collective dimensions, grounded and manifested in our own local setting.

In his recent book (*Self Come to Mind*), Antonio Damasio discusses the human capacity to recognize one's own being in features of the external world (natural and cultural things, events, works). The world offers us a mirror in which to track the turns of our identity. He offers an example of his own experience of this capacity.

> It is an object that helped him construct, interpret, ponder and crystallize his identity, or at least his idea of it. It came to him in the early 1970s, when he was in medical school at the University of Lisbon. The sculpture, made by a woman he had just begun dating (a fellow neuroscience student and a sculptor named Hanna Costa), is a little terra-cotta figure of a man seeming to fight his way forward in a storm. And it all but cried out to Damasio with a mysterious urgency. "Somehow I felt that it was me, or belonged to me," he recalled. "Even though she had done it before we met." The doctor was even more convinced that it was a sculpture of his favorite boyhood hero: Tintin, the boyish blond reporter and detective whose comic-book adventures, written by Georges Remi (a k a Hergé) from the 1930s to the early 1980s, delighted generations of European children. Dr. Damasio was one of them, having found endless inspiration in Tintin's feats of derring-do and the restlessly inquisitive mind that dispatched mystery after mystery with faultlessly astute reasoning and a killer right punch. (Coleman)

In a review of Damasio's book, Ned Block pointed to one significant area of disagreement, not with Damasio's example, but with how the capacity is interpreted. It reflects not so much "self-consciousness" as "phenomenal" consciousness, related to Merleau-Ponty's "flesh."

> But there is also a different kind, as anyone who knows what it is like to have a headache, taste chocolate or see red can attest. Self-consciousness is a sophisticated and perhaps uniquely human cognitive achievement. Phenomenal consciousness by contrast—what it is like to *experience*—is something we share with many animals. A person who is drunk or delirious

> or dreaming can be excruciatingly conscious without being wakeful, self-aware or aware of his surroundings. (Block)

For the purposes of flash reason this disagreement is beside the point. It is important rather to mark a capacity for experience of identity as the one augmented through concept avatar, whose skill set is flash reason organizing dromosphere information sprawl into a consultation on being. The function of *measure* in image metaphysics is this event of recognition (belonging to me, enowning). Avatar is activated from the side of the mirror: It recognizes me. I am the orchid, avatar the wasp (the lesson of rhizome). "Letter" reminds us, at the same time, that embodied experience is complexity itself.

A swimming pool may teach me something about my attunement to life, then; not just something about myself, but about my community, my world, if I am prepared to be a Champollion to the hieroglyphics of my locale. This extrapolation from the models and application to myself are the challenge and opportunity of choragraphy in electracy. What is the ethical dimension of maintaining the proper balance of chemicals in pool water? What is the politics of my struggle to purify the water in which my family swims? What is the metaphysics of a luxury whose leisure function belies the deteriorated fragility of its mechanical functioning? It is an engine of measure, a paragon of *concinnitas.*

I understand that the feeling I associated with the ponds of childhood memory was one of security, certainty, order (the bourgeoisie constructed it as habitus). Hence the fetish power of the frog. How much of my disciplinary devotion to putting order into a body of heterogeneous information draws upon that unforgettable page in the coloring book with the cattails, redwing blackbird, frog on the lily pad scene? What about the passage from innocence to experience that includes lessons in ecology, of a Darwinian food chain underlying this bucolic image? *I love to see that Nature is so rife with life that myriads can be afforded to be sacrificed and suffered to prey on one another,* says Thoreau (201), undeterred by accident and death; *tadpoles which herons gobble up, and tortoises and toads run over in the road.* The idea of order in Gainesville: Frog @ Pool.

Pool maintenance teaches responsibility: to be not the child who plays in the water, but the one who balances the chemicals and enforces rules for safety. Here is another relay for concept avatar: parent with swimming pool. In the large frame of society, the pool is a mortification. Children, mortgage, the entire farm—where did they come from? Decision + time. The pool in its materiality shows me something, makes me confront something—my own class position, the patriarchal mood of my values—that otherwise readily slip out of sight and out of mind. It is measure as such. The critical power of the project depends upon this anchor or grounding of theories and emotions in the maker's own material existence, which then may be included in the act of reading and writing. In this scenario (Walden) pool is avatar, that is, consultant, with frog in the hole. I went to Spain to escape the pools of responsibility, only to be admonished by Emerson's wisdom: *Travelling is a fool's paradise. At home I dream that at Naples, at Rome, I can be intoxicated with beauty and lose my sadness. I pack my trunk, embrace my friends, embark on the sea and at last wake up in Naples, and there beside me is the stern fact, the sad self, unrelenting, identical, that I fled from. I seek the Vatican and the palaces. I affect to be intoxicated with sights and suggestions, but I am not intoxicated. My giant goes with me wherever I go* (Emerson 187).

11 Hegemony

The Empty Universal

The political potential of hole (for avatar as collective agency) may be seen in the notion of hegemony. Perhaps the most relevant theorist of hegemony for flash reason is Ernesto Laclau (who collaborates on some projects with Chantal Mouffe). Laclau clarifies the fact that hegemony is a kind of logic. Machiavelli based his innovations on the tradition of *phronesis*, of practical reason as a judgment about the appropriate fit between immediate circumstances and the maxims expressing some principle. The problem of fitting rules to cases involves inference, and is a version of the ancient problem of the relationship between universals and particulars. The problem for collective identity in modernity is the loss of the universal measure with which to construct an accord. The reservoir of maxims lost authority in the era of science, and the industrial city vacated tradition in favor of pop culture. Here is the challenge for concept avatar. Each previous epoch was able to call upon some "common sense" consensus on the general mediator capable of hegemonizing any subaltern or minority position. The Classical Polis (friendship), God (faith) in the Medieval period, Reason (science) in the Enlightenment. The last contender for a universal in the epoch of the bourgeoisie was Utility (Bentham). Today exchange is managed by the commodity sign (universal equivalent). Electracy proposes: *sinthome*. Letter. As Laclau explains, the consensus is that there must be a mediating universal to provide a quilting point of order, but it must remain empty, since there is no *sensus communis*. Concept avatar counsels negentity. In electracy, the universal is distributed.

Laclau's contribution to the discussion is to show the logic by which hegemony is able to foster alliances across disparate and incommensurable identity groups. The transitional character of Laclau's project as ontology is revealed in his promotion of a fundamental linguistic feature—the two axes of language, selection (paradigm, metaphor, condensation) and combination (symtagm, metonym, displacement)—to a social logic. Having in mind Jakobson's structuralist observation that what resembles, assembles—or that in the poetic function the axis of selection is mapped onto the axis of combination—we could say that hegemony is to politics what poetry is to literature (thus opening it to flash reason). The challenge of creating collective coherence for multitude is the one that motivated Gramsci to promote hegemony in the first place—the need to create alliances or partners for the working class among other groups in the society. Laclau generalizes the problem beyond the ideological categories such as class: it is not just a matter of a class recognizing itself as a collective being, but of a collective intelligence as such. Group formation in this logic works not by "persuasion," but by "identification" (an insight achieved previously by Kenneth Burke in his grammar and rhetoric of motives). It is the difference between a rhetoric of persuasion and a tropology (a rhetoric of evasion) according to Bloom.

One group is able to attract other groups to its position, and in so doing serves as a proxy for the universal. Some particular stance of opposition against an oppressive regime, for example, does double duty in that it also represents opposition in general. The historical example is the Solidarity movement in Poland, which became the rallying point for "revolution" across society as a whole. The logic of this aspect of the process is that of "equivalence," which works like hypotyposis in Kant's reflective judgment. The identification is not based on mimetic resemblance between two positions, but on a proportional ratio: one group is positioned in its situation similarly to the way the hegemonic group is positioned (A : B :: C : D).

> Why does the equivalential aggregation have to express itself through the universal? The answer is to be found in what we said about the formal structure on which the aggregation depends. The "something identical" shared by all the terms of the equivalential chain—that which makes the equivalence possible—cannot be something positive (that is one more difference which could be defined in its particularity), but proceeds from the unifying effects that the external threat poses to an otherwise perfectly heterogeneous set of differences (particularities). The "something identical" can only be the pure, abstract, absent fullness of the community, which lacks, as we have seen, any direct form of representation and ex-

> presses itself through the equivalence of the differential terms. (Laclau *Emancipation(s)* 57)

In other words, to adapt Kant's distinctions, the people must be thought in terms of multitude in a politics of the sublime. What is the clasp or attractor capable of gathering and holding together this assemblage?

The other logic operating in hegemony is that of difference, understood (and this is Laclau's insight) in Derrida's deconstructive sense (*différance*). As Laclau explains, Derrida's spectral hauntology is only the point of departure for this logic, which develops the alternative ratio of anomaly (bachelor machine). Derrida's explicit politics, as expressed for example in his reading of Marx, takes up Heidegger's theory of *Ereignis* or event: the recognition that time is out of joint, that any decision in the present works within an historical delimiting framework of prior decisions that create a vector, a trajectory partly determining the choice. The radical stance of this aspect of deconstruction, which Derrida names aporia, is that the future remains open, and that the meaning of history as a whole, like any individual sentence, is constructed retrospectively through the displacements and delays of time. "The role of deconstruction is, from this perspective, to reactivate the moment of decision that underlies any sedimented set of social relations. The political and ethical significance of this first movement is that, by enlarging the area of structural undecidability, it also enlarges the area of responsibility–- that is of the decision" (*Emancipation(s)* 78). Belatedness is structural.

While this openness to the future is crucial to hegemonizing the multitude, there is a more basic feature of "difference" as a logic. In an increasingly fragmented condition, the logic of *differance* (conduction or the fourth mode of inference) moves across all levels of discourse, crosses every border and boundary, following a network that has always been operative in language, but which apparatus shifts brought to the fore. The inferential powers of this logic were first systematically demonstrated in Freud's cases. Laclau cites Freud's Rat Man case as his example of the "verbal bridge" made of signifiers separated from any signifieds, and hence creating a short-cut through information, to produce unforeseen (topological) connections with similar signifiers in otherwise incommensurable semantic domains. In other words: the hole. Laclau shows what the hole is for.

> Freud's "Rat Man," through "verbal bridges," constructed a "rat complex," partly through meaningful associations—for example, rat = penis, for rats spread diseases such as syphilis, and so on—but partly also through purely verbal associations which have nothing to do with meaning—"Raten means installments, and leads to the equation of rats and florins; Spielratte means gambler, and the Rat Man's father, having incurred a debt gambling, becomes drawn into the rat complex." The importance of this dissociation of truth from meaning for hegemonic analysis is that it enable us to break with the dependence on the signified to which a rationalist conception of politics would have otherwise confined us. What is crucial is not to conceive the hegemonic process as one in which empty places in the structure would be simply filled by preconstituted hegemonic forces. There is a process of communication of the empty signifiers by the particularities which carry out the hegemonic sutures, but this is a process of mutual contamination; it does operate in both directions. For that reason it leads to an autonomization of the signifier which is decisive to the understanding of the political efficacy of certain symbols. (Laclau, "Identity and Hegemony" 69)

A review of Derrida's theories and practices along these lines will show more clearly what is meant by a "score" as the hegemonic band of the multitude. The universal as rathole.

Trait

A "trait" in literate metaphysics refers to the property, attribute, or feature associated with an object as thing. To understand the innovations in judgment needed to bring prudence into electracy, we need to learn from Derrida how to compose with the trait. Heidegger showed that philosophers and poets begin in the same position with respect to being, between nature and language (at the beginnings of literate metaphysics). Both grasp the world by means of traits, but with different purposes and therefore with an attention to different traits. Philosophers isolate those essential traits that make a thing what it is (name its being), which they identify by means of definitions, propositions, resulting in concept formation. They are concerned with the true-false axis, supported by declarative statements (propositional logic). Poets are more interested in what does not appear, but which must be evoked through accidental traits that produce atmosphere, to sustain a mood through feeling (the pleasure-pain axis). Electracy does not replace the oral or literate metaphysics, but supplements them with a new dimension of reality.

Heidegger problematizes this basic distinction, since his proposal is that another different metaphysics was potentially available at the beginning of literacy in the example of poets and the other arts, and may still be learned from poets in our own day, such as Hölderlin. There is a way to perform ontology by poetic means. Derrida pushes this proposal into a dimension of writing that he observes in Heidegger's argument. His goal is to bring out a new possibility of trait. This new trait brings out the full potential of the Rat Bridge invoked by Laclau. Derrida focuses his commentary on Heidegger's decision to make language do some productive work, to rub two semantic groups together in order to produce sparks. "Two families, so to speak, of words, nouns, verbs and syncatagoremes, form an alliance, engage, cross each other in this contract of the trait in the German language. It is on the one hand the 'family' of *Ziehen* (*Zug, Bezug, Gezuge, durchziehen, entziehen*), and on the other, the 'family' of *Reissen* (*Riss, Aufriss, Umriss, Grundriss,* etc.). To my knowledge the role which this crossing plays has never been remarked or at least thematized" ("The Retrait of Metaphor" 27).

What interests Derrida is the "difference," that is, the articulating relationship that Heidegger creates by his thinking of the metaphysical trait through the surplus value of meaning generated when these families are juxtaposed (a parallax linguistics). He is acting on Heidegger's insight, that ontology is an emergent effect of writing, and so shifts attention to what language can do, language as force, rather than form/matter relationships in nature.

> It happens and comes about only in effacing itself. Inversely, the trait is not derived. It is not secondary, in its arrival in relation to the domains, or the essences, or to the existences that it cuts away, frays, and refolds in their re-cut. The re- of re-trait is not an accident occurring to the trait. It rises up (s'enleve) in allowing any propriety to rise up, as one says of a figure on a ground. But it is lifted neither before nor after the incision which permits it to be lifted up, neither substantially, acciden-

> tally, materially, formally, nor according to any of the oppositions which organize so-called metaphysical discourse, (29)

This re-trait is an "emergent" effect, we would say in the language of autopoiesis.

When the theorists say that the multitude is ontological, they mean that in the new logic of hegemony we are constructing reality (but not the Real). Derrida demonstrates some of the creative resources of language available for the enterprise, beginning by showing the formal means, noted by many others, by which philosophical concepts are composed in the manner of emblems. Metaphysicians, Derrida suggests, are bad poets, in that they write "white mythology"—creating metaphors that hide or erase themselves. What interests Derrida is not any particular metaphor (or trope) that may be found within the philosophemes (beginning with the sun, the heliotrope, and the figurative connection between light, sight, the eye of the mind, idea, from theater to theory), but in demonstrating the surplus value still available within "trait" itself (the virtual or potential dimension of being). To take just the German term *Zug*, for example, the dictionary inventories an extraordinary range of signification recorded in this word: drawing, pulling, stretch tension tug stroke (rowing); move (chess); draught (animal), tractor (mechanical), railway train; march, marching, passage, progress, procession, expedition, migration, flight, flock, herd, school; drift (of clouds), range (of mountains), row (of houses), current (of air); retinue, gang, band, troop, squad, section; span, yoke (of oxen); strokes of a pen, line, outline, feature, characteristic, trait, lineament, attraction, sympathy, bent, disposition, inclination, bias; drawing power, impulse, gulp, draught (of drink), whiff, puff of smoke, pull on a pipe (toke), set of strings, chords, grip, bell-pull, rifling (gun barrel). Imagine the student of comparative literature, reading Heidegger, coming to the term *Zug*, and reaching for a dictionary.

Derrida's experiment with trait as *Zug* passes through musicology, for it is this musical analogy that directs us to the conductive passage of differance. The connotations of *Zug* have been used in music theory to name the passage through sound created and experienced in the movement of a musical composition.

> Schenker developed the notion of *Zug* in his commentary (1921) on Beethoven's Piano Sonata op.101. . . . By merging directed tonal motion with a teleological effect of striving and

> fulfillment, Schenker saw how motion between two consonances could be generalized into directed motion across the whole composition. Technically, *Zug* refers to a linear progression that passes between lines or triadic voices. But Snarrenberg also unpacks many other connotations of *Zug*, such as trait or characteristic (as in a motive), a linear configuration, the action of pulling, a dynamic progression, and "the complex motion of a train, departing, traversing intermediate points, arriving at a destination." The traversal of a *Zug* is the execution of an intention, even in the face of resistance, delay, or diversion. Step 3 was the effect of *Ursatz*. Finally, in *Der freie Satz* (1935), Schenker imagines the entire piece as an elaboration of a single *Zug*—an *Urline*-Zug—in counterpoint with a bass arpeggiation. Hence the piece as a whole, coterminous with a single conceptual triad, becomes the ultimate context for the effect of passing, the dynamic of striving and fulfillment from departure to goal. (Spitzer and Michael 40)

Here we have Derrida's addition to the "bridge," taking up Kant's aesthetic hypotyposis, Freud's verbal bridge, and Laclau's hegemony, to propose a movement of inference through discourse in this musical fashion (existential refrain). What is the feeling of attraction-repulsion? *Zug* names a force of movement, of passage (a thought train). This is how the musical side of language supports inference (the hole). The terminology evokes several contexts important to flash reason. The most obvious is the connection with jazz, which, as the commentators note, promoted rhythm to at least an equal status with melody. The blues was said to have found in the sounds of locomotives a substitute for the talking drums of African tradition. Listeners claimed that in the trumpet solos of Louis Armstrong they could hear the call of the train whistle, and the response from the ensemble of the pumping pistons and the rumbling boxcars (Murray). This theme extends also to formal features: a musical bridge is a modulation to a different key (in jazz to an unrelated key), creating an effect of intensification.

The other echo is philosophical, with Spinoza's understanding of human essence in terms of "*conatus*," defined as the striving of every creature to persevere in its own being. "The *conatus* with which each thing endeavors to persist in its own being is nothing but the actual essence of the thing itself. . . . It is clear from the above considerations that we do not endeavor, will, seek after or desire because we judge a thing to be good. On the contrary, we judge a thing to be good because we endeavor, will, seek after and desire it" (Spinoza 109). Spinoza's extension of *conatus* into the politics of multitude is central to Antonio Negri's collaboration with Michael Hardt on a theory of globalization. *Zug* instantiates striving: concept avatar is immanent, does not descend, but strives.

The pull of *Zug* at the same time recalls the tradition of commonplaces and topical composition that Bloom found at work in the repetition drive of the unconscious structured like a language. Or to be more precise: structured as commonplaces (Gestalts). Roland Barthes described the experience of using the places to compose as that of working a machine.

> This network is a montage. One thinks of Diderot and his machine for making stockings: "It can be seen as a single and unique reasoning whose conclusion is the fabrication of the object . . . " In Diderot's machine, textile material is fed in at the beginning, and at the end, it is stockings which emerge. In the rhetorical machine, what one puts in at the beginning, barely emerging from a native aphasia, are the raw materials of reasoning, facts, a "subject"; what comes out at the end is a complete, structured discourse, fully armed for persuasion. (Barthes, "The *Aide* to Memory" 51)

"The enthymeme has the pleasures of a progress, of a journey," Barthes suggests. "One sets out from a point which has no need to be proved and from there one proceeds toward another point which does need to be proved; one has the agreeable feeling (even if under duress) of discovering something new by a kind of natural contagion, of capillarity which extends the known (the opinable) toward the unknown" (60). The pleasure, he adds, is like that of completing a given pattern or grid, such as a crossword puzzle. The topics provided this "grid" for production.

> A subject (*quaestio*) is given to the orator; in order to find arguments, the orator "passes" his subject over a grid of empty forms: from the contact between the subject and each compartment (each "place") of the grid (of the Topics) appears a possible idea, an enthymematic premise. There existed in Antiquity a pedagogic version of this procedure: the chreia or "useful" exercise was a test of virtuosity given to students

> which consisted in "passing" a theme through a series of places. Taking his inspiration from ancient Topics, Lamy, in the seventeenth century, proposes the following grid: genre, difference, definition, enumeration of parts, etymology, conjugations (this is the associative field of the verbal root), comparison, repugnance, effects, causes, etc. Let us suppose that we must produce a discourse on literature: we "dry up" (with good reason), but fortunately we possess Lamy's Topics: we can then, at least, ask ourselves questions and try to answer them: to what "genre" will we attach literature? Art? Discourse? Cultural production? If it is an "art," how does it differ from the other arts? How many parts are we to assign to it, and which ones? What does the etymology of the word suggest to us? (66)

Passage

An inspiration for Derrida's bridge is Cézanne. In *Truth in Painting* Derrida takes up the logical implications of Cézanne's innovations in pictorial space, which in their graphics demonstrate how ontology extends beyond writing into imaging (from grammar to graphic design). "Putting in question against the trait as a signature, whether this signature passes via the proper name known as patronymic or via the idiom of the draftsman sometimes called *ductus,* I explore in its logical consistency the system of duction (production, reproduction, induction, reduction, etc.). This amounts to treating the trait, its unity and divisibility, otherwise" (10). The operation opens logic to a fourth inference, conduction, whose movement through information follows the trait, both as a graphic or a phonic mark. Hole conducts. The categorial function of gathering features into a set works by means of shared syllables, or letter pairs. Derrida applied this logos at different scales, with a range of primary sources, from the philosophy of Hegel to the objects and drawings of Gerard Titus-Carmel.

In the essay around Titus-Carmel's series of drawings, "The Pocket Size Tlingit Coffin," Derrida explores the "ductus" meaning the way a personal style (manner) signs a work as surely as does a proper name (I discussed this experiment in *Applied Grammatology*). The larger question is his testing of Heidegger's crossed semantic domains, creating the pull of the *Zug* through designed or discursive space and time.

> *Tirer*: To draw lots, to draw cards, to draw to one's end, etc. There is an idiom—or rather an idiomatic effect—of the tirer. I understand it in two senses: the idiom of the line drawn but also the idiom of the word tirer and of all the ways it is treated in the language. Later, elsewhere, draw all this discourse on lines drawn, draw it across toward where the two "families" cross—that of *Riss* (the broaching, the contour, the frame, the sketch, the plan, the précis, etc.) and that of *Zug* (trait, to draw, to attract, to withdraw, the contract gathering all the features). (193)

The insight is that the (bachelor) machine of places extends beyond discourse into the multi-modal graphical user interface in general.

It is important to note that the trait crosses media, forms, modes. Its full potential Derrida finds in Artaud's late "drawings," produced during his madness. That he was sick, Derrida noted, did not prevent him from saying the truth. The truth in painting, in fact. The drawings were exhibited along with Artaud's writings of the period, in which Artaud declared in his title the metaphysical nature of his project ("*Mise-en-Scene* and Metaphysics") (Derrida, "To Unsense the Subjectile" 84). The text treats in part a painting by Lucas van Leyden, *Lot and His Daughters,* which allegorizes the metaphysical intent of Artaud's trait. The *mise-en-scene* of the painting, showing God visiting His Judgment upon the city, invokes the etymological significance of "category" in its original Greek sense: the handing down of an indictment in a court of law (as Heidegger noted in his discussion of Aristotle). "It is again the breach of a surface or a support, by a 'force of destruction' coming from above, hurtling from the sky toward the underneath, toward the substratum of the surface or of the support, bombarding it, rending it apart. At once a visible 'bombardment' with 'solar bombs' and a 'resonant rending.' . . . Artaud is describing *Lot and His Daughters*" (87). We are given a glimpse here of Artaud's Allegory of Prudence.

Electracy transforms the parergon of judgment from law to art (from true-false to pleasure-pain). The question is: how may graphics support ontology beyond language? At stake is a conductive logic to link rules with cases. The manner of the drawings convey that part of metaphysics Heidegger named *aletheia*, to establish that Being is not simply that which is permanently present, but that it comes and goes, appears, presences. Heidegger is naming what the Greeks intuited in the term *phusis* (nature), referring to the upsurge of life, the blossoming forth. A witnessing of this energy is captured in Artaud's marks. Part of the relevance for us in this particular example of trait is that Artaud's marks are hybrids, suggesting the possibilities for an image category, crossing all established categorial borders. "This is why I shall propose to give another sense to the word pictogram in order to designate this work in which painting—the color, even if it is black—drawing, and writing do not tolerate the wall of any division, neither that of different arts nor that of genres, nor that of supports or substances" (78). This "new language" unites in one modality the means of writing, music, color, and drawing (multi-modal composing).

The title of the essay names the dimension opened for ontological work by Artaud's example: "to unsense the subjectile." The subjectile names a hinge region, a fractal dimension between subject and object, augmenting the interval working in every binary (every concept). The thought of the subjectile is carried in Artaud's performances that spill over all the limits and conventions: the cigarette burns through the supporting medium, the repetitious stubbings of the pencil marks. The categorial work or gathering action of the manner is a manifestation of the "drawing" of trait as the force of *Zug* as train, or (strange) attractor. It figures what Derrida elsewhere calls "chora" (*khora*), the regional space of "*genos*" in Plato's *Timaeus,* within which becoming is sorted into (given the stamp of) being. "*Parergon*" is another synonym, with each of these notions and their interrelationship being part of Derrida's attempt to show this dimension of categorial force (of energy). Derrida generates "*parergon*" out of Kant's *Critique of Judgment,* to name those decorations or supplements that mark off a border, making possible a form, shape, idea, *eidos*, as part of his shifting of metaphysical tropes from sight (*theoria*) to taste (gustation). The subjectile articulated through the modality of trait captures for ontology the dimension of manner, intensity, vividness (the values of lived experience).

The ultimate parergon in relation to Kant's system, Derrida suggests, is the *vomi*, the vomited, the absolutely repulsive, beyond the sublime even, to be associated with everything "abject," to remind us that the aesthetic axis is not just attraction, but attraction-repulsion. A figure for the *parergon* as frame, setting inside/outside hinges, is the *passe-partout*, the empty frame, like Laclau's empty universal, into which may be inserted any content. It is the hole, the open, the gap, strike zone, abyss maintained by the object @, temp of desire, effigy of avatar. This gap is what electracy opens in the dimension collapse of dromosphere. Breathing room for the operant subject. The important operator is that the frame is mobile (imagine it as a film director, using her hands to frame off a section of a scene, conducting mise-en-scene as a contemporary "templum"). An immediate fit is with hand-held devices displaying augmented reality. There is a "strike zone" in every situation. Hole lends itself to mixed reality.

The political stakes are high, in the adaptation of chora, parergon, subjectile as the categorial practice of a new hegemony. Such is the challenge: a hole attractor. We see the politics of abjection (of pure repulsion) in Palestine/Israel today. Can it happen t/here? As we speak. The choral category, organized by trait, is holistic (the "w" elided in advance) rather than analytic. A multitude is not one, not whole, but hole. "I shall take it to mean especially," Derrida says of Artaud's pictograms,

> the trajectory of what is literally understood to cross the border between painting and drawing, drawing and verbal writing, and, still more generally, the arts of space and the others, between space and time. And through the subjectile, the motion of the motif assures the synergy of the visible and the invisible, in other words theatrical painting, literature, poetry, and music. Without any totalization and taking due account of the subjectilian wall, of this dissociation in the body of which the singularity of the event made into work will always be marked. ("Unsensing the Subjectile" 78–79)

Consulting with the mad, vanguard of conduction. Image ontology emerges within this manner of remarking.

Rta

We learn in a footnote that Derrida has been using the Rat Bridge for his "trait-ment," finding it already at work in Artaud's proper name, as an embodiment of the abject. "For a reading of this ra, grammar of the future and clearing of the throat, a semantic ramification and a frenzied death rattle, we would have to bring together all the ra's and all the rats of Artaud, starting with those to be heard in his own name: Ar-Tau" (154). The singularity of Artaud's symptom (the motif of degradation, filth, shit) becomes a *sinthome*, in Lacan's terms, the symptom enjoyed, embraced as the one point of direct connection with the Real. Laclau observes that the new hegemony works in this same way. "I have attempted to show in *On Populist Reason* how the logic of hegemony and that of the Lacanian object *a* largely overlap and refer to a fundamental ontological relation in which fullness can only be touched through a radical investment in a partial object—which is not a partiality within the totality but a partiality which is the totality" ("Constructing a People" 651). He is in the region of flash reason, whose task is to bring global Internet ratio up to speed.

What has to be enacted for a multitude is a hegemonic logic and space that is coheres at this level of the unsensed, or, in our terms, by developing absensibility. The multitude gathers as a distributed one. Derrida's choral category and its conductive trait offer this possibility, being a non-objective ontology, so to speak (he is a Cézanne of metaphysics). The electrate apparatus, after all, is forming in the conditions of spectacle, the waning of Abstract space, the waxing of Differential space, co-existing in the transition of Contradictory space of homogenous fragmentation (to use Henri Lefebvre's terms for the production of modern space). All the *topoi* of good form and sense are dissolving in Bataille's formless. As Derrida appreciated, the relay for the category adequate to these conditions could be found in Cézanne: to do for metaphysics what Cézanne did for painting. The active term in discussions of Cézanne's invention is *passage* in Derrida's sense of trait, the force of musical (aesthetic) coherence. As Ezra Pound wrote in the *Pisan Cantos*, when the mind swings by a grass blade, an ant's forefoot shall save you. The hole, that is, is an aesthetic logos (vortex). Your white-crowned pigeon, your *gelato*, your frog. Promo for the empty universal (the floating signifier): your *sinthome* here.

Derrida's merging of semantic domains based on certain syllables (tr, gl, ra) mimes Cézanne's uniform brushstrokes that ignore the outlines of individual things (literate categories), in favor of producing the "little sensations" of color perspective (parallax), triggering potential lichettes.

> The primary method [Cézanne] arrived at was based on two simple visual phenomena—the obvious assumption that if one object or plane overlaps another the former must be in front of the latter, from the observer's viewpoint; and the fact that cold colors—blues and greens—tend to recede and warm

> colors—reds, oranges, yellows—to advance. By exploiting the effects of overlapping forms and juxtaposed warm-to-cold color planes, Cézanne was able to diminish greatly the importance of converging and diverging lines and still achieve distinct spatial effects. (Murphy 80)

And just as Cézanne's scenes remained recognizable as figures, so too do Derrida's "traitises" remain semantically cogent. The effect of their respective innovations is to make it possible to see and to think an emergent reality (a new ontology). Happily, rhetoric and painting share the term "color." Mary Ann Caws summarized the formal power of passage:

> The term "passage" may be taken as the corridor between moments, situations, states, at once spatial, temporal, psychological, sociological, and anthropological, its rites openly acknowledged. It is the place of ritual and psychological transformation, the moment of shift and displacement of sentiment, the consciousness of a textural turn. The notion of passage has also been extended to painting and sculpture, where it marks the instant of change, of colors blending one into the other, planes intersecting or of objects intersecting with the surrounding air, and so on. Originally associated with Paul Cézanne and the cubists, this sort of passage is a useful concept also for the critical eye. Moreover, the idea may be likened to the *relais* in the weaving of a tapestry, that is, the moment at which there is a marked change of color or figure. The varied techniques of joining patterns, covering over or disclosing passage or change, and the concept of rest between patterns—another shift, a relay as in a game, a relief between night and day—may also be useful in order to gain a different perspective on textual techniques. Connected with this guiding metaphor is the essential notion of the step (pas, Latin *passus*) both as in the steps of a stair, and also as in the steps of a walker or a passerby, in the "passos" of Luis de Gongora, Breton's lost steps, and Louis Aragon's reference to the actual covered gallery Passage de l'Opera," all alluded to here. (11–12)

What weaves the mass into a multitude is a circulation of traits, configured as emblems (each marking a *sinthome*), which taken at face value may appear as non-sense. But each marks the site of *conatus*, of a striving to persevere in one's own being, a life force (self-preservation) that is the motivation of all prudence. Trait as *Zug* functions as this trajectory, an attractor force pulling us through a situation, a thought, a text, a database, serving as decorum for undergoing vectorial dynamics in life. The figure I came upon when first opening Kafka's diaries was a scene of passage (being yanked by his hair up through several floors of a residence, to burst out through the roof tiles above the city). Such was the force field of Kafka's *sinthome*. What must be realized to fully appreciate hole hegemony is that the reality constructed for metaphysics with this operator is sited in your body—the urbanization of embodiment, Virilio might say. Testing the principle of hole, I noticed the letters turning from RAT to ART. What about RTA? Is RTA a dead end or a passage? Google answered. In the Vedic religion, *Ṛta* (Sanskrit, "that which is properly joined; order, rule; truth") is the principle of natural order which regulates and coordinates the operation of the universe and everything within it. There is Rta hole. *Alcántara* is from an Arabic word for bridge. Ponte Trajan mapped onto electracy. Arjuna receives Rta from Krishna. The hole mediated by concept avatar, itemizing choral coherence: art, rat, rta, tar.

In the railroad museum giftshop, I purchased a wooden whistle that simulated the mournful wail of a night train of blues refrains. When I tooted the toy, there occurred a Proustian memory, in which a shared sensation brings into the present a fragment of lost time. Immediately appeared a scene of South Center Street, Miles City, Montana, 1949, in the rental house backing on the Northern Pacific Railroad tracks. Mother was hanging laundry on the lines in the back yard, where I was playing next to one of the poles. Through the sheets flapping in the breeze I saw the stranger approaching from the direction of the boxcars parked on the siding. He carried a rucksack. Arriving at the back fence, he said something to my mother, who went into the house and reappeared after an interval with a small bag, which she handed to the man whom I now identify as "hobo." She had given him a sandwich, and judging by the visits from similar characters in the months that followed, he must have chalked the hobo sign for "kind-hearted lady" (a grinning cat) somewhere near our house. We moved the next spring, leaving future tenets to live up to this (blues) legend.

12 Counsel

Disaster

Coordinating idiot with event, concept avatar consults. In flash reason, the crisis (the disaster itself) is avatar. Avatar intimates, gives a sign: accident (the Big No): the writing of the disaster. Agency in electrate subject formation is distributed, collective. Our Allegories are networked in cyberspace. Disaster avatar as consultation in my case (supplying history's macrocosm for memory's microcosm) is the Cabot-Koppers Superfund site, located in my hometown, Gainesville, Florida (but you have your own visit from Pandora). It is a test for the Allegory of Prudence: to take counsel from a disaster, to frame "accident" as transference. A guiding question: who decided to pollute the drinking water of my region with dioxin? The conventional answer: *oops*. But the direction from Virilio to foreground accident by-product as sign in an electrate metaphysics envisions a necessary (fatal) accident. To bring this sign into flash ratio (hole) we inventory the scene for potential emblems.

The Cabot-Koppers site, located on NW 23rd Ave in the City of Gainesville, consists of the western half of a designated Federal Superfund site due to contamination with wood treating chemicals in site soils and groundwater. The eastern half is the Cabot site which contains groundwater contamination from past pine tar, pine oil and charcoal production. Investigation of the source areas conducted by Beazer in April, May and June 2004 indicated that creosote type materials were present in the upper and lower Hawthorn Group formations at the site at depths of approximately 60 to 100 ft below ground surface in several of the 4 primary source areas at the site. Additionally for the first time significant groundwater contamination was detected in one well (FW-6) installed into the upper zone of the Floridan Aquifer near the North Lagoon contaminant source area at depths of approximately 150 ft below land surface. The depth of this found contamination in the Hawthorn and Floridan Aquifers was unexpected and presented a potential threat to the City of Gainesville's Murphree Wellfield (Cheryl).

The City of Gaineville recently directed its Regional Utility Company to stop buying utility poles from the Koppers company (there are 120 million utility poles in service in the United States), and the company now is closed. Koppers continued up to the present to use the Superfund site for wood treatment, the activity that caused the original pollution of the area. Here is an initial term for figural inquiry: utility pole. The pole figures metaphysical causality. *That for the sake of which* . . . The pole is merely a means to an end, a tool. We did not want the pole as such, for itself alone. Aristotle's four causes: What is it made from? What is its form? What produced it? For what purpose? We may ask: what is the utility of the pollution of Gainesville's wellfield? How well are we (what is our wellness)? We have poles *in order to* . . . The hole turns about a pole. The metaphysical (categorial) issue is: pollution versus purity.

Heidegger articulates the ontological dimension of cause: *Worumwillen*. *Dasein* is this for-the-sake-of-which, referring to my concerns, creative of *world*. It is hard to keep track of everything. Lacan's @ (the object a), the fetish, is not what is desired but the object cause of desire (standing in). Avatar. The wires supported by utility poles figure lines, vectors, making appear the force-field framing our situation. Americans: we who are poisoned by the utility pole (this phrase is a figure). Is *utility* itself the cause? Utility names one of the historical universals, each one functioning as Measure for its epoch: Polis; God; Reason; Utility; Commodity. Utilitarianism declared collective well-being as its criterion of value, as did Commerce. Have we come full circle today, at least linguistically? Not "Polis," but only "pole is." Becoming pole. A polar imbalance (favoring one extreme). What is the other pole magnetized with "utility"? "Futility"? Virilio proposed "Finitude" (disasters measure the outer limit of progress). "Fatality" at least. Perhaps we should follow those power lines to see where they lead, and to hold responsible those we find at the other end (that is to say, us)? Choragraphy maps *dharma*: you-are-here is karma. *Sinthome* hegemony.

Fatal strategy (how we become what we are) leaves remediation to conventional consultants, in order to consider accident from a different perspective, to determine what in the event is irreparable, that is, what in the event concerns ethos, character. A parallax strategy of consulting. The disaster is an inheritance. Event (*Ereignis* is Heidegger's term) refers to this received decision, what is given as gift, a duty to be paid by receiver. The past is well-preserved. In the event of the Koppers site, the activity resulting in pollution began in 1911, and the pitch pine tar was used to treat utility poles, and any other wooden entity requiring preservation. Pine tar is a by-product formed as the result of distilling pine wood at high temperatures, forcing it to decompose. Once the wood breaks down, it results in the formation of charcoal and a gum-like substance, tar. When the tar is further distilled, oils are removed from it, creating the by-product pine tar pitch. The history of this product goes back six centuries, with the original use being the treatment of ship hulls. Pine tar is an important link in the story of invention tracked in episode seven ("The Long Chain") of *Connections* (James Burke), and is a good example of *technics*, referring to the autonomous, interdependent ontologies of technology and human culture. The original source of pine tar (Scandinavian forests) used by the British and other European fleets was cut off due to war, replaced by the New World colonies as primary supplier, primarily the Southern states. The evolution of inventions, passing through a series of accidents, mistakes, chance connections traced by Burke, evolves from pine tar through coal tar eventually on to plastics. Fatal strategy places accident in its collective historical dimension. We are on the TAR bridge. *Avapinetar.*

Contrast: Scenario

Heuretics suggests running a CATTt, to correlate the scene of the accident with concept avatar (the "tar" pitch is sounding through *daimonion*). William Poundstone's *Prisoner's Dilemma* is a source for Contrast. This account of the passage from pure research (Von Neumann's invention of "game theory") to public policy formation (American foreign policy, specifically U. S. nuclear strategy) during the Cold War, establishes that part of the problem for which fatal strategy is the alternative. We retain public policy formation, choosing a specific disaster (accident) and its related policy options, while updating strategy for international relations in the new conditions of terrorism. The first step in filling the Contrast slot is to inventory primary attributes of the source example. We need to understand how game theory evolved into public policy, in order to locate opportunities for fatal games. In keeping with the heuretic method, we identify one primary feature of the source to translate into an instruction for our CATTt. That feature is the example of the variation on Prisoner's Dilemma known as Chicken. We are reminded that Lacan used Prisoner's Dilemma as hypotyposis to relate the intersubjective experience of subject in the Imaginary register (the struggle for recognition of the Other).

Bertrand Russell is credited with identifying this model of human conflict in his book *Common Sense and Nuclear Warfare* (1959). The relevant instruction comes from Russell's use of the 1955 film *Rebel Without a Cause* (starring James Dean) as a metaphor for nuclear stalemate. "In the movie, spoiled Los Angeles teenagers drive stolen cars to a cliff and play a game they call a 'chicken run.' The game consists of two boys simultaneously driving their cars off the edge of the cliff, jumping out at the last possible moment. The boy who jumps out first is 'chicken' and loses" (Poundstone 197). Russell saw this game as an emblem for "brinksmanship." The metaphor was picked up in subsequent discussion, and contributed to the discourse surrounding the Cuban Missile Crisis. It is now a commonplace of contemporary commentators on current affairs, for example, in recent descriptions of the debate over raising the debt ceiling in the United States Congress (deadline August 2, 2011). Instruction (to clarify our alternative): select a pop film narrative to use as a metaphor or emblem for articulating or expressing a narrative scenario relevant to your disaster/accident. Hollywood the sage, preserved by pine tar.

The relationship between the policy of brinksmanship and the film *Rebel Without a Cause* noted by Bertrand Russell recalls a more general observation made by Richard Slotkin. Slotkin observed that US policy planners and Hollywood scriptwriters draw upon the same "mythologies" in the formulation of their scenarios.

> *Rio Grande* thus appears to be in some sort of dialogue with history. Film and event "speak" to each other—event lending political resonance to the fiction, the fiction providing mythological justification for particular scenarios of real-world action. They did so in the first instance (1950) not because one necessarily caused or influenced the other, but because the conceptual categories which shaped the scenarios developed by both movie-makers and policy-makers were drawn from the same cultural lexicon, the same set of mythological models. But once the "cult of the cavalry" was established as a

> major division of American mythic space and was seen to be responsive to the course of political events, its fictive rationales and heroic styles of action (especially as embodied in the symbolic persona of John Wayne) became functional terms in public discourse and symbols of the correct or heroic response to the challenges of the Cold War. (Slotkin 364)

Slotkin adds that an entire complex history is condensed into an emblem consisting of John Wayne in his cowboy persona associated with a motto (the right man with a gun). The emblem communicates in a flash (flash reason) US counterinsurgency strategy from Vietnam to the present, as evidenced by the Navy SEALS code name for Osama bin Laden ("Geronimo"). The relevance to flash reason is not so much in terms of matching films with specific strategies, but locating the ethos (limit, character)—but we could also say "fantasy"—guiding the screenplay/policy. Frank Rich in a review of the Coen Brothers remake of *True Grit* (the original starring John Wayne), makes the point.

> Talk about Two Americas. Look at *The Social Network* again after seeing *True Grit*, and you'll see two different civilizations, as far removed from each other in ethos as Silicon Valley and Monument Valley. While *The Social Network* fictionalizes Mark Zuckerberg, it mines the truth of an era—from the ability of the powerful and privileged to manipulate the system to the collapse of loyalty as a prized American virtue at the top of that economic pyramid. In contrast to Mattie's dictum ["You must pay for everything in this world one way or another. There is nothing free except the grace of God"], no one has to pay for any transgression in the world it depicts. (WK10)

The legibility of collective decision as ethos in policy and cinema suggests a heuristic device: to use popular narratives as probes to locate fundamental assumptions (the common scenarios, the fantasies) organizing decision in individual and collective situations. The instruction is to explore such a connection with a Target disaster, keeping in mind that we are documenting an aspect of Contrast in order to examine our common sense expectations, relative to concept avatar. What is *dharma*, for us, keeping in mind that the difference between us and Arjuna is that our Law may be amended. Ethos is call. Pathos is response (origin of the blues).

Burning Rivers

An abstract of the film *A Civil Action* (1998) exemplifies the environmental pollution scenario. Jan Schlickmann (John Travolta) is a cynical lawyer who goes out to 'get rid of' a case, only to find out it is potentially worth millions. The case becomes his obsession, to the extent that he is willing to give up everything—including his career and his clients' goals, in order to continue the case against all odds. This is how many stories begin: the ordinary world is disturbed, interrupted by some interference in one or the other economies of exchange (love, money, language). Narrative has its own way of confronting *problem,* in other words, even when it is dramatizing argument, as in this instance. The attitude of the voice is given, but indirectly, evoked at the level of discourse, through the inflections provided by style. The experience of *identification* is the sign of understanding: message received.

The three steps of form also function in this mode, ordering the three acts of the standard screenplay: 1. the ordinary world (home) is disturbed, and the character must choose to answer the call; 2. the first encounter with the problem, the opponent, but none of the usual behaviors suffices. The character must make a fundamental decision: to become what one is (to enact anomaly); 3. with this transformation the character becomes protagonist (or not), and succeeds in restoring order to the world (or not). Travolta, playing the lawyer Schlickmann, at the moment of decision, changes from a selfish exploiter of the misery of others to a champion of right and justice. The axis of narrative is: right-wrong. This structure does not reflect actual historical experience, where in reality the corporations manage to avoid responsibility most of the time for the "non-intentional" ruin they create in their pursuit of profit. The point of the story, rather, is the promotion of a value, ethics, a metaphysics of agency in which change happens in the world only through the action of individuals, who assert their will against the determining forces of nature and society. This mode of identity is selfhood, native to literacy. Agency in electracy shifts to a group or "operant" subject (accessed through concept avatar). Avatar mediates between "I" and "We."

A Civil Action shows the symptom that may also be present in my Superfund site. The lawyers believe that someone must have seen something that could provide evidence for the actions of the corporation. Finally they find a witness who saw the river on fire at night. The river fire points in at least two directions, as do the images we see in dreams:

one leads into the public history of culture, to show the family relations of the symptom. Greek Mythology talks of five rivers separating the land of the living and the dead. Phlegeton was one of them—the River of Fire. It burned but did not consume any fuel. This same river figures in Dante's *Divine Comedy* which describes what dead souls undergo. Phlegeton is in the outer ring of Circle Seven reserved for those violent against others. The other direction is the chain of my personal associations. This symptom intimates the propensity of things in my existential project. It is a kind of prophecy, like the one the witches told to MacBeth, that he "will not be killed until the *Birnam* Wood moves to Dunsinane Hill." The *burning* may be heard again in Birnam. The Koppers disaster includes charcoal, perhaps the ashes of this fire. But it is not the scene itself that is my symptom, but something of that sort, expressing a bachelor machine of oxymorons (burning rivers, moving woods), marking a path through the scene of my disaster, leading to the surprise. To receive the sign the consultant must take it personally. These are the devices of allegory, of divination.

The Travolta film shows the kind of stories told about disasters in popular culture (we can't help but regard him as "Michael" in our context). It foregrounds the two predominant ways of saying being in our practices: as evidence (true and false, the axis of science) and as story (right and wrong, the axis of morality institutionalized in religion). In fatal strategy both modes are subordinated to a third kind: figure (the axis of pleasure-pain). Moreover, the particular scene of this "smoking gun" is a pivot, opening a way beyond both modes, becoming independent as a sign. The corporations in our case have accepted responsibility and negotiated compensation, even while the full catastrophe is still in progress and is irreparable (fatal). For many years, the clay in the Upper Hawthorn Group was assumed to be a barrier to downward migration of contamination into the Floridan aquifer. As recently as 2002, this assumption changed. Sampling data from 2003 revealed that contamination was widespread in the Hawthorn Group ("Second Five-Year Review Report" EPA). Surprised? *Laugh now, cry later.*

Theory: *Obscenario*

The effect of working through the sources of the CATTt is the emergence of a conversation (intertext) between and among the readings. The specifications of instructions in one text call out correspondences in subsequent texts. For example, the instruction from Contrast is to appropriate some popular narrative (Hollywood movie) as a probe to identify relative to disaster an operative mythology. This instruction is further motivated by the context of matching and replacing the role of game theory in public policy formation. An important feature of this Contrast is the use of scenario form, narrative structure, to represent strategy alternatives. There are many studies of this practice, and some of the basic principles include the goal of identifying and changing the mental models of decision makers, in order to envision possibilities for actions anticipating tendencies, trends, propensities of events in the future. In short, scenarios are formulations of deliberative reason, of collective or institutional prudence. It is common to propose three alternatives, between the poles of best and worst case. Peter Schwartz in *The Art of the Long View* identified a collection of plot templates: winners and losers, challenge and response, evolution, revolution, cycles, the lone ranger, "my generation." It goes without saying that the narrative form itself supplies a set of assumptions: a model of human agency, the role of action to transform situations, the whole actantial structure familiar to students of literature. The common sense of our habitus is that stories guide decisions both personal and political. Recent complaints about President Obama's leadership are that he has failed to provide a clear narrative. But there is an additional dimension available for deliberation. Fatal strategy assumes a different relation between agent and world from that organizing narrative form or documentary argument.

Avatar consulting does not oppose story design (*Darstellung*), but probes into region by pushing away from convention. The challenge posed by the 9/11 Commission to policy makers requires going beyond Hollywood scenarios (such as those composed for Homeland Security by the Analytic Red Cell Unit) to an electrate configuration of potentiality (*Entstellung*). Yes, I await the call from Washington. The elementary narrative exploited so efficiently in popular culture is an account of a subject who desires an object of value and sets out to get it, and who is transformed by the process. This is ethos. The accomplishment of the quest manifests the principal modalities of human capacity, the qualities of will, duty, power, and knowledge. Decorum display. It is worth reviewing scenario dynamics, since these undergo distortion (*Entstellung*) in dromosphere. These qualities are expressed as modalities of doing and being in the narrative and discourse, and it is this modalization that may lend itself to inclusion in ontology. In semiotic theory, a narrative correlates three axes of interaction (Martin and Ringham). The axes put in relation six actants (functions) constituting the minimal units of any narrative: Sender-Receiver, Subject-Object, Helper-Opponent. These are the positions of ethos enacted in scenarios: a map of decorum. The following review is from Martin and Ringham's handbook:

1. Communication. The modality of the axis of communication is "knowing" (cognitive, epistemic), referring to the internal state of mind of actants (ignoring, deceiving, etc). A story is first of all a communication in a specific culture and historical period. It is a message in which a Sender persuades/manipulates a Receiver, and a Receiver interprets/resists, relative to an Object of Value. The Sender is simultaneously any or all of the culture collectively, the author, an authoritative character in the story, a caregiver (reading the story to a child); the Receiver is also the culture, the Subject, another character in the story, the one reading or listening. The meaning of the story as a whole results from the axiology (system of value relations in the paradigm) and ideology (specific beliefs enacted in the syntagm) created within the text. The story has a point of view, and the purpose of the communication is to express it. When we ask after the wisdom of literature, we want to know the purport of these axiologies and ideologies (formal and thematic presentations of values). The story (Cinderella is a prototype) communicates a message about what is important in life and how to get it.
2. Desire. The modalities of the axis of desire are "wanting" (will) and "having to" (duty). Subject and Object are created together, interdependent, with the state of wanting-to-be and wanting-to-do initiating the becoming of the Subject as such. The Subject begins in a condition of separation (disjunction) from the Object of Value. The syntax of the narrative develops as transformation, a mediation, bringing the Subject into conjunction with the Object. This process is characterized as a practical syllogism: Major premise = the desire; Minor = the means; Conclusion = the action. Cinderella desires to have a

life, to be loved and respected, and the event of the royal ball incarnates this desire.

3. Performance. The actants of this axis represent the competence of the Subject, in the positions of the Helper and the Opponent or Anti-Subject. The modality is being-able-to, or power. The syntax of action stages three tests, gauging the worthiness of the Subject, the confrontation or decision that accesses the Object, and recognition or evaluation of the success (or failure). The Opponent is Cinderella's step-mother and step-sisters, who are Subjects in their own right (Anti-Subjects), but this is not their story. The Helper (donor) is the magic fairy, who provides the accessories Cinderella needs to accomplish her winning of the Prince. The Object of Value is tracked through the transformations of mediation between poles by means of a figure, a circulating item that is exchanged between or among actant positions. The famous glass slipper is a token of this circulating type. When politicians appeal to the proverb about "kicking the can down the road," they may not be aware that this "can" alludes to *posse*, the modality of "I can." If you cannot, then you must delay the action. The problematic posse is a primary concern of concept avatar. Brand hears "entourage," but avatar interrupts: im/potence.
4. Discourse: the surface vocabulary is organized into a series of figures. The other dimension of text besides narrative is discourse, including all the other features of language and style. This is the dimension opened for ontological development in electracy. The lexicon of exposition describing Cinderella's beauty, poverty, hard circumstances; the step-relatives' ugliness, meanness, selfishness; the Prince's wealth and so forth, is already accessible to Natural Language Programming and semantic ontology.

The challenge of hole to the technological register of electracy is in the design of the lexicon to express the axiology of the story, by means of isotopies created among the terms of the exposition, to bring this dimension into database construction. Gathering isotopies into a figure (Gestalt) is the work of *obscenario*. Egent inventional consultants compose *obscenarios* for deliberative decision. The descriptions are organized as binary oppositions (beauty-ugly, rich-poor, clean-dirty, high-low, happy-sad, kind-cruel). The elementary isotopy is life-death (for the individual), correlating with good-bad/evil. The alignments of these figures with Cinderella's happiness guarantee the wisdom of the story will not be missed, a wisdom reiterated by Marilyn Monroe in the film *Gentlemen Prefer Blondes*, or Julia Roberts in *Pretty Woman*, and still with us today in many popular texts, however stereotyped and out of fashion it may be. Concept avatar opens wisdom formation to social media. Popular narrative expresses habitus. *Poncif* in play. The task of concept avatar is to change habitus (to access attitude at the deepest level of its formation). Our consultation counters ethos with pathos, following a Brechtian separation of tracks: knowledge, duty, hope need not be synced. Player negotiates with avatar.

In narrative terms, player with avatar is hero with helper (donor). In *True Grit,* the hero is Mattie Ross, the fourteen-year-old girl who seeks justice for the murder of her father. She hires Marshal Rooster Cogburn to get the job done, making him the donor figure. The weakness of the American *dharma* may be seen in this arrangement. Screenplay guides are careful to differentiate between mentors (who remain in the familiar world of home) and donors (denizens of "Hades"). Our donors have shifted or evolved from consultants or guides to mercenaries. Krishna is sage. He does not fight Arjuna's battle, but delivers a revelation of *dharma* and karma, leaving Arjuna to decide. Arjuna's role is "warrior," but to be what he is he must choose it (a forced choice, Žižek would say). This mutation of roles and positions in American wisdom (ethos) is a fundamental imbalance and may be rectified in electracy. Concept avatar as *Bildung* opens a passage to this restoration of the function of donor as sage. It supplements the narrative axes with a modality of manner (vividness, the life feeling as value). Pathos as trope does not impose knowledge or will on accident, but becomes accident (as persona), to acquire its wisdom. The passage from scenario to trope, from hero's story to sage's figure, is by way of the "circulating object."

We look for instruction towards this goal in the central argument of our Theory (Baudrillard) regarding figures of the transpolitical, which declares the end of (narrative) scene as such.

> The transpolitical is the transparency and obscenity of all structures in a destructured universe, the transparency and obscenity of change in a dehistoricized universe, the transparency and obscenity of information in a universe emptied of

> event, the transparency and obscenity of space in the promiscuity of networks, transparency and obscenity of the social in the masses, of the political in terror, of the body in obesity and genetic cloning. . . . The end of the scene of the historical, the end of the scene of the political, then of the scene of fantasy, the end of the scene of the body—the irruption of the obscene. The end of the secret—the irruption of transparency. (*Fatal Strategies* 45)

The dromosphere requires transpolitics. The relevant point is that a goal of our strategy is to do for the obscene what scenario did for scene: *obscenario*.

Fatal strategy helps decision makers accomplish collective prudence, by drawing upon the "ecstasy of communication" (*Entstellung* or distortion) in the same way that game theory drew upon the "theatrics of alienation" (*Darstellung* or presentation). We need to learn from Theory the formal resources of the *obscenario*. The principle is: accident intimates the Real, in a way that requires translation. Concept avatar does not compete with conventional consultants and their narrative scenarios, but opens a parallax dimension in which individuals consult accidents as donors, to undergo the collective register of Being (to experience measure on behalf of a hegemonic logos). The consulting procedure is not a scenario, then, but an emblem, an Allegory of Prudence. The accident measures collective will and as *daimon* says No.

The Accident Replies

Target instruction is to receive the accident as a sign, but (Contrast) not as narrative (which is too slow). Player with avatar expressed as consultant with accident (the accident is Krishna explaining *dharma* to the player, or *daimon* whispering Nemesis). Disaster is uncanny (it is Nemesis, retribution). Theory refines this instruction. These specs begin with one of the primary moments of Theory's response to Target's call:

> This liquidation of metaphor, this precipitation of the sign into brute, senseless matter, is a thing of murderous efficacy. It is of the same order as the meaningless event, the catastrophe, which is also a blind reply, without metaphor, of the world as object to man as subject. It's always like this that

> destiny becomes specific: at a given moment, at a given point, signs become objects, impossible to turn into metaphors, cruel, without appeal. They cut short any decipherment, become confused with things (which is why fate is a dreamer, with the unintelligible instantaneity signs and words have in dreams). The strategy of the object, like that of the woman in the story [her suitor admired her eyes, so she sent him one of her eyeballs], is to be confused with the thing desired. (*Fatal Straegies* 153)

The imperative is not to explain the accident, but that the accident explains us. Exceeding all rhetoric, it offers itself as a hypertrope for thinking with the Real, to experience collective measure, eco-limit. Some terminology is clarified in this statement. "Fatal" as modifier in French means "predestined" before it means "lethal." A "fatal strategy" is one that maps this default trajectory, this entropy: what cannot be otherwise. Fatal strategy recognizes what is self-evident in the accident. Hypertely (excrescence to the extreme) is our version of "entelechy" (disaster marks the threshold measure). The crisis is the lack of measure, absence of operant subject needed to manage *technics*. This shift to obscene (overlooked) figure is an answer to the challenge posed to electracy by the dromosphere of dimension collapse. The reason why "scene" disappears is because media (information) and event have merged: information and world coincide (precession of the simulacrum). What the Greek language singing Homeric epics was to literacy, the ubiquitous entertainment broadcasting of pop culture (including all journalism, Internet searches, database archives) is to electracy. Philosophy (literate metaphysics) was created out of written Greek culture (mythos into logos). Electrate metaphysics must be created out of the signifying materials of information culture (logos into pathos). What we seek from Theory is an instruction for how to manage this readymade discourse, how to construct an ontology of second nature. The accident sign is to electracy what the Greek word *eidos* was to literacy (raw material for metaphysics).

Baudrillard's qualification of the catastrophe as "pure" alludes to his instruction for us, to be found in his discussion of Baudelaire and the inception of "pure art" in Bohemian Paris. Cabaret (Paris as the Athens of electracy) enabled pure aesthetics, from which emerge the devices of an image metaphysics. The blind reply of the Real (the obscene) is the end of literate metaphysics (the excrescence overrunning all literate categories), not the end of signification. Bataille characterized these conditions of category pollution as "formless." Chora or hole as electrate catetory gathers topics into holisitic region. The *topoi* (*doxa*) coexisting in the accumulated representations of a city scene (for example) become combined through the work of formless into one atmosphere, emergent *Ort*. The function of formless as a logic is to declassify,

> an action that simultaneously 1) lowers or debases objects by stripping them of their pretension—in the case of words, their pretensions to meaning—and 2) declassifies, or attacks the very condition on which meaning depends, namely the structural opposition between definite terms. . . . The categorical blurring initiated by the continual alteration of identity within this work is precisely what Bataille means by formless. It is not just some kind of haze or vagueness in the field of definition, but the impossibility of definition itself due to a strategy of slippage within the very logic of categories, a logic that works according to self-identity—male, say, or female—stabilized by the opposition between self and other: male versus female, hard versus soft, inside versus outside, life versus death, vertical versus horizontal. (Krauss, *Bachelors* 5, 7)

The result of formless is not chaos but region, vortex, *Zug*. It is felt beyond thought. To call it "category" is a catachresis.

Category pollution (information sprawl) requiring new modalities of classification, is a point of transition into electracy facilitated by concept avatar. To test this functionality we need to apprehend the traits of an accident-sign, in order to outline its communicational system (a preliminary step). "If the waves of meaning, if the waves of memory and historical time are receding, if the waves of causality around the effect are fading (and the event today comes at us like a wave; it doesn't travel only 'over the waves'—it is a wave indecipherable in terms of language and meaning, decipherable only and instantly in terms of color, tactility, ambiance, in terms of sensory effects)" (*Fatal Strategies* 36–37). In short, the sign received from *technics* as autonomous ontology consists of what Sartre called in his ontology *qualia* (to anticipate our surprise). Part of the implication concerns the apparatus: that cinematography (the optical unconscious) is required to record the properties of the dromosphere (so far in excess of human faculties). The graphics of abstract art afford means to articulate as logic the forces manifested in the material break-up of accident. A scene of material pollution, then, instructs us on metaphysics. This new logic begins in my capacity to be affected by a modest detail from my situation designed as figure. The challenge is to extend the Allegory of Prudence into a practice of hegemony. Your *sinthome* as universal-for-a-day.

Seduced's Epiphany

Our game is not "Prisoner's Dilemma," but "Seduced's Epiphany." To receive the accident we occupy the position of object, within the field of event (following Baudrillard's advice). The *obscenario* as figure brings this value into reach of experience: it intimates the life-death ratio. The instruction for how to compose an *obscenario* comes from Modernism in general, Baudelaire in particular, and his strategy of becoming commodity (Benjamin). In pop terms we seek the magic tool or circulating prop (the glass slipper, the purloined letter, in Lacan's famous study), as shorthand (flash) revelation of the vectors structuring the *Ort*. As alternative to the calculation of game theory, with its grid of all rational options, fatal strategy assumes that if you locate the object-cause-of-desire (fetish, magic tool) you identify the unavoidable choice (our collective existential project). The electrate "thing" is (like) a commodity. In place of expanding into a narrative scenario, the consultation locates the event force in this universal substitutability.

> No longer to explain things and to set their value in objective criteria and in an unbounded system of references, but, on the contrary, to implicate the whole world in a single one of its details, an entire event in a single one of its features, all the energy of nature in a single one of its objects, dead or alive—to find the esoteric ellipsis, the perfect shortcut toward the pure object, the one which is not involved in the division of meaning, and which shares its secret and power with no other. (*Fatal Strategies* 146)

To communicate at light-speed, a sign must be compressed. This detail is the very one we are exercising in the Allegory of Prudence, following the passage of reflective judgment, which departs from the local particular ("locontology"). Flash reason.

Fatal strategy as formless derives from the arts invented in Paris, adapting to the shocks of industrial cities. The trauma of alienation, of reification, separates us from the experience of agency. Agency and hence decision as such move elsewhere, outside, neither spirit nor self, but into the collective order, as operant subject. It returns—the re(com)pressed—in the form of event, accident, and this effect is what fascinates, since the accident is us (*Problems B Us*). These uncanny conditions of alienation (of exile) demonstrate the obsolescence of our narrative ethos, which still promotes individual agency as the force of change. That is the experience of self (or will). It fails to recognize the impoverishment of lived experience in dromosphere and the emergence of brand as vehicle of commodified identity. The accident is uncanny in its revelation of agent impotence. Like Oedipus, we must point to ourselves when the Sphinx of disaster poses its question. We do not want to hear it, such that the hole is at the same time a knot of resistance. Derrida arrives at the hole from this direction, citing Freud's original hypotyposis for the dimension of Real: the navel.

> There is often a passage [a place, *eine Stelle*] in even the most thoroughly interpreted dream which has to be left obscure; this is because we become aware during the work of interpretation that at that point there is a tangle [*Knäuel*, like a ball of yarn] of dream-thoughts which cannot be unraveled and which moreover adds nothing to our knowledge of the content of the dream. This is the dream's navel, the spot where it reaches down into the unknown. The dream-thoughts to which we are led by interpretation cannot, from the nature of things, have any definite endings; they are bound to branch out in every direction into the intricate network of our world of thought. It is at some point where this meshwork [*Geflecht*] is particularly close that the dream-wish grows up, like a mushroom out of its mycelium. (Freud qtd. in *Resistances* 14)

This navel, whether as hole (Lacan) or knot (Derrida), is the *Stelle* of structural limit (measure). The unknown concerns the mystery of resistance to knowing, related to the overwhelming: that there is a morbidity in our nature and our ethos, that resists well-being. Electracy destabilizes the received terms of the aporia, by exploiting the alignment between the dream navel and digital networks. Concept avatar conducts a passage to a practice adequate to this alliance: flash reason goes by way of the Tar bridge. Derrida calls attention not to the logic of conduction but the resistance to solution (in transference), which he considers to be the more valuable discovery of psychoanalysis. Yes, that the best "solutions," based on expert knowledge, are nonetheless rejected, disavoed, refused, is in itself a justification for pursuing a supplemental consultancy (the EmerAgency). What is the intelligence of disavowal? Derrida proposes a portmanteau of his own, *poleros*, combining politics and eros, to name a cause of the aporia: practical reason is conducted within the ethos of seduction and resistance (restance) (10). Concept avatar extends the thought to fatality: *polnemesis*.

The conduct of the cure through transference demonstrate the axis of attraction-repulsion at work structuring the field of decision. The optimism of identifying the hole/knot (umbilicus, mycelium) as a structural condition (irreducible and irreparable) is that it adds a functionality to the recognition that the defense mechanisms of the unconscious are versions of rhetorical tropology. Policy formation in the public sphere is neither *Vorstellung* nor *Darstellung* (neither representation nor presentation), but *Entstellung* (distortion, organized by the deferral and displacement of differance). In hegemonic struggles, competing parties practice a rhetoric of evasion (disavowal, repression) against the opponent's rhetoric of persuasion (reflecting the constitutive antagonism of all relationships in society). At the same time, these evasions may be mapped, and positions tracked to their crypts, since the movement of defense is necessarily tropological. At the same time, it is important to recall that we are referring to a thought that happens elsewhere, outside, as unclaimed or alienated experience. The hegemonic strategy is to send a probe-trigger through the by-ways of tropology.

The extimacy of communication needed to consult on accidents framed as hole/knot goes beyond narrative scenarios to figural *obscenarios*, and this latter mode constitutes the practice of the EmerAgency. The goal is not to compete with empirical explanations, but to evade the disavowal that prevents me from undergoing the event. Opinion is shallow; attitude is deep. Narrative is shallow; figure goes deep. The relays for egents (electrate agents) are found in modernist poetics, Baudelaire's correspondences first of all, followed by all the variations (Eliot's objective correlative, Rilke's *Weltinnenraum*, Joyce's epiphany, Pound's vortex, Benjamin's dialectical image, Freud's *unheimlich*). The allegory has become immanent, the commodity is anagogical. The lyrical image registers in the microcosm the shock of the disaster in the macrocosm. Baudrillard learns from Baudelaire how to receive the oracle of the Real by treating problem symptoms as miniaturizations (*mise-en-abyme*). Suddenly the Real manifests itself everywhere. Our pain poses the question of *Befindlichkeit* (Heidegger, how do things stand, for me, for my situation in the world?). The disaster answers: obesity, cancer, terror (as metaphysical tropes). Events are not contingent aberrations, nor necessary determinisms, but "realizations" of potentiality. Events fascinate. The fundamental operating device of consultation: some feature of the outside scene adopted as a flash portrait of being. The instruction now is enhanced by the accident sign: look for a commodity (the circulating prop). Identify the obscene commodity, object cause of desire. What seduced (possessed) me (us) to treat wood? The stakes of the Allegory of Prudence are raised in this gambit, extending its application from mapping personal measure, to locating that measure within the event (*Ereignis*) of collective decision. The consistency of the gambit is that we are learning to simulate Krishna's revelation to Arjuna: *dharma*. Decision has a history.

Taste

The idea of order at Cabot-Koppers Superfund site. The soil in and around the Koppers site in Gainesville, Florida, is contaminated (polluted) with dioxin, a by-product of the wood treatment process that, locally at least, began in 1911. What is the temporality of pollution? It is fatal in the sense of predestined, even primordial, a gift/poison out of the past, monumental, archival, and also in the sense of lethal, deadly, undermining well-being, assuming that its natural movement down into the acquifer is irreversible. The fetish detail of this event is dramatized in the documentary television series, *Connections*, by James Burke, a series that anticipates and contributes to the discussion of *technics* (machine ontology).

> It was this concern for ships' hulls that was to lead, within a hundred years, to an invention that is present in almost every modern home [plastic]. As the ships sailed more often into tropical waters, their wooden hulls were attacked by a tiny mollusc called *teredo navalis*, which lived in those waters, and which bored into the hulls with devastating results. The only protection against the mollusc was a thick layer of a

> mixture of tar and pitch smeared over the bottom of the ship. At the beginning of the eighteenth century most of this material came from Scandinavia and the Baltic, from the unit of Sweden and Finland joined under the Swedish crown. Over the previous two hundred years most of Europe had become increasingly dependent on northern timber, as the forests of England, France, Spain and Portugal had become more and more depleted. The timber was used to build ships and to produce the tar and pitch. The best kind of wood for making tar and pitch was pine, which was cooked slowly in pits until the tarry substance ran out of the charring wood, to be collected and distilled and then shipped in barrels. In 1700 the Russians, whose northern ports froze over in winter, decided they needed a warm-water port on the Baltic, and moved against Sweden-Finland. The war that followed totally disrupted supplies. Fortunately for the English, there was one other source of supply—which they owned—in the new American colonies. (194–95)

Is this the zipped detail, the fetish? It was the encounter of wooden ships with the mollusc that caused the swerve (clinamen), the turn (-vert, trope), sending the manufacture of pine tar and pitch to America, and ultimately to Florida.

Derrida says everything passes through the mouth in economimesis (the metaphysics emergent from taste tropes). We retrace the uncanny path of event (return to sender), of passage and coming to pass (find the *Zug* of attraction-repulsion). Why were the trading ships entering warmer waters, where they encountered *teredo navalis?* Look around this decision to notice the force, the economy: we are in the spice trade. Pepper plants are native to southern India, and pepper has been used in Indian cuisine since ancient times. Black pepper was so valuable that it was used as money. In its decline Rome paid "protection" to the Visigoths in the form of tons of black pepper. The "spice" trade was originally primarily the "pepper" trade. Competition over control of the trade pushed the Portuguese to find a water route (alternative to the land routes controlled by Venice). The story is familiar from there. The lesson of this history for fatal strategy is to trace the accident as Nemesis, in the ancient sense of retribution (recalling that Schelling translated this Greek term into German as *unheimlich,* the source for Freud's "uncanny"). Our desired spice came with a "free *gift*." A rule of *obscenario*: product plus by-product (every invention is a happy-meal). Pandora + box.

The accident records our gesture, creating a field of action around Flesh, that is, human embodiment. The umbilicus as synecdoche. People developed a passion for the pungency of pepper. A revelation of the Real: our capacity to be affected. *Pungency*. You are the hole disaster (networked punning). If you have a mouth, you are complicit. Pepper is not really a preservative. It was rather flavor that sent the accident: taste. Chora in *Timaeus* sorted chaos into the four elements: earth, air, fire, water. This system remains relevant as metaphysics, if not as physics, especially if we specify the elements as the four flavors: sweet, bitter, salty, sour. The fifth element was ether (quintessence), and *umami* (savoriness) the fifth flavor. Refinements on the classifiction add pungency (pepper) and astringency. *A Billion Wicked Thoughts,* by the cognitive neuroscientists Ogi Ogas and Sai Gaddam, reports on a datamining study of search engine entries, used to help identify a set of sexual cues hard-wired into human neural circuitry. The cues accounting for human sexual desire are analogous to the five taste cues discerned by the human tongue (Yang).

Embodiment is categorial, projected into a metaphysics and beyond, into 'Pataphysics, through electracy. The genealogy of the Gainesville Superfund site is exemplary in part because of its association with Kant's *Critique of Judgment,* given the foundation of electrate metaphysics on the faculty of taste as the basis of aesthetic judgment, the sensorium oriented by un/pleasure. Such is the third axis, supplementing right-wrong (orality, religion, narrative) and true-false (literacy, science, evidence) with attraction-repulsion (electracy, entertainment, figure). Check your event for its bit of Flesh. Wisdom traditions devoted most of their attention to coping with this by-product of embodiment (to no avail). Such is the uncanny lesson of concept avatar, confounding in its unreceivable self-evidence. Why are there bridges and orchards? What is the wisdom of pepper? The institutions go right past it. It is obscene.

Analogy: Tropology

Greek (literate) metaphysics introduced the terminology of substance/accident relative to nature (*phusis*). Electracy supplements the resultant science by taking into consideration the modification of nature by *technics* (Stiegler). Accident manifests the encounter of *technics* with *phusis* (the two ontologies) revealing macromeasure for the apparatus of electracy. It is a version of Nietzsche's crossroads, for a collective subject: find the point at which the aphorism of culture crosses the anecdote of *technics*. The motivation for this reach is that *sinthome* (character) must be adequate to the function of hegemony. The CATTt instructions indicate that the accident sign is a figure, a trope, and the terms of the figure are specific to a given event. In the frame of bachelor machine logic, we recall Jarry's initial definition of 'Pataphysics, as

> the science of that which is superinduced upon metaphysics, whether within or beyond the latter's limitations, extending as far beyond metaphysics as the latter extends beyond physics. Ex: an epiphenomenon being often accidental, pataphysics will be, above all, the science of the particular, despite the common opinion that the only science is that of the general. Pataphysics will examine the laws governing exceptions, and will explain the universe supplementary to this one. (Jarry 21)

Bok's *'Pataphysics* makes the instruction precise. The lesson is found in the breakout of Surrationalist 'Pataphysics as art practice into three "declensions": *anomalos* (principle of variance); *syzygy* (principle of alliance); *clinamen* (principle of deviance).

A difficulty of heuretics is its heuristic nature: how should we respond to this appearance of three tropes in our Analogy source (the cabaret bachelor machine)? We could simply accept Bok's terms, and apply one of them to figure the accident. But then we notice the invented nature of Bok's figures. Syzygy is borrowed from astronomy, for example, naming originally one or the other of two points in the orbit of a celestial body either in opposition to or conjunction with the sun. The term is generalized to refer to any unity achieved through coordination of alignment. It is worth noting that Bok describes Bloom's revisionary ratios as 'Pataphysical. The invention of rhetoric is ongoing. Bok's creative move guides the instruction: identify in the technical discourse of your event a process that may be generalized into a trope or figure of thought. What is the tropical operation implicit in the Koppers Superfund accident? The answer depends on further clarifying the trait of the accident sign available in the vocabulary of its inscription.

We need to receive the whisper (intimation) from the Superfund site, to learn the uncanny discourse of Nemesis. We inventory the peculiar operations of the figure in the accident as avatar, or *daimon* (intimating the specific nature of macro-limit) by observing the *technics* of the scene. What does *technics* intimate? Pine tar, obtained by cooking pine wood, involves the distillation of an organic substance (wood in this case, but coal also is treated in this way). Wood, the fifth element, carries a fifth metaphysical cause. Aristotle proposed four causes operating in physical reality — four dimensions of explanation. Applied to Koppers production of Pine Tar, the causes are:

1. Material: *that out of which a thing comes to be, as a constituent in the product.* The raw material is wood (pine trees).
2. Formal: *the formula of what it is to be the thing in question.* How is Pine Tar produced, the chemistry of distillation, the cooking of pine wood that produces the tar.
3. Efficient: *the origin of the movement or rest.* The makers, Cabot-Koppers corporations are responsible and get credit for the production.
4. Final: *the end or aim, the purpose of the thing in question.* Pine Tar was produced in order to (that for the sake of which) treat wood, to preserve it from deterioration in the environment. These four causes must be supplemented with a fifth dimension, active in events of purposeful modification of nature.
5. Gift: *the by-product, unintended consequences of the process.* It is "gift" in the macaronic sense appropriated from the German word: gift/poison. Pine distillation that produces Pine Tar also produces charcoal. Charcoal is a welcome present. The other by-product is creosote, an unwelcome poison. The production of pine tar at the Cabot-Koppers site, beginning as early as 1911, and continuing until 2010, resulted in environmental disaster.

Instruction: count five causes; Material, Formal, Efficient, Final, Gift. It is an electrate update of *cause.*

Aristotle prepares us by using as analogy for the relation between matter and form, the process by which a craftsman transforms "wood" (matter) into "table" (form). Our concern is with wood processed into pine tar and *creosote.* The process is "distillation," which gives us an operant term, the equivalent for the Koppers emblem of Bok's syzygy or clinamen. Distillation includes vaporization and condensation. To distill (the dictionary supplies all the concepts) extracts a concentrate. By extension, distillation is any concentration, essence, or abstraction. The process is a purification. A preliminary review of the vocabulary supplied by the Rat/Tar Bridge (the hole, the choral word gathering the potential meanings) shows that my accident already employs one of the cardinal tropes: metaphor (condensation). The instruction was: look for a burning river. We promote the effect into a proverb: *purification pollutes.* The vocabulary resonates with descriptions of the commodity form itself (pine tar as paragon of commodity as such). Commodity as a relation of universal exchange perform a reduction, "which we might as well call the analysis, the decomposition or destructuration of the thing into its most elementary components (if there are any)—ought to reveal, as if by distillation or purification, the common core which exchangeable things share, the likeness on the basis of which they can be put into relation, measured proportionally" (Keenan, 110). This abstracting distillation empties out (kenosis) the properties of a thing, erases all difference, but leaving always a certain fatal remnant, personified as ghost or spectre by Marx (and Derrida after him), that returns to haunt the measure of value. "There is nothing of them left over but this very same ghostly objectivity, a mere jelly of undifferentiated human labor" (Marx, qtd in Keenan 115). This ghostly jelly is gift cause.

A purpose of concept avatar is to include this fifth cause in public policy calculations of well-being. Part of the meaning of a sign is its relational difference in a system. One system articulating the possibilities of *distillation* as generator of signification is alchemy (a precedent for elemental metaphysics retrieved by numerous vanguard artists, including Duchamp). James Elkins develops a systematic hypotyposis between alchemy and the craft of painting, to explore the potential meanings of painting beyond language into the direct figurations of materiality (how materials occupy the mind). The first transcendental meaning of distillation in alchemy, he noted, is as a metaphor for resurrection. His application of how distillation works in painting, however, is the insight relevant to flash reason.

> In alchemy, distillation is when the substance gives up its mundane body and becomes spirit, and in painting, it is when the paint ceases to be paint and turns into colored light. Al-

> though the Christian metaphors run deep and thick here, the fundamental concept is religious in a more general sense. On an empty canvas, a blob of yellow paint is a wet sculpture, a hanging adhesion on the linen threads, coated in a slowly thickening elastic skin. But if I step back far enough, it may become a yellow sun, shining in a white sky. In that moment the paint distills into light: it moves without my noticing from its base oily self into an ethereal abstraction. (Elkins 125)

This step back is what avatar conceives. It is the metamorphosis of Becoming into Being. Distillation is one step in the larger alchemical method of transmutation (transvaluation), seeking the philosopher's stone (wisdom). Elkins tracks the full circuit, including coagulating, cohobating, macerating, reverberating, to understand how elements occupy the mind. His account offers a short-cut for translating the material operations of your accident into tropical figures.

Figuration is the device that EmerAgency egents (consultants) add to narrative scenarios (it is the formal means of the *obscenario*). The passage from literal to figurative signification is a dead metaphor by now, in that it is common to see references to "distilling" of ideas, or concentration of materials. Of particular relevance is the description of distilling atmosphere from objects (applied to the box assemblages of Joseph Cornell, for example). In this preliminary inquiry we are accumulating instructions. A still is the apparatus of distillation, also read in our context as "still life," or "film still." Paronomy pushes us further into "still": motionless (adjective); stillness (noun); even now, nevertheless (adverb); *quieten* (verb). The Old English origin is to be fixed, stand. *Stelle*, in short (further evidence of the relevance of this scene to my Allegory). This vocabulary coming from the technical thing in the scene of counsel (*der Rat* in German) accumulates into design instructions for the *obscenario*: a still life (*nature morte*), perhaps a version of the atmosphere of *Silent Spring* (1962), Rachel Carson's book documenting the lethal effect of pollution (pesticides in particular) on birds, credited with helping start the environmental movement. For my Allegory of Prudence I was already alerted by Frog @ Walden Pond to look for a passage from motion to stillness. Cabot-Koppers supplies the textbook.

There is a more directly relevant meaning of the stillness counseled by accident avatar, as explained by Roger Shattuck, who names the cumulative stance (*Stelle*) of vanguard Paris as *stillness.* This passage was noted previously, in our discussion of the cabaret academy, and now we find a site of application.

> The paintings, poems, and compositions of the Banquet Years [1885–1914] turn back upon themselves and lie quiet. They imply that by being sufficiently still, by becoming for an instant exactly identical with ourselves, nothing more nor less, we can allow the universe to move around us. This is the meaning in art of relativity. An object in motion has difficulty taking into account other motions. Only by achieving rest, arrest, can we perceive what is happening outside ourselves. Simultanism, the third voice of life, signifies an approach to immobility and thus an extremely sensitive attunement to the infinite universe. Baudelaire, Bergson, and cummings are all describing this state. Arrest is achieved not by absence of power to move, but by an equilibrium of forces, whence the dynamic nature of works we call modern. (Shattuck 350–51)

The emblem of stillness as stance, invoked by Jarry in his 'Pataphysical plans for a time machine, is the gyroscope: "Like a gyroscope, it sustains itself by a concentration of forces in self-reflexiveness, art turning upon itself. This inwardness reveals itelf in a posture of total arrest—the justaposition of parts around a moment of profound awareness" (351). *Simultanism* (Orphism) is Apollinaire's name for bachelor machine logic. It is the logic of flash reason against the Internet accident, and its application in concept avatar supports this experience of time/out. The immediate lesson is: avatar intimates in the vocabulary of your accident. The formal design of the Allegory is now defined: *construct a gyroscope*—map the movement around a still point through which you experience awareness of jouissance polarity (attraction-repulsion).

Element

I am learning from accident avatar how to figure hegemony (collective prudence). One goal of the consultation is to learn how to generalize from the particular reading to an image pataphysics (electrate equivalent of category). The general category of a relevant tenor for the accident vehicle is Merleau-Ponty's "Flesh" (hear the *ponte*). Merleau-Ponty's extension of ontology beyond substance and language is an important resource for flash reason. Merleau-Ponty (like Heidegger) recognized that the logic of a new metaphysics was invented within modernist arts, especially in Cézanne's painting and Proust's novel. Just as "Being" is an effect of, and happens only within, alphabetic writing, so too is "Flesh" (Merleau-Ponty's ontological category) an effect of thought's encounter with imaging. Graphic design is the grammar and syntax of this mode of articulating "wild" or brute nature of embodied experience (*jouissance*). In the context of electracy, for operating the interface-databases of a digital apparatus, phenomenology and deconstruction (experience and language) are allies. Nature proper may not be a *forest of symbols*, but MUVE's (multi-user-virtual-environments) are or could be. The immediate interest for fatal reason is Merleau-Ponty's retrieval of the term "element" to replace "substance" in discussing ontological flesh la chair.

> The flesh is not matter, is not mind, is not substance. To designate it, we should need the old term "element," in the sense it was used to speak of water, air, earth, and fire, that is, in the sense of a *general thing*, midway between the spatio-temporal individual and the idea, a sort of incarnate principle that brings a style of being wherever there is a fragment of being. The flesh is in this sense an "element" of Being. Not a fact or a sum of facts, and yet adherent to location and to the now. For if there is flesh, that is if the hidden face of the cube radiates forth somewhere as well as does the fact I have under my eyes, and coexists with it, and if I who see the cube also belong to the visible, I am visible from elsewhere, and if I and the cube are together caught up in one same "element," this cohesion, this visibility by principle prevails over every momentary discordance. (138)

Flesh names the metaphysics of embodiment. This updating of "element" suggests the appropriateness of locating the categorial potential of the accident sign in its distribution of elements. The nature of this sign is revealed in the materiality of the product and by-product of the commodity scene. Stimilli wondered how one of the elements, "air," came to name the aura or expression of a unique face. The context of Flesh as element calls attention to the absence of wood in Western cosmology, wood being the fifth element in the Chinese system. Nemesis, like wood, is suppressed in the tradition, benched in favor of Elpis. Could "wood" be the "air" of "disaster?" Here is an opportunity for concept avatar, to develop the analytical powers of all the elements in the way that "air" expresses physiognomy. "Air" historically combined with "aura" to blend the atmosphere of landscape with individual physiognomy. Perhaps "wood" may combine with "spectre" to blend similarly the atmosphere of disaster with a collective look. Is there not something *creosotic* about corporate conduct? The Cabot-Koppers wood treatment plant produced pine tar (pitch). The production of pine tar is the vehicle for our tropic accident. What is pine tar pitch as element (as metaphysics)? We are on the Tar Bridge.

Merleau-Ponty is not the only one to use Bachelard's *Water and Dreams* as a relay for developing *element* as a replacement for "substance" in image metaphysics. Sartre takes Bachelard's psychoanalysis of things as a point of departure for summarizing his own existential psychoanalysis, in the final section of *Being and Nothingness.* In the context of flash reason, we may consider this lengthy text to be a philosophical unpacking of the epiphany dramatized in the novel *Nausea.* Sitting on a park bench, Antoine Roquentin (the protagonist of *Nausea*) receives the event of being-in-itself, of *Dasein* (there is, *es gibt, il y a*) recognized in a tree root. The material *quality* associated with the root is viscosity, stickiness. The term used in *Being and Nothingness* is *visqueux,* and the translator notes that his choice of "slimy" as the primary variant could just as well have been "sticky." Sartre's phenomenology is on display in his claim that such *qualia* are ontological, constituting objective revelations of what is there, of being-in-itself. Being-for-itself (consciousness, the *cogito*) becomes what it is, self-aware of its own project, its passion, its direction, its intention within a situation, through the appropriation of *qualia.*

Through intentionality, consciousness experiences its nothingness, its nature as hole (its absensibility, absense-ability), as uncanny relative of responsibility. By means of extimacy (chiasmatic outside-in), of poetic correspondences, being-for-itself (human consciousness) attempts to coincide with being-in-itself, become what it is, to put the stamp of being on becoming, as Nietzsche proposed, transposing the project of entelechy into autopoiesis on behalf of the entire Western tradition. Such is our impossible responsibility as operant subject for *technics.* The existentialist caveat is the reminder that such coincidence is a trait of God, and is not possible for creatures of finitude. The aporia is not only that there is no sexual relation (as Lacan said, that is, no guarantee, just because you are sexed), but there is no self relation either (identity is not guaranteed). Agamben helps us understand this structural limitation: it concerns the temporality of pleasure (idiocy). This ontological function of element constitutes a background also for Baudrillard's obscene. Through *qualia* humans undergo the Real as aesthetic measure, supplementing the quantitative measures of conventional consulting.

Mary Douglas read Sartre's discussion of viscosity as a material inquiry into the tension between purity and pollution in classification metaphysics. "Viscosity, Sartre says, repels in its own right as a primary experience. An infant, plunging its hands into a jar of honey, is instantly involved in contemplating the formal properties of solids and liquids and the essential relation between the subjective experiencing self and the experienced world. The viscous is a state half way between solid and liquid. It is like a cross-section in a process of change" (38). These are the terms of the Allegory. The materiality of your external scene intimates the feeling of your standing-now. Phenomenological intentionality (consciousness [inside] is always necessarily consciousness of something [outside]), and poetic epiphany converge on this device. Prudence is viscous (repellently adhesive). The Real intimates via earth air fire water. Viscosity connects concept avatar with the emerging paradigm of "flow," as noted in the cfp for the journal *Space and Culture.*

> The notion of "flow," most widely known from the work of Deleuze and Irigaray, occurs repeatedly in social theory. Associated with a paradigm shift within cultural studies and sociology from the analysis of objects to processes, it is also linked by geographers to the notion of "nomadism" and the breakdown of the fixity of boundaries and barriers. More poignantly, it is the lived experience of the global mass migrations and movements of refugees. In effect, the dominant metaphors for discussion of socialty have swung from models of affinithy to those of viscosity" (Shields 2).

Shields adopts from Deleuze a set of "imminent qualities" for analyzing flow in all its manifestations (beginning with desire). To vector and viscosity he adds volume, rhythm (rather than speed), associated with amplitude, frequency, intensity (4). These qualities are associated with the values of manner (style). The evidentiary effect of flow relative to Accident is augmented by the conductive inference relating the theory and its example in Sartre's argument. It begins with the fact that Sartre's ontology is grounded in taste, literally, using one's preferences in flavors to note the axis of attraction-repulsion (pleasure-pain), the aesthetic axis, constituting singular categorial measure. The claim is not that being-in-itself has the same feeling for everyone, but that Sartre's first-person undergoing of being occurred through his repugnance for stickiness, and his personal instance is generalizable (each one finds his/her own measure in experience). Habitus formats our bodies, including a complete sensorial encyclopedia, an ethology in fact, that underwrites hypotyposis and tropology in general. That students find it difficult to understand poetry shows the impoverishment of experience in our techno-scientific ethos. The emergency avatar addresses concerns this formatting of nature by culture (pathos of ethos). The primal undergoing of embodiment from infancy onwards constructs a felt orientation constituting a kind of *sensus communis.* Artists in all media have always exploited this formatting, demonstrating in practice the potential viability of Kant's proposal for an aesthetic bridge between pure and practical reason (Being and Becoming). The framing of the senses is "common" or universal to the degree that it assumes embodiment, but it is open to the infinite variation of particular experience. We undergo Eros as bittersweet. Is *daimon* saltysour? Nemesis, the astringentumami?

The relevance of the hole is not only scholarly (the elaboration of another instance of the ontological potential of "element"), but because one of the primary examples Sartre gave of a viscous substance is "pitch," or pine tar.

> I have projected it into the world by my original project when faced with the sticky; it is an objective structure of the world and at the same time an antivalue; that is it determines an area where sticky objects will arrange themselves. Henceforth each time that an object will manifest to me this relation of being, whether it is a matter of a handshake, of a smile, or of a thought, it will be apprehended by definition as sticky; that is, beyond its phenomenal context, it will appear to me as constituting along with pitch, glue, honey, etc., the great ontological region of stickiness. (*Being and Nothingness* 774)

Eureka. An implicit link between *Nausea* and *Being and Nothingness* is the fact that pine tar is usually produced through the processing of pine tree roots and stumps (although the tree in *Nausea* is a chestnut). The key point for an image metaphysics is that this classification functions beyond language, through felt embodiment, brought into ontology through aesthetic design. The ontology of manner(s), opening to electracy the stubbornness with which symptom adheres to jouissance (the stickiness of gift).

Embodied Wisdom

The preliminary lesson for electrate consultants is that the accident sign figures elemental metaphysics. Or, in terms of our framing experiment, the accident sign is how avatar addresses player as egent (counsel on public policy, representing the axis of well-being). The tradition reminds us that *daimon* is personal, specific to me (guardian angel, spirit guide to invoke some of the pop personifications). Not every accident whispers to every consultant. The consultancy is distributed. As Emerson said, your eye is placed to notice that particular ray; the gate is for you alone. You are categorial, not category itself, which is simply to say that avatar requires apparatus, the EmerAgency coordinates a group or distributed egency augmented in the digital apparatus. The accident of the Superfund site in Gainesville (as prototype) involves precisely pine tar (pitch), produced at the Cabot-Koppers site since 1911 for the treatment of wood. The surprise of this (lucky) find (*trouvaille*) is an epiphany in my Allegory, aligning my circumstances with event (as distinct from history). The complete figure is: the production of pine tar and its poisonous by-product expresses the relation of being-for-itself with being-in-itself (Sartre's elemental ontology), meaning that by-product is ontological (byplay, paralogy). Reflective judgment generates a macrocosm out of a particular microcosm. The oracular impact of this connection, as prototype for fatal counsel in general, is due to the materiality of my accident matching Sartre's exemplary element. Divination is a strategy, an attitude, a reading effect, whose evidentiary power has always relied upon a chance switch between coincidence and fatality. The surprise of this conductive link is augmented by the presence of my signature in Sartre's account: glue (as in my email address, constituted by my initials + a French "e," glue@ufl.edu). The accident sign functioning within the hole of the Rat-Tar-Art-Rta Bridge advises me on the most relevant frame for receiving communications from the other ontology of *technics*, and even from the Real as such. My hometown disaster is Exhibit A for existentialist metaphysics. So is yours.

The conductive vortex in my experiment joined the Koppers pine tar with Sartre's ontology, producing the makings for a collective emblem of prudence. The cause-effect scenarios of the Army Engineers overlook gift. It is an emblem, constructed as vehicle (pine tar production) and tenor (existential psychoanalysis of things). What does it say (what is its counsel)? The accident sign exhibits a quality (*quale*), to be organized by elements in an image classification native to digital technologies, an insight for further invention, learning how to map the viscosity and vector of jouissance. This capacity of imaging is the equivalent of Aristotle's discovery of propositional logic. Caveat: propositional logic still structures our relational databases. In short, our databases are Ptolemaic. Meanwhile, communication between human and machine ontologies emerges in the obscenity of elemental accidents. This logic of *quale* morphics (arts equivalent to quantum mechanics, generating qualitative measures of well-being to supplement our lop-sided reliance on quantity) is under construction, but the prototype in Gainesville manifests the principle: accidents are avatars of seeming (reveal the nature of the Real) through *qualia*. One result is an insight into the General Accident: *embodiment is disaster*, thus answering our hypothetical question with a metalepsis: an ancient taste for pepper put dioxin in my water. The emblem is a pepper mill (a hand mill), marked with the icon warning "poison" (skull and crossbones). Pepper Mill with Dixoin @ Cabot-Koppers: the idea of order at a Superfund site. This pepper mill adds to the collection that includes the hand mills of Kant and Duchamp, emblems of hypotyposis as ratio. The ratio is manifested today in the Internet meme, scene of a police officer using pepper spray on students participating in the Occupy movement. Pepper weaponized.

The accident explains karma: *your body is killing us.* Heidegger called it the overwhelming, the aporia. It is your animal, thematized in the Aesopic tradition of fables. Do you love pepper? *Smile now, cry later.* What does flash reason propose? A new wisdom of embodiment, supporting experience of the collective potentiality of taste. There is a reason why Rabelais (Gargantua) is the godfather of the Parisian cabaret, and Ubu Roi his heir. *Appetite.* Who will have designed the *app* that projects our distributed epiphanies into an "*appiphany*" of *technics*? The literate apparatus invested in a science that augmented through tools the energy available in nature, with the contemporary prototype being nuclear energy. *Jouissance* names an energy specific to human embodiment. Our future will be determined by how this energy is augmented and directed in electracy (*The Matrix,* inspired by Baudrillard, as worst-case scenario). This wisdom is to electracy what philosophy is to literacy, and will take the form of media *qualia* capturing the little sensations, including the complexity of *jouissance*, the *lichettes,* to access for well-being the constructivist (ontological) powers of attraction-repulsion (the knot/hole).

Keep in mind that our allegory exercise is in the context of an apparatus program. The accident-sign is dialogical. The prospectus is that distributed *sinthomes*, augmented and networked digitally, function as operant governor of *technics*, negotiating between humans and machines. We forgot Being, but avatar remembers. Interfaced with the other ontology, avatar reminds organics and *technics* alike about distinctions between *creosote* and *gelato. Technics* knows not from happiness. Corporations, churches of capitalism, are like horses: they will consume (us) to death. This institutional site of the emergence of electracy through the commodity sign inherently lacks measure. Apparatus theory reveals the challenge: attraction-repulsion needs its own institutionalization (science had to break with religion; entertainment needs to break with capitalism). Well-being needs an army. Such is the emergency. The human-*technics* rhizome is a co-dependency, and the mutating equipment must take into account the condition of human thriving (that-for-the-sake-of-which). Given the materiality of my Superfund accident, perhaps a pinetree knothole would be a good logo for my Superfund *obscenario.* The task of concept avatar is to facilitate the design and testing of *quale* morphics against the General Accident. The habitus emerging in social media is already training you for it. Got taste?

13 Wisdom

One more variation on the Allegory, apprenticed to Titian's family portrait as Prudence. The device is evident by now, but I will make one more pass, one more attempt to put the stamp of Being on Becoming. I am consulting with a situation, seeking in it the little sensation giving satisfaction by means of a detail that draws the world into shape, idea (*eidos*), figuring the decision (but you will have made your own decision), giving me its source that is limit, measure, destiny. This exercise maps an attractor (the category system of electracy) through a measure of (un)happiness, to locate a kind of gyroscope in experience. The gyroscope shows both the dynamic structure of our hypotyposis but also its navigational function: a GPS of Being. The family is gathered at the house we rent occasionally on the ocean near Ponte Vedra Beach (listen to the bridge). It is the same group more or less that gathered in Key West and Florence, with some variation. Parvathi's aunt is visiting from India, driving from Georgia with her son and his wife and daughter. Lee's work kept him in Texas, but Anita and Tyson are here with the significant addition of Anjali, my granddaughter. It is May, the weekend of Mother's Day, with the stated purpose of the vacation to celebrate multiple generations of moms.

An early morning walk along the shore, a little after sunrise, up before the rest of the household for a change (in honor of Nietzsche), but Anjali will have most of them busy by the time I return. The house is three stories, plenty of bedrooms and baths, with private access to the beach via a long boardwalk, similar to every other house along this stretch of the Atlantic. A blue crab senses my approach, but not until I am close enough to notice its movement despite the perfect camouflage; the top of its exoskeleton is an exact simulation of the sandy beach from which the tide is just now withdrawing. *Live hidden,* some sage advised, which turns my thoughts to prudence. Giorgio Agamben provided a version of my fantasy in *The Idea of Prose,* the opening section, "Threshold," in which he recounts the anecdote of Damascius, the scholarch incumbent when the emperor Justinian closed the Athens school of philosophy in 529 AD. Damascius thus was the last diadoch of pagan philosophy. Fearing persecution, the diadoch and a few helpers went into exile, seeking refuge at the court in Persia. Such is the fantasy: *the sage in exile.*

The scholar fled to a strange land, far from home. Holed up in a house in an old section of a Persian city, Damascius intended to devote his remaining years to a project with the title *Aporias and Solutions Concerning First Principles.* Would this not be a good subtitle for *Avatar Emergency?* The question was perhaps aporia itself, meaning that it was impossible to resolve, since it concerned the single supreme beginning of the Whole, whether this beginning was itself beyond the Whole (the temporality of the absolute Whole). The very unknowability of the question is part of the fantasy, because the scene is not only about the work, but the life devoted to it: the dilapidated residence in the old city, the Syrian housekeeper shopping at the outdoor market, the total engagement with an ultimate perplexity, thumbing whatever manuscripts he was able to salvage from the Academy. There is wine and solitude, thought and writing. The attraction of the anecdote is not only this situation of exiled scholar, but also the nature of the problem addressed, and the manner of its solution. Call it philosophy as poem, or the thought of a feeling. A guiding image dissolved the perplexity.

> And so it was that as he was writing one night the image suddenly sprang to mind that would guide him—so he thought—through to the conclusion of his work. It was not, however, an image, but something like the perfectly empty space in which only image, breath, or word might eventually take place. Or, rather, it was not even a space, but the site of a place, as it were, a surface, an area absolutely smooth and flat, on which no point could be distinguished from another. He thought of the white stone yard of the farm where he had been born, at the gates of Damascus, where the peasants threshed the wheat in the evenings to separate grain and chaff. Wasn't what he was searching for exactly like the threshing floor, itself unthinkable and unspeakable, where the winnowing fans of thought and language separated the grain and chaff of everything? (Agamben, *The Idea of Prose* 33)

The winnowing fans . . . of thought (hypotyposis).

The diadoch undergoes a time image, a dialectical conjunction of a childhood anecdote with a philosophical aphorism of thought. This repetition in time, constructed into an emblem, is the gyroscope. The provenance of this image comes as no surprise to anyone familiar with Plato (and who would be more familiar than the diadoch?). In *Timaeus* Plato proposed a new dimension of metaphysics, dubbed chora (space, region), as interface for Being and Becoming. To communicate the nature of this dimension, which, as generator, is neither intelligible nor perceptible directly, Plato relied on bastard reasoning, that is, mythos. The primary image of chora is that of threshing, since like winnowing chora sorted chaos into the fundamental elements of the cosmos (earth, air, fire, water). Plato in turn borrowed the image from the Eleusinian mysteries, the cults ritualizing fertility, in whose ceremonies stone phalloi were hidden in winnowing baskets. Orpheus's descent into Hades is just one of the avatars referenced in the mysteries (what Bloom calls the lie against time), to account for the rhythm of life-death-life.

The value Damascius added to the thought was to receive the founder's metaphysics through Aristotle's revision of it. Aristotle, that is, collapsed Plato's transcendental dualism into a temporal unfolding immanent in the world. Becoming received the stamp of Being not through participation with the Ideas in chora, but entelechy (being-at-work-staying-itself), a thing becoming what it is immanently in time. Aristotle thought of chora as potential (*dunamis*), whose end or purpose is realized in actuality (*energeia*) from the essential nature of what an entity is (acorns become oaks). The mystery was human entelechy or end, of course, identified as Happiness in principle, actualized as the Good. The aporia of Aristotle's ethics is the same as the fault of Epimetheus: "Happiness" and "Good" are floating signifiers. The transcendental status of these terms left open to invention the particular realization of the end. The gap (hole) separating Becoming from Being is time, structured as the difference between potentiality and realization. Damascius further refined the image when he began to write.

> Suddenly he remembered the passage in the book on the soul in which the philosopher compared the potentiality of the intellect to a tablet on which nothing is written. Why had he not thought of it before? It was this that he had unceasingly

> pursued by the light of the brief flash of the unglimpsable, blinding halo. The uttermost limit thought can reach is not a being, not a place or thing, no matter how free of any quality, but rather, its own absolute potentiality, the pure potentiality of representation itself: the writing tablet! (34)

The flash of insight.

Writing supplies the anchor for conceptual hypotyposis, to figure the event of limit. The project in fantasy is just this hybrid of first philosophy and lyric poetry, the device that transforms sensation into a thought: not just any thought, but thought itself. Pure thought (pure art). The insight anticipates Derrida's metamorphosis of being into text, or Lacan's formula of the subject, by exploiting the ontological analogy. "What could not cease from writing itself was the image of what never ceased from not writing itself. In the one was mirrored the ungraspable other" (*Idea of Prose* 34). Such is the *more* of hole, and Damascius's figure of a still smooth surface center of a vortex, a world (the Ister) gathered around threshing as material and spiritual production. His moment of insight is recreated in the animated film *Ratatouille*—a movie about a Rat (if this comparison is not too humble): when the food critic tastes the chef's ratatouille he is transported instantly to childhood, tasting his mother's own recipe (Proust's madeleine). The pleasure of the fantasy is in this effect of accessing the invisible ineffable by means of some humble object or gesture, available through the devices of art. The insight happens at the intersection of an aphorism of thought (chora) and an anecdote of life (seasonal winnowing): a rhizome of lyrical abstraction. This crossroads is augmented in electracy, networked with databased hole: brainstorming the aporia with low-focus browsing attention, Damascius experienced the trigger *when the emotion associated with a childhood place matched the problem structure.* It is Proust's formula for Time Regained, applied to conceptual invention. The lesson resonates with the wisdom of concept avatar. "He now believed that he understood the sense of the maxim stating that by knowing the unknowable it is not something about it we know, but something about ourselves. That which can never be first let him glimpse, in its fading, the glimmer of a beginning" (*Idea of Prose* 34). The thought is sublime, in Kant's sense, and it must have consoled the diadoch, the last official successor of Plato. Might the wisdom not be condensed into a variation on a proverb? *To someone whose only tool is a writing tablet, everything looks like a text.* Yes, but I am with the diadoch, perplexed by an impacted abstraction, and scanning the scene for counsel. Through the unknowable we learn something about ourselves. The unknowable, the navel, where the dream-wish arises like the mushroom from its *mycelium.*

*

Turning back towards the house, I encounter several temporary tide pools left by the withdrawing waves. There are two pools not far apart, both busy with darting shadows showing the presence of many small fish. One pool is already isolated, while the other still connects to the tide through a deep channel carved in the pliant sand by the surf. The outflow in the deep channel is swift. Nearing the steps to the walkway over the dunes leading back to the house I turn for a moment in response to the cry of gulls gathering over and around the isolated pool. The scene evokes an image, forming an analogy. Hypotyposis. The newspaper that Sunday carried extensive reports of the end of Osama bin Laden, tracked down to his hideout exile in Abbottabad, Pakistan. His compound near an elite military school in this prominent city was valued at over a million dollars, but his existence remained nearly as confined as if he lived in his legendary cave. It is a caveat for those who would romanticize exile.

The penultimate hideout was more modest, being in Chak Shah Muhammad, a small village of poultry farms and wheat fields. There are many imponderables to occupy the thoughts of an exile: mayhem and terror in bin Laden's case, with one ear scanning for helicopters. There might be a screenplay in this event: a child recalling the chance meeting with the Guest one afternoon, and the conversation they had that opened a way (out). Why begrudge a man locked up for years with several wives a little pornography (the thumb drives). His command goes out into the world, and then he waits. It is another scene available for Prudence, if you like, showing the devout terrorist cloistered with a crowd of women and children. Documents and money were sewn into his change of clothes, ready for a quick departure at a moment's notice, assuming he would be tipped off to any American plans by his associates in Pakistan's special services. Fantasy is your quick-change outfit, an extra dimension just outside here and now. But the choppers come for everyone, eventually.

The tide pools resonating with the news triangulate to my own decision circumscribed around me. The setting of this house on the ocean where my family is beginning another morning routine is a kind of anamorphic stain, awaiting the cylindrical mirror of an object x (or @) to become legible. The experience of this shift into more is uncanny: a visit from avatar. Locating this extra scene of fantasy reconnects electrate avatar with brand. Brand in Second Life pretends complete control over manifestation, as if virtuality were protean. This role of fantasy in online brand (restricted) "avatar" is the point of departure for general (emergent) avatar, when your image splits and folds upon itself. "Aaron Green," the Freudian psychotherapist, disclosed to Janet Malcolm (in *Psychoanalysis: The Impossible Profession*) that through his training analysis he discovered that unconsciously he wished to be a beautiful woman. According to most accounts he can join the club, since the majority of sexpot female "avatars" in Second Life are played by men. Capacity to be affected means: capacity to fantasize. When brand becomes reflexive, an interface receiving universal *sinthome* as well as projected self, it becomes potential *daimon*. This folded dis/course is the virtual scene (dromos) of the coming politics.

*

We are seeking what Damascius sought, and what was sought by the entire tradition of which we are the diadochi: chora—the Moment when order appears (figure from ground), the Moment when a frog becomes an emblem, when metaphysics distills from *gelato*. Avatar counsels chora, and to receive it I have to construct an emblem, an icon (the Allegory). Electracy emerges out of a hypotyposis with literacy, mediated by concept avatar. You don't remember literacy, but It does. A chief lesson from the history of literacy is the extent to which nearly every language practice in every institution was based on some application of Aristotle's categories in particular, and Classical Greek metaphysics in general. And this point is as true for the use of images as for texts. A task for flash reason is to separate the ratio of imaging from literate metaphysics. Gombrich observes, for example, that the iconic allegories of the kind represented by Titian's *Prudence* were designed as "painted definitions." When such works are described as "personified concepts," the phrase must be understood literally, in that the selection of features used in the personification followed the rules of essence, of substance and attribute, which also guided propositional predication. Concept avatar, counselor of passage, is a personified concept. This tradition is the one that we exploit in transition from literacy to electracy, by designing a persona for concept avatar to render present in crisis the archive. The persona and anecdote pass into electracy, leaving the abstractions in the database. The iconology used in the formation of emblems—a practice inspired by the hermetic understanding of Egyptian hieroglyphics—was based explicitly on Aristotle's use of definition to sort out essence and accident.

> "The category of images which are the subject of this discourse [writes Ripa] corresponds to the definition . . . which can conveniently be expressed by means of the human figure. Because just as man is always a particular man in the same way as a definition is the measure of the defined, so the accidental form which appears external to him can be the accidental measure of the qualities to be defined." But how are we to account for the fact that the same concept can be represented in so many different ways, as Ripa himself was anxious to demonstrate in his book? We are referred to Aristotle's distinction of the four types of definition, corresponding to his four types of causes, the material, the efficient, the formal and the final. The deviser of visual definitions is equally free to characterize a concept according to any of these approaches, illustrating, say, the cause or the effect of Friendship. "When by this method we have become distinctly aware of the qualities, the causes, the properties and the accidents of a definable concept on which the image can be based, we have to look for the similitudes that exist between these concepts and material things and which function as substitutes for the words as used in the images and definitions of the orators." (Gombrich 142–43)

It might be, as the emblematic treatment of the Seven Arts indicated, that when it came to dealing with the ultimate mysteries, that theology would have to relieve prudence as the guide to thought. Nonetheless, as Roy Wagner shows in the case of the theological invention of the Eucharist, this reasoning also relied on Aristotle's principles of substance and accident.

> The doctrine of transubstantiation was developed from the realist philosophy of the previous epoch, and was based on the assumption of the essential reality of conventional conceptual or verbal categories. The imperceptible type-essence, or universal, inherent in every particular thing according to

> its kind, was called the *substantia*. The sensuous, perceptible aspects that differentiate the thing from others of its generic were called *accidentia*. On this basis, "the idea of transubstantiation is that in the consecration of the elements the *substania* change but the *accidentia* remain the same. The *substantia* of the bread and wine become the *substantia* of the body and blood of Christ. The *accidentia* remain the same, and the *accidentia* are all that remain of the original bread and wine." This made the ground of being, the divine presence in communion with clergy and worshipers, a kind of disembodied trope, like a figure of speech moving independently of language. (104)

The terms undergoing mutation resound in this passage: the accident sign gives disaster as transubstantiation. "Element" replaces "substance" in image metaphysics, and Flesh remains corporeal. Bread and wine as body and blood, yes, but immanently so. Wagner demonstrates the flexibility and inventiveness of this trope, which he argues is the core figure of the entire Western tradition. He shows that this structure of substance and accident has been able to support, and perhaps even direct, every shift in worldview experienced during the epoch of literacy.

> The "age of scientific discovery," of Copernicus, Galileo, Columbus, and Magellan, and the outbreak of the Protestant Reformation, were two sides of the same coin. Accidentia was discovered as nature, not in Erigena's sense of the figurative manifestation of God, but as a new, secular ground of being, in the very epoch in which *substantia*, the presence of God, was determined by Luther and others to be a function of human faith. Thus the epoch of Reformation was the point at which Western culture, not having a stabilizing ritual, fell through its figure-ground reversal. (111)

And now, after the commodity reformation, in the epoch of Entertainment? *Technics* speaks accident.

The icon in Byzantium functioned at the opposite pole of the Eucharist, to convey the absence of God from the world, and this creative absence (absensibility) is what chora thinks. The institutional "economy" of all emblematic modes, in any case, share a structure made most explicit during the iconoclastic controversies of the Byzantine era in the defense of religious imagery authored by Nikephoros. The special relevance for us in Marie-Jose Mondzain's account of iconophilia is that the doctrine relied explicitly on Greek philosophy. St. Paul made the connection between Christ as the incarnation of God on earth and the work of the Church to extend this visibility (appearance). God appeared as revelation (epiphany), the event of the universal given in an instant of time. The icon mode was invented to negotiate the difficult relationship between the visible and the invisible, the apophantic and the kataphantic, through which "enigma" was used to think "mystery." It is the source of that idiom: *a mystery wrapped in an enigma.* Today the referent is human embodiment, the incarnation of subjects as Flesh, whose nature is to produce nonsensory effects. You see the theme: every feature of the complex history of the West was thought, structured, and communicated through the system of categories invented in the Academy (Lyceum). Implication: every feature of the electrate apparatus will have been thought, structured, and communicated through the network of attractors invented in the Cabaret. You cannot run ahead of this shape, this event (*Ereignis*). It is messianic, if you please, and as fatal as electricity.

The icon was considered to be a practice of prudence in several respects: 1. Icon as the "guile" of God for extending globally the authority of the Church into the realms controlled by the political power of the Emperor; 2. truth should not be expounded coldly, but with the rhetorical vividness of the orators in order to seduce the flesh; 3. the teachings of the church must be adapted to the prejudices and human limitations of the audience (Mondzain 48, 59). Greek concepts of space were used to theorize the doctrine of incarnation, beginning with chora in Plato's *Timaeus,* the receptacle wherein Being and Becoming could interact. "The Virgin's clothing is as beautiful as heaven and earth, as vast as the universe. The space (*khora*) of the virginal body where Christ finds the form of his carnal periphery, the membrane that defines his terrestrial place, and the space of the consecration of the ecclesial body are all simultaneously identified with each other" (161). The icon, the Virgin womb, and the Church have a relational rather than a representational connection. "The icon reiterates and perpetuates in turn the implantation of the Word within the virginal border, a uterine khora traversed by divine breath, sustained by the voice of the herald" (101). This relational order, vacated by the old metaphysics, constitutes the empty universal Now. In any case, we have to consider closely our Western tradition of incarnation, even while welcoming the global agreement on the value of figural descent as a relay for electrate subject invention.

Nikephoros also made use of the Greek notion of *kenosis* (void) in this theological context. The incarnation is kenotic, not only because it opens the place of God in the world (that is, avatar), but that this place appears under the sign of dereliction and death. The Son is in self-exile from God who is outside the world. *Kenosis* is used to theorize this presence of an absence.

> The meaning of this cannot be understood without examination of the doctrine of *kenosis*, which I take to be a system of thought concerning an emptiness that makes place for the light of real, natural, and transfigured matter. Only then does it become possible to glimpse that element that has the ability to become imaginal flesh rendered visible in iconic flesh. *Kenosis* has often been interpreted solely from the aspect of divine condescension as referring only to the humility, poverty, and nudity of the Messsiah. The "form of the slave" of which Paul speaks would in this sense be nothing but terrestrial exile, far from the Father's glory. But in the debate over the image, the question of the incarnational emptiness takes on a whole new amplitude, because it perpetuates the emptiness of the *Parousia* in the very form of the iconic memorial. (95)

Terrestrial exile.

Image pataphysics may be understood as a secularization of this operation, with commodity sign inheriting the functionality of icon. The abject figure in electracy, responsible for the kenotic opening of life, is your *sinthome* (Lacan's appropriation of Marx's surplus value for identity formation). To understand the challenge of this function of embodiment in the new apparatus we need to learn how *descent* was practiced historically. The mystery remains the same: negentity; absensibility, hole through which life as force happens. The kenotic nature of the icon has been secularized in our era by Lacan's object @, Laclau's hegemony (the empty universal) and Heidegger's *aletheia* (truth as disclosive withdrawal), to mention some of the most prominent versions. The Ragpicker (*chiffonnier*) as modern hero is the Parisian artists's contribution. It is the structure of an opening in imaginal space-time created by a disclosive withdrawal of the Real, with some object/letter as placeholder promoted to the status of Thing. This structuration produces an image attractor, whose operation we approach through concept avatar: a kenotic hollowing out within some existing support, a framing from which emerges more signification through tropological flow.

Mondzain generalizes the lessons of the icon to all art.

> The greatest western pictorial works of art also necessarily concern an existential relation to the presence of an emptiness, although in a place where this is not always perceived. By this we mean that in their secret emptiness, they remain faithfully indifferent to representation, in order to maintain a *skhesis,* a *pros ti,* where mimetic polarities are linked together, between the spectator and their invisible center. All great art is kenotic. (92)

It is the emptiness of the commodity sign. The practical point of avatar emergency is that, because you are a human being, you have felt this kenotic *Zug.* Lacan's insight is that the Church as institutionalization of Mary's Womb, opening a place for God in matter, is a projective manifestion of a human capacity that must be updated for each epoch. Freud literalizes this update in his hypotyposis, naming the mother's genitals as the ultimate uncanny place. Psychoanalysis, our guide to electrate embodied logic (hole), exists practically as cure for inhibition and anxiety, as contemporary heirs of *daimon* and demon. Lacan at some point recognized the ambivalence in this genealogy, from genius to symptom, which motivated his final version of cure: *savoir-y-faire.* Yes, we have to revisit the entanglement of genius with madness. When you take your Allegory of Prudence, you will get it, and be at ground zero of the coming apparatus.

The point is useful for our extraction of flash reason from the tradition of virtue in general, and prudence in particular. The formal functioning of the icon, as explained by Nikephoros, was never mimetic or representational in the way feared by the iconoclasts, who rejected any limitation on the divine. The icon is an abstraction, a proportional relationship, that Nikephoros modeled on Aristotle's categories, to think the icon (or emblem, in our context) as being to line and color what definitions were to words (83). Merleau-Ponty's turn away from substance to element takes this direction. The icon was a pictorial *eidos*, delineating the face of the divine accessible to humans. The icon is not itself the Image, since the latter is a prototype or archetype, akin to a Platonic Form. The icon is an attractor, but not only to seduce the human eye (and seduction must be extended to cover all experience of *Zug*). It attracts the divine gaze upon us as well (the uncanny event in which the world looks back). Brand within commodity abstraction functions as icon to attract the attention of Internet avatar.

> What is at issue is the specification of something in the foundation of the imaginal gaze that always necessarily involves a problematic of withdrawal and vacuity. It is this that is also undoubtedly the "secret" of the image, by which I mean that which it both secretes and hides, and which Paul gave voice to in his formulation of the specular enigma. What is an enigma? The providing of meaning to hidden words, a cryptic word that suddenly exposes what was until then a pure mystery. (Mondzain 81–82)

Byzantine mosaics include icons of the Pantocrator. Your *sinthome* is Pantocrator-for-a-Moment, Pantattractor. An ad-vert on the universal: *your letter here.* The challenge of concept avatar is to think the revenant, ghost, viscous jelly of body that fatally adheres to *jouissance*, resisting exchange, substitution, circulation. It is this position fallen (abjected) outside of exchange that allows sinthome (character) to function as measure of value. Deconstruction approached this problematic through prosopopoeia, Schizoanalysis through faciality. Allegory of Prudence rehearses candidates for this (distributed) office.

*

The tide pool comes close to the feeling I recognize as avatar, that is, measure of my decision, but is not it. Exile, yes, but not trap, nor hideout. "Exile" is how sages describe the feeling of remaining within an ego boundary, separated out and isolated from the universe, clinging to the wheel of suffering that is living (that's me). The riddle of striving: *to what end?* You glimpse the Gate, but what lies beyond the threshold? Antigone knows. Bataille proposed *transgression* as the probe to force threshold to appear, but Baudrillard found that today the probes escape gravity and become hypertelic (capital-driven consumer as horse eating itself to death), like space shots without mission control. Without measure, we consume until we pop (the next Big Bang). Some mystics speak of an oceanic feeling of union with the universe, while others fold the absolute onto the quotidian, and find ecstacy in a sand dollar. This tradition archives precedents inventoried by concept avatar, whose function is first-person undergoing of the actions of a distributed group subject—a kind of simulation of Kant's Categorical Imperative.

History delivered us (this family) to Ponte Vedra, adhering to some cosmic etiquette. The variations x are infinitely gradable, and the Real appears continuously, available for counsel at any moment. What is the attitude expressed in the situation? All you need is for some feature of the setting to look at you, some objective point of reference locating the attractor of the region, the pole star of the whirling stain. The gyroscope updates chora. That such diverse sources would share the vortex as emblem is less surprising when one is reminded of the importance of the "whirlpool" figure in the cosmology of world civilizations. Ancient peoples observed the turning of the heavens around a central hole or pole that they figured in an image of a millstone. A mythology of world-ages was expressed in narratives of a cosmological machine that ground out peace and prosperity in a golden age, but that eventually collapsed into the bottom of the sea opening a hole to the land of the dead in a story of decline and fall from one world-age to the next. In the mythological narrative the movement of the stars and the phenomenon of the Milky Way were figured as great rivers, underground (the night sky). Sky and earth are a chiasmus. Tradition exploited ambiguous etymologies, allowing the hybrid semantics joining "air" with "aura," physiognomy and landscape (area). Various phenomena of "lights in the sky," from halo to corona, were associated with "area." "The Greeks called such shining lights threshing-floors (areas) because generally the places set aside for threshing grain were round," Pliny wrote (qtd. In Stimilli, 66). "A passage such as this may provide the missing link to connect the topical and the elemental meaning of 'aria,'" Stimilli notes, referring to a passage culminating in Leonardo's chiaroscuro, and sfumato.

I imagine Damascius and his epiphany, when he beheld the threshing floor. Giorgio de Santillanà and Hertha von Dechend in their study of the relation of the story of Hamlet (Amlohdi) to this tradition, refer to *Timaeus* as "that 'topos' from which come and to which return all 'rivers' of cosmological thought" (305). They clarify the cosmological reason for the winnowing basket as Plato's metaphor for chora (space).

> The soul of man is not only reincarnated again and again, but it is subdivided further and further, since mankind multiplies

> as does the grain to which man is so frequently compared. This simile—misinterpreted time and again by the fertility addicts—ought to be taken seriously and literally. The demiurge did not create the individual souls of every man to be born in all future, he created the first ancestors of peoples, dynasties, etc., the "seed of mankind" that multiplies and is ground to mealy dust in the Mill of Time. (308)

The pepper mill of time.

Associated with this cosmological image is the whole Timaeic tradition of persuasion, a synthesis of the Platonic and Biblical accounts of creation (bringing order out of chaos): a practice of "ornamentation" or "decorum" that actualizes or perfects what otherwise remains only *potential* in the character of a person (Briggs 68). Or, in Cicero's terms, the analogy is of the rhetor as gardener drawing forth the seed into nature's plant (81). Shattuck cites Tolstoy (a statement made at the end of his life) to clarify the gyroscope emblem of stillness. "I have keenly experienced consciousness of myself today, at 81 years, exactly as I was conscious of myself at five or six years. Consciousness is motionless. And it is only because of its motionlessness that we are able to see the motion of that which we call time. If time passes, it is necessary that there should be something which remains static. And it is conciousness of self which is static (January, 1910)" (qtd. in Shattuck 352). That is what I seek, something to hold open the still center, avatar of consciousness, pathos as gyroscope.

*

Not far from the steps of the walkway, and just above the residue of foam and detritus marking high tide, is a small heap of sand. It is the "castle" Anjali constructed last evening, her first one, just a mound, a pile still showing marks of a toy shovel. The trigger fires: *the idea of order at Ponte Vedra,* the sand castle as cylinder making legible the anamorphic stain of circumstance; the sand castle as gyroscope, as pole star, as avatar. This is what the t/rope looks/feels like. It registers immediately with the archive of culture, the symbols of tides erasing castles built of sand, as time erases the works of humanity and circumstances refute dreams. It is pathos (attitude, character, direction) replying to ethos (dharma), in our American Religion of self-reliance. You have to step back from the sand pile for the distillation event to occur, the metamophosis into spirit, the gestalt shift from ground to figure.

I understand now that all the things promoted to emblem in my exercises evoke the gyroscope, pole star of the vortex attitude creates out of time. There are no "edges" in nature, we know, but they may be extracted from contours, such as the one traced by the moving surf, the shoreline, the Atlantic horizon, the shift of hue between sky and sea (aria). The only vertical in the shot is Anjali's pile, or is it a heap (a distinction found in the origins of category formation)? *You bring your grain of sand to the seashore* (overheard in a seminar).

Entertaining that sentiment exaggerated in my emblem the tone Agamben observed in the diadoch's exile. That was my decision, to be a scholar (fantasy successor). It has to do with a particular idiocy noted also by Nietzsche in his contempt for thumbing. The tone turns on the metaphysics of entelechy, of becoming what you are (operant of *technics*). The point is central to electracy, since it involves the axis of attraction-repulsion, the dimension of embodiment targeted by concept avatar (weather maps and ocean currents figure the *Zug*). A temporality beyond the received figures of cycles and lines (olive orchards and Roman bridges, nature and history, oral and literate cosmologies) is available in the state of Pleasure, Agamben explains, referring to Aristotle's definition. "Pleasure is that whose form in every instant is fulfilled, perpetually taking place, which is to say, outside of time" (*The Idea of Prose* 71). Potentiality, Agamben adds, is the contrary of pleasure, because it is never enacted, never achieves its end. "The pain of potentiality disappears, in fact, the instant in which it passes into act. But there are forces everywhere—even within ourselves—which constrain potentiality to hang fire within itself. Power grounds itself on these forces; power is the isolation of potentiality from its act." *Power* articulates epochs.

Is this the commonplace of scholars who hang fire, unable to pass to the act, preferring ascetic pain as a condition of possibility? Study or *studium,* Agamben observes, has no rightful end and does not desire one. He refers to Plato's seventh letter, also Nietzsche's source. "Only after a long, studious rubbing together of names, definitions and knowledge is the spark struck in the mind which, in enkindling it, marks the passage from undergoing to undertaking" (64). It is illumination for idiots like me. Etymology associates *studium* with a shock or impact, relating studying with stupefying. The student is between grasp and release, discovery and loss, agent and patient (such is the rhythm). "Nothing resembles it more than the condition which

Aristotle, contrasting it with the act, defines as 'potential.'" This long dwelling in potential explains the sadness of the scholar, Agamben says, whose gloom derives from the postponement of the deed (65). They don't tell you this in the brochure. His insight clarifies the specific point at which EmerAgency (inventional) consulting takes over from conventional (empirical) consulting. Our narrative scenarios assume the connectivity between *velle* and *posse* (where there is a will, there is a way). There is, however, a tradition of "the coming philosophy," from Kant through Benjamin to Deleuze, whose persona is Bartleby, that identifies an inevitable separation of being-able-to, of potency, from will and act, and this is the virtual dimension articulated by the figural distortions of hole. *Resistance* stops argument and narrative. CNN host Anderson Cooper, commenting on a segment he calls "keeping them honest," observed: "It just surprises me when we meet people who are misinformed and don't seem to be willing to alter their viewpoint" (Bauder). *Symptom.* Anderson Cooper cannot change your stand, but you can. Concept avatar does not work at the level of opinion or story, but by the parallax means of figure. The positive aspect of this separation is that kenotic withdrawal positions you within potentiality (the virtual), whose entailment is a metamorphosis of habitus itself (such is the goal of figural *obscenarios*).

I recognize the truth in Agamben's assessment of study, especially since getting the turn in the olive orchard as towards knowledge and away from act (as hanging fire). The sage withdraws, and passes an age rubbing books and notes in hopes of striking a thought. It keeps you busy. The Ancient Greek *daimon* became psychologized as anxiety, we are told, and Lacan in Seminar X revised the loss expressed in this mood from castration to impotence as the site of separation. Plato in the famous letter insisted that nothing of his true doctrine could be found in his writings, because it only was confided esoterically. Today books are esoteric. Who has the patience for those theory chapters? Concept avatar as donor has infinite patience. There is only one way to *gnosis*: "Acquaintance with it must come rather after a long period of attendance on instruction in the subject itself and of close companionship when, suddenly, like a blaze kindled by a leaping spark, it is generated in the soul and at once becomes self-sustaining" (Plato 1589). The chorus reprimanded Antigone for her uncanniness, reminding her that the hearth must remain canny. I join the chorus preaching prudence in a bullfrog voice, *tr-r-r-oonk, ko-ax, ko-ax.*

Gnosis (activating *daimon*) brought you to this pass, this herm or cairn marking the way, Anjali's sand heap. Kneeling to look at it more closely (and to snap your portrait), you feel the *Zug*, Rta, the pull of attraction turning the region of *Ort* into a vortex. The great metalepsis promised in the revisionary ratios happens: this close-up becomes to your electracy what the threshing floor was for the diadoch's *First Principles*, separated only by the "w" of w/hole. This feeling is not *Agon*, as Bloom insisted, (Kafka, Titian, Damascius are not rivals) but one of the other fundamental ludic modes, *Ilynx*, the game of vertigo of which a child spinning into dizziness is the prototype. Damascius left his work unfinished, unpublished, judging it to be superfluous. I recognize that assessment, but I pass along concept avatar to the diadochi, just in case there could be more to it.

You are ambivalent about idiot, but as Lacan advised, the prudent response to the encounter with measure (*sinthome*) is *savoir-y-faire. Sand castle @ Ponte Vedra Beach* attunes my decision with one of the first figures of the tradition constituting my reality (*studium*). *Time is a child playing with droughts. The lordship is to the child* (Heraclitus). Olive Orchard @ Alcántara; White-Crowned Pigeon @ Key West; Gelato @ Firenze; Frog @ Walden; Pepper Mill @ Koppers Superfund; Sand Castle @ Ponte Vedra Beach. The *poncif* is set. Perhaps some next generation of iTunes "Genius" can take it from here. A collection of totem animals emerged from the mycelium to accompany my anecdotes, in any case, although their iconography resists interpretation: cat, rat, frog, pigeon, donkey, corresponding to Titian's wolf, lion, and dog. "As" as object @, gathering not only Eros, but all the personifications of becoming what you are: Genius, Necessity, Fortune . . . Goethe meant well when he replaced Retribution with Hope. "Elpis" would be a good name for a cat, and perhaps the hobo sign for "kind-hearted lady" grins over all the occasions of finding measure. Life endures and happiness happens because sometimes someone makes a sandwich for a bum.

The turn from Becoming to Being passes through attitude (inclination). Take the measure of "family": what is it worth? One of Audubon's rarest birds? All the *gelato* in Italy? A grandchild's first sand castle? You wanted to know *what is there?* Kant put it this way: *what can I know? What ought I do? For what can I hope?* The tradition replies: there is, *es gibt, il y a.* The work of four decades comes down to this! In this register, Heidegger advised, we are not thinking but thanking.

I first read that in graduate school and passed the test without getting it. What was missing was event, intimating "what gives" through the fatal It (*Es*): it rained. It familied. The beach before, and the beach after, and in between: *Yes*.

On the porch, hosing off sandy feet, I see my family through the sliding glass doors (along with my own reflection). I would prefer to pack the car and drive home immediately, to start writing, but my Syrian housekeeper has other plans, and she is right. They wave me in, holding up the espresso pot. Something sizzles in a pan on the stove, but it will be too *spicy* for my taste. Smiling, auntie from India says something that may be in the idiom of the *Bhagavad Gita*. Anjali has her bucket and shovel, ready for another visit to the beach. Some day soon I will tell her the story. "Once upon a time in Ancient Greece there lived an old diadoch," and she will ask: "What's a diaduck?"

Figure 5. *Ponte Vedra Prudence (after Titian)*, Gregory L. Ulmer.

Afterword: Class Portrait With *Daimon* (A Remix)

The Mares that are able to take me as far as I want to travel had so taken me once they'd set me down on the Daimon's *Way—for it is She that takes the Knower through each town.*

I started tending bar for the money but also because I was so bashful in school that it would force me to talk to people. I worked at the Alta Club for six years and really got to know a lot of people. While I worked out there, I met this guy and was going to marry him. M and his brother were musicians and had a gig one night and on the way home his brother was driving and they hit a cement post on the bridge and he got killed. After a while I got laid off from the Alta Club and went on unemployment for about three months.

The problem of knowledge assailed me with insoluble difficulties. What they say about it in books brought me no light. On one particular night I experienced a dreamlike ecstasy. Suddenly I was wrapped in gentleness; there was a blinding flash, then a diaphanous light in the likeness of a human being: Helper of souls, Imam of wisdom, Primus Magister, whose form filled me with wonder and whose shining beauty dazzled me. He greeted me so kindly that my bewilderment faded and my alarm gave way to a feeling of familiarity. And then I began to complain to him of the trouble I had with this problem of knowledge.

Then I went to work at the VA Hospital as an LPN. I worked in the Nursing home but got to be too hard on my back and a job came open in the Supply Department so I put in for it as it was in the sterilization department and with my LPN license, I figured I had a good chance for it. I ended up getting the Lead Medical Supply tech. I worked in the nursing home for six years and the next twenty-four years in the Sterile Supply department. I retired in January 2009.

The female form of Zanni–Zanne—is a lady's maid, not a lower servant, and unlike them her comedy never springs from some deformity of body or character. Her names might be Colombina, Spinetta, Licetta, Smeraldin, Oliva, Nespola. The older, plainer servetta would have had slow earthy movements, enlivened by swift movements of arms or feet in defense or attack, and perhaps unexpected acrobatic skills.

Right after I retired, my left leg started shaking and the doctors thought I had Parkinson's disease but then both legs started shaking and my mouth moves all the time like I'm chewing gum. After a few tests, the neurologist decided it was Tardive Dyskinesia from one of the medication I was on and there is no cure for it. The only time I don't shake is when I'm sleeping. And while they were trying to figure that out, I found out I had breast cancer last April. Had surgery and they got it all. Went through chemo and now I am on Tamoxifen for the next five years.

But come, and I will instruct you. And you must take back home with you what I say—whether in fact there are only these two ways for thought to travel; Either: "It is" (and also) "That it is not," is not (and this is the path of which one ought to be persuaded for it leads to truth).

At the end of one year, I married a fellow music major and we decided to head east to try to go to the Eastman School of Music in Rochester, New York, a school known enough to eager and naïve kids like us to make it an attractive idea. We worked to get money to buy a used car, packed it with groceries, and headed east in freezing January. Long before reaching our goal, we ran out of food and money—finding ourselves in Cleveland, OH. Rather than live in the car any longer, we decided instead to check out the music school there and try to get in. Unbeknownst to us, it turned out that the Cleveland Institute of Music was a top conservatory—and there we were—already in town! Our marriage didn't last, but I got a scholarship and eventually worked my way through the Institute. Upon graduating in 1968, I found myself saying that I was moving to New York City. What on earth I had in mind, I don't know, but I had the idea that the greatest music comes from New York—and so I pointed myself in that direction.

In whatever form it happens to take, and whatever its cause, exile—at its start—is an academy of intoxication. And it is not given to everyone to be intoxicated. It is a limit-situation and resembles the extremity of the poetic state. Is it a favor to be transported to that state straight off, without the detours of that discipline, by no more than the benevolence of fatality? Think of Rilke, that expatriate de luxe, and of the number of solitudes he had to accumulate in order to liquidate his connections, in order to establish a foothold in the invisible. It is not easy to be nowhere.

When my mom was diagnosed with lung cancer, she and my dad came to live with us. I "retired" to take care of her. She was on hospice, and I gained a tremendous respect for the program. After she passed away, I looked for a way to become involved with the hospice program here. There were no openings, but I took a position at Holy Rosary so that I would have one foot in the door. A few years later, the position of Nurse Manager of the Hospice Department came open. I got the job. The time with hospice will always be a treasured memory for me. I had a very special staff and we took care of some very special people.

There is no excuse for playing The Captain like a slightly irritable bank-clerk! The head, shoulders, chest, hips, legs and feet, should never be allowed to rest in their normal alignment. There should always be counterbalance and contrary direction. The Captain's gestures are broad and powerful. He is a coward, but he is not physically weak; in fact he is a world-class athlete—when he's running away.

After ten years I quit and pursued my hobby, archery. With two partners we opened an indoor archery, shooting lanes and pro shop. Fortunately I was gifted in this sport and became quite good, went to the National Archery Shoot held in Las Vegas, finished anywhere from third to what's your name again. Found out that if you don't have another business to go with archery it is hard to make a living, shifted to managing a sporting goods store, became a fishing specialist, fishing and rod making, assisted in teaching rod making and fly fishing. You would think that picking one seasonal business would have taught me, slow learner, that seasonal business also needs another sideline to make it viable.

Or: 'It is not' (and also) 'That it is' cannot be (and I say that this is an unconvincing road: it doesn't turn). You cannot know what in fact has no being—this is impossible and you cannot speak of it.

My main memories of that day are of photos on the walls showing horrific automobile wrecks with graphic dead bodies, and then a tour of the jail that included seeing a square (about 3' x 3') on the second story floor that enclosed an area serving as a trap door for hangings. As the years went by I came to view both as contrived to scare us (haven't we all put up pictures for one-day occasions?—and capital punishment in M. C.?—come on). However, a little research revealed that yes, there were two judicially mandated hangings in the jail, both in 1935. And who knows, maybe the justice of the peace actually liked looking at those auto wreck pics day after day (but I doubt it).

Arlecchino, the simpleton from Bergamo, the servant of a skinflint of a doctor, is obliged, through the meanness of his master, to wear a costume made of different colored patches. He is a foolish buffoon, a roguish servant who seems always to wear a cheerful grin. But see what is dissembled by the mask: Arlecchino, the all-powerful wizard, the enchanter, the magician; Arlecchino, the emissary of the infernal powers. The mask enables the spectator to see not only the actual Arlecchino before him, but all the Arlecchinos who live in his memory.

I became a donut fryer with a friend that had two donut shops, was fun, but like the commercial of the time "I had to get up and make the donuts," decided that three in the morning is not a good time to go to work. Worse seven pm is a lousy time to have to go to bed when you have small kids. Moved into restaurant management, worked at an establishment that wasn't fast food, but not sit down fancy either. We called it " half fast." Did that until I got a call from a place that sold, serviced, and rented construction equipment. I became a parts manager and purchasing agent. My job was to figure out how to cut inventory to manageable size. Not a small task, as roughly a third of the inventory was obsolete.

The Eighth Climate is the mundus archetypus, *the world of Images and archetypal Forms. Actually, the only universe that possesses dimensions and extent is the one that is divided into eight climates. Seven of them are the seven geographical climates with dimensions and extent which are perceptible to the senses. The Eighth Climate is the one whose dimensions and extent can only be grasped by the imaginative perception. This is the world of autonomous Images and forms.*

Fifteen years ago I had an episode of irregular heartbeats, went in and found out I had a major blockage, fixed it with a stint. Ten years later again irregular heart beat, went in another blockage. When they went in to place the stint, they ran the catheter through the artery wall, so had to get out. Six weeks later I had to go back in and have it done again. Being seventy plus pounds overweight is probably why I have high blood pressure, Diabetes, high cholesterol and other associated probs. Seems my arm and mouth are in a conspiracy, every time my elbow bends, my mouth thinks it should have something put in it.

When your active Imagination will have attained all its perfection and all its plenitude, your capacity will expand till it makes possible the impossible, till it contemplates suprasensory realities of the Imagination under a sensory mode, till it understands allusive signs and deciphers the secret of the diacritical points of letters. Then you will have woven a garment from these suprasensory realities; when you have put it on, open for yourself a door giving access to the sesame.

I was on national television in 1967 for a minute on *The Joey Bishop Show.* Taped in California, Joey sometimes let audience members ask questions of his guests. Knowing this, I purposely sat in an aisle seat as that is where previous shows indicated a greater chance of being picked. Mickey Rooney was a guest that day. Knowing that he had been married many times and was a short man I asked him how tall his wife was. Before Mickey could answer Joey answered for him, "He doesn't care how tall they are. He's marrying his whole high school class, one woman at a time!"

The Pierrot movements are completely individual. Start by gently raising the right arm to the side and above the head, then lowering it till the hand takes a position shielding the eyes, in the mime of "looking." It is held briefly in this position as the left hand is lifted to the side, and above the head. The right hand is then lowered, its place being taken by the left hand in the same "looking" gesture. This is repeated: right, left, right, left in a continuous movement of inward flowing circles.

After high school, I got into dance; working at a couple studios in San Diego. Set out to conquer the world, armed with a dogged naivety and a fierce ignorance, I expected rainbows day after day. I bumbled along with an idealistic view of wonderment, which swiftly cracked into pieces as I married the wrong man. I'll gloss over this part of my life, except to say the greatest happenings to come out of the drudge were my two amazing children.

One ends up in exile for a variety of reasons and under a number of circumstances. Some of them are better sounding, some worse, but the difference ceases to matter already by the time one reads an obituary. On the bookshelf your place will be occupied not by you but by your book. And as long as they insist on making a distinction between art and life, it is better if they find your book good and your life foul than the other way around. Chances are, of course, that they won't care for either.

Alaska was still beckoning, so I traveled up there a few more times. On one of my treks, I met a tall, handsome stranger who said things like, "Never cower. Stand tall and walk into the storm like you own it!" and "Never take on a job, a horse, a town or people detrimental to your personal freedom." This whetted my interest. I liked his frankness, boldness, humor and free will. Turned out he was an ex-Nevada cowboy and ex-US Federal Marshal. Didn't hurt that he looked like Gregory Peck either. Married him.

When you have thoroughly understood what this is about, you will observe that the imaginative power (the Imaginatrix) which belongs to the soul of the universe, and itself including everything included by the other imaginative powers (those of the Animae coelestes*), is the substratum and epiphanic place of this interworld. It is called the* mundus archetypus *because it contains the Forms of everything existing in this world, and because it is the archetype of all the Forms of the individuals and essences existing on the plane of divine knowledge.*

I'm involved in a local hospice to help women and children victims of domestic violence, in honor of the memory of Barb Jones Bender. I feel the reason we're here on the earth is to help others. I've come up with several inventions and am in the process of procuring copyrights and patents. I would feel ashamed if I died without making some significant contribution to humanity. This quote from Teddy Roosevelt has been a touchstone through my life. "Far better to dare mighty things, to win glorious triumphs, even though checkered by failure, than to take rank with those poor spirits who neither enjoy much nor suffer much, because they live in a gray twilight that knows not victory nor defeat."

And on it there are many indications that Being is unengendered, that it cannot be broken apart (for it is whole, without parts), that Being does not fluctuate, that it has no end. It never was. It never will be. It is all NOW—one continuum.

I developed a love for the medical world during Viet Nam as a Red Cross Volunteer in Florida. I ultimately went back to college for another five years to get a BS degree in Nursing at CSU Fresno. By then I was certain that a double BSer was the right fit for me!—no more college! I loved my surgical time in Nursing, but my passion was Home Health, Hospice and Public Health Nursing. I did my career in a remote desert town in Ridgecrest, CA. near China Lake Weapons Center. My final twenty years were spent as a hospital administrator specializing in Quality and Risk Management.

And now I must dissuade you not only from taking that one of these two courses but also from another upon which mortals wander double-minded not knowing anything for only ineptitude straightens the errant thought in their minds. They are carried along blind and obtuse—these utterly astonished ones, this indiscriminate horde—by whom the 'to be' as well as the 'not to be' are thought of as the same and at the same time not the same and that the track down which everything passes is backward turning.

One of the most interesting experiences in my life was serving on a capital murder trial in Bakersfield, CA in 2008. I was one of twelve jurors selected from a pool of over six hundred. I had to drive four hours each day for four months to serve on that jury. I was the foreman/ woman, and we found Vincent Edward Brothers guilty of murdering his wife, four-year-old son, two-year-old daughter, six-week-old son and his mother-in-law. He is now in San Quentin prison awaiting his death. I was so proud to be part of that process and learned so much about myself and my personal and spiritual convictions.

Everything man pictures to himself, all that he really perceives, whether through intelligible or sensory perception, whether in this world or in the beyond, all these things are inseparable from man himself and cannot be dissociated from his essential "I." More precisely, what is essentially the object of perception is something that exists in himself, not in something else.

In the fall of 1966 I decided I had outgrown M. C. and went to Houston, TX to visit my brother and check out the action. Worked briefly for Union Carbide, Linde Division, as a dispatcher and enjoyed weather. Feeling homesick I returned to M. C. to visit and ran into J. With much planning and forethought we decided Los Angeles needed our presence. In LA I trained and worked as a lathe operator for Lockheed Aircraft. I found this work to be tedious and boring and so moved on. On to Green River, WY working construction for Peter Kiewitt and Sons, summers and attending U of Montana, Missoula, for couple of years. Good times, but went to Houston for Christmas and played golf in December and I was hooked. No more cold weather.

For the truth of the matter is that exile is a metaphysical condition. At least, it has a very strong, very clear metaphysical dimension, and to ignore or to dodge it is to cheat yourself out of the meaning of what has happened to you, to doom yourself to remaining forever at the receiving end of things, to ossify into an uncomprehending victim.

Being too young to sit around I worked in the Renovation and Restoration industry for six years. Most of the work was for insurance companies where the insured experienced a loss from water, wind, hail or fire. In 2003 I drove for Werner Industries (the Blue Trucks) hauling to Wal-Mart stores from the warehouse in Tomah, WI. S and I divorced 2003 and I hooked up to a travel trailer and hit the road for several years then ending up back in M. C. I worked for Coffee Cattle

Co managing their Liscom Creek Ranch fifty miles south of M. C, off Tongue River, for a couple years.

For the narrow rings are filled with unmixed fire and the next ones are full of the night and a tongue of flame shoots out. In the middle of this is the Daimonness who steers all things and she commands the commingling and the hateful births of everything.

My greatest passion though is unquestionably animals. There's a real plethora of pets around our house, and we're pretty crazy about them all. Several years ago I quit packing into the Bob Marshall Wilderness, and have sold all my horses, but there's still a mule named Gertie here to remind me of those days. There are eight cats scattered between the house, barn and garage. They have lovely and improbable names like Phoebe, Elaine, Zoe and Eilleen (what else would you call a cat who was born with one front leg and one back one?). We have two West Highland Terriers: Alfie is perfect in every way, Sophie is psychotic. And within the last month we've adopted a beagle/basset cross from the pound. Some folks are too smart to take in (and fall in love with) a nine-year-old dog, but not me.

Exile brings you overnight where it normally would take a lifetime to go. If this sounds like a commercial, so be it, because it is about time to sell this idea. Because I wish it had more takers. Perhaps a metaphor will help: to be an exiled writer is like being a dog or a man hurtled into outer space in a capsule (more like a dog, of course, than man, because they will never bother to retrieve you). And your capsule is your language. To finish the metaphor off, it must be added that before long the passenger discovers that the capsule gravitates not earthward but outward into space.

Sixth of June 1962 found me with a shaved head at MCRD (Marine Corps Recruit Depot) San Diego, CA. What a shock for a young man from Montana. After boot camp and ITR (Infantry Training Regiment) at Camp Pendleton, I married classmate M. M. and was stationed at NAS (Naval Air Station), Memphis, TN for a short tour then on to NAS Jacksonville, FL. After attending "A" school we moved to MCAS (Marine Corps Air Station) Cherry Point, NC. I was stationed at Cherry Point until 1965 when I moved to Atsugi, Japan then on to Iwakuni, Japan before going into Viet Nam where I was stationed at Da Nang. During the time at Cherry Point, M and I decided that we didn't like each other so she returned to M. C. and a divorce.

We should at this point give a brief outline of the question of Hurqalya, of the description of that universe and its situation among the planes of being. Roughly, the word Hurqalya refers to the mundus archetypus, the world of Images, the world of autonomous Figures and Forms. It is also called the Eighth Climate, referring to the fact that the philosophers and learned men of former times divided the Earth into seven climates. The universe of Hurqalya is above all these climates, and is not included within their visible boundaries.

I have had a fabulous life. I have wonderful friends all over this country. I have fallen in love again at this young and tender age with a guy who came back to Montana like I did! Life is sweet. Memories are to be cherished. My mom always wrote to me in college and ended her letters with "Think Positively." It's good wisdom.

Take a big breath and then, with a sigh, exhale every bit of air from the lungs. When you think you've done that, raise the shoulders and shake the body, with "Ha! Ha! Ha! Ha!" Still without taking a breath. Time now for a big breath and a repeat of the sequence, a little quicker, this time varying the pitch of the "Ha's," high and low. If everyone does this together, the infectious nature of laughter ensures that the room soon shakes with genuine laughter.

Sources

Autobiographical statements, graduates of CCHS, 1962, personal emails, 2011.

Corbin, Henry.*Spiritual Body and Celestial Earth.* Trans. Nancy Pearson. Princeton: Princeton UP, 1977. Print.

Grantham, Barry. *Playing Commedia: A Training Guide to Commedia Techniques.* Portsmouth: Heinemann, 2000. Print.

Robinson, Marc. *Altogether Elsewhere: Writers on Exile.* Boston: Faber and Faber, 1994. Print.

Stein, Charles. "Notes Toward a Translation of Parmenides." *Being = Space x Action Io #41.* Ed. Charles Stein. Berkeley: North Atlantic Books, 1988. Print.

Works Cited

Aarseth, Espen J. *Cybertext: Perspectives on Ergodic Literature.* Baltimore: Johns Hopkins UP, 1997. Print. .

Abrams, M. H. *Natural Supernaturalism: Tradition and Revolution in Romantic Literature.* New York: Norton, 1971, Print.

Agamben, Giorgio. *The Coming Community.* Trans. Michael Hardt. Minneapolis: U of Minnesota P, 1993. Print.

—. *Idea of Prose.* Trans. Michael Sullivan and Sam Whitsitt. New York: SUNY P, 1995. Print.

—. *Potentialities: Collected Essays in Philosophy.* Palo Alto, CA: Stanford UP, 1999. Print.

—. *Infancy and History: On the Destruction of Experience.* New York: Verso, 2007. Print.

Altieri, Charles. *Painterly Abstraction in Modernist American Poetry: The Contemporaneity of Modernism.* New York: Cambridge UP, 1989. Print.

—.*The Particulars of Rapture: An Aesthetics of the Affects.* Ithaca: Cornell UP, 2003. Print.

Anderson, John M. Introduction. *Discourse on Thinking* by Martin Heidegger. New York: Harper and Row, 1959. Print.

Arendt, Hannah. *The Life of the Mind. One: Thinking; Two: Willing.* New York: Harvest, 1978. Print.

Aristophanes. *The Complete Plays of Aristophanes.* Ed. Moses Hadas. New York: Bantam, 1962. Print.

Aristotle. *The Ethics of Aristotle.* Trans. J. A. K. Thomson. New York: Penguin Books, 1976. Print.

Armer, Alan A. *Writing the Screenplay: TV and Film.* Belmont, CA: Wadsworth, 1988. Print.

Aumont, Jacques et al. *Aesthetics of Film.* Trans. Richard Neupert. Austin: U of Texas P, 1992. Print.

Bai, Matt. "After the Tuscon Shooting, Is the Anger Gone?" *New York Times* 16 Jan. 2011: WK1. Print.

Ballard, Bruce. *The Role of Mood in Heidegger's Ontology.* Lanham, MD: UP of America, 1991. Print.

Ballard, Edward G. *Philosophy at the Crossroads.* Baton Rouge: Louisiana State UP, 1971. Print.

Barabasi, Albert-Laszlo. *Linked: How Everything is Connected to Everything Else and What it Means for Business, Science, and Everyday Life.* New York: Plume Books, 2003. Print.

Barthes, Roland. *Camera Lucida: Reflections on Photography,* Trans. Richard Howard, New York: Hill and Wang, 1981. Print.

—. *Critical Essays.* Trans. Richard Howard. Evanston: Northwestern UP, 1972. Print..

—. *Image, Music, Text.* Trans. Stephen Heath. New York: Hill and Wang, 1977. Print.

—. *New Critical Essays.* Trans. Richard Howard. New York: Hill and Wang, 1980. Print.

—. *Roland Barthes.* Trans. Richard Howard. New York: Hill and Wang, 1977. Print.

—."The Old Rhetoric: an *aide-mémoire.*" *The Semiotic Challenge.* Trans. Richard Howard. New York: Hill and Wang, 1988. 11-94. Print.

Basho, Matsuo. *Back Roads to Far Towns.* Trans. Cid Corman and Kamaike Susumu. Hopewell, N.J.: Ecco Press, 1996. Print.

Bataille, Georges. *Visions of Excess: Selected Writings, 1927–1939.* Ed. Trans. Allan Stoekl. Minneapolis: U of Minnesota P, 1985. Print.

—. *Encyclopaedia Acephalica.* London: Atlas, 1995. Print.

Bateson, Gregory. *Mind and Nature: A Necessary Unity.* New York: Bantam, 1979. Print.

Bauder, David. "Keeping Them Honest." *The Gainesville Sun* 14 Jun. 2011: Print.

Baudrillard, Jean. *Fatal Strategies.* Trans. Phil Beitchman and W. G. J. Niesluchowski. New York: Semiotext(e), 2008. Print.

—. *Seduction.* Trans. Brian Singer. New York: St. Martin's Press, 1990. Print.

Beaujour, Michel. *Poetics of the Literary Self-Portrait.* Trans. Yara Milos. New York: New York UP, 1991. Print.

Beistegui, Miguel de. "'Homo Prudens'" Raffoul and Pettigrew 117-134..

Bell, Ian F. A. *Critic as Scientist: The Modernist Poetics of Ezra Pound.* New York: Methuen, 1981. Print.

Benjamin, Walter. *Illuminations.* Trans. Harry Zohn. New York: Schocken, 1969. Print.

—. *The Arcades Project* Trans. Howard Eiland and Kevin McLaughlin, Cambridge, MA: Harvard UP, 1999. Print

—. *The Writer of Modern Life.* Trans. Howard Eiland et al. Cambridge, MA: Harvard UP, 2006. Print.

Berlinski, David. *The Advent of the Algorithm: The 300-Year Journey from an Idea to the Computer.* New York: Harcourt, 2000. Print.

Berthoff, Warner. *Literature and the Continuances of Virtue.* Princeton: Princeton UP, 1986. Print.

Blanchot, Maurice. *The Space of Literature.* Trans. Ann Smock. Lincoln: U of Nebraska P, 1981. Print.

—.*The Writing of the Disaster.* Trans. Ann Smock. Lincoln: U of Nebraska P, 1986. Print.

Block, Ned. "What Was I Thinking?" *NY Times.* 26 Nov. 2011: BR21. Print.

Bloom, Harold. *Agon: Towards a Theory of Revisionism.* New York: Oxford UP, 1982. Print.

—. "Poetic Crossing: Rhetoric and Psychology." *The Georgia Review.* 30 (1976):. Print.

—. "The Breaking of Form." *Deconstruction & Criticism.* Eds. Harold Bloom et al. New York: Seabury Press, 1979. 1-31. Print.

Blumenberg, Hans. *Shipwreck with Spectator: Paradigm of a Metaphor for Existence.* Trans. Steven Rendall. Cambridge, MA: MIT P, 1997. Print.

—. *The Legitimacy of the Modern Age.* Trans. Robert M. Wallace. Cambridge, MA: MIT P, 1983. Print.

—. *Work on Myth.* Trans.Robert M. Wallace. Cambridge, MA: MIT P, 1985. Print.

Boddy-Evans, Marion. "Painting in the Style of the Old Masters." *About. com.* About.com, 2011. Web. 19 Dec. 2011.

Bok, Christian. *Pataphysics: The Poetics of an Imaginary Science.* Evanston: Northwestern UP, 2001. Print.

Bourdieu, Pierre. *The Rules of Art: Genesis and Structure of the Literary Field.* Trans. Susan Emanuel. Palo Alto, CA: Stanford UP, 1996. Print.

Bowker, G. C., and S.L. Star. *Sorting Things Out: Classification and Its Consequences.* Cambridge, MA: MIT P, 1999. Print.

Bracher, Mark, et al., eds. *Lacanian Theory of Discourse: Subject, Structure, and Society.* New York: New York UP, 1994. Print.

Briggs, John C. *Francis Bacon and the Rhetoric of Nature.* Cambridge, MA: Harvard UP, 1989. Print.

Britt, Aaron. "Avatar." *New York Times Magazine.* New York Times Magazine. 8 Aug. 2010. Web. 19 Dec. 2011.

Brogan, Walter A. *Heidegger and Aristotle: The Twofoldness of Being.* Albany: SUNY P, 2005. Print.

Buci-Glucksmann, Christine. *Baroque Reason: The Aesthetics of Modernity.* Trans. Patrick Camiller. Thousand Oaks, CA: Sage, 1994. Print.

Burgess, Thornton W. *Old Mother West Wind.* New York: Grosset & Dunlap, 1910. Print.

Burgin, Victor. *In/Different Space: Place and Memory in Visual Culture.* Berkeley: U of California P, 1996. Print.

—.*The Remembered Film.* London: Reaktion Books, 2004. Print.

Burke, James. *Connections.* New York: Simon & Schuster, 1995. Print.

Burke, Kenneth. *A Rhetoric of Motives.* 1950. Berkeley: U of California P, 1969. Print.

—. *Language as Symbolic Action*. Berkeley: U of California P, 1966. Print.

Burnham, Jack. *Great Western Salt Works: Essays on the Meaning of Post-Formalist Art.* New York: George Braziller, 1974. Print.

Butler, Judith, Ernesto Laclau, and Slavoj Žižek. *Contingency, Hegemony, Universality: Contemporary Dialogues on the Left.* New York: Verso, 2000. Print.

Cage, John *M: Writings '67'72.* Middletown: Wesleyan UP, 1974. Print.

Calasso, Roberto. *K.* Trans. Geoffrey Brock. New York: Knopf, 2005. Print.

Campbell, Joseph. *The Hero with a Thousand Faces.* Princeton: Princeton UP, 1972. Print.

Carrouges, Michel, et al. "What is a Bachelor Machine?" *The Bachelor Machines.* New York: Rizzoli, 1975. Print.

Carruthers, Mary J. *The Book of Memory: A Study of Memory in Medieval Culture.* Cambridge, UK: Cambridge UP, 1990. Print.

—. *The Craft of Thought: Meditation, Rhetoric, and the Making of Images, 400–1200.* Cambridge, UK: Cambridge UP, 1998. Print.

Carson, Anne. *Eros the Bittersweet.* London: Dalkey Archive Press, 1998. Print.

Carter, Judy. *Stand-Up Comedy: The Book.* New York: Dell, 1989. Print.

Casey, Edward S. *The Fate of Place: A Philosophical History.* Berkeley: U of California P, 1998. Print.

Cate, Phillip Dennis, and Mary Shaw, eds. *The Spirit of Montmartre: Cabarets, Humor, and the Avant-Garde, 1875–1905.* New Brunswick: Rutgers UP, 1996. Print.

Caws, Mary Ann. *A Metapoetics of the Passage: Architextures in Surrealism and After.* Hanover: UP of New England, 1981. Print.

Chaitin, Gilbert D. *Rhetoric and Culture in Lacan.* New York: Cambridge UP, 1996. Print.

Chernyakov, Alexei. *The Ontology of Time: Being and Time in the Philosophies of Aristotle, Husserl and Heidegger.* Boston: Kluwer Academic Publishers, 2002. Print.

Cixous, Helene. *Readings: The Poetics of Blanchot, Joyce, Kafka, Kleist, Lispector, and Tsvetayeva.* Trans. Varena Andermatt Conley. Minneapolis: U of Minnesota P, 1991. Print.

Cheryl, http://protectgainesville.org/tag/cabot-inc/ (1/13/12).

Coleman, David. "In His Own Image." *New York Times.* 6 Jan. 2011: ST5. Print.

Cooper, Lane. *The Rhetoric of Aristotle.* New York: Appleton-Century-Crofts, 1960. Print.

Copleston, Frederick. *A History of Philosophy, Vol 3: Late Mediaeval and Renaissance Philosophy.* Garden City: Image Books, 1963. Print.

Corman, Cid. Introduction. Basho 9-11.

Cosgrove, Denis, ed. *Mappings.* London: Reaktion Books, 1999. Print.

Damasio, Antonio. *Looking for Spinoza: Joy, Sorrow, and the Feeling Brain.* New York: Harcourt, 2003. Print.

Davenport, Guy. *Objects on a Table: Harmonious Disarray in Art and Literature.* Washington, D.C.: Counterpoint, 1998. Print.

Dean, Greg. *Step by Step to Stand-Up Comedy.* Portsmouth, NH: Heinemann, 2000. Print.

de Certeau, Michel. *The Mystic Fable.* Trans. Michael B. Smith. Chicago: U of Chicago P, 1992. Print.

—. *The Practice of Everyday Life.* Trans. Steven Rendall. Berkeley: U of California P, 1984. Print.

De Duve, Thierry. *Kant After Duchamp.* Cambridge, MA: MIT P, 1998. Print.

—. *Pictorial Nominalism: on Marcel Duchamp's Passage from Painting to the Readymade.* Trans. Dana Polan. Minneapolis: U of Minnesota P, 1991. Print

Deleuze, Gilles. *Cinema 2: The Time Image.* Trans. Hugh Tomlinson and Robert Galeta. Minneapolis: U of Minnesota P, 1989. Print.

—. *Foucault.* Trans. Sean Hand. Minneapolis: U of Minnesota P, 1988. Print.

—. *Francis Bacon: The Logic of Sensation.* Trans. Daniel W. Smith. Minneapolis: U of Minnesota P,2003. Print.

Deleuze, Gilles, and Felix Guattari. *Kafka: Toward a Minor Literature.* Trans. Dana Polan. Minneapolis: U of Minnesota P, 1986. Print.

—. *What Is Philosophy?* Trans. Hugh Tomlinson and Graham Burchell. New York: Columbia UP, 1994.

Derrida, Jacques. *Aporias.* Trans. Thomas Dutoit. Stanford: Stanford UP, 1993. Print.

—. *Politics of Friendship.* Trans. George Collins. Verso, 1997. Print.

—. *Resistances of Psychoanalysis.* Trans. Peggy Kamuf et al. Stanford: Stanford UP, 1998. Print.

—. *The Other Heading: Reflections on Today's Europe.* Trans. Pascale-Ane Brault and Michael B. Nass. Bloomington: Indiana UP, 1992. Print.

—. "The Retrait of Metaphor." *Enclitic.* 2.2 (Fall1978): Print.

—. *The Truth in Painting.* Trans. Geoff Bennington and Ian McLeod. Chicago: U of Chicago P, 1987. Print.

—, and Paule Thevenin. "To Unsense the Subjectile." *The Secret art of Antonin Artaud.* Trans. Mary Ann Caws. Cambridge, MA: MIT P, 1998. Print.

Detienne, Marcel, and Jean-Pierre Vernant. *Cunning Intelligence in Greek Culture and Society.* Trans. Janet Lloyd. Chicago: U of Chicago P, 1978. Print.

Devlin, Keith. *Mathematics: The Science of Patterns.* New York: Scientific American Library, 1997. Print.

Dobyns, Stephen. *Best Word, Best Order: Essays on Poetry.* New York: St. Martin's Griffin, 1997. Print.

Dodds, E. R. *The Greeks and the Irrational.* Boston: Beacon Press, 1957. Print.

Donald, James. *Imagining the Modern City.* Minneapolis: U of Minnesota P, 1999. Print.

Douglas, Mary. *Purity and Danger: An Analysis of Concepts of Pollution and Taboo.* Boston: Routledge & Kegan Paul, 1966. Print.

Duchamp, Marcel. *Salt Seller: The Writings of Marcel Duchamp (Marchand du Sel).* Eds. Michel Sanouillet and Elmer Peterson. New York: Oxford UP, 1973. Print.

Eco, Umberto. *Kant and the Platypus: Essays on Language and Cognition.* Trans. Alastair McEwan. San Diego: Harcourt, 1997. Print.

—. *The Aesthetics of Chaosmos.* Trans. Ellen Esrock. Cambridge, MA: Harvard UP, 1982. Print.

—. *The Search for the Perfect Language.* Trans. James Fentress. Oxford, UK: Blackwell Publishers, 1995. Print.

—. *Semiotics and the Philosophy of Language.* Bloomington: Indiana UP, 1984. Print.

Eleb, Danielle. *Figures du Destin: Aristote, Freud et Lacan ou la Rencontre du Réel.* Ramonville Saint-Agne, France: Editions Eres, 2004. Print.

Elkins, James. *What Painting Is.* New York: Routledge, 2000. Print.

Emerson, Ralph Waldo. *Selected Prose and Poetry.* Ed. Reginald L. Cook. New York: Hot, Rinehart and Winston, , 1963. Print.

Environmental Protection Agency (EPA). "Second Five-Year Review Report for Cabot Carbon/Koppers Superfund Site. U.S. Army Corps of Engineers. 2006. Web. 29 Jan. 2012. www.epa.gov/superfund/sites/fiveyear/f2006040001087.pdf 8/10/11.

Evans, Dylan. *An Introductory Dictionary of Lacanian Psychoanalysis.* New York: Routledge, 1996. Print.

Fernald, James C. *Funk and Wagnalls Standard Handbook of Synonyms, Antonyms, and Prepositions.* Rev. ed. New York: Funk and Wagnalls, 1947. Print.

Fictioc, Mihaela. *The Beautiful Shape of the Good: Platonic and Pythagorean Themes in Kant's Critique of the Power of Judgment.* New York: Routledge, 2002. Print.

Fishel, Catharine. *Redesigning Identity: Graphic Design Strategies for Success.* Gloucester, MA: Rockport, 2000. Print.

Foucault, Michel. *The Order of Things: An Archaeology of the Human Sciences.* New York: Vintage, 1973. Print.

Freud, Sigmund. "Notes Upon a Case of Obsessional Neurosis." *Three Case Histories.* New York: Collier Books, 1963. Print.

—. "The 'Uncanny.'" *On Creativity and the Unconscious.* New York: Harper and Row, 1958. 123–159. Print.

Freydberg, Bernard. *Provocative Form in Plato, Kant, Nietzsche (and Others).* New York: Peter Lang, 2000. Print.

Friedman, Thomas L. *The Lexus and the Olive Tree.* New York: Anchor Books, 2000. Print.

Garver, Eugene. *Machiavelli and the History of Prudence.* Madison: U of Wisconsin P, 1987. Print.

Gasché, Rodolphe. *Of Minimal Things: Studies on the Notion of Relation.* Stanford: Stanford UP, 1999.

—. *The Idea of Form: Rethinking Kant's Aesthetics.* Stanford: Stanford UP, 2003. Print.

Gefin, Laszlo. *Ideogram: History of a Poetic Method.* Austin: U of Texas P, 1982. Print.

Gelernter, David. *The Muse in the Machine: Computerizing the Poetry of Human Thought.* New York: Simon and Schuster, 2002. Print.

Giles, Cynthia. *The Tarot: History, Mystery, and Lore.* New York: Simon & Schuster, 1992. Print.

Gilloch, Graeme. *Myth and Metropolis: Walter Benjamin and the City.* Cambridge, England: Polity Press, 1996. Print.

Golding, John. *Marcel Duchamp: The Bride Stripped Bare by her Bachelors, Even.* New York: Viking Press, 1972. Print.

Gombrich, E. H. *Symbolic Images: Studies in the Art of the Renaissance.* New York: Dutton, 1978. Print.

Gramsci, Antonio. *Selections from the Prison Notebooks.* Trans. Quintin Hoare and Geoffrey Nowell Smith. New York: International Publishers, 1971. Print.

Gray, Richard T. *Constructive Destruction: Kafka's Aphorisms.* Tübingen: Max Niemeyer Verlag, 1987. Print.

Greimas, Algirdas Julien, and Jacques Fontanille. *The Semiotics of Passions: From States of Affairs to States of Feeling.* Trans. Paul Perron and Frank Collins. Minneapolis: U of Minnesota P, 1993. Print.

Grojnowski,Daniel *The Spirit of Montmartre: Cabarets, Humor, and the Avant-Garde, 1875–1905.* Ed. Phillip Dennis Cate and Mary Shaw. New Brunswick: Rutgers State UP, 1996. Print.

Grossmann, Reinhardt. *The Categorial Structure of the World.* Bloomington: Indiana UP, 1983. Print.

Guattari, Felix. *Chaosmosis: An Ethico-Aesthetic Paradigm.* Trans. Paul Bains and Julian Pefanis. Sydney: Power Publications, 1995. Print.

—. *Molecular Revolution: Psychiatry and Politics.* Trans. Rosemary Sheed. New York: Penguin Books, 1984. Print.

Hamilton, Edith. *Mythology: Timeless Tales of Gods and Heroes.* New York: Mentor, 1953. Print.

Hans, James S. *Socrates and the Irrational.* Charlottesville: U of Virginia P, 2006. Print.

Hansen, Mark B. N. *Bodies in Code: Interfaces with Digital Media.* New York: Routledge, 2006. Print.

—. *New Philosophy for New Media.* Cambridge, MA: MIT P, 2006. Print.

Harari, Roberto. *How James Joyce Made His Name: A Reading of the Final Lacan.* Trans. Luke Thurston. New York: Other Press, 1995. Print.

Hardt, Michael, and Antonio Negri. *Multitude: War and Democracy in the Age of Empire.* New York: Penguin, 2004. Print.

Harriman, Robert, ed. *Prudence: Classical Virtue, Postmodern Practice.* University Park, PA: Pennsylvania State UP, 2001). Print.

Heidegger, Martin. *An Introduction to Metaphysics.* Trans. Ralph Manheim. New Haven: Yale UP, 1959. Print.

—. *Contributions to Philosophy (From Enowning).* Trans. Parvis Emad and Kenneth Maly. Bloomington: Indiana UP, 1999. Print.

—. *Hölderlin's Hymn "The Ister."* Trans. William McNeill and Julia Davis. Bloomington: Indiana UP, 1996. Print.

—. *Nietzsche, Volume II: The Eternal Return of the Same.* Trans. David Farrell Krell. San Francisco: Harper and Row, 1984. Print.

—. *On Time and Being.* Trans. Joan Stambaugh. New York: Harper and Row, 1972. Print.

—. *Pathmarks.* Ed. William McNeill. New York: Cambridge UP, 1998. Print.

—. *Poety, Language, Thought.* Trans. Albert Hofstadter. New York: Harper and Row, 1971. Print.

—. "The Basic Problems of Phenomenology." Trans. Albert Hofstadter *Pratt Journal of Architecture.* .2 (1988). Print.

—. *The Fundamental Concepts of Metaphysics: World, Finitude, Solitude.* Trans. William McNeill and Nicholas Walker. Bloomington: Indiana UP, 1995. Print.

—. *What Is Called Thinking?* Trans. J. Glenn Gray. New York: Harper and Row, 1968. Print.

Herrmann, Douglas J., ed. *Memory in Historical Perspective.* New York: Springer Verlag, 1988. Print.

Hersh, Seymour M. "Selective Intelligence." *The New Yorker.* 12 May 2003: 44–51. Print.

Hirsch, Edward. *The Demon and the Angel: Searching for the Source of Artistic Inspiriation.* New York: Harcourt, 2002. Print.

Hirshfield, Jane. *Nine Gates: Entering the Mind of Poetry.* New York: HarperCollins, 1997. Print.

Huizinga, Johan. *Homo Ludens: A Study of the Play Element in Culture.* Boston: Beacon Press, 1950. Print.

Huson, Paul. *Mystical Origins of the Tarot.* Rochester, VT: Destiny Books, 2004. Print.

Hyde, Lewis. *Trickster Makes This World: Mischief, Myth, and Art.* New York: North Point, 1998. Print.

James, David E., ed. *To Free the Cinema: Jonas Mekas & the New York Underground.* Princeton: Princeton UP, 1992. Print.

Janicaud, Dominique, and Jean-Francois Mattei. *Heidegger from Metaphysics to Thought.* Trans. Michael Gendre. Albany: SUNY P, 1995. Print.

Janis, Harriet and Sidney. "Marcel Duchamp, Anti-Artist." *Marcel Duchamp in Perspective.* Ed. Joseph Masheck. Englewood Cliffs, NJ: Prentice Hall, 1975. Print.

Japaridze, Tamar. *The Kantian Subject: Sensus Communis, Mimesis, Work of Mourning.* Albany: SUNY P, 2000. Print.

Jarry, Alfred. *Exploits and Opinions of Doctor Faustroll Pataphysician.* Trans. Simon Watson Taylor. Exact Change Press, 1996. Print.

Joyce, James. *A Portrait of the Artist as a Young Man.* New York: Viking Press, 1964. Print.

Kafka, Franz. *The Blue Octavo Notebooks.* Ed. Max Brod. Cambridge: Exact Change Books, 2004. Print.

—. *The Diaries of Franz Kafka, 1910–23.* Ed. Max Brod. Trans. Martin Greenberg. Middlesex, England: Prergrine Books, 1964. Print.

—. *The Trial,* Trans. Willa and Edwin Muir. New York: Schocken Books, 1995. Print.

—. *Zürau Aphorisms.* Ed. Roberto Calasso. Trans. Geoffrey Brock and Michael Hoffman. New York: Schocken Books, 2006. Print.

Kahn, Victoria. *Rhetoric, Prudence, and Skepticism in the Renaissance.* Ithaca: Cornell UP, 1985. Print.

Karcher, Stephen. *The Illustrated Encyclopedia of Divination.* Rockport, MA: Element Books, 1997. Print.

Katz, Ephraim. *The Film Encyclopedia.* New York: Putnam, 1979. Print.

Kearney, Richard, *The Wake of Imagination: Toward a Postmodern Culture.* Minneapolis: U of Minnesota Press, 1988. Print.

Keenan, Thomas. *Fables of Responsibility: Aberrations and Predicaments in Ethics and Politics.* Stanford: Stanford UP, 1997. Print.

Kekes, John. *Moral Wisdom and Good Lives.* Ithaca: Cornell UP, 1995. Print.

Klingmann, Anna. *Brandscapes: Architecture in the Experience Economy.* Cambridge, MA: MIT P, 2007. Print.

Koelb, Clayton. *Kafka's Rhetoric: The Passion of Reading.* Ithaca: Cornell UP, 1989. Print.

Koesler, Arthur. *The Act of Creation,* New York: Dell, 1964. Print.

Kracauer, Sigfried. *Theory of Film: The Redemption of Physical Reality.* New York: Oxford UP, 1960. Print.

Krauss, Rosalind E. *Bachelors.* Cambridge, MA: MIT P, 1999. Print.

—. *The Optical Unconscious.* Cambridge, MA: MIT P, 1994. Print

Krell, David Farrell. *Daimon Life: Heidegger and Life-Philosophy.* Bloomington: Indiana UP, 1992. Print.

—, and Donald L. Bates. *The Good European: Nietzsche's Work Sites in Word and Image.* Chicago: U of Chicago P, 1997. Print.

Kristeva, Julia. "Ellipse sur la frayeur et la séduction spéculaire." *Psychanalyse et Cinéma: Communications* 23: (1975). Paris: Seuil. Print.

—. *Revolution in Poetic Language.* Trans. Margaret Waller. New York: Columbia UP, 1984. Print.

Krysa, Joasia, ed. *Curating Immateriality: The Work of the Curator in the Age of Network Systems.* Brooklyn, NY: Autonomedia, 2006. Print.

Kundera, Milan. *Testaments Betrayed.* Trans. Linda Asher. New York: HarperCollins, 1993. Print.

Lacan, Jacques. *My Teaching.* Trans. David Macey. New York: Verso, 2008. Print.

—. "Television." Trans. Denis Hollier, Rosalind Krauss, and Annette Michelson.*October.* 40 (1987): 5–50. Print.

—. *The Four Fundamental Concepts of Psychoanalysis.* Ed. Jacques-Alain Miller. Trans. Alan Sheridan. New York: Norton, 1978. Print.

—. *The Seminar of Jacques Lacan: Book VII, The Ethics of Psychoanalysis 1959–1960.* Ed. Jacques-Alain Miller. Trans. Dennis Porter. New York: Norton, 1992. Print.

Laclau, Ernesto. *Emancipation(s).* New York: Verso, 1996. Print.

—. "Identity and Hegemony: The Role of Universality in the Constitution of Political Logics." Butler et al. 44-89.

—. *On Populist Reason.* New York: Verso, 2005. Print.

—. "Why Constructing a People Is the Main Task of Radical Politics." *Critical Inquiry.* 32.4 (2006): Print.

Latour, Bruno. *We Have Never Been Modern.* Trans. Catherine Porter. Cambridge, MA: Harvard UP, 1993. Print.

Lechner, Joan Marie. *Renaissance Concepts of the Commonplaces.* New York: Pageant Press, 1962. Print.

Lee, Rensselaer W. *Ut Pictura Poesis: The Humanistic Theory of Painting.* New York: W. W. Norton, 1967. Print.

Leiris, Michel. *Manhood: A Journey from Childhood into the Fierce Order of Virility.* Trans. Richard Howard. New York: Grossman Publishers, 1963. Print.

Lefebvre, Henri. *The Production of Space.* Trans. Donald Nicholson-Smith. Cambridge, MA: Blackwell, 1991. Print.

Lorca, Federico Garcia. "Play and Theory of the *Duende.*" *'Deep Song' and Other Prose.* Trans. Christopher Maurer. New York: New Directions, 1975. Print.

Lyotard, Jean-Francois. *Discours, Figure.* Paris: Klincksieck, 1978. Print.

—. *Driftworks*. Ed. Roger McKeon. New York: Semiotext(e), 1984. Print.
—. *Duchamp's Trans/formers: A Book*. Venice, CA: Lapis Press, 1990. Print.
—. *Lessons on the Analytic of the Sublime*. Trans. Elizabeth Rottenberg. Stanford: Stanford UP, 1994. Print.
—. "Sensus Communis." *Judging Lyotard*. Ed. Andrew J. Benjamin. New York: Routledge, 1992. 1-25. Print.
—. *The Inhuman: Reflections on Time*. Trans. Geoffrey Bennington and Rachel Bowlby. Stanford: Stanford UP, 1991. Print.
—. *The Differend: Phrases in Dispute*. Trans. Georges Van Den Abbeele. Minneapolis: U of Minnesota P, 1988. Print.
Lysaker, John T. *You Must Change Your Life: Poetry, Philosophy, and the Birth of Sense*. University Park: Pennsylvania State UP, 2002. Print.
Machiavelli, Niccolo. *The Ruler*. Trans. Peter Rodd. Chicago: Great Books Foundation, 1966. Print.
MacIntyre, Alasdair. *After Virtue: A Study in Moral Theory*. Notre Dame: U of Notre Dame P, 1981. Print.
McLuhan, Marshall.. *From Cliché to Archetype*. with Wilfred Watson, New York: Pocket Books, 1971. Print.
—, and Eric McLuhan. *Laws of Media: The New Science*. Toronto: U of Toronto P, 1992. Print.
Macnab, Maggie. *Decoding Design: Understanding and Using Symbols in Visual Communication*. Cincinnati: How, 2008. Print.
McQuire, Scott. *Visions of Modernity: Representation, Memory, Time, and Space in the Age of the Camera*. London: Sage, 1998. Print.
Mann, Wolfgang-Rainer. *The Discovery of Things: Aristotle's Categories and their Context*. Princeton: Princeton UP, 2000. Print.
Marchand, Roland. *Advertising the American Dream: Making Way for Modernity, 1920–1940*. Berkeley: U of California P, 1986. Print.
Marin, Louis. *To Destroy Painting*. Trans. Mette Hjort. Chicago: U of Chicago P, 1995. Print.
Martin, Daniel. *Montaigne et la Fortune: Essai sur le hazard et le langage*. Paris: Librairie Champion, 1977. Print.
Martin, Bronwen, and Felizitas Ringham. *Dictionary of Semiotics*. New York: Cassell, 2000. Print.
Mathieu, Georges. *De la revolte a la renaissance: Au-dela du Tachisme*. Paris: Gallimard, 1972. Print.
Meadows, Mark Stephen. *I, Avatar: The Culture and Consequences of Having a Second Life*. Berkeley, CA: New Riders, 2008. Print.
Merleau-Ponty, Maurice. *The Visible and the Invisible*. Trans. Claude Lefort. Northwestern UP, 1968. Print.
Mitchell, W. J. T. "Metamorphoses of the Vortex: Hogarth, Turner, and Blake." *Articulate Images: The Sister Arts from Hogarth to Tennyson*. Ed. Richard Wendorf. Minneapolis: U of Minnesota P, 1983. 125-168. Print.

Mirzoeff, Nicholas. *An Introduction to Visual Culture.* New York: Routledge, 1999. Print.

Moakley, Gertrude. *The Tarot Cards Painted by Bonifacio Bembo for the Visconti-Sforza Family.* New York: New York Public Library, 1966. Print.

Mondzain, Marie-Jose. *Image, Icon, Economy: The Byzantine Origins of the Contemporary Imaginary.* Trans. Rico Franses. Stanford: Stanford UP, 2005. Print.

Morford, Mark P. O., and Robert J. Lenardon, eds. *Classical Mythology.* 6th ed. New York: Longman, 1999. Print.

Morphet, Richard, and Robert Rosenblum. *Encounters: New Art from Old.* London: The National Gallery, 2000. Print.

Moss, Ann. *Printed Commonplace-Books and the Structuring of Renaissance Thought.* Oxford: Clarendon Press, 1996. Print.

Murphy, Richard W. *The World of Cézanne.* New York: Time-Life Books, 1968. Print.

Murray, Penelope. *Genius: The History of an Idea.* New York: Basil Blackwell, 1989. Print.

Myskja, Bjorn K. *The Sublime in Kant and Beckett: Aesthetic Judgment, Ethics and Literature.* New York: Walter de Gruyter, 2002. Print.

Negri, Antonio. *Subversive Spinoza: (Un)contemporary Variations.* Trans. Timothy S. Murphy et. al. New York: Manchester UP, 2004. Print.

—. *The Savage Anomaly: The Power of Spinoza's Metaphysics and Politics.* Minneapolis: U of Minnesota P, 1991. Print.

Nicholls, Angus. *Goethe's Concept of the Daemonic: After the Ancients.* Rochester, NY: Camden House, 2006. Print.

Nietzsche, Friedrich. *Ecce Homo.* Trans. Walter Kaufmann. New York: Vintage Books, 1969. Print.

—. *The Gay Science.* Trans. Walter Kaufmann. New York: Vintage Books, 1974. Print.

—. *Thus Spoke Zarathustra: A Book for Everyone and No One.* Trans. R. J. Hollingdale, Baltimore: Penguin Books, 1961. Print.

The 9/11 Commission Report..New York: WW. Norton, 2004. Print.

Novak, Marcos, "Liquid Architecture in Cyberspace." *Cyberspace: First Steps.* Ed. Michael Benedikt. Cambridge, MA: MIT P, 1992. 225- Print.

O'Brien, Tim. *The Things They Carried.* New York: Penguin, 1990. Print.

Ong, Walter J. *Ramus: Method, and the Decay of Dialogue.* Cambridge, MA: Harvard UP, 1983. Print.

Oosterhuis, Kas. *Hyperbodies: Towards an E-motive Architecture.* Boston: Birkhauser, 2003. Print.

Oring, Elliott. *The Jokes of Sigmund Freud.* Philadelphia: U of Pennsylvania P, 1984. Print.

Panofsky, Erwin. *Meaning in the Visual Arts.* Garden City, NY: Doubleday Anchor Books, 1955. Print.

—, and Dora Panofsky. *Pandora's Box: The Changing Aspects of a Mythical Symbol.* Princeton: Princeton UP, 1962. Print.
Pasolini, Pier Paolo. *Lutheran Letters.* Trans. Stuart Hood. Manchester: Carcanet New Press, 1983. Print.
Pérez-Gómez, Alberto. *Built Upon Love: Architectural Longing after Ethics and Aesthetics.* Cambridge, MA: MIT P, 2006. Print.
Peter, Rozsa. *Playing With Infinity: Mathematical Explorations and Excursions.* Trans. Z. P. Dienes. New York: Dover, 1976. Print.
Pleynet, Marcelin. *Painting and System.* Trans. Sima N. Godfrey. Chicago: U of Chicago P, 1984. Print.
Pound, Ezra. *The Cantos of Ezra Pound.* New York: New Directions, 1996. Print.
Poundstone, William. *Prisoner's Dilemma.* New York: Anchor Books, 1993. Print.
Proust, Marcel. *Swann's Way.* Trans. C. K. Scott Moncrieff. New York: Vintage Books, 1970. Print.
—. *The Past Recaptured.* Trans. Andreas Mayor. New York: Vintage Books, 1971. Print.
Raffoul, Francois, and David Pettigrew, eds. *Heidegger and Practical Philosophy.* Albany: SUNY P, 2002. Print.
Rajchman, John. *Truth and Eros: Foucault, Lacan, and the Question of Ethics.* New York: Routledge, 1991. Print.
Reale, Giovanni. *A History of Ancient Philosophy, III: The Systems of the Hellenistic Age.* Trans. John R. Catan. Albany: SUNY P, 1985. Print.
Rich, Frank. "The One-Eyed Man Is King." *The New York Times* 23 Jan. 2011:.WK10 Print.
Ricoeur, Paul. *The Rule of Metaphor.* Trans. Robert Czerny. Toronto: U.of Toronto P, (1981), 1981. Print.
Rilke, Rainer Maria. *The Notebooks of Malte Laurids Brigge.* Trans. M. D. Herter Norton. New York: Capricorn, 1958. Print.
Robins, Kevin. *Into the Image: Culture and Politics in the Field of Vision.* New York: Routledge, 1996. Print.
Rossi, Paolo. *Logic and the Art of Memory: The Quest for a Universal Language.* Trans. Stephen Clucas. Chicago: U of Chicago P, 2000. Print.
Rothenberg, Jerome, and Diane Rothenberg, eds. *A Symposium of the Whole: A Range of Discourse Toward an Ethnopoetics.* U of California P, 1983. Print.
Rugoff, Ralph, ed. *Scene of the Crime.* Cambridge, MA: MIT P, 1997. Print.
Sachs, Joe. Introduction. *Metaphysics* by Aristotle. Trans. Joe Sachs, Santa Fe, NM: Green Lion, 1999. Print.
Sanbonmatsu, John. *The Postmodern Prince.* New York: Monthly Review Press., 2004. Print.

Santillana, Giorgio de, and Hertha von Dechend. *Hamlet's Mill: An Essay on Myth and the Frame of Time.* Boston: David R. Godine, 1977. Print.

Sartre, Jean-Paul. *Being and Nothingness: A Phenomenological Essay on Nothingness.* Trans. Hazel E. Barnes. New York: Washington Square Press, 1966. Print.

—. *The Philosophy of Jean-Paul Sartre.* Ed. Robert Denoon Cumming. New York: Vintage, 1965. Print.

Serres, Michel. *Angels: A Modern Myth.* New York: Flammarion, 1995. Print.

—. *The Parasite.* Trans. Lawrence R. Schehr. Baltimore: Johns Hopkins UP, 1982. Print.

Shah, Idries. *The Pleasantries of the Incredible Mulla Nasrudin.* New York: Dutton, 1971. Print.

Shattuck, Roger. *The Banquet Years: The Origin of the Avant-Garde in France 1885 to World War I.* New York: Vintage, 1968. Print.

Shlain, Leonard. *Art and Physics: Parallel Visions in Space, Time and Light.* New York: William Morrow, 1991. Print.

Shields, Rob, "Flow," in *Flow: Space and Culture—the Journal*, 1, 1997. Print.

Slomkowski, Paul. *Aristotle's Topics.* New York: Brill, 1997. Print.

Slotkin, Richard. *Gunfighter Nation: The Myth of the Frontier in Twentieth-Century America.* New York: HarperCollins, 1992. Print.

Spinoza, Baruch. *The Ethics.* Trans. Samuel Shirley. Indianapolis: Hackett Publishing, 1992. Print.

Spitzer, Leo. *Classical and Christian Ideas of World Harmony.* Baltimore: Johns Hopkins UP, 1963. Print.

Spitzer, Michael. *Metaphor and Musical Thought.* Chicago: U of Chicago P, 2004. Print.

Stewart, Susan A. *Nonsense: Aspects of Intertextuality in Folklore and Literature.* Baltimore: Johns Hopkins UP, 1989. Print.

Stiegler, Bernard. *Technics and Time, 1: The Fault of Epimetheus.* Trans. RichardBeardsworth and George Collins. Palo Alto: Stanford UP, 1998. Print.

—. *Technics and Time, 2: Disorientation.* Trans. Stephen Barker. Palo Alto: Stanford UP, 2009. Print.

Stimilli, Davide, *The Face of Immortality: Physiognomy and Criticism*, Albany: SUNY Press, 2005, Print

Summers, David. *The Judgment of Sense: Renaissance Naturalism and the Rise of Aesthetics.* New York: Cambridge UP, 1987. Print.

Surette, Leon. *A Light from Eleusis: A Study of Ezra Pound's Cantos.* Oxford: Clarendon Press, 1979. Print.

Thomson, Garrett, and Marshall Missner. *On Aristotle.* Belmont, CA: Wadsworth, 2000. Print.

Thoreau, Henry David. *Walden and Civil Disobedience.* Ed. Owen Thomas. New York: Norton, 1966. Print.

Tisdall, Caroline. "Historical Foreword." *Metaphysical Art.* Ed. Massimo Carra, et al. Trans. Caroline Tisdall. New York: Praeger, 1971. 7–16. Print.

Titian. *Allegory of Prudence.* 1565. *Wikipaintings.* Web. 19 Dec. 2011.

Trilling, Lionel. *Sincerity and Authenticity.* Cambridge, MA: Harvard UP, 1971. Print.

Ueda, Makoto. "Basho on the Art of the Haiku: Impersonality in Poetry." *Japanese Aesthetics and Culture: A Reader.* Ed. Nancy G. Hume. Albany: SUNY P, 1995. Print.

Ulmer, Gregory L., *Heuretics: The Logic of Invention.* Baltimore: Johns Hopkins UP, 1994. Print.

—. *Internet Invention: From Literacy to Electracy.* New York: Longman UP, 2003. Print.

Verhaeghe, Paul. "Lacan's Answer to the Classical Mind/Body Deadlock: Retracing Freud's Beyond." *Reading Seminar XX.* Eds. Suzanne Barnard and Bruce Fink, Buffalo: SUNY P, 2002. Print.

Virilio, Paul. *Open Sky.* Trans. Julie Rose. New York: Verso, 1997. Print.

—. *Politics of the Very Worst; An Interview by Philippe Petit.* Trans. Michael Cavaliere. New York: Semiotext(e), 1999. Print.

—. *The Information Bomb.* Trans. Chris Turner. New York: Verso, 2000. Print.

—. *Unknown Quantity.* New York: Thames and Hudson, 2003. Print.

Virno, Paolo. *A Grammar of the Multitude.* Trans. Isabella Bertoletti, James Cascaito, and Andrea Casson. New York: Semiotext(e), 2004. Print.

—. *Multitude Between Innovation and Negation.* Trans. Isabella Bertoletti. New York: Semiotext(e), 2008. Print.

Voruz, Veronique. "Acephallic Litter as a Phallic Letter." *Re-inventing the Symptom: Essay on the Final Lacan.* Ed. Luke Thurston. New York: Other Press, 2002. Print.

Wagner, Roy. *Symbols that Stand for Themselves.* Chicago: U of Chicago P, 1986. Print.

Weber, Samuel. *The Legend of Freud.* Palo Alto: Stanford UP, 2000. Print.

Weir, David. *James Joyce and the Art of Mediation.* Ann Arbor: Michigan UP, 1996. Print.

Whiting, Cecile. *A Taste for Pop: Pop Art, Gender, And Consumer Culture.* Cambridge: Cambridge UP, 1998. Print.

Wing, Betsy. Translator's Introduction. *Poetics of Relation* by Édouard Glissant. Trans. Betsy Wing. Ann Arbor: U of Michigan P, 1997. Print.

Yang, Wesley. "Sex, Lies and Data Mining." *The New York Times Book Review.* 31 July 2011: BR16, Print.

Yates, Frances A. *The Art of Memory.* Chicago: U of Chicago P, 1966. Print.

Zeitlin, Marilyn, ed. *Bill Viola: Survey of a Decade.* Houston: Contemporary Art Museum, 1988. Print.

Žižek, Slavoj. "A Hair of the Dog that Bit You." in Mark Bracher, et al. 46-73.

—. "Hitchcockian 'Sinthoms'." *Everything You Always Wanted to Know about Lacan (but Were Afraid to Ask Hitchcock).* Ed. Slavoj Žižek. New York: Verso, 1992. 125-128. Print.

—. *The Sublime Object of Ideology.* New York: Verso, 1989. Print.

—. *Welcome to the Desert of the Real! Five Essays on September 11 and Related Dates.* New York: Verso, 2002. Print.

Zupancic, Alenka. *The Odd One In: On Comedy.* Cambridge, MA: MIT P, 2008. Print.

—. *The Shortest Shadow: Nietzsche's Philosophy of the Two.* Cambridge, MA: MIT P, 2003. Print.

Index

About the Author

Gregory L. Ulmer is Professor of English and Media Studies at the University of Florida, where he teaches courses in Hypermedia, E-Lit, and Heuretics. He is Joseph Bueys Chair in the European Graduate School, Saas-Fee, Switzerland, where he teaches a summer seminar on electracy and heuretics. He is coordinator of the Florida Research Ensemble, a creative arts research group first formed in the late 1980s, focusing on choragraphy through "Imaging Place" since the mid 1990s. Ulmer's books include a grammatology trilogy (*Applied Grammatology*, 1985; *Teletheory*, 1989; *Heuretics*, 1994). A second trilogy on the virtual consultancy known as the EmerAgency applies grammatology and heuretics to the invention of electracy, especially concerning the practices of aesthetics, ethics, and politics in the conditions of dimension pollution that Paul Virilio describes as the *dromosphere* (society of the spectacle). The published works are *Internet Invention* (2003), *Electronic Monuments* (2005), and *Miami Virtue* (2011). He is theorist for *E*, a collaboration with colleagues in the US and Canada investigating text mining and visualization for a poststructural web ontology.

Photograph of the author by the University of Florida Publicity Department. Used by permission.

www.ingramcontent.com/pod-product-compliance
Lightning Source LLC
LaVergne TN
LVHW091020080826
845145LV00002B/312

9781602352896